W9-CBX-327

EIGHTH EDITION

THE
PRINCIPLES
OF PHYSICAL
EDUCATION

JESSE FEIRING WILLIAMS, M.D., Sc.D.

EMERITUS PROFESSOR OF PHYSICAL EDUCATION
COLUMBIA UNIVERSITY, NEW YORK

W. B. Saunders Company
PHILADELPHIA AND LONDON   1964

Spanish Translation, Buenos Aires, 1954

Japanese Translation, Tokyo, 1957

To My Students of Physical Education
Teachers College, Columbia University
1911 – 1941

PREFACE

At one time, which seems too long ago, much of my leisure was spent in games. They had an importance then that other interests could scarcely rival. Later, I was thrilled by the Sword Dances that Cecil Sharpe brought to America, and particularly by the *Flamborough*. Wrestling, boxing, and tumbling were always challenging. It is still pleasant now, although the skill is gone, to recall the hours spent with Gustav Bojus in learning the handspring, the flip, and the snap-up. At the time the activities were sufficient; later one thought about them. Why were they so eagerly indulged? What were the values for a developing boy? What is their significance today in the larger arena of community, state, and national affairs?

For a span of nearly forty years this book has been concerned with such questions. But, today, more searching inquiries impend. The games of youth were played at the very beginning of this century. The Spanish-American War had ended; it had been brief and meant little to a boy immersed in games. Later, two wars involved the principal nations of the world and let loose revolutionary forces of great scope and magnitude. Children are quite unaware of these forces as they continue their play, even though they live in an environment where adults are uncertain, fearful, and often frustrated. When one ponders physical education in this mid-century and considers its purposes, the larger problems of American life crowd into the foreground and the most pressing issues come to the top. It is no longer sensible to consider chiefly the biological aspects of physical education; this area of education must also be examined in the light of political, economic, and social concepts.

Every informed person is aware that economic, social, and political forces are shaping nations anew. Schools and colleges, like other social institutions, are feeling the impact of questions hurled at them by citizens who are vitally interested in the purposes proposed, the methods used, and the direction of programs. Physical education is also questioned. There is quick acceptance of the functional skills that are taught, recognition of its vigorous activities as the sure source of vitality in the people, and approval of its wholesome interest in play and recreation. But what is physical education doing to foster respect for the dignity of the individual? What are its plans for developing courage and self-reliance? What is its contribution to tolerance? What is its essential role in the continuing drama of the American Way of Life?

The above paragraphs are from the Preface of the Sixth and of the Seventh Editions of this book. The questions raised ten years ago continue to require answers. Today we are living in what is called the Space Age, but for some time to come physical education must be primarily concerned with our human problems on Earth. And these problems grow increasingly urgent: the delinquent behavior of young people, dishonesty in sports, intolerance, physical deficiencies of youth and adults, sedentary habits, the hazards of leisure time, the increase in nervous tension and emotional disturbances. These evidences of social stress and personal failure are the product of many forces and no single agency can overcome them. All of education must be responsible for their solution. Because of their complexity, physical education may be dismayed at the enormity of the task and wonder if it does not have a unique function to which it can be devoted. Getting an easy answer, some teachers wish to concentrate on "physical fitness." Of course, withdrawal into a narrow exclusiveness is no answer at all, because the responsibility of physical education to young people in their social development, in their play and recreation, in their health practices, in their racial and religious attitudes, and in their philosophic values remains. In this situation the present revision continues to present the view that physical education is an education of the potentials of the whole person through physical activities, rather than an exclusive education of the physical.

Dr. Eleanor Metheny, in writing of the meaning of human movement, concludes a very significant statement with these words:

> Will recognition of the meaning implicit in our movement experiences

materially alter our physical education curriculum? I think not. Our curriculum is made up of the kinds of movement experiences that children have long found meaningful because we have never been able to sell normally intelligent children experiences that were not meaningful to them.

Will it be easy to sell this concept of the meaning of human movement to those people we call "the administrators"? No. It will not even be easy for us to incorporate this concept into our own educational creeds. But I believe that we can do what we must do in our own moment of history. And I believe that only as we are able to identify the *meanings* and values that we, ourselves, so highly prize in our movement experiences can we hope to find a permanent place for physical education in the *meaning-centered* curriculum that will meet man's needs for discovering his own identity as a human being in an impersonal universe of space.[1]

This is my last revision of this book, not because of omens or prophecies but because of the passing years. In this farewell to the profession, I greet all those who help the young to develop their potentials in organic strength, in functional neuromuscular skills, in zest for life, and in devotion to those kinds

[1] Eleanor Metheny, "The Unique Meaning Inherent in Human Movement," *The Physical Educator*, March, 1961, p. 7.

of living that are good for the individual and good for our American republic.

Jesse Feiring Williams

Carmel, California

CONTENTS

CHAPTER THREE

Physical Education in a Democracy — Political Concepts ..   53

CHAPTER FOUR

Physical Education in a Democracy — Economic Concepts ..   98

CHAPTER FIVE

Physical Education in a Democracy — Social Concepts 135

CHAPTER SIX

The Nature of Man — His Biological Foundations 182

CHAPTER SEVEN

The Nature of Man — His Psychological Foundations 243

CHAPTER EIGHT

The Historic Role of Physical Education in the Problem of Adjustment to Life 275

English Physical Education, 296. Russian Physical Education, 301. Physical
Education in Other Lands, 304. American
Physical Education, 304. The Rise of a
Professional Association, 311. The Preparation of Physical Education Teachers,
313. Questions and Problems for Discussion, 314. Reference Readings, 315.

CHAPTER NINE

What is the Curriculum? 319. What is
the Course of Study? 320. Steps in Preparation of a Curriculum, 320. The Situation, 321. The Individual To Be Educated,
322. The Aim of Physical Education,
323. The Objectives of Physical Education, 329. The Curricular Materials of
Physical Education, 350. Sources of Curricular Materials, 352. 1. Adapted Activities, 352. 2. Games, Sports, Athletics,
Play, Equitation, Aquatics, 353. 3. Dance,
355. 4. Self-testing Combat and Self-defense Activities, 356. 5. Fundamental
Skills, 357. 6. Out-of-Door Activities of
the Camp, 359. What Part Has Gymnastics in the Curriculum? 359. The Place
of Drill in the Curriculum, 361. When
is a Person Physically Educated? 362.
Questions and Problems for Discussion,
364. Reference Readings, 365.

CHAPTER TEN

Scientific Method, 369. Methods and Objectives, 370. The Range of Objectives,
372. Many Methods, and One is Best,

374. Principles of Method in Technical Learnings, 376. Principles of Method in Associated Learnings, 379. Principles of Method in Concomitant Learnings, 389. "Group Process" as a Method, 396. Unifying Learning Experiences, 402. Questions and Problems for Discussion, 403. Reference Readings, 404.

THE SOURCES AND DATA OF PRINCIPLES OF PHYSICAL EDUCATION

THE SOURCES AND DATA OF PRINCIPLES OF PHYSICAL EDUCATION

The unexamined life is not worth living by any man.

Socrates.

But there are risks in every act of life, and therefore we always keep in mind adverse possibilities and sharpen our intellect to perceive clearly the reality in the midst of which we act.

Croce.

Women in Greece expecting to have children, kept in their rooms the images of beautiful gods, in the expectation that those constant images would operate toward the beautifying of their eventual children. It was a hope as dubious as it is touching. But that images of beauty, goodness and truth do affect action, or put differently, that ideals stimulate behavior, release energies, and incite to enterprise, movement and adventure is beyond the possibility of doubt.

Edman.

AN ANCIENT HERITAGE

Physical education bears an ancient heritage. Its sources rise out of the nature of man, its variations reflect the changing economic, industrial, religious, and cultural environments of all people, and its purposes demonstrate the dominant ideas of the time and the place. Some of the early sources of physical education are very old. According to Gunsun Hoh, "The authentic history of China begins with Huang-ti in the year 2697 B.C.,"[1] and this leader advocated wrestling, archery, sword play, and military and ceremonial dancing. These activities were designed to serve military purposes. The ancient cultures of India, Egypt, Babylonia, Assyria, Persia, Greece, Carthage, and Rome also give evidence of this same purpose to use physical education to train youth in warlike activities.

With the exception of Greece all these early efforts in physical education had little to offer to Americans who looked to history for examples of significant practice. Greek physical education, however, in its training of the young and especially in its great athletic festivals at Olympia, Corinth, Delphi, and Argolis, has been a rich source of inspiration and practical procedure. Civilized societies have always felt the need for the physical education of its members, except during the Middle Ages in Europe when asceticism in the early Christian Church set a premium on physical weakness in the vain hope that this was the path to spiritual excellence. With the breakup of the Graeco-Roman society, "after its physique had been permanently undermined by the Hannibalic War,"[2] the fall of the Roman Empire was followed by an *interregnum* that was dominated by the ideas and practices of the Christian Church.

From the tenth to the fourteenth centuries European societies that had been vassals of Roman power succumbed to the

[1] Gunsun Hoh, *Physical Education in China*, Shanghai, Commercial Press, 1926, p. 2.

[2] Arnold J. Toynbee, *A Study of History* (abridged by Somervell), New York, Oxford University Press, 1947, p. 11.

3

prevailing ascetic ideas. The Renaissance of the fifteenth and sixteenth centuries broke through the gloom and despair of the Middle Ages, and with the discovery of Old Greek manuscripts a more rational view of the nature of man appeared. One of the earliest efforts to revive physical education in the education of the young developed at Mantua, Italy, in 1423 when Vittorino da Feltre undertook the education of the sons of Marquis Gran Francisco Gonzaga. In addition to classical studies, his program included dancing, riding, fencing, swimming, wrestling, archery, ball games, and other activities of a knightly education. So successful was the project that other pupils enrolled in the school, called La Casa Giocosa. In time most of the princely houses of Italy were represented in the school together with pupils from some foreign countries. Over the years other schools appeared in which physical education shared some responsibility for the education of youth.

In an assessment of this ancient heritage, students will be impressed with the fact that men of accomplishment in other fields found time to write about and to give support to early efforts to develop physical education. Of those who advocated physical education, three men expressed their ideas in such striking phrases that their words should be remembered by all teachers of physical education.

Michel de Montaigne (1533-1592), the eminent French essayist, wrote: "I would have his outward behavior and mien, and the disposition of his limbs, formed at the same time with his mind. It is not a soul, it is not a body, that we are training up; it is a man, and we ought not to divide him into two parts; and as Plato says, we are not to fashion one without the other, but make them draw together like two horses harnessed to a coach. . . . Inure him to heat and cold, to wind and sun, and to danger that he ought to despise. Wean him from all effeminacy in clothes and lodging, eating and drinking; accustom him to everything, that he may not be a Sir Paris, a carpet knight, but a sinewy, hardy, and vigorous young man."

John Locke (1632-1704), an Oxford graduate, attained considerable notice in publishing his *Essay Concerning Human Understanding*. When he published *Thoughts on Education*, he had a receptive audience. In this treatise he advocated a spartan type of education for the young. He wrote: "Keep the body in strength and vigor so that it may be able to obey and execute the orders of the mind. . . . A sound mind in a sound body* is a short but full description of a happy state in this world; he that has these two has little more to wish for; and he that wants either of them will be little the better for anything else. . . . He whose mind directs not wisely will never take the right way; and he whose body is crazy and feeble will never be able to advance in it." For activities he advised swimming, fencing, riding, and wrestling. His views are summed up in these rules: "Plenty of open air, exercise and sleep; plain diet, no wine or strong drink and very little or no physic; not too warm and strait clothing; especially the head and feet kept cold, and the feet often used to cold water and exposed to wet."

A third great leader of this period was a Frenchman, Jean Jacques Rousseau (1712-1778), who wrote an educational romance entitled *Emile*. In this book he championed the free spirit, worth, and dignity of the individual as against the rigid social and moral doctrines of his time. He could not accept the Christian doctrine of original sin and taught that man was naturally good; it was his environment that made man selfish and evil. He advised vigorous activities for youth: "Let him," he wrote, "learn to make jumps, now long, now high; to climb a tree, to leap a wall. Let him always find his equilibrium, and let all his movements and gestures be regulated according to the laws of gravity long before the science of statics intervenes to explain them to him." Some of his more memorable phrases sound familiar today:

> The body must needs be vigorous in order to obey the soul; a good servant ought to be robust. The weaker the body the more it commands; the stronger it is the better it obeys. If you would cultivate the intelligence of your pupil, cultivate the power it is to govern. In order to learn to think, we must exercise our limbs, our senses, and our organs which are the instruments of

* The satirist Juvenal said the same thing: "Orandum est, ut sit mens sana in corpore sano" (a sound mind in a sound body is a thing to be prayed for).

our intelligence; and in order to derive all the advantage possible from these instruments, it is necessary that the body which
furnishes them should be robust and sound.

The philosophic and educational views of Locke and
Rousseau soon began to bear fruit. Two schools appeared that
incorporated many of these new and novel ideas. One was the
Philanthropinum founded by Johann Bernhard Basedow in
1774 at Dessau; the other the Schnepfenthal Educational Institute founded by Christian Gotthilf Salzmann in 1784, at
Schnepfenthal near Gotha. Both schools were in German terri-
tory. Although the Philanthropinum was the pioneer institution,
Schnepfenthal lasted longer and became more famous because
of the contribution made to it by its teacher of physical education, Johann Christoph Friedrich Guts-Muths (1750-1839). Guts-
Muths taught at the Institute for nearly fifty years and is recognized today as one of the great pioneers of modern physical
education. His fame rests in part upon two books: *Gymnastics
for the Young* and *Games*. Three other men, Franz Nachtegall
(1777-1847), Per Henrik Ling (1776-1839), and Friedrich Ludwig
Jahn (1778-1852), made memorable contributions in the development of physical education. Nachtegall in Denmark is properly
credited with the construction of the first gymnasium in modern
times; Ling and Jahn organized and developed two national
systems of gymnastics that not only gained wide acceptance at
home but also played an important part in the early development
of physical education in the United States.

From this brief glimpse of the heritage of physical education and its beginnings in modern times it is apparent that a full
historical account would be richly rewarding to the student of
physical education and quite indispensable for an adequate
appreciation of the field.[3] Additional historical material is presented in Chapter 8.

As the student reads the history of his major field, he will

[3] The following books will be helpful:
Ainsworth, Dorothy S. *The History of Physical Education in Colleges
for Women*. New York, Barnes, 1930.

understand that the early pioneers conceived of physical education according to the then prevailing ideas of human personality,
of man's place in nature, and of the social forces that played upon
him. Much of what these leaders did he will approve; some will
appear to be of little use or value. As he thinks about these first
efforts and contemplates the role that physical education should
play today he may properly conclude that every society in the
course of its life is confronted by what Toynbee calls, "a succession of problems which each member has to solve for itself as
best it may."[4] What German and Swedish leaders did in the eighteenth century represents their responses to challenges that came
from their societies. Today in the United States leadership of
physical education is also confronted by a succession of problems. It is the general argument of this book that the challenges presented are best met by conceiving of physical education as an education through the physical.

AN EDUCATION THROUGH THE PHYSICAL[5]

Physical education is an old and fundamental education.
The first physical educator was the parent who taught his son

---

Footnote 3 continued

Dorgan, Ethel J. *Luther Halsey Gulick (1865-1918)*. New York, Teachers
College, Columbia University, 1934.

Elliott, Ruth. *The Organization of Professional Training in Physical
Education in the United States*. New York, Teachers College,
Columbia University, 1927.

Leonard, Fred E., and Affleck, George B. *A Guide to the History of
Physical Education*. Philadelphia, Lea & Febiger, 1947.

Schwendener, Norma S. *A History of Physical Education in the United
States*. New York, Barnes, 1942.

[4] Arnold J. Toynbee, *op. cit.*, p. 3.

[5] The paragraphs of this section are from the author's contribution to
the Yearbook (1951) of the American Association for Health,
Physical Education and Recreation, *Developing Democratic Human Relations,* although the ideas expressed were formulated
earlier and printed in an article by the author in the *Journal
of Higher Education,* May, 1930, entitled, "Education Through
the Physical."

to throw a spear, to climb a tree, to leap a brook, to do all those things that were important for a youth to learn in the tribal life of uncivilized man. Over the centuries the civilized social scene has changed tremendously, ways of living have profoundly altered, and new stresses have pressed upon the old biological patterns of man. And yet the patterns remain; the organism still retains the structures, organizations, and functional demands that long ago appeared. The need to learn how to throw a spear has passed, but the need to throw remains; the need to climb a tree is gone, but the urge to climb appears in every child; the need to leap a brook rarely occurs, but the necessity to leap arises again and again in the urgent jumpings and leapings of youth. The patterns developed by nature are old and fundamental forms that emerge out of a tribal past and insistently make their demands in a highly industrial and complex present.

It has been the unfortunate heritage of physical education to conceive of its programs in physical terms alone because its activities were so obviously physical. When mind and body were thought of as two separate entities, physical education was obviously an education *of* the physical; in similar fashion mental education made its own exclusive demands. But with new understanding of the nature of the human organism in which wholeness of the individual is the outstanding fact, physical education becomes education *through* the physical. With this view operative, physical education has concern for and with emotional responses, personal relationships, group behaviors, mental learnings, and other intellectual, social, emotional, and esthetic outcomes. Although important and not to be neglected, it is quite insufficient to develop strength of muscles, bones, and ligaments, to acquire motor skills, and to secure physical endurance. The dichotomy of body *and* mind has been abandoned in scientific circles. Physiology, psychology, sociology, and modern philosophy recognize the fact of organismic unity. Furthermore, not only is the individual a whole but he is also one with his environment, so that the total situation includes the whole person in all his aspects and the environment with which he reacts and interacts in all his responses.

This recognition of man's organismic unity and environmental dependence has required that physical education be *in fact* an education through the physical and hence take into account not only the technical learnings of a physical experience but also the associated and concomitant learnings that inevitably accrue. It is therefore absurd to limit one's objectives to physical outcomes; other outcomes emerge also. Recognition of the whole does not require minor respect for the physical; by virtue of the activities themselves the physical will always have a major role. Nor should there be any apology for its prominence in the proper education of young people. Anyone disposed to regard the physical lightly should remember that the physical, as well as courage and intelligence, was present at Bataan and Okinawa and persists as a part of everything that is good and true and beautiful. Nothing could be meaner than to miscall it. It asks for no supremacy, knowing full well the ugly distortion in the human being when it has an exclusive role. The balance and harmony sought by the Greeks is, in modern terms, an education of the whole person in which the physical takes its proper place in the unfolding of the intellectual, social, emotional, and esthetic powers of the individual.

This emphasis upon the education of the whole person runs the risk that the physical may be neglected because of the pressing demands of the intellectual and because of the high compensation that an industrial society pays for mental skills. Nevertheless, that risk should be run. Force and strength without humane direction are too terrible to contemplate. All persons should know that vigor and vitality of peoples are dependent upon muscular exercise for their development and entirely for their maintenance, and that, aside from the conditioning influences of heredity and favorable nutrition, vigorous physical education is the indispensable means today for national strength. But it should never be forgotten that vitality that is ungenerous, beastly, and knavish is no proper objective for any division of education. Let the sponsors of physical education have deep convictions about the tremendous importance of vigor and vitality in peoples; let them assert, time and again, and everywhere, the strategic and imperative role of muscular activity in development, but let them guard against an unworthy exclusiveness that leaves them devoted to strength with no cause to serve, skills with no function to perform, and endurance with nothing worth lasting for.

THE BASIS OF AN EDUCATION THROUGH THE PHYSICAL

When man was viewed as separate body, separate mind, and separate spirit, it was logical to seek separate outcomes. If the body is merely physical and separate, then development of the body as such, and without regard for mental and emotional results, is a sound objective. On the other hand, if the human individual is a unified organism, then his physical education must take into account what happens to his ideas, thoughts, feelings, and emotions as he engages in physical activities. Is there evidence that man is a unified organism? What is it?

Good Things Go Together. The famous psychologist Edward L. Thorndike believed that in general good things go together and that high intelligence is likely to be associated with superior qualities in other traits. This view is strongly supported by studies of Professor Lewis N. Terman at Stanford University.[6] From a study of 1500 persons with an I.Q. of 140 and over, he concluded that individuals of this intelligence level are appreciably superior to unselected individuals in physique, health, and social adjustment, and markedly superior in moral attitudes. Thirty years later in a restudy of his test group he found that mortality, insanity, and alcoholism were below those of general groups.

Thorndike's and Terman's studies illustrate a basic unity in the organism. It is further supported by Professor Hartman, who writes: "Educational psychology cannot neglect the body, for the elementary reason that that is all the human being *has* and *is*. In this sense, physical education (or education through

---

[6] Lewis N. Terman, "The Discovery and Encouragement of Exceptional Talent," *American Psychologist,* June, 1954, p. 221.

the physical) is the only kind that takes place or can possibly occur."[7]

Good things do go together in nature. The finest achievements of mind and the most exalted behavior in character are properly admired because, like fine muscular coordinations, they are of the same flesh and blood. They are not the exotic products of a separate mind but true sons of the same soil that bears bone and muscle; all are applauded because they serve the complete harmony of man. The desire for truth, beauty, and justice, the zeal for competence in work, and the yearning for good will toward men may seem far removed from the physical. They are remote in the sense that the forces in their favor have to work diligently to make them even partial aims and yet they reside in the body of man himself and come from the activities of his physical cells.

Herrick stresses this dependence of mind upon physical sources when he writes:

> ". . . there is nothing in our experience, there are no mental powers, no skill in ratiocination or logical analysis, no capacity to forecast future events, no flights of imaginative fancy, which do not depend directly or indirectly upon sensory data. . . . We surpass the brutes in our capacity to use the data so provided and to supplement our limited and in some cases defective sense organs by artificial aids, such as spectacles and microscopes, but never can our thinking transcend the realm of sense experience. The most abstruse metaphysical speculation, in common with the highest flight of poetic fancy and the keenest aesthetic appreciation, are earth-bound within the limits set by our physical sensory equipment.[8]

James-Lange Theory of the Emotions. In 1884 William James, and independently, C. Lange in 1885 announced an explanation of emotional behavior that indicated the unitary character of the human organism. James gave the following exposition of his view:

[7] George W. Hartman, *Educational Psychology*, New York, American Book, 1941, p. 46.

[8] C. Judson Herrick, *Neurological Foundations of Animal Behavior*, New York, Holt, 1924, p. 43.

Our natural way of thinking about the . . . emotions is that the mental perception of some fact excites the mental affection called the emotion, and . . . this latter state of mind gives rise to the bodily expression. My theory, on the contrary, is that the bodily changes follow directly the perception of the exciting fact. Common sense says, we lose our fortune, are sorry and weep; we meet a bear, are frightened and run; we are insulted by a rival, are angry and strike. The hypothesis here to be defended says that this order of sequence is incorrect, that the one mental state is not immediately induced by the other, that the bodily manifestations must first be interposed between, and that the more rational statement is that we feel sorry because we cry, angry because we strike, afraid because we tremble and not that we cry, strike, or tremble, because we are sorry, angry, fearful, as the case may be. Without the bodily states following on the perception, the latter would be purely cognitive in form, pale, colorless, destitute of emotional warmth. We might then see the bear, and judge it best to run, receive the insult and deem it right to strike, but we should not actually *feel* afraid.[9]

The significance of this theory is that bodily changes constitute the physical basis for the conscious state we call emotion.

Postures as Evidence. Additional evidence of unity is given by certain well-known facts of posture. The various postures an individual assumes are not the product of physical factors alone. They also reflect psychological and physiological states and conditions. Typically the slave crouches, the general strides, and the coward slinks. But even more is involved. If a person is sad and depressed, the assumption of an erect and happy pose produces an emotional change and presently a feeling of courage and self-assurance does ensue. And the opposite is also true.

DEFINITION OF PHYSICAL EDUCATION

It is apparent on every hand that the accumulated social inheritance presents a staggering load to be acquired by

[9] William James, *Principles of Psychology*, New York, Holt, 1893, pp. 449 ff.

each new generation. When youth had only a few skills to learn or one or two legends to memorize, the task of education was simple indeed. Now, selections must be made. Likewise in physical education, the great wealth of material in physical activities, the wide range of objectives, and the increasing mobility of local situations demand careful selection of material. All motor experiences are physically educative, but some are worth more in effects produced and in kinds of effects than others. With these considerations in mind a well-known definition of physical education should be stated here: *Physical education is the sum of man's physical activities selected as to kind, and conducted as to outcomes.*

This definition takes into account the fact that a selection of activities must be made and that outcomes are important. Selection as to kind requires appreciation that activities vary in value and hence that some are obviously better than others for securing the outcomes desired. When one chooses one thing from among many, unless caprice controls, principles are necessary to which the activity is referred. Principles reflect the dominant ideas and urgent needs of people. Although muscular and mechanical needs persist, it is not practical to use only the principles that serve such purposes. The social and moral necessities of today place upon all forms of education the responsibility of keeping selections broad and inclusive enough to minister to these necessities also. Certainly these grim days do not demand any "back to the body" movement, but rather a selection of physical activities that contribute to democratic human relations, that will offer opportunity for the individual to be tolerant, generous, kind, and friendly, that will encourage manifestations of self-reliance, independence, and adventurous spirit, and that will make primary the goal of a strong and positive personality.

And the phrase, "conducted as to outcomes," means of course that the outcomes needed by America will be sought. There will, therefore, be emphasized physiological results, growth and developmental outcomes, neuromuscular skills, interests, attitudes, and habits. Habits and attitudes of healthful living and interest in wholesome recreation are the concern and responsibility not only of health education and recreation but of physical education as well. While health education and recreation will devote more time to the development of healthful habits and attitudes, and recreational interests, their achievements will always be conditioned by the patterns of social life that other forces help to shape. To the proper purposes of health education and recreation, physical education has a unique opportunity to contribute in its training and conditioning routines, in its athletic ideals, and in its functional leisure-time skills.

Let us see how this definition can be employed in a practical situation. Suppose that a parent objects to physical education for his son because, in the parent's words, "He gets all the exercise he needs in mowing the lawn and doing his paper route." It must be admitted that children get some physical education in various motor activities out of school. Every motor experience has some outcomes, even if trivial and of little worth.

It is exactly at this point, however, that physical education should be prepared to guide uninformed opinion. All physical activities are not of equal worth, even when narrowly conceived outcomes are sought. Many activities are too mild to stimulate sufficiently the organic systems in growing youth. Moreover, when other than physical outcomes are considered, the *selection* and *conduct* of activities become highly discriminating. Now, it is clear that certain motor activities can develop wholesome interests in the out-of-doors, in sports and dance that yield functional carry-over skills and can arouse the purpose to live in certain ways and not in other ways.

PHYSICAL EDUCATION IN THE MODERN WORLD

It should not be supposed that the concept of an education through the physical has always prevailed or is even now universally accepted. Over the years social, economic, and political influences have operated to use physical education for varied purposes. Even its application to human needs has been varied, and it is not surprising, therefore, to find in the modern world diverse forms of physical education. Innumerable proposals have been made, many programs have been practiced, and a countless number of plans have been rejected or abandoned. There are today numerous systems of gymnastics, different ways of organizing and conducting sports and games, and sharply conflicting theories of dance. In addition to the more or less regular forms of physical education, there are curious types of massage or treatment cures, special breathing methods, exercises to cure eye defects, and other irregular forms of physical movement.

Although physical education is exceedingly diverse in its expression, the many ideas embodied in a bewildering array of activities may attest to its vitality and energy rather than represent a weakness. Indeed, recent developments and expansions would so indicate. However varied the pattern from nation to nation, the idea that people should be physically educated has won a real place in the national life of virile peoples. World War I gave a new emphasis to physical education; World War II made it secure. The combatant nations adopted the idea of fitness, irrespective of the causes which it was made to serve. Hitler gave to strength a spurious supremacy that aroused more antagonisms than it subdued, but it did cause his opponents, threatened by their weakness, to recruit and develop all that they possessed of vitality, energy, and endurance to meet the challenge that he hurled at them. American military departments were compelled by the grim nature of the struggle to establish quickly extensive programs of physical education, and today the three services continue physical education as a real part of the training of military personnel.

But the modern movement for a wider use of physical education is not limited to the military forces. In schools, in universities, on playgrounds, in clinics, in hospitals, in numerous organizations engaged in welfare work, and in industry physical education has won a place of respect and usefulness.

In the light of varied and highly diverse programs of physical education, it is apparent that guides are needed. Such guides for any profession are the principles of the profession to which all its members can refer; they are a compass at all times, a light to those in doubt, an assurance to the inexperienced.

THE NATURE OF PRINCIPLES

Principles are general concepts based either upon pertinent scientific facts or upon philosophic judgment that arises out of insight and/or experience. The meaning of this statement may be illustrated by the diagram in Figure 1.

PRINCIPLES FROM SCIENTIFIC FACTS

Facts, as such, in scientific circles are regarded as approximations to truth. At the moment of their demonstration they stand as truth until further investigation alters them. The scientific person holds that truth is discoverable, not that it is discovered. His position is not final; it is tentative and not dogmatic. While the nature of fact or truth is scientifically regarded as tentative, the many data from anatomy, physiology, psychol-

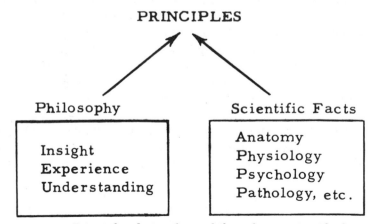

Figure 1.   Principles derive from philosophy or scientific facts.

ogy, and other pertinent sciences are so well established that principles can safely be formulated from them.[10]

Darwin in his study of animal life learned many related facts. From these he derived the principle of natural selection. Cannon studied the adjustments that man makes in maintaining a state of physiological balance and from these he derived the principle of homeostasis.[11] At times, principles are established so clearly that they seem to be irrefutable and come in time to have the sanction of a natural law such as the law of gravitation.

There are numerous principles of physical education that are based upon scientific fact. Thus, the principle that distinguishes in physical education between certain stunts on apparatus for boys and similar activities for girls is based upon the facts of anatomy and physiology, which point to a need for different activities for the two sexes at certain age levels. The principle that breathing should follow as a result of activity, and be an expression of physiological need rather than reflect methodology rests upon certain established facts of physiology, pathology, and psychology. The principle that dance should be an objective, expressive activity rather than a subjective, self conscious movement resides in the nature of dance as well as in the psychological backgrounds of the activity.

The different sciences contribute variously to the determination of principles. For example, anatomy provides information regarding the use of the foot in walking, biology traces an instructive lesson in the developmental stages of vital organs, physiology presents the facts of respiratory need, psychology reveals the laws of learning, embryology makes clear the meanings of growth and of development, anthropology offers an explanation for movements of climbing and hanging. Reliance upon these sciences insures correct principles in the technical

[10] D. B. Van Dalen, "The Nature of Facts," *The Physical Educator,* March, 1958, p. 20. This article gives an illuminating discussion of the nature of facts.

[11] W. B. Cannon, *The Wisdom of the Body*, New York, Norton, 1932. The word *homeostasis* designates the ability of the body cells to maintain a state of balance with respect to the constantly changing conditions that arise during the activities of the cells.

aspects of physical education. Principles derived from scientific facts will be stated in later chapters in connection with the facts that support them.

PRINCIPLES FROM PHILOSOPHY

Insight, understanding, and experience rather than scientific facts are the philosophic basis of principles of government and social organization. The democratic concept of social life expresses its goals in terms of principles such as the dignity of man, equality of opportunity, and worth of the individual man. These principles tend to be unique for the national culture that upholds them. For this reason it is unlikely that systems of physical education can be successfully imported from foreign lands; with respect to certain nations such importation is impossible. While principles relating to man's nature are relatively permanent, and, if based on scientific fact, are adaptable to any people anywhere on biological grounds, the tremendous differences in social, political, and, at times, environmental status are so great that imported systems are usually worthless.

There are many examples of principles of physical education that derive from the philosophy of freedom. The following are illustrative: All children should experience an adequate physical education; the good of the individual rather than the good of the institution should control in managing athletics; discipline of self should be sought rather than the formal discipline of authority; in accordance with their ability pupils should share in planning and managing their activities. Principles based upon philosophic insight and understanding will be stated in later chapters in connection with the argument for their use.

DO PRINCIPLES CHANGE?

Principles based upon well-established facts do not change. The straight foot position in walking, the opposition of arms and legs in locomotion, breathing as related to activity, the learning of form before adding speed to movement—these and similar principles are apparently unalterable. Indeed, the sciences of anatomy and physiology are so well developed that it is doubtful if there will be any considerable change in the principles of physical education based upon these sciences.

In the area of principles derived from philosophic concepts, less assurance of stability can be given. While there are many who believe strongly in the ideas of freedom incorporated in our governmental institutions, there are others who would give up independence, self-reliance, liberty of action, and other traits for economic security, governmental solution of problems of persons, and bureaucratic management of affairs. The present ideological conflict between the East and the West centering in Russia and the United States may produce more uniformity, more regimentation, and more dependence upon government in American life. If this change should occur and thoroughly pervade American life, then the principles of the dignity of man, self-discipline, self-reliance, and the worth of individual personality would also change.

THE SERVICE OF PRINCIPLES

One difference between a profession and a trade is that the former is guided by principles based upon scientific facts and/or philosophic concepts, while a trade is guided only by rules, methods, and directions. These rules may be based upon scientific fact, but the artisan need have no knowledge of them. The characteristic of a profession is its reliance upon facts of nature and/or philosophy as the basis for determination of procedure.

The employment of principles in the training of teachers is justified by the demands of the job. Young people may readily learn a considerable number of motor skills and may appear to the inexperienced person to be qualified to teach the skills they know. If a teacher of physical education had no other responsibility than teaching motor skills to any or all persons, then professional major departments could abandon their libraries and close their lecture halls. But in teaching physical education there are decisions to be made regarding programs, adjustments for individual differences to be effected, various proposals of school officials and laymen to be accepted or rejected, and a wide range of teaching and learning problems to be answered. To recognize and to face competently these important demands requires a much wider preparation than is represented by learning motor skills and nothing more.

An opinion or belief that exercises a directing influence on selection of subject matter or procedure in teaching may have the force of a principle, but it may not be valid in its operation. It may be nothing more than a superstition, a taboo; it may have back of it a body of misinformation. Information may vary tremendously in its validity, both with respect to the accuracy of the data and also with reference to the point of view maintained in deriving the principle.

It is a significant thing that one may uphold a belief based upon untruth as steadfastly as if it were resting on secure foundations in fact. Nevertheless, it is important to remember that the word "principle" implies truth. One meaning of the word connotes primary substance, cause, fundamental truth. It is in this spirit that the words "eternal principles" are used. While it is recognized that beliefs based upon taboo, inaccurate information and traditional practices may have the force of principles in directing effort, use of the term "principle" to imply a foundation in scientific fact and/or philosophy is highly desirable.

The service of principles in a discussion of controversial questions is particularly great if those who represent different views will submit their opinion to its test. Suppose A, wishing to gain good posture, joint flexibility, and muscular strength for children as soon as possible, would advise a certain type of systematic gymnastics. B, considering other things more important in the developing period of childhood, is opposed to such a systematic and artificial activity. Continual emphasis upon individual views avails nothing and may even lead to derogatory remarks and senseless criticism. Suppose on the contrary that

B refers the whole question to the principles of the child's nature, his native drives and urges, the need for education in practices which will not only give muscular strength and agility, but also will shape attitudes and foster skills in activities for living. Suppose, in addition, that B refers to the tendencies in physical education today and shows that books and programs recommend the view which he is proposing.

This reference of disputed practices to principles may lead to agreement on the validity of the principles and so settle the question or, if disagreement persists, the controversy is now on a different level and is apt to be free from recrimination, distrust, and personal criticism. The questions of ballet dancing for children, football for girls, interschool athletics for elementary school children, and numerous others should be considered in similar fashion.

THE PRINCIPLE OF RELATIVE VALUES

Regardless of the value we place upon any technical exercise or motor skill, physiological result or social value, we will always be confronted by the principle of relative value with respect to the opportunity available and the greatness of the need. Physical education alert to fundamental principles will be ready always to formulate its program in realistic fashion.

The changing world today demands vigorous youth. The automobile and the airplane now dominate national life. Their effective use demands fine coordination between hands, feet, and eyes, accuracy in judgment of speed and distance, physical courage and readiness in response. Our changing world also presents problems in the use of leisure, in the prevention of delinquency, in the development of satisfactions and emotional sanity. Failure to recognize the changing world in which we live condemns all human effort to dead purposes and nonexistent needs. To propose for American schools programs devised for children of another land living under tremendously different conditions is to ignore the lessons of history. To conduct physical education in the United States today without reference to the persistent problems of our social scene or regardless of the biological shortages revealed in modern life is to miss completely its real function.

Principles of physical education must be set up which reflect the facts of our changing world in the mirror of that future world that we, in our best moments, most desire. The problems of urban congestion, transportation, and leisure time, and the general disregard for law in comparison with problems of how to throw farther, to dance longer, or to stretch more, are on quite a different level of importance. The former deserve immediate attention and devoted study; concentration on alignments, stretchings, toe pointings, and methods of lengthening the punt are of less value. Nevertheless, the scientific technical facts that enrich, perfect, and justify the practice of physical education in its varied forms are not to be neglected. They are important. There is need for more precise information on a great many vexing problems of procedure. Evaluation of these guides as of less importance than the ones that reflect the changing social and political problems in modern society does not render them worthless. They are significant, but here as elsewhere in education the purpose is more important than the tool. The social direction of human effort is to be considered as paramount.

THE APPLICATION OF PRINCIPLES

If one is convinced that a principle is true, that a body of facts is sound, that a certain program is required by the considerations of theory, then one is obligated to put into operation, as far as possible, the practice which will illustrate the theory. There are those who will say, "The theory is good; the principles are acceptable as theory, but they will not work; they are not practical." This attitude is precisely like one which would accept honesty as good theory, but would note that it was not practical in the modern world.

Many of the desirable things to be done in physical

education do not have wide general approval. There are newspapers which continue to call physical education a "frill"; there are educators who do not understand play, and there are citizens who believe that the sole function of the school is to train the mind. These often oppose a rich program of physical education but will tolerate a drill program with its gross absurdities and impoverished outcomes. The duty of physical education is clear. Whatever programs are best for the finest development of youth, whatever facilities are necessary, the leadership of physical education is everywhere obligated to realize them.

Leaders in physical education who accept the theory or principles at any point are bound to give practical expression to that intellectual agreement or appear completely foolish. Moreover, one who proposes the theory, or states the principles, or assembles the facts is no more responsible for demonstrating their practical application than he who accepts them. The test of leadership is precisely here: to help others to see what is so clear to you. The only way to lead in physical education is to lead. To make prevail that which appears impractical, but which we are convinced is true, is at once the challenge and the test of our conviction and our leadership.

PRINCIPLES AND EXPEDIENCY

How far shall one go in adherence to principles? Shall one abandon principles when it appears expedient to do so? Every teacher, at some time in his professional career, faces issues that test his devotion to principles. How he resolves the issues depends largely upon his professional ideals.

Abraham Lincoln in making his "House Divided" speech in 1858 was confronted by an issue in which principle and expediency were at stake. Before making the address, he read it over privately to some friends. All of them, except Herndon, his law partner, objected to the Biblical quotation: "A house divided against itself cannot stand." His friends argued that he would lose votes if he made this reference. Lincoln made his decision in these words: "I would rather be defeated with this expression in the speech, and uphold and discuss it before the people, than be victorious without it."

Lincoln knew the facts about the Missouri Compromise, the Kansas-Nebraska Act, the Dred Scott decision of the Supreme Court, and in the light of these facts he arrived at the principle expressed in his "House Divided" speech. Moreover, he felt obligated to discuss with the people the principle that he saw so clearly. Friends advised expediency. The politically smart course appeared to require deletion of this part from his address, but devotion to the idea of discussing the truth, as he saw it, led him to reject expediency.

Numerous occasions arise to test the principles of a professional person. Consider the following:

A local American Legion Post requests the school administration to substitute military drill for the program of physical education for boys.

The political leadership of a community supported by the local newspaper advocates a program of athletic competition in all elementary schools with an elimination tournament and award of championships in boxing, football, baseball, basketball, and track.

A textbook publisher requests an author to delete a discussion of evolution from a hygiene text because of criticism from and a loss of sales at certain institutions.

Expediency and compromise are the easy way. Why quarrel with the American Legion? Why risk a position by opposing a local political force? Why discuss evolution and lose royalties? The answers to such questions are always personal; the individual must decide. It should be remembered, however, that expediency and compromise of principles are always fraught with danger to personal integrity. One may give way on a minor principle in order to gain a major one, or one may accept a present defeat in view of a promise of a later victory. The ultimate test, however, is a professional rather than a personal advantage; a cause served rather than personal profit gained.

And that test is not easily made, especially if one is disposed to rationalize his actions. Some persons readily salve an expedient act with the unction of professional good when honest analysis of the problem would reveal personal gain as the bene- factor of the treatment. In these conflicts of the personal and the social, the skeptic is likely to declare that all behavior is selfish and that even the father who goes without food in order that his child may be fed gets more pleasure out of the idea of food for his child than he does from the taste of food on his own palate. Whatever sophistry one may accept in such an argument, the crucial question in this particular situation would seem to be: Which is the better father—the one who feeds himself or the one who feeds his child?

Something like this is the kind of test that a teacher of physical education must make in considering a problem involv- ing principles. Shall he teach breathing exercises at the request of the West Point General who is president of the institution and asks him to do so? Shall he offer a state program of physical edu- cation that will meet the demand of an uninformed but powerful chairman of an important committee of the legislature?

Help in finding the right answers may come from asking other questions. Would a teacher of science instruct his students in astrology, spontaneous generation, or phrenology at the re- quest of a superior official who believed in these notions? Would a physician use leeches in treating disease if requested by a pa- tient to do so? Would a compromise with principles be in order in such circumstances? If the answer is "no" to these questions, under what conditions would the answer be different? It is the counsel of experience that advises compromise when two oppos- ing positions arise in a group from which action is expected or perhaps required. There may be no gain if action is blocked and a possible gain if a middle course between the opposing views can be discovered and accepted. This sort of compromise is inevitable in legislatures, and appears often in the work of educational committees. The compromise leaves each group still loyal to its proposals, whatever they may be, until such time as more experience or more information will lead to abandonment of the position taken or to acceptance by those now in opposition.

QUESTIONS AND PROBLEMS FOR DISCUSSION

1. In what ways do old biological patterns of behavior persist?
2. Why should the notion of separate mind and body lead to educational programs that are restricted to mental or physical outcomes? What is the heritage of physical education?
3. In what ways does the concept of education *through* the physical change the range of objectives for physical education? What is the evidence that good things go together?
4. Does education *through* the physical imply less attention to physical outcomes? Explain.
5. What are the risks incurred by one who is interested in the education of the whole person? What risk does the football coach run when he is interested in pupils' achievements in mathematics, social science, chemistry, and other studies?
6. Give a definition of physical education. Is chopping wood physical education? Is sweeping the porch, milking the cow, carrying newspapers? How would you rate these in comparison with swimming, basketball, or dance? Explain your rating and the reasons for your decision.
7. What are some of the forms of physical education today? Are some of these likely to be better than others? How could the goodness of them be determined?
8. What are principles?
9. What are scientific facts? What is the attitude of the scientist toward truth?
10. What principle did Darwin develop from scientific facts? Can you suggest how useful this principle has been?
11. What principle did Cannon develop from scientific facts?
12. What principles are derived from philosophy? When Jefferson wrote: "We hold these truths to be self-evident, — that all men are created equal; that they are endowed by their Creator with certain unalienable Rights; that among these are Life, Liberty, and the pursuit of Happiness," from what source did Jefferson draw?
13. Do principles change? Explain. Why should principles from philosophy be less stable than those from scientific facts?
14. How can principles serve in the solution of a problem where there are differences of opinion?
15. What is the meaning of relative values? How does this meaning apply in consideration of principles?
16. To what extent is it the duty of a teacher to put theory into practice?

17. How far should one go in adherence to a principle? What do you think of Lincoln's decision? What do you think of the advice given by Lincoln's friends?
18. What answers would you be inclined to give to the problems raised by the American Legion, the political leader, and the publisher? Explain your position in each instance.

REFERENCE READINGS

Brownell, Clifford L., and Hagman, Patricia. *Physical Education: Foundations and Principles*. New York, McGraw-Hill, 1951.

Bucher, Charles A. *Foundations of Physical Education*, 3rd Edition. St. Louis, Mosby, 1960.

Cowell, Charles C. *Scientific Foundations of Physical Education*. New York, Harper, 1953.

Davis, Elwood C. *The Philosophic Process in Physical Education*. Philadelphia, Lea & Febiger, 1961.

Larson, Leonard A. *The Foundations for Physical Education*. Madison, University of Wisconsin, Extension Division, 1962.

Morehouse, Laurence E., and Rasch, Philip J. *Sports Medicine for Trainers*, 2nd Edition. Philadelphia, Saunders, 1962.

Oberteuffer, Delbert, and Ulrich, Celeste. *Physical Education*. New York, Harper, 1962.

Raymont, Thomas. *Modern Education: Its Aims and Methods*, 4th Edition. New York, Green, 1958.

Shepard, Natalie M. *Foundations and Principles of Physical Education*. New York, Ronald Press, 1960.

CHAPTER TWO

PHYSICAL EDUCATION AS EDUCATION

Does our progressive civilization, while it makes ever greater demands on the qualities of its bearers, does it not tend to impair, has it not always in the past actually impaired, the qualities of the peoples on whom it makes these increasing demands?

McDougall.

And yet mankind does not renounce its longing and its demand for a more just, more gentle and more civilized world, that is, for a more human world, in which all rights will be protected; in which every good deed will find help and encouragement; in which hardships and sorrows will gradually diminish or will be transferred to a higher plane than that of cutting one another's throat; in which war will be abolished, not the metaphysical war that is inherent to life itself, but the war which continues the barbaric custom of bloodshed, massacres, cruelties, and torments.

Croce.

Free democracy permits everyone to take part in life as a cultural agent, and not merely as a pawn.

Barzun.

PHYSICAL EDUCATION — AN ASPECT OF EDUCATION

When an individual joins a group and becomes an active participant in its activities, he not only enlarges the scope of his own interests but he also becomes responsible for the purposes to which the group is devoted. When physical education in schools and colleges identified itself with general education, the old and exclusive interest in physique, strength, and motor skills was enlarged to encompass a wider range of objectives. But even more significant than this shift in physical education purposes was the proper concern of physical education with the stated purposes of education itself. In a very real sense, the purposes, programs, and organization of schools and colleges are the concern of physical education, not only because this area is an aspect of education and shares in its total effect on American life but also because it has quite properly a responsibility, like other special areas of education, to help form the purposes of education, to help shape its programs, and to help determine its organization.

EDUCATION IN A REVOLUTIONARY ERA

American education in all institutions is confronted by an unprecedented state of affairs as a result of the economic, social, and political forces loose in the world today. To meet the challenges of these times the help of all educational forces is needed. Both public schools and institutions of higher education are wrestling with problems that call for re-examination of old and well-established policies and procedures.[1] There are many critics of the schools but it should be remembered that criticism of the achievement of education is merely one expression of the general atmosphere of discontent that is world wide.

[1] Thomas W. Mahan, "The Problem of a Democratic Philosophy of Education," *School and Society,* September 27, 1952.

There is no valid reason to lose faith in American education; its problems will be solved even as the American dream of a republic will be fulfilled.

It is heartening to recall that the political and social revolutions in England and France in the seventeenth and eighteenth centuries provided education with rich materials for instruction which for more than a century have nourished the ideals of free peoples. These great cataclysms of society, so tragic for many individuals of one generation, always carry the possibility of great good for following ones. The unrest, uncertainty, and deep concern for the future that mark so plainly the mood and manner of American life today represent the ferment of new ideas in a world of rapid change. Out of this fermentation some clear layers are separating out. It is becoming increasingly clear that whatever social structure emerges out of the present American distress, the health of all is a national asset, the physical education of all children and youth is an imperative need, and the recreation of a community has profound relationship to health, happiness, and good citizenship.

In the light of such convictions, any citizen may properly request that educational leadership concern itself in substantial ways with reasonable measures for guiding and promoting the normal growth of young people. It is easy to dwarf and distort the young organism. This may occur in the home. However faulty in this respect the home may be, it is the clear responsibility of the schools to protect against needless loss the precious quality of native vitality of the young, to develop the innate powers of skill, strength, and endurance in every child, and to promote the wholesome interests of all in the outdoors.

The schools are invariably blamed for any conspicuous failure of youth. When a youth shows poor posture, awkward movements, and inability to play, the American home may escape censure and the popular criticism against "frills" in education may be forgotten, but the program of the schools is remembered. When a youth exhibits bad health habits, the notions and customs of the home are excused but the school's part in the product is assigned. When a youth fails to show the kinds of behavior demanded by society, indeed, when juvenile delinquency bursts forth in a community, the discipline, ideals, and purposes of the home are not mentioned, but the school's policies and programs are widely criticized.

We agree with Thomas Jefferson, who swore "eternal hostility to tyranny over the mind of man," but this sort of autocratic domination should not be confused with rigorous and consistent teaching, which society should exercise in moral and political values. Young people need to learn the rules of custom, courtesy, morals, and religion. When the behavior of young toughs with no sense of personal responsibility is excused as due solely to environmental lacks, social control through education has failed. Civilized and responsible behavior thrives in an urbane environment but that alone is not sufficient.

There is a good deal of sentimental gush about freedom of the individual, which in part is answerable for delinquent individuals. Donald O. Hebb, Professor of Psychology at McGill University, although aware of the tradition of English liberty, writes as follows:

> We do not bring up children with open minds and then, when they can reason, let them reason and make up their own minds as they will concerning the acceptability of incest, the value of courtesy in human relations, or the desirability of democratic government. Instead we *tell* them what's what, and to the extent that we are successful as parents and teachers, we see that they take it and make it a part of their mental processes with no further need of policing.[2]

This sort of statement conflicts, of course, with the general idea of personal freedom. Nevertheless, wherever the behavior of the free individual becomes license to ignore the rights of others, then that freedom needs direction and even restraint. Freedom of the individual to do as he pleases must be judged in the light of what pleases him. If it pleases him to

[2] Donald O. Hebb, "The Role of Experience," *Control of the Mind, Man and Civilization* (Seymour M. Farber, Editor), New York, McGraw-Hill, 1961, p. 52.

bully others, to steal what is not his, or to trample on the freedom of others, then he must be re-educated, if possible, or restrained. Any other policy leads to social chaos.

THE SEARCH FOR EDUCATIONAL PURPOSES

Some of the difficulties confronting educational leadership arise out of confused purposes. An old question constantly recurs: "Shall education seek to develop good individuals or good citizens?" Some persons would say that there is no conflict here; the good individual is the good citizen. But in actual school procedures conflicts arise between those who seek to develop the full potentialities of the human personality and those who seek to train him to become a good citizen.

In these turbulent days of conflicting national ideologies, the issue in education tends to center more and more in this area of the individual and the citizen. Certainly, totalitarian governments are concerned primarily in training citizens, and citizens of a kind that will support the State; in this effort the individual is of little importance and the State is supreme. And just as surely, the free nations that believe in the worth of the individual, the dignity of man, and the sacredness of personality tend to conceive of their purposes in terms of the individual.

There is, however, no basic conflict between the good individual and the good citizen unless goodness in the former excludes relationships with others and goodness in the latter requires conformity to a *status quo*. Education in American schools generally seeks to secure both. When it has been wise, its programs for citizenship have retained what was best in individuality and its programs for self-expression and self-realization have been social as well as personal. However difficult may appear to be the theory of dual purpose, the practice is even more so. To find a balance between the needs of the individual and the needs of the State is the persistent challenge to education in the United States; it is a challenge also to physical education.

PUBLIC OPINION AND EDUCATIONAL PURPOSE

The ideas of the time and place shape educational effort. When education appears at one time to stress citizenship and in another era to regard individual personality as its chief goal, the schools are responsive to the prevailing ideas of the time and place. Over the years, elementary education has exhibited these singular stresses and, even today, either the individual or the citizen may appear to some teachers to be more important.

In colonial days the school was owned, supported, and controlled by the parents of the community. The school committee were the fathers of the children who attended the school. It was a local project and insured local interest. The teacher to be employed and the subjects to be taught were determined by the committee. The teacher boarded with local families during the school term. In some communities the pastor of the local church was the teacher; in all communities the school was closely identified with the church. This close relationship of the family, church, and school placed the emphasis in education upon citizenship.

But colonial life in its simple agrarian society passed away. Industrial development and the growth of manufactures in shop and factory replaced home industries. Populations congregated in large cities. The little red school house could not meet the demands of these new conditions and educational purposes, policies, and administrations changed. Instead of the close relationship of the family, church, and school, diversity grew rapidly; the local school lost much of its independence through the development of state departments of education, trained teachers and superintendents, accreditation agencies, and standards for curricula, buildings, and teachers.

As the schools changed the old emphasis upon moral precepts, character formation, and citizenship became less prominent. New interests appeared. These centered in child study and the learning process. Many of the old beliefs about the nature of the child were challenged by discoveries in several of the biological sciences: The notion of the child as a minia-

ture adult gave way to the concept of the child as a developing
organism; the idea of free will was modified by recognition of
the influence of environmental conditions and physiological
factors; and the separateness of mind and body was abandoned
in view of the overwhelming evidence of organismic unity.

In addition to these shifts in concepts about child nature,
studies in psychology announced revolutionary ideas about
learning. The old adage that "practice makes perfect" was denied by Thorndike's Law of Effect, which stated that learning
was more effective when satisfaction was experienced by the
learner and less effective when dissatisfaction prevailed. Practice was still important, but now interest in what one practiced
and satisfaction from the practice were more important than
repetition. And the age-old belief in general qualities such as
obedience, determination, reasoning, and the like that could be
developed through the study of certain subjects was forced to
retreat before the evidence that learning was specific; it was a
shock to teachers to discover that neatness in a school theme
did not guarantee neatness in the laboratory, in personal appearance, or in housekeeping. Some subjects that had held prominent positions in the curriculum because of their supposed
efficacy in training the mind in reasoning, logical thought, and
clarity of expression gradually lost influence as the abilities they
developed did not transfer to other areas.

THE DILEMMA CONTINUED

The secondary school continued to face the same problem that confronted the elementary school, complicated somewhat by the demand to provide every youth with the best preparation possible for intelligently choosing and competently
following a career. The junior college movement and the availa-
bility of university education as well as the influence of vocational education complicated the purpose of education to
attain the highest level of self-direction possible for the individual's own development as a person and as a responsible

citizen. In these complexities, the purpose of making a good citizen might be lost in concentration upon passing the college entrance examination or in gaining a competent introduction into vocational life. And yet every person must learn not only how to make a living but also how to live with himself and with others in a complex, competitive, and industrial society.

It is clear that the needs of the individual as a person and as a citizen must continually be sought. That such dual purpose is not impossible is indicated by a statement on the needs of youth presented by the Educational Policies Commission as follows:

1. All youth need to develop saleable skills and those understandings and attitudes that make the worker an intelligent and productive participant in economic life. To this end, most youth need supervised work experience as well as education in the skills and knowledge of their occupations.
2. All youth need to develop and maintain good health and physical fitness.
3. All youth need to understand the rights and duties of the citizen of a democratic society, and to be diligent and competent in the performance of their obligations as members of the community and citizens of the state and nation.
4. All youth need to understand the significance of the family for the individual and society and the conditions conducive to successful family life.
5. All youth need to know how to purchase and use goods and services intelligently, understanding both the value received by the consumer and the economic consequences of their acts.
6. All youth need to understand the methods of science, the influence of science on human life, and the main scientific facts concerning the nature of the world and of man.
7. All youth need opportunities to develop their capacities to appreciate beauty in literature, art, music, and nature.
8. All youth need to be able to use their leisure time well and to budget it wisely, balancing activities that yield satisfactions to the individual with those that are socially useful.
9. All youth need to develop respect for other persons, to grow in their insight into ethical values and principles, and to be able to live and work cooperatively with others.
10. All youth need to grow in their ability to think rationally,

to express their thoughts clearly, and to read and listen with understandings.[3]

It is important to notice all the items in the statement of the Educational Policies Commission. Apparently, items 2, 3, 8, and 9 are especially applicable to physical education, but all of them have significance for the teacher of physical education who is interested in the education of the whole person. It should be clear from this statement as well as from many similar ones that physical education is a real part of education in schools and colleges today; it is not only accepted but sought. Its future depends upon its continued contribution to the complete education of individuals and citizens.

EDUCATION AND WORLD CONFLICT

Public education in America has always given some attention to national aspirations, ideals of freedom, and patriotic purposes. Since World War I, this effort has increased, and since the close of World War II, the policies and programs for Americanism have been sharpened and improved. But, in general, this has not restricted freedom of the individual. The nature of principles that guide free peoples, however, is at once a blessing to persons and a hazard to the state. They provide a wide field of choice for all persons without the restriction of commands, the bluster of authority, and the heavy hand of a police state. They protect not only the good citizen but also those who have no love for America and little regard for its institutions. This latter danger must be alertly faced.

In education, principles of freedom not only guarantee

[3] Educational Policies Commission, *Education for All American Youth,* Washington, D.C., National Education Association, 1944, pp. 255-256. See also: Educational Policies Commission, *The Central Purpose of American Education,* Washington, D.C., National Education Association, 1961.

academic freedom for teachers but also give a full opportunity to experiment in educational methods and with curricular materials. Generally, this freedom is not abused. Educational leaders are sensitive to the perilous dangers of these days and within their limitations serve the ideals of the republic as well as do other responsible citizens of the state. Limitations exist in persons of all professions. There are professors of education who expound at length upon economic and social theories concerning which they have no evident competence and only bad taste to guide them. There are educational theorists who invent, propose, and adopt policies and programs that are at best experimental. But these freedoms should not be curtailed. When the views of professors become sufficiently obnoxious, the correction will come either from colleagues or from their own experience with naïveté; and experimentation with educational method and curricular materials is essential for progress. Absurd proposals will be advanced, faulty methods will be tried but the search for better ways to develop better persons and better citizens should continue.

It is necessary to consider all methods and all programs of instruction not only as experimental approaches to better education but also in relation to the very obvious and insidious attacks upon American democracy. Thus, the academic freedom of scholars, guided by intellectual honesty and enlightened by the standards of a scholarly profession, must not become a shield for the insidious propaganda of antagonistic ideologies. It is a matter of fact and record that communism has made determined efforts to infiltrate our schools and colleges. But the protection of the nation in the field of ideas must come from the scholars themselves. Education can be as alert to protect principles of freedom as set forth in the Constitution and Bill of Rights as it is to teach the truth revealed in scholarly studies. Scholarly accomplishment does not inoculate against communist infection, and even professors can be misled by clever and unscrupulous persons, but there is no patriotic élite with enough ability to tell education how to police itself.

THE CONTRIBUTION OF PHYSICAL EDUCATION TO EDUCATION

The identification of physical education with education exists today because physical education made two important decisions. In one decision it changed its purposes and modified its programs of mass calisthenics and formal drill; in the other decision it accepted the responsibility given by wise educational leadership to be interested in and concerned with the whole program of the school or college.

These decisions were based upon the understanding that physical education had a contribution to make to the education of the individual and the citizen. That contribution arises out of four possible developments: (1) development of organic systems, (2) development of neuromuscular skills, (3) development of interest in play and recreation, and (4) development of standard ways of behavior.

DEVELOPMENT OF ORGANIC SYSTEMS

The organic systems are the great vital organs and their associated structures: circulatory, respiratory, digestive, excretory, endocrine, skeletal, and nervous systems. Their development to highest functional levels is dependent upon physical activity that uses vigorously the large muscles of the trunk and hip joints. These large muscular masses make demands upon the vital organs to increase their functions in order to meet the needs of the muscles (Fig. 2). The vigor and vitality of a person resides in the functional ability of these vital organs, and their functional powers are developed in childhood and youth by physical exercise. There is no alternate route that one can take; moreover, this development must occur in childhood and reach its fulfillment in youth.

The small muscles of the arms contribute little to this development, and mild exercises are of minor value. Therefore, in order to gain the development needed for vitality, the

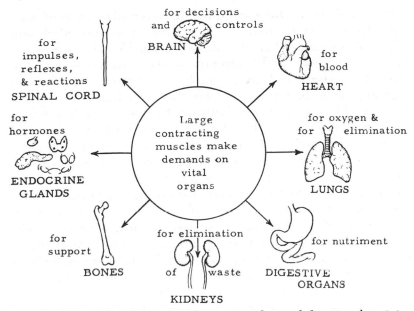

Figure 2 How the large muscle masses demand functional activity of the vital organs.

child must run and jump, climb and hang, pull and push, wrestle and test himself in many ways with others of his kind.

It is nature's way to develop the internal vital systems by muscular exercise. There is no other way. All of life in its varied manifestations of energy flows from the functioning of the vital organs. It is important to discuss the relations of muscular exercise to these vital systems: muscular, nervous, circulatory, respiratory, digestive, eliminative, and endocrine.

The Muscular System and Exercise. The nutrition of muscle depends in part upon the activity of the muscle. Other things being equal, a moderately used muscle is better nourished than one less used or unused. Use causes the muscle cells to increase in size. This is called *hypertrophy*. Disuse results in *atrophy*. In the latter there are progressive chemical changes, and when these are long standing, there is replacement of muscle cells with connective tissue. Atrophy is accompanied with a loss of strength. When the atrophied muscles are used again (as after an illness), the atrophy is soon overcome and the size of a muscle and its strength are restored. Muscles are supplied with blood by vessels that penetrate the muscle bundles. The tissue spaces between the muscle cells serve as exchange places to receive the nourishing substances brought by the blood and to discharge the waste products from the muscle cells. These exchanges depend upon osmosis and diffusion, although muscular contractions greatly facilitate the exchange. These contractions add something in additional waste products, but the general effect of exercise is improvement of the quality of the fluid in the spaces around the muscle cells.

A muscle with its nerve is a functional unit. Without its nerve a muscle is a helpless mass, and the motor nerve without its effector muscle is a futile structure. The two together comprise a neuromuscular or psychomotor unit.

The Nervous System and Exercise. Development of the nervous system is promoted by movement. When the individual animal gained the ability to move from one place to another, new experiences could arise, and these required responses from the nerve structures to surrounding objects and forces. Sessile creatures fixed to one place never achieve the nervous development possible in mobile ones. Moreover, muscle and nerve (neuromuscular unit) developed in close relationship (Fig. 3); in low life forms such as sponges contractile elements developed before nerve elements appeared.[4] Later on, as cells became more specialized, it was the development of muscles that dragged into existence nervous, circulatory, respiratory, digestive, eliminative, and endocrine systems. Descriptive anatomy and physiology often give the impression that these vital systems are quite independent. Nothing could be further from the truth. All are intimately related through nerve impulses and chemical secretions. Herrick calls attention to this

[4] C. Judson Herrick, *Neurological Foundations of Animal Behavior*, New York, Holt, 1924, pp. 81, 86, 90.

Figure 3. Diagram of a primitive neuromuscular unit. After Parker.

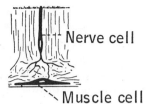

Nerve cell

Muscle cell

in the following: "The unity of the organism in all complex animal bodies appears to be dependent upon the presence of a highly efficient conducting apparatus."[5]

The pattern in all education today is to require scientific evidence for our decisions. It is interesting, however, to read a statement like the following written nearly 100 years ago, with no scientific data offered:

> Well might we touch upon the condition of the nervous system of the people of our own and many other countries at the present time. They are indeed highly strung! Yet mental excitation is boundless and increasing. Rapid travelling, cheap and abundant literature — every desire appealed to, every want forestalled! Surely we require no additional loads to be cast upon this nervous system, but we need a better harness for its control and guidance.[6]

Even then, Blundell knew that moderate exercise reduces nervous tension, and Josephine L. Rathbone repeats this excellent advice as she writes: "It is possible to reduce tension and bring about relaxation by rhythmic exercises for the extremities and trunk."[7]

The Circulatory System and Exercise. In one-celled organisms the circulation of needed materials through the cell membrane is relatively a simple process. However, when the animal is composed of many cells those not in contact with the ex-

[5] *Ibid.,* p. 250.
[6] John W. F. Blundell, *The Muscles and Their Story,* London, Chapman & Hall, 1864, p. 4.
[7] Josephine L. Rathbone, *Relaxation,* New York, Teachers College, Columbia University, 1943, p. 93.

ternal environment need some means of transporting nutrients to the inner cells and of removing their waste.* This dual function is served by the circulation.

The different vital systems make varying demands upon the circulation. During digestion of food the alimentary tract is very demanding, and during exercise both the circulation and respiration are accelerated. In vigorous exercise the muscles are gorged with blood to bring nutrient materials to the active cells and to remove their waste. In carrying on this circulation the heart is the prime agent in propelling blood not only to the muscles but—such is the nature of the vessels—to all parts of the body. In the return of blood to the heart, there are several aids to the circulation, with muscular contraction the most important factor in returning blood from the legs.

Regular doses of exercise slow the heart rate and increase the strength of the heart beat. Typically, athletes have a slower heart rate than nonathletes. Cardiologists today agree that exercise does not injure the normal heart. Some persons with heart defect are benefited by prescribed amounts of exercise, but individuals with an infection should be quiet rather than active during temperature periods.

Students today are not likely to be familiar with R. Tait McKenzie's book *Exercise in Education and Medicine.* It is now out of print, but if library copies are available, Chapter IV, "The Effects of Exercise on the Heart," is well worth reading.[8]

Respiratory System and Exercise.   The lungs are enlarged and the respiratory muscles strengthened by regular exercise. Running develops lung capacity more surely than breathing exercises. Many years ago Fernand Lagrange, in one of the first books on the physiology of exercise, advised running for boys, and dancing for girls, for chest development. Exercise requires oxygen and produces carbon dioxide; the interchange in these

* The calculated number of cells given by Ruth Moore is 1,000,000,-
    000,000,000. See Ruth Moore, *The Coil of Life*, New York,
    Knopf, 1961, p. 380.
[8] R. Tait McKenzie, *Exercise in Education and Medicine*, Philadel-
    phia, Saunders, 1915, pp. 50-62.

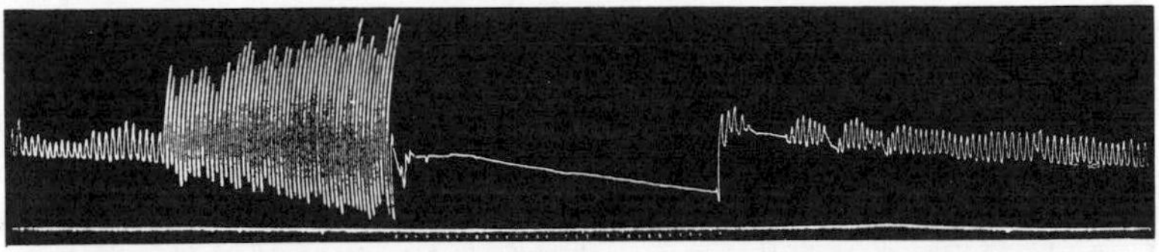

Figure 4. Forced breathing for a period of two minutes is followed by apnea lasting for three minutes. This is succeeded by periodic breathing of the Cheyne-Stokes type which persists for a minute or so before normal breathing is resumed. (After Douglas and Haldane. From Best and Taylor: "The Living Body," Henry Holt and Company.)

gases occurs in the lungs. Normally in quiet states, in which the respiratory rate is about 14 times per minute, there is an equilibrium in respect to the two gases. This condition of respiration is known as *eupnea*. If one forcefully breathes for 90 seconds at the rate of 30 times per minute, an interval will ensue in which there is no breathing (Fig. 4). This condition is called *apnea;* it is due to a scarcity of carbon dioxide. The period of apnea persists until carbon dioxide has accumulated sufficiently to restore the normal breathing rate.

In running races of a mile or more a well-known phenomenon is "second wind." This gives sudden relief to the agony of breathlessness and is an adjustment of the heart and lungs to the increased demand for oxygen and elimination of carbon dioxide. The mile runner usually gets this relief during the third quarter of the race. Its onset and efficiency seem to be improved by training.

Digestive System and Exercise. The demand of the muscles for nutrient materials tends to improve appetite, increase food consumption, and to cause increased activity of all the digestive organs. The outcomes are delayed. Vigorous exercise soon after eating may cause digestive disturbances due to inhibition of the digestive juices. Since sugar is the chief nutrient used by the muscles, its presence in the blood increases during vigorous exercise. Emotional stress also increases the blood sugar, probably an adaptation in preparation for an emergency. If the emergency fades, the excess of sugar is eliminated by the kidneys.

Athletes before a game invariably give a positive test for sugar in the urine but never after they have played.[9]

Eliminative System and Exercise. Waste is eliminated from the body by the lungs in expired air, by the skin in perspiration, by the kidneys in the urine, and by the intestines in the feces. Muscular exercise influences the functioning of these organs. The lungs eliminate carbon dioxide from the blood—this is one of the waste products of exercise.

The perspiration is composed mainly of water with some salts in solution, but the skin is not an important organ of elimination except for purposes of temperature control; in this function evaporation of water from the surface of the skin is cooling.

The kidneys are the main eliminative organs. One of the waste products of exercise is lactic acid; some of this is eliminated in the urine. Other waste substances in the urine are urea, creatine, uric acid, purine compounds and chlorides, sulfates, and phosphates. Some of these are derived from protein metabolism and come from other cells in addition to the muscles.

The waste left after digestion of food is not regarded as an excretion of the eliminative system, but it must be removed and exercise aids in this function. This waste comes mainly from food materials. At the end of some 20 feet of travel the food, now entirely liquefied and changed chemically, enters the colon in its first portion, the cecum. If one could travel over this tract and on reaching the cecum wished to take a side trip, he could visit one of the old ruins to be found in man, the vermiform appendix. This remnant of a by-gone age remains as silent testimony of other days, but it plays no part in the activity of a twentieth century colon.

In its course through the colon water is lost from the food mass; hence as it reaches the sigmoid it has become semisolid. During its stay in the colon bacterial activity has been marked. Along the way it has associated with a motley crowd that has given it a bad name; there are chemicals of putrid odor, decomposing bits of undigested food, bacteria, and a mass of pigments,

[9] C. P. Hickman, *Physiological Hygiene,* New York, Prentice-Hall, 1937, p. 77.

fatty globules, the varied remnants of the company encountered in the tract.

Muscular exercise that strengthens and maintains the tone of the muscles of the abdominal wall plays a large part in normal functioning of the alimentary canal.

The Endocrine System and Exercise. Little is known about the specific effects of exercise on endocrine functions. These organs of internal secretion play a large part in metabolism, influence growth and development, and are very active in emergencies, in emotional states, and in the development of sex characteristics. It is reasonable to assume that exercise, by improving circulation, helps to maintain their efficiency.

DEVELOPMENT OF NEUROMUSCULAR SKILLS

The human individual is skill-hungry; at an early age the child begins his search for skills and repeats his runnings, jumpings, throwings, and climbings a countless number of times. The skills he himself selects to learn are all related either to his hereditary past or to the actual present. He may be taught all sorts of skills but only those that are functional contribute to his education. Functional skills are either utilitarian or recreational. The utilitarian skills are walking, running, sitting, standing, lifting weights, climbing stairs, carrying objects, and other neuromuscular coordinations employed in daily life. The recreational skills are innumerable coordinations that function in games, sports, athletics, dance, and self-testing activities. These illustrate the functional use of skills and suggest their educational contribution as the individual enters into recreational activity at various age levels.

Moreover, physical education in functional neuromuscular skills is full-time education. It is not a subject to be studied thirty minutes a day and then forgotten. Instead it lives on in the many activities of clubs, after-school play, vacations, and all of life.

This kind of physical education carries over into life if

the skills are functional. There are some persons who teach movements that have no relation to any conceivable natural activity of man; they give the dubious justification that such movements are hard to do and therefore good for one. The reasons for teaching nonfunctional skills are various. Pupils are asked to bend over and touch the floor with the fingers without bending the knees; movements that hurt, like medicine that tastes bad, are often regarded as good for people. But this exercise has no functional use whatever. In picking up an object from the floor, the proper coordination is to bend the knees. Indeed, this is very important in lifting heavy objects, since one should lift with the thigh rather than the back muscles. Trying to touch the floor without bending the knees puts strain on the sacroiliac joint and may cause injury. Football players are exercised in "grass drills"; erroneous justification—to warm up the players, but the "drill" is usually given after the players have been passing and kicking the ball, running and dodging for fifteen to twenty minutes. Moreover, the movements in these "drills" are quite unrelated to the skills required in football. In practice for golf, baseball, or basketball the athlete will do exercises which are real parts of the activity. He does not warm up by doing "duck walks," push-ups, and other unrelated movements. Pupils engage in shuttle relay races and at times are given a basketball to carry while they run; false justification— to give variety to the activity, but in the game of basketball the player is taught *not* to run with the ball.

DEVELOPMENT OF INTEREST IN PLAY AND RECREATION

To awaken and to keep alive an interest in wholesome play and recreation is a real contribution to the education of the individual. All children express early an interest in play. To the casual observer the play may appear to be mere "fooling," but it is nature's way of development. As the child grows older he gains more controls, and as skill increases, the possibilities of the activity are appreciated. Now interest intensifies and expands. Learning such a simple game as hopscotch may lead the individual to spend many hours in this activity, while rope-jumping may open up so many exciting coordinations that the jumper will practice for hours until satisfaction comes. It is from such simple experiences in childhood that the individual goes on to more complex games, and later in life carries over into adult years the interest in handball, golf, tennis, swimming, and dance.

This kind of physical education is leisure education. The activities it promotes not only arouse interest in recreation but also prepare the individual to find satisfaction in it. The relationship of skill in an activity to participation is simple and direct. The dub in any motor experience gets no fun from a poor performance and soon drops the activity because it provides no satisfaction. Proficiency and participation go together.

DEVELOPMENT OF STANDARD WAYS OF BEHAVIOR

Behavior is learned. Every experience leaves a behavior deposit in the habits and attitudes of the individual. Physical education is one of the vital means of education in civilized behavior because the young care deeply about these experiences in which they participate. Learning to be generous, kindly, fair, friendly, and tolerant when participating in vital experience is learning that takes and lasts. When an individual strongly desires to win a game and learns to temper this desire by the higher control of fairness, or tolerance, or generosity, he is started on the path of civilized behavior that contributes to good citizenship in a community or nation.

But youth does not arrive at this condition of civilized action alone. The behavior is taught and leaders are responsible for the teaching. Improvement in human behavior in any area of action depends upon persons who exemplify kinds of behavior that the young desire to imitate; more is accomplished by good example than good precept, and precept that is not illustrated is probably worthless. Fair, generous, kindly, and tolerant behavior fails of achievement in the young when teachers miss the chance to be excellent examples, when parents neglect to support ethical decisions, and when citizens generally excuse poor behavior in professional sports and place winning above everything else.

At the Sequoia Junior High School in Fresno, the record for the rope climb event (15 feet) was 2.1 seconds. The following is an account by the physical education instructor of an experience in teaching standard ways of behavior:

> For three years Bobby Polacio, a 14½-year-old ninth grade Mexican boy, has trained and pointed, and, I suspect, dreamed of breaking this record. It has been his consuming passion; it seemed his whole life depended upon owning this record.
>
> In his first of three attempts Bobby climbed the rope in 2.1 seconds, tying the record. On the second try the watch stopped at 2.0 seconds flat, a record! But, as he descended the rope and the entire class gathered around to check the watch, I knew I must ask Bobby a question. There was a slight doubt in my mind whether or not the board at the 15 foot height had been touched. If he missed, it was so very, very close — not more than a fraction of an inch — and only Bobby knew this answer.
>
> As he walked toward me, expressionless, I said, "Bobby, did you touch?" If he had said "yes" the record he had dreamed of since he was a skinny seventh grader and had worked for almost daily would be his, and he knew I would trust his word.
>
> With the class already cheering him for his performance, the slim, brown-skinned boy shook his head negatively. And in this simple gesture, I witnessed a moment of greatness.
>
> Coaches do not cry. Only babies cry, they say. But as I reached out to pat this boy on the shoulder, there was a small drop of water in each eye. And it was with effort, through a tight throat, that I told the class: "This boy has not set a record in the rope climb. No, he has set a much finer record, a real genuine record for you and me and everyone to strive for. *He has told the simple truth.*"
>
> I turned to Bobby and said, "Bobby, I'm proud of you. You've just set a record many athletes never attain. Now, in your last try, I want you to jump a few inches higher on the take off. You're going to break this record."
>
> After the other boys had finished their next turns and Bobby came up to the rope for his last try, a strange stillness came over the gymnasium. Fifty boys and one coach were breathlessly

set to help boost Bobby Polacio to a new record. He climbed
the rope in 1.9 seconds! A school record, a city record, and perhaps close to a national record for a junior high school boy.

When the bell rang and I walked away, now misty-eyed, from
this group of boys, I was thinking: "Bobby, little brown skin,
with your clear, bright, dark eyes and your straight trim, lithe
body — Bobby, at 14 you are a better man than I. Thank you for
climbing so very, very high today."[10]

THE NEW EDUCATION

The old problem of education to develop the individual
both as person and as citizen remains. In a society of free men
no other purpose is possible. And that purpose can be advanced
by an intelligent cooperation of all the forces in education today.
In such a society, properly conceived human needs and properly
conceived national needs fuse, coalesce, and become one. The
needs of the individual for physique correspond to national
needs for vigor and vitality in citizens. The needs of the personality for belonging correspond to national needs for patriotism and love of country in citizens. Neither persons nor the nation need be exalted or debased. Proper planning for education
will lead us to think of benefits to the nation without which
persons are bereft, and benefits to persons without which there
would be no nation. There is no national good, if it is unable to
prove itself good for persons and there is no personal good, if
it is unable to support and strengthen national life. Physical education accepts the challenge of this dual effort given to education.

QUESTIONS AND PROBLEMS FOR DISCUSSION

1. Why have the objectives of modern physical education enlarged? Discuss the limitations upon individual freedom
   that you would advise as educational policy.

[10] By permission of *The Journal of the California Teachers Association,*
February, 1962, p. 21.

2. To what extent should physical education be concerned with the purposes of education? Explain your answer.

3. What are some of the outcomes of the world-wide revolutionary movement that are of interest to physical education?

4. Why should educational leadership be interested in physical education?

5. Who is responsible for the following: poor posture, awkward movement, bad health habits, juvenile delinquency in high school pupils? To what extent do you think that the individual himself is responsible?

6. Why is a democratic society interested in the individual as both a person and a citizen? Under what conditions has education wisely sought both objectives?

7. What was the nature of the school in colonial America?

8. Why was the little red school house abandoned?

9. What changes did psychology and child study bring to the school?

10. Is there any reason why interest in personal achievement should interfere with development of the good citizen?

11. What approval or disapproval do you give to the statement of the needs of youth by the Educational Policies Commission?

12. What four contributions does physical education make to education?

13. Why does the development of organic systems contribute both to the person and to the nation? What effects on the vital organs are produced by exercise?

14. Why does the development of functional skills contribute both to the person and the nation?

15. Explain how an interest in play and recreation may be good for the individual and of value to the community.

16. Explain how fine behavior is an advantage to the individual and to the nation.

17. What are the organic systems? What kinds of activity develop these systems? Discuss the effects of exercise upon the organic systems.

18. What are functional skills? Name some nonfunctional skills which you have learned. Discuss the warming up exercises used in golf, baseball, basketball, and football. Explain why touching the floor with the hands, knees being straight, is a poor exercise.

19. What is a standard behavior? How is it established?

20. What is the meaning of the statement that physical education is "universal and timeless"?

21. Why should physical education avoid an exclusive emphasis upon the physical?
22. What is the full import of the idea that all manifestations of life arise out of the physical organism?
23. Why should "Bowl games" be tested by the purposes behind them?
24. Discuss fully the concept that physical education should join hands with general education.
25. Describe how the needs of the individual and the nation may fuse in physical education.

REFERENCE READINGS

Abernathy, Ruth. "Implications for Physical Education in the Current Re-Examination of American Education." *Journal of Health—Physical Education—Recreation*, January, 1961, p. 19.

American Association for Health, Physical Education and Recreation. "Athletics in Education: Platform Statement." *Journal of Health—Physical Education—Recreation*, September, 1962, p. 24.

American Association for Health, Physical Education and Recreation. *Developing Democratic Human Relations Through Health Education, Physical Education and Recreation.* First Yearbook. Washington, D.C., 1951.

Bishop, Thelma. "Values in Sports." *Journal of Health—Physical Education—Recreation*, September, 1962, p. 45.

Brace, D. K. "Ethical Standards for Personnel Connected with Intercollegiate Athletics." *Proceedings of the College Physical Education Association*, 1958, p. 132.

Bruner, Jerome Seymour. *The Process of Education.* Cambridge, Harvard, 1960.

Conant, James B. *The American High School Today: A First Report to Interested Citizens.* New York, McGraw-Hill, 1959.

Elkins, Wilson W. "Physical Education: Part of the General Education Program." *Journal of Health—Physical Education—Recreation*, February, 1961, p. 25.

Gruber, Frederick C. (Editor). *The Emergence of the Modern Mind.* Philadelphia, University of Pennsylvania, 1958.

Gwynn, John Minor. *Curriculum Principles and Social Trends*, 3rd Edition. New York, Macmillan, 1960.

Hutchinson, John L. (Editor). *Leisure and the Schools.* American Association for Health, Physical Education and Recreation. Fourth Yearbook. Washington, D.C., 1961.

Kelley, Earl C., and Rasey, Marie I. *Education and the Nature of Man.* New York, Harper, 1952.

Kozman, Hilda C. (Editor). *Group Process in Physical Education.* New York, Harper, 1951.

Martin, Phyllis C., and Vincent, Elizabeth L. *Human Development.* New York, Ronald Press, 1960.

Nash, Jay B. "Education for Leisure—A Must." *Journal of Health—Physical Education—Recreation,* January, 1960, p. 17.

O'Keefe, Pattric R., and Aldrich, Anita. *Education Through Physical Activities: Physical Education and Recreation, Elementary Grades,* 3rd Edition. St. Louis, Mosby, 1959.

Paschal, Elizabeth. *Encouraging the Excellent.* New York, Fund for the Advancement of Education, 1960.

Prescott, Daniel Alfred. *The Child in the Educative Process.* New York, McGraw-Hill, 1957.

Report of Committee on Aging. "Education of Children and Youth for the New Era of Aging." *Journal of Health—Physical Education—Recreation,* March, 1962, p. 24.

Rockefeller Brothers Fund. *The Pursuit of Excellence: Education in the Future of America.* Garden City, N. Y., Doubleday, 1958.

Tibbits, Clark, and Donahue, William (Editors). *Aging in Today's Society.* Englewood Cliffs, N.J., Prentice-Hall, 1960.

PHYSICAL EDUCATION IN A DEMOCRACY — POLITICAL CONCEPTS

PHYSICAL EDUCATION IN A DEMOCRACY* – POLITICAL CONCEPTS

Do you want to be a free human being standing on your own feet, accepting the responsibilities, as an effective member of society?

Dewey.

The realism which underlies the criterion of the good society . . . cautions against expecting it to come into the lives of men and nations too easily . . . philosophical, political, economic and religious beliefs are not the only things making society and history what they are. There are famine, disease, climate and countless other non-ideological factors. Also there are the ignorance, the lassitude, and the bursts of impulsive, misguided frenzy in each one of us and in mankind. And there are the hardened habits, institutions and sentiments formed by the partial, inadequate and often outmoded values of the past.

Northrop.

*Although the government of the United States is a republic and not a democracy in the exact meaning of the word, the latter term is generally used to indicate the form of the American government since the ultimate power resides in the people.

DEMOCRACY—A MORAL SYSTEM

In the earliest social groups of man, the headman of the family or clan or tribe held power over the members of the group. The activities of primitive life gave a kind of training which served the tribe or in due time it ceased to exist. A great weakness in this early group life was the waste in time, energy, and wealth in quarreling or war, due largely to the fact that few concepts existed defining the moral relationships among men. From these early chiefs or headmen, the step to king and emperor was easy and the change from a wandering or nomadic life to village and larger community life carried along the customs, traditions, and rituals of despotic rule by an all-powerful leader.

These organizations of men, held together by fear or tradition or ritual, were despotisms. The king ruled; the people obeyed. In this situation man is a slave either to a king or a tradition. Somehow, somewhere, one man got the idea that he disliked this sort of thing. He rebelled. If he gained followers, he dethroned the ruler and became a king himself. This usually changed nothing for the people. One king might be more benevolent than another or more selfish and tyrannical than another. The despotism remained. Somehow, somewhere, the idea arose that man himself, as a person, is something of real worth, *in and of himself*. This was a revolutionary idea in a group where men were chattels to be bought and sold, killed or imprisoned as the ruler pleased. This idea was further expounded by a carpenter by the name of Jesus who preached the doctrine of the sacredness of the personality. A new force had appeared in human society that in a few centuries was to change the ideas of millions of men about government, rulers, and human relations.

In 1776 the American colonies rebelled against England and set forth their notion about political matters in the words of Jefferson:

We hold these truths to be self-evident, — that all men are created equal, that they are endowed by their Creator with certain unalienable Rights, that among these are Life, Liberty and the pursuit of Happiness. That to secure these rights, Governments are instituted among Men, deriving their just powers from the consent of the governed. . . .

Lincoln further defined the idea set forth by Jefferson in the Declaration of Independence. He used the words, "government of the people, by the people, for the people."

This idea of government is called democracy, a word of Greek origin meaning people and authority. The idea of democracy deals with the relationship among men in which it is proclaimed that people have certain natural rights, "natural because they belong to all men by virtue of their being men."[1] While the development of democratic institutions arose as protest against taxes, arbitrary government, imprisonments, interference with trade, denial of trial by jury, and other tyrannies of ruling groups, democracy is basically a moral system rather than an economic system. Its foundations are the supremacy of the human personality and the brotherhood of mankind.

As a moral system democracy rests upon belief in a Supreme Being who created all men equal, belief in the development of the human personality, and belief in a definite relationship of the person to this Supreme Being. Because of this relationship man has "certain unalienable rights" and therefore these cannot be abrogated by any power on earth.

DEMOCRACY AND EDUCATION

In the political conflicts of these days much of the debate centers on economic problems. This is because economic issues are generally the particular and practical areas of disagreement. The American colonists objected to taxation, but behind that issue was the conviction about "certain unalienable rights." The

[1] William F. Russell, *The New "Common Sense,"* New York, Macmillan, 1941, p. 75.

meaning of liberty and freedom lie beneath these discussions of economic questions and come to the surface when economic issues become acute and dangerous to the basic freedoms of man.

Moreover, the culture of a society tends to shape the philosophy of government. Jefferson was aware of the power of a cultural pattern in shaping political institutions; he feared that the growth of manufactures and trade might impair the democratic forms of life in which he so strongly believed. But manufactures and trade have developed and increased. The cultural pattern of modern industrial America is established and the nation cannot go back to the simple agricultural society that Jefferson admired. Maintenance of democracy in America must depend upon its present sources.

Democracy and its institutions can persist only if people love them. John Locke in the eighteenth century taught that a democracy could survive if the people were educated to understand it and do their part as citizens of it. Education must give respect for law, teach the citizen to take his place in government, and show him how to apply in his whole life those moral principles of democracy that underlie the concept of government by free men. Such moral education must center its efforts on the activities of the young who can learn by experience the meaning of equality of opportunity, dignity of the human personality, individual responsibility for outcomes, and other moral concepts of democratic life. Some of these concepts will arise and must be taught in physical education. Four of these, equality of opportunity, personal worth, individual responsibility, and self-achievement, relate directly to physical education.

EQUALITY OF OPPORTUNITY

The Declaration of Independence says, in Jefferson's words, "all men are created equal." In many ways this is a strange idea. Every day the evidence shows that all persons are not equal in strength, in agility, in intelligence, indeed in almost every trait. Moreover, physical education accepts the principle of individual differences among persons. But the equality that Jefferson had in mind was not biological equality but political equality. The practice for centuries had been to play favorites, to grant special privileges, to have one kind of justice for friends and another for enemies. The idea of equality in a democracy has come to be equality of opportunity.

This concept is of great interest to education because it underlies the whole process of developing the young. Only as every child has an opportunity to develop his unique and inherent powers and capacities can the fullness of himself be realized and the nation receive the contribution of his life. There are several points at which this concept applies in the conduct of physical education; as such they are principles.

In school and college all should have equal opportunity in a basic and general program of physical education.

In the survey of the schools of a mill town in an eastern state, it was observed that the program of physical education varied greatly in the schools of the community. In the schools attended by the children of the mill hands, the program was mainly calisthenics and formal drill; in the schools on the hill attended by the children of mill owners, professional and business persons, the program was rich with dance, swimming, tennis, and athletic games. After the survey the program was changed, but its existence illustrates the fact that at times leadership is quite unaware of the danger to democracy that resides in favoritism and special privilege and in denial of equality of opportunity.

Equality of opportunity may be violated in facilities and equipment as well as in program. If all are to have equality of opportunity, then the placement of a swimming pool in a school is not determined by the economic or social status of the neighborhood which the school serves, the budget allowance for expendable items is not set by political considerations in which privilege operates, and the use of piano or phonograph for dance is not settled by favoritism of one teacher over another.

It should not be supposed that differences in opportunity

always mean venal behavior of those who make decisions. Equality of opportunity is a reality with which physical education must be concerned but it does not require that the opportunity be always identical. The difference will be illustrated in the following application of the principle.

Needs, interests, and abilities of the participants should serve to determine the differences in opportunity to be offered.

There are differences in individuals that justify differences in programs. The justification arises out of the purpose to meet individual needs, interests, and abilities. Therefore it is sound to offer special instruction in order to meet needs, to offer a choice of activities in order to meet interests, and to offer elementary and advanced instruction in order to meet abilities.

Special instruction is readily justified for handicapped individuals. The entire rehabilitation program or the restricted class program rests upon this principle of individual need.

But this principle should not be distorted in its application. In the school survey of an eastern city, a high school teacher of physical education was observed conducting a class of boys. He tossed out a basketball to the class, and while most of the boys engaged in a free-for-all type of basketball game and the smaller boys stood around, the teacher used the period to instruct two boys in sprints on the running track of the gymnasium. Special instruction for the few with corresponding neglect of the many is poor teaching, and a violation of democratic principles.

The application of this principle is severely tested by the way in which physical education teachers distribute their time to athletes and nonathletes. Certainly there is no justification for a teacher of physical education to give time in special instruction to the superior performer if this means neglect of the ordinary pupil or student. The entire athletic team program in school and college is an education of an élite. It should be done only if all other individuals in the group are getting a chance to be physically educated.

The principle of interest presents a problem because the interests of young people are limited by experience. Teachers should interpret the principle of interest to refer to type of activity rather than a specific form of it. For example, college students with no experience in lacrosse are not likely to be interested in it but their basic interest in games is sufficient reason for the teacher to introduce them to this sport.

Moreover, there is another important consideration in this problem. The policy of public education rests upon the assumption that the educated person will become not only a better individual but also a better citizen. In the latter role he will be expected to return to society in his social behavior something that corresponds to the energy, effort, and time given to his education. If this view is maintained in physical education then it is reasonable to expect that the general program of physical education will educate the individual in the dub class to the level where he participates in physical activity and enjoys doing so. Such continued participation over the years is evidence of wholesome leisure time interest and surely contributes to at least one aspect of good citizenship. And by the same token, individuals whose instruction requires more energy, effort, and time of a staff in the complex activities of interscholastic or intercollegiate sport should be expected to return more to society, not only in their physical performance but also in their behavior as citizens.

The champion athlete is an excellent organism; the demands upon him for physical performance are enormous. He can run and jump better than most persons. At times, he must feel himself possessed of greater vitality and in command of more power; at these times he excels. But neither educational philosophy nor public opinion should be satisfied with superior physical performance alone. Education holds that an élite has obligations that all nobility rightfully feels. The privilege of the superior person lies not in concessions or favors but in conquests. Jose Ortega y Gassett expresses a similar thought in the following: "The excellent man is urged by inner necessity to appeal from himself to some standard beyond himself, superior to himself, whose service he freely accepts."[2] In this

---

[2] Jose Ortega y Gassett, *The Revolt of the Masses*, New York, Norton, 1932, p. 69.

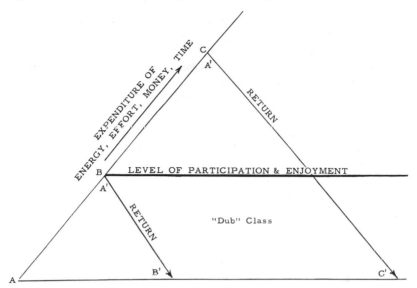

Figure 5. This diagram illustrates the principle that a greater expenditure on the education of an individual requires that the social investment should be matched by the individual return, that A'B' will be equivalent to AB; and that the greater investment in AC places correspondingly greater obligations upon the excellent man as indicated in A'C'.

view, then, the ordinary performer makes no great demands upon himself and is content to be at all times what he already is. The excellent man, however, makes great demands upon himself and is in perpetual servitude to new standards to which he can and does repair. Interscholastic and intercollegiate athletics will never be "overemphasized" if the participants in these rigorous sports become increasingly the excellent citizens, the shining examples of character and behavior for the youth of a nation to imitate (Fig. 5).

PERSONAL WORTH

Two views of life and government exist in the world today. In one the State is supreme and the individual exists to serve the State; in the other the individual is supreme and he creates and maintains the State. The two views are opposite. Either the State is first and man is second, or man is first and the State is second. Either man is a cog in a machine, a number, a statistic, or he is a personality, a being of worth in and of himself.

Democracy believes in the personal worth of every individual. "The worst slavery comes when the individual is a means and not an end, and exists only for the State and its rulers."[3] There are several applications of this concept to physical education.

All persons should have the opportunity to develop their own unique qualities.

Believing in the worth of the individual personality, physical education will offer a program which will give the individual an opportunity to achieve his potential powers. Therefore, physical education is opposed to mass regimentation, mass calisthenics, mass drills which aim at uniformity of response. There are, however, some situations in life where uniformity is required. It is sufficient to seek it in the situation that demands it; there is no need to involve other experiences with its routines.

In an orchestra, the players are directed by a leader in an effort to secure a mass effect and yet each person makes a unique contribution with a particular instrument. In an army, uniformity of action is at times required but aside from parades and the inevitable waiting in lines, the individual soldier adjusts his action to the field situation. The day of the phalanx is gone. The modern soldier seeks cover, attacks in scattered squads, and avoids the mass formation so typical of the parade. In fire drills in school, mass order is required and uniformity of response is essential. These regimentations are accepted as means; they should never be sought as ends. The notion that formal drill was a good "discipline" for youth is correct if regimented persons who implicitly obey the orders of the State are desired. But in a democracy, where initiative, self-discipline, and ability

[3] William F. Russell, *The New "Common Sense,"* New York, Macmillan, 1941, p. 49.

to take charge of oneself are educational goals, then formal drill for the general development of the citizen is a mistake and a waste of time.

Acceptance of the principle of personal worth implies that self-expression is desirable.

When an individual has an opportunity to express himself, he reveals what he has to say, what is his inner self — his convictions, standards, beliefs, fears, and faith. These revelations have a double significance. In the first place, they put the individual on record with his associates; and secondly, they put him on record with himself. The latter is more important.

Sometimes, individuals can recognize how foolish are their ideas and attitudes only when they are exposed to public view. And again, how noble when they are expressed. This is not a mere matter of being "on the record" but in a very real sense a process of self-revelation. Certainly, one can express only what one is; otherwise the expression is a fraud, a stupid posturing that fools no one.

This identification of expression with the inner self ought to emphasize the importance of achieving the full possibilities of personal worth, all that is within the power of each individual to become. The possible state of man is always greater than the actual state. Or in language of the athlete, the height that one can jump now is less than the height that can be attained by continued effort. And this difference in performance is reflected in the personality. Browning stressed this difference in "Paracelsus" in the lines:

> Are there not, dear Michael,
> Two points in the adventure of the diver,
> One — when a beggar, he prepares to plunge,
> One — when a prince, he rises with his pearl?
> Festus, I plunge!

An activity is expressive as it enlarges the meaning of the experience for him who engages in it and releases forces and energies that reveal to some extent the drives from within the individual. Expression is a creative act but one does not create out of nothing. Every expression is based upon impression and all the antecedent experiences and reactions of life. Creation has no magical source from which expression rises; differences in ability to create are partly inherited and partly the product of experience. The building of anything—a boat, a book, a poem, a dance—depends upon antecedent sensory stimuli to which the individual has reacted according to the state and condition of the organism at that time. A girl essays to do a creative dance. What can she do? Only what she has at the time to bring to this activity.

Moreover, self-expression has been advocated as a release mechanism. Repression of the personality has caused neuroses and the literature of psychiatry is replete with cases of this kind. But it should not be supposed that repression is never required in modern life or never desirable. On the contrary, repression lies at the center of self-control. The impulse to retaliate is natural; the impulse to be generous is learned. Physical education in all its games faces the need to teach children to curb unsportsmanlike behavior. This is repression. On the positive side, it seeks to help children manifest sportsmanship. When physical education is wise, it helps youth to find a balance between repression and expression, knowing that neither is an end in itself but only a means for the realization of the real worth of the individual personality.

The content and conduct of activities should provide opportunities for self-expression.

Some activities in physical education are barren experiences in the area of personal development. They may provide moderate exercise but they never allow Mary or John to be the persons they now are or in attitude to be the persons they are capable of becoming. On the other hand, activities such as dance in its various forms, games, and sports are rich in expressive content.

And the conduct of activities should provide for self-expression. Since development of initiative, independence, reliability, and such traits arise as particular and not as general qualities, it is essential to give them exercise in as many situations as possible. The conduct of a sport such as football may resemble the regimentation of formal drill although the activity itself has numerous opportunities for the players to make decisions and to be reliable. The consistent effort of rules' committees to restrict the action of coaches during the playing of the game testifies to the fact that coaches generally have not thought of football *as an educational experience* for youth but *as a contest to be won.* It should be said, of course, that coaches are the captives of an emotional situation that has been allowed to develop in school and college sport. This explanation of their behavior does not invalidate the force of this principle.

Nor should it be held that winning is, itself, an achievement of bad odor. Disapproval with "winning at all costs" sometimes leads to condemnation of any victory at all. This is nonsense and violates the principle of personal worth. Indeed, achievement inevitably makes comparisons; some persons achieve greatly and others less so. After recognition of this fact, the next step of the teacher is to help those of less ability to find the horizons at which their achievements can be seen clearly by themselves and from which there are "take-offs" for further effort. Levels of achievements are personal.

INDIVIDUAL RESPONSIBILITY

All that an individual is at any one time is the product of his inheritance plus all of his experiences. For example, the health of an individual, like other personal qualities, is probably for all persons never so fine as it might have been. Whatever the shortages in physical environment, whatever the uninspiring examples that adults give to youth, whatever the influence of the group into which he happens to fall, the greatest loss in personal development is represented in the failure of an individual to get a glimpse of the finer person he might become *with some effort on his part.* In a time when economic opportunity and physical environment are properly given large responsibility for what happens to children, it is supremely

Figure 6. Diagram of the three forces that shape an individual person.

important to arouse young people to their share in personal responsibility for outcomes and consequences. Society has its obligations but individuals are also responsible. Society presents handicaps; individuals are to overcome them. Society gives an inheritance; individuals are to realize all their personal resources. Society offers opportunity; individuals are to grasp them and realize in themselves their full potentialities (Fig. 6).

In these days, it is important to stress individual responsibility. For some time in the past and in the thinking of some persons at the present time, individual responsibility is not important. It is held that the individual is to rely upon government to make decisions and to look to government for individual security. This view is contrary to the democratic tradition and denies the principles that underlie American life. If individuals are to develop a sense of individual responsibility they should face and accept responsibility and have a share in determining arrangements that condition outcomes and consequences. As individuals make choices, so they should be responsible for their selections; as they share in decisions so they should be responsible for outcomes. It is the strength of democratic philosophy that individuals may shape the pattern of national life; it is the weakness of democratic practice that individuals fail to accept responsibility for the life that has been made.

Individuals should share, according to their abilities, in the management and conduct of physical education activities.

It is a common practice to use pupils and students as managers in various sports, to train squad leaders for gymnastic groups, and to select pupils as monitors for various situations. These opportunities may be rather sterile experiences with few chances to express ideas, to help make schedules, and to participate in business affairs or they can be rich and rewarding. It is a mistake to give to youth responsibilities too large for them to bear, but they should never be criticized for attempting more than could be accomplished.

There are several approaches to the conduct of physical activities.[4] In one the teacher directs and the children obey. Children who do not respond well to this approach are considered "disciplinary problems." After children with this kind of experience leave school, they lack self-direction since no one is around to command specific responses. Rudderless as adults, they have no inner compulsions to lead them to engage in physical activity.

There is also the abortive attempt to have pupils share in the conduct of activities by appointment of one pupil to take the roll, one to collect the balls at the end of a period, and another to watch for fouls during a game. These are minor concessions to the need for all pupils to be responsible for the way an activity proceeds; and this overall responsibility can come only when all have had a share in setting up the goals of the activity and in planning for their accomplishment.

Individuals should share, according to their abilities, in the planning of programs in physical education.

The purpose to have individuals share in the planning of what they are to experience is one of the most difficult democratic processes to use. In the early years of school life this procedure often fails; the range of individual experience is so small that little of value can be contributed to the program. But that little should be used, be allowed to grow, and be kept alive by increasing opportunity and responsibility. As the individual matures, larger opportunities should be offered. In high school and

---

[4] Ruth Cunningham and associates, "Group Discipline," *National Education Association Journal*, January, 1949.

college, the individual should suggest areas of interest and problems to be studied that seem important to him. This sort of sharing needs to be enriched by the suggestions of the teacher. To regard the student as the sole source of guidance in planning a program is to ignore the range and depth of experience that the teacher ought to possess.

In the process of sharing responsibility for decisions, the principle of majority rule should be used. Effort should be made to keep time-consuming procedures to a minimum, to avoid arousing recalcitrant attitudes in minorities, and, when differences are sharp and not readily harmonized, to keep the decision in the hands of the teacher.

SELF-ACHIEVEMENT

In many rigid social systems, the future of a youth is determined by the class into which he is born. The sons of peasants remain peasants and the sons of noblemen also belong to the nobility. While wide differences exist among Americans at birth, nothing but ability or opportunity can prevent a poor boy from becoming the head of a large corporation, a great physician, a governor, or President of the United States. Ability may not be sufficient or opportunity expressed in environment and associates, and education may be inadequate, but nothing else can keep a youth from self-achievement.

The essence of this situation is the competitive character of American life in which the better man advances to larger responsibility. Since competition is so large a part of physical education, it is important to examine this concept of self-achievement in the light of both competition and cooperation.

Competitive intercollegiate sport when diverted to commercial ends places in jeopardy its educational values.

Any thoughtful student of social forces in American life could have prophesied a generation ago the trend in development that college athletics would take. Sport is a part of the culture as definitely and as fully as working conditions, clothing, language, tools, and machines. The ideals of individual liberty are variously realized and in politics and economics the doctrine of *laissez faire* and rugged individualism widely prevailed. A culture which permitted the amassing of great personal fortunes with widespread poverty and impaired opportunity is precisely the culture which would give free play to the notions of graduate managers for the achievement of athletic supremacy. Proselyting, scouting, professionalism and commercialism in sport are the natural products of a way of thinking, a mood and a manner of acting. It is obvious that the oft-expressed desire to develop practices of English sport in the American culture denies the very basis upon which English sport rests. It is a cultural expression. It flowers from the traditions, customs and ways of behaving that compose English character and English life.

Sport in the American scene is as truly American as mass production. Even the report of the Carnegie Foundation for the Advancement of Teaching,[5] thorough, comprehensive, and generally fair, had no significant effect upon athletic practices. Today, more than three decades after its publication, subsidization of athletes is more open and probably more general. Intercollegiate sport reflects the ideas, standards, and behavior of the culture in which it exists. *Laissez faire* in economics and rugged individualism in intercollegiate sport are products of the time and place.

But there is no fixed and final status about any cultural climate. Ultimately, American life becomes what those who shape its destiny desire, and intercollegiate sport is in the hands of those who control its conduct. Their hands need to be upheld by an informed public opinion because college sport is no longer the concern of faculties and students only; it has become an important interest of chambers of commerce, special "bowl" committees, newspapers, and gamblers. In 1962-1963, there were more than fifteen intersectional "bowl" games in football, played under the auspices of commercial organizations; in recent years the Madison Square Garden basketball games have been

[5] Bulletin No. 23, Carnegie Foundation for the Advancement of Teaching, 1929.

followed by scandals, arrests for bribery, and evidence of corruption of college athletes. In Russia the athlete participates for the State, which rigidly controls his behavior; the cynic might well remark that in America he participates for a promoter with a "cut" on the side, but his behavior is his own decision.

But cynicism is not helpful in the solution of the persistent problems of intercollegiate sport. Such an attitude would lead to the inevitable acceptance of the gambler and briber in the locker room, and easy endorsement of the newspapers that print the odds on different athletic contests.

It seems very clear that the only approach to the present situation is to continue the effort to establish machinery for the enforcement of standards. Whatever professional associations are developed for this purpose, the duty of every teacher to promote sportsmanlike behavior among players will always remain.

Competition in physical education activities should always reflect the highest standards of sportsmanship.

The tendency to classify all forms of competitive effort in a single category leads to error. Competition in games can always be a striving for excellence; competition in business tends to become a striving after more things or more power over others. To view competition in games as either in fact or in necessity a parallel to competition in business is to indulge a bias and to ignore the facts. On the contrary, proper competition in sport is one of the best examples of the kind of competition that enlightened business leaders seek to develop. In both sport and business, excellence rather than privilege, performance rather than unfair advantage can be realities.

The ability to see in social phenomena ways of future action or kinds of behavior that have implications for education is a constructive approach to planning for educational outcomes. To discern in examples of competitive effort and in cooperative performance the essential principles that might be captured for educational method and made, through teaching of children, to appear as ways of behaving in the lives of men and women is the task of an alert and professional education. On the contrary, the adoption of slogans and the uncritical acceptance of terms portray a wishful thinking. We may announce that we are for cooperation and against competition for a variety of reasons, but it is important to remember that terms become significant not by designation but because of the fact that vital phenomena are described. To place competition and cooperation as terms at the extremes of human behavior is the procedure of the propagandist, but the phenomena require a more constructive analysis. Moreover, careful scrutiny of the matter will reveal that these terms stand for kinds of behaving of enormous range and that wide variations exist in competitive effort and in cooperative performance.

By definition competition is an act of seeking what another is endeavoring to gain at the same time and cooperation is an act of working jointly with others to a common end. Examples of these two forms of behavior are legion.

There may be competition by two or more men for the same girl, two or more boys in the same race, two or more railroads for the same traffic, two or more religions for the same soul. These may manifest the finest qualities of the human spirit in fairness, in tested excellence, in freedom of choice, in purpose to deserve, in service to mankind. But these qualities exist in persons and not in the process. It is possible to have a world in which men do not compete for a woman. In old China parents selected the mates for their children. Freedom of choice, purpose to deserve do not arise as qualities out of such a situation. It might be possible to have a world in which boys would not run a race, religions would not compete for the same soul, and men would always step aside for others so that public offices never would be filled, but neither historical experience nor present life knows such a world.

There are other examples of competition. There is competition that seeks and obtains unfair trade practices, special privileges in tariffs, subsidies, bonuses or bounties for particular groups, that achieves exploitation of performers for commercial gains, that elevates self through destruction of another, that cooperates with others to "box" an opponent in a race, that uses brass knuckles or emery dust, that leads to corruption of officials, that lies, cheats, and destroys. These qualities exist, however, in the behavior of persons; they are not inherent in competition. They arise in actions and reactions of persons living in a world of varying standards and reflect, therefore, the values in life that operate in society, that is, in individuals.

These latter examples are not any more truly the characteristic or unique product of competition than are the former. The products of competitive effort may range from a fine sense of fair play to corruption of officials, from purpose to deserve to purpose to deceive, from tested excellence to boxing an opponent, from the golfer counting all his strokes to the one who makes an alibi for poor performance.

Cooperation should be sought in physical education activities.

There are many examples of cooperative effort. There may be the cooperation of a community in selecting good men for office or cooperation of a political party for power, plunder and privilege; cooperation of persons for schools, libraries, parks and playgrounds or cooperation of persons for elimination of so-called "frills"; cooperation of educational institutions for friendly, courteous, generous, athletic contests or cooperation of educational institutions to control free speech, free inquiry, and independent action.

These variations in cooperative performance are not inherent in the thing called cooperation, but represent qualitative attributes of individuals. A method of cooperation in itself is not bound to produce either fine or baleful results; these depend upon the ends that are served.

By a fallacious analysis, competition may be made to appear socially bad and cooperation socially good. To designate all that is evil in competition as the litter it is bound to breed, and all that is excellent in cooperation as the fair flower of its process is neither accurate nor in accord with the facts.

With respect to origins, both kinds of behaving, competitive and cooperative, find their drives in biologic traits. Thorndike writes:

Every human being . . . tends by original nature to arrive at a status of mastery or submission toward every other human being and even under the more intelligent customs of civilized life somewhat of the tendency persists in many men.[6]

All except the most fervid environmentalists acknowledge this trait in original nature. Regarding cooperation there is less evidence to support its biological origin, but Zuckerman reports that it exists in the social life of monkeys and apes.[7]

This possible biological origin of these ways of behaving indicates that they are not the product of a particular social system. Moreover, there is no evidence that these traits have produced particular social organizations. Fascistic and communistic states demand cooperation with the forces in power, but the abdication of individual intelligent cooperation and enthronement of slavish obedience are an essential condition of dictatorial government. Social life makes any individual peculiarly what he is. Fascism and communism produced in Italy, Germany and Russia the kind of citizens that the dictatorships demanded. The halting and often confused democracy in American life produces Americans with the qualities and ways of behaving that are the product of action and reaction in American society. Educated men and women in America do not openly snatch for things nor cry for what they want. Approved social behavior does not sanction slugging an opponent in a football game. There are, however, behaviors that all thoughtful persons condemn, but only the naive theorist would suppose that behavior in sport was to be interpreted apart from the ideas, customs and traditions of the time and place. Much of amateur athletics today corresponds to rugged individualism in economics or to militant nationalism abroad and has about the same justification. But to observe that practices in competitive athletics may emulate the jungle standards of the market place is quite different from de-

[6] E. L. Thorndike, *The Original Nature of Man*, New York, Teachers College, Columbia University, 1919, p. 93.

[7] S. Zuckerman, *The Social Life of the Monkeys and Apes*, New York, Harcourt Brace, 1932, p. 294.

claring that jungle standards inherently belong with any particular social organization.

Competitive and cooperative behavior can be modified by education and experience.

Human traits may be accentuated or weakened by education and social experience. Tendencies to certain kinds of behavior are altered by the actions and reactions of the individual in various situations. The hope of public education in character development rests upon this basis. Therefore, it is the practice among enlightened social groups to weaken by various forms of disapproval the kind of behaving that is selfish, against group welfare, and subversive to social good, and likewise to strengthen those responses of behavior that are highly regarded. Those who consider all competition as antisocial are disposed to see in cooperation the panacea for a socially disturbed world and in this respect are like those socialists who contend that . . . "the collective ownership of the means of production will produce a 'classless' state, inhabited by a race of men who are purged of acquisitiveness and aggression . . . ."[8]

Milovan Djilas, the Yugoslav, imprisoned for writing the book *The New Class* (1957), shows that socialism in power in Russia for over forty years has not produced a "classless" state and in fact is developing a new aristocracy of Communist leaders.

But for Americans, generally, social good has no reality except in terms of the individuals composing the group. The concept of a state, outside of, beyond, and above the persons that comprise its citizenry is for Americans a strange doctrine. Although gradually over some sixty years the ideology of collectivism has gained adherents in American life, there still remains a strong belief in the importance, worth, and dignity of individual personality. This regard for the individual rather than for a state explains much of the political philosophy of democracy with its well-known phrases; all men are born free and equal; the rights of the common man; individual liberty; freedom of speech.

[8] Walter Lippmann, *The Good Society*, Boston, Little, Brown, 1937, pp. 78-83.

Interest in the individual personality, rather than regimentation for a state has dominated American education since the beginning. And the role of competitive activities in the development of the individual is widely appreciated. In the early years of childhood, play is largely cooperative, but before the years reach two figures, the question is, as Lee writes, "Who is the better man, or the greater or more endurable in some respects?"[9] This is the beginning of self-realization, and stronger than the desire to impress others is the child's impelling drive to test himself. To identify himself, to discover his own reality — this is one sure outcome of the competitive situation. Even so severe a critic of competition as Bertrand Russell writes: "Competition and cooperation are both natural human activities and it is difficult to suppress competition completely without destroying individuality."[10]

Physical education in its competitive activities should help to maintain the principle that struggle is important in the development of the personality.

Administrative measures in education must take into account the various abilities and needs of children, but the drive behind all education for social ends must come from the philosophy that portrays the goals and gives meaning to the process. There are many reasons for believing that the good life is characterized by struggle. Struggle to realize self gives some fiber to the personality that alone makes life worth living. If competition of all kinds could be eliminated in life, what sort of watery human being would result? If this sort of noncompetitive life were to ensue, then doubtless we are at the climax of civilization and less can be said for its continuance than many of us suppose.

William James some years ago in a famous lecture to students commented on what makes a life significant. He wrote with prophetic vision of the planned and purposed society, without risks, inequalities, or dangers, now advocated so strongly by

[9] Joseph Lee, *Play in Education*, by permission of the Macmillan Co., Publishers, New York, 1916, p. 186.
[10] Bertrand Russell, *Education and the Modern World*, New York, Norton, 1932, p. 237.

totalitarians, and of that democratic system of free enterprise with its continual struggle to improve and enrich individual personality:

> A few summers ago I spent a happy week at the famous Assembly Grounds on the border of Chautauqua Lake. The moment one treads that sacred enclosure, one feels one's self in an atmosphere of success. Sobriety and industry, intelligence and goodness, orderliness and ideality, prosperity and cheerfulness, pervade the air. It is a serious and studious picnic on a gigantic scale. Here you have a town of many thousands of inhabitants, beautifully laid out in the forest and drained, and equipped with means for satisfying all the necessary lower and most of the superfluous higher wants of man. You have a first-class college in full blast. You have magnificent music — a chorus of seven hundred voices, with possibly the most perfect open-air auditorium in the world. . . . You have kindergartens and model secondary schools. You have general religious services and special club-houses for the several sects. You have perpetually running soda-water fountains, and daily popular lectures by distinguished men. You have the best of company and yet no effort. You have no zymotic diseases, no poverty, no drunkenness, no crime, no police. You have culture, you have kindness, you have cheapness, you have equality, you have the best fruits of what mankind has fought and bled and striven for under the name of civilization for centuries. You have, in short, a foretaste of what human society might be, were it all in the light, with no suffering and no dark corners.
>
> I went in curiosity for a day. I stayed for a week, held spellbound by the charm and ease of everything, by the middle-class paradise, without a sin, without a victim, without a blot, without a tear.
>
> And yet what was my own astonishment, on emerging into the dark and wicked world again, to catch myself quite unexpectedly and involuntarily saying: 'Ouf. What a relief. Now for something primordial and savage, even though it were as bad as an Armenian massacre, to set the balance straight again. This order is too tame, this culture too second-rate, this goodness too uninspiring. This human drama without a villain or a pang: this community so refined that ice-cream soda-water is the utmost offering it can make to the brute animal in man; this city simmering in the tepid lakeside sun; this atrocious harmlessness of all things, — I cannot abide with them. Let me take my chances again in the big outside worldly wilderness with all its sins and

sufferings. There are the heights and depths, the precipices and the steep ideals, the gleams of the awful and the infinite; and there is more hope and help a thousand times than in this dead level and quintessence of every mediocrity.'[11]

It is the duty of physical education to promote not only fine sportsmanship but also sound notions of the competitive process.

Critics of competition in sport have a good case when the attack is made upon unfair and unsportsmanlike behavior, but it is ridiculous to claim that the competitive act seeks the humiliation of the opponent. Nothing could be further from the truth. Sportsmen do not desire to humiliate opponents. The countless numbers of competitive activities in schools today are not run to humiliate opponents. Small, cruel boys and some adults who are still growing up act in this way, but the code of fair endeavor is built upon the standard expression "May the better man win." For those who lose, there is no humiliation unless a faulty education has taught them to expect always to be right and never to lose. Educational policy for a general practice, however, cannot be derived from the limitations of emotionally abnormal children. Such children should have the supervision in activities that their special problems require, but they are the special cases that illustrate the principle of individual differences. Therefore, children who are **humiliated** when their team loses need special care, exactly as others do who are timid, shy, secretive, unduly sensitive, fearful, and vain.

To set a standard of social activity which is based upon the abnormal response of a player who is humiliated when he loses in games would correspond to establishing a diet based upon carious teeth and inability to masticate, or a standard of honesty based upon the behavior of a kleptomaniac.

Physical education leadership should be alert to recognize and condemn those practices in which the competitive situation is manipulated so that a contestant can win unfairly, in which the urge for power or prestige manages affairs so that the com-

---

[11] William James, *Talks to Teachers on Psychology and to Students on Some of Life's Ideals*, New York, Holt, 1900, pp. 268-271.

petition is unequal, and in which the "winner" and his achievement are exploited to his great disadvantage for commercial or other gains.

PERSONALITY AND THE STATE

After World War I and particularly after certain European experiments in government, serious questions were raised in some quarters about democracy. These questions raised the issue between democracy and other forms of government and are epitomized in the query, "Can democracy cope successfully with the modern problems of an industrial age?" After December 7, 1941, this question was set aside in the eagerness to mobilize the nation's power for winning World War II. Political and public differences over New Deal policies were held in abeyance, and all strove to assemble the resources of the nation. In the first months of 1942, our forces had scarcely begun to fight, and yet the spirit of cooperation and willingness to sacrifice ran high. The old freedom in enterprise disappeared and not only soldiers but also civilians came under the regulations of a central authority.

For the duration of the war, there was little discussion of the totalitarian theories of social organization. The vital examination of democratic philosophy and procedures which had been carried on for ten years was put aside in a concerted effort to crush totalitarianism.

One may accept the fact that such centralization of authority and effort is essential in war, and yet have faith in democratic values, and seek to maintain enthusiasm for liberty and freedom. Since the end of World War II, and especially since the first sessions of the United Nations, the discussion about democracy and totalitarian communism has been constant and often charged with great emotion. All of education is concerned with the outcome of the present disagreement in world affairs; all Americans have a stake in democracy, respect for personality, the rights of man, and the freedoms that we know and enjoy.

For a hundred years, between 1828 and 1929, there was a gradual, though perhaps needlessly slow, growth in the development of democratic ideals. These were embodied in such phrases as, "the worth of the common man," "the rights of the common people," and "respect for personality." This regard for personality was expressed some years ago; it is good to recall it today.

> In the whole world there is nothing more sacred than human personality, and the right of that personality to shape and to direct its own beliefs and its own conduct, subject only to being held responsible for results which infringe the like rights of others, is absolute and supreme. There is, and can be, no public interest apart from the interest of the individuals of whom the public is composed.[12]

Impatient for values, those who wish immediate social good seek a monopoly of social power. Intolerant of the slow process of social evolution that is dependent upon education and inherent in the democratic process, they desire an ascendency over the group that will enable them to do the thinking and planning for the mass who are to remain the docile instruments of their vision. Such control inevitably leads to tyranny. Suzanne Labin, in *The Anthill* (1961), records an interesting anecdote about Confucius as follows:

> After leaving a province burdened by the exactions of a tyrannous overlord, Confucius and his disciples came to a wood where they observed an old woman weeping by an open grave. The sage stopped and sent one of his disciples to inquire the cause of the woman's distress.
> "The father of my husband was killed here by a tiger," she replied. "And then my husband also. And now my son has suffered the same fate."
> "But why then," the sage inquired, "do you stay on in such a dangerous neighborhood?"
> "Because at least there is no tyrannous government in these parts," the woman explained.

[12] Nicholas Murray Butler, "Three Types of Mind," address delivered at the opening of the academic year of Columbia University, September 22, 1926.

Confucious now turned to his disciples.
"Mark the poor woman's words," he said. "An oppressive government is worse for the people than a tiger."

Contemporary American culture is marked therefore with sharply conflicting ideas of government, with a renewal of interest in the meaning of democracy, and with a rather critical examination of those political forms which oppose or attack its principles.[13]

Physical education should never allow its program to be used for creating a docile and regimented people.

In these crucial days physical education, a field that will be used early by any authoritarian group that might attain power, must assay anew the democratic philosophy, and if convinced, must hearken to democratic ideals. The contrasts are sharp indeed in the authoritarian and democratic views of national organization. The marching groups, the regimented discipline, the external controls mark both the Fascist and Communist ideologies. With these belong mass drills, compulsory military service in peace time, the regimentation of peoples in thought and action. A democracy has no need for docility and submissiveness in its citizens. It does not set out to **mold** any individual. Rather it attempts to be sensitive to the wants of the personality, to awaken desire for better wants, and to give opportunity for the individual to realize himself.

It is interesting to note that even before the dastardly attack on Pearl Harbor, considerable agitation arose for regimentation of youth through physical education. After war came, the cry for drills, calisthenics, for rigid gymnastics — the stupid exercising of muscles leaving the minds and emotions free to oppose or submit to authority — was heard everywhere. It has been difficult always for people to believe in democratic processes; it is more difficult to practice them.

The leader of a servile people could readily arrange for all the ordinary processes and activities of life. Such control

---

[13] Laurence K. Frank, *Society as the Patient*, New Brunswick, Rutgers, 1949. Max S. Marshall, "Competition: for Better or Worse?" *School and Society*, November 22, 1952.

could avoid largely the numerous irritations, inefficiencies, and futile efforts that mark a democracy. But it was this sort of control that the founders of America tried to escape from when they dared to leave their homes in Europe to build anew in a wild and unknown continent. The American dream[14] is not compatible with such social order, however secure it may now appear. Since the powers for the development of a democratic social order come from the people themselves, it is delegated to representatives with the reservations that operate in the tenure of public officials. These powers enable the people to shift the emphases in the social order as new ideas, inventions, and industrial development present new problems, or as science discovers new facts, or as old superstitions are discarded. The democratic state may in 1860 allow human slavery and in another century provide old age pensions, workmen's compensation, and social security for black as well as white. But in a democracy the powers remain in the people.

This contrast in totalitarian and democratic philosophy is quite properly a parallel to the static and dynamic views of human nature. When the individual is merely an item in the national account to be employed for national ends, his abilities are catalogued, and he is assigned to predetermined tasks. When, however, the individual is a personality to be developed, whose future is still to be discovered, then the dynamic character of all experience takes on added significance in his education. Thus, physical education can drill a group of boys for regimented purposes, or it can accept a variety of responses in games, sports, and vigorous activities, always seeking to discover their best reactions, to strengthen their best habits, and to arouse their best emotions and attitudes.

Thus is the issue joined.

Physical education, like all vital agencies of national life, should be ready to serve the nation during war.

It would have been quite impossible 50 years ago for even the most far-seeing of men to predict the course of events in

---

[14] James Truslow Adams, *The Epic of America*, Boston, Little, Brown, 1931.

world affairs over the next half-century. Indeed, the expectations of men of good will in the early years of the 1900's were contrary to the course that developed. Then, the prospects for complete abolition of war were believed to be based on realistic judgments. It was argued that development of international trade and means of rapid communication would lead to international understanding and bring about universal and lasting peace.

In 1910, four years before "the guns of August" opened World War I, *The Great Illusion*, by Norman Angell, had just been published. The book later was translated into eleven languages. It won a large following who accepted the thesis that financial and economic independence of nations made war impossible.

The notion that war between modern nations was impossible was primarily an English view. In Germany, however, General von Bernhardi and other militarists declared that "war is a biological necessity" and is "the natural law upon which all the laws of Nature rest, the law of the struggle for existence."

Over and through the years, in spite of the urgings of men of good will to strive for international agreements to abolish war as national policy, reliance upon military virtues had persisted. Loyalty, courage, and patriotism were associated with war and as virtues were widely approved. Could such virtues be achieved by activities other than war? An answer to that question was given by William James in his memorable study, "The Moral Equivalent of War."[15]

The State with the king at its head is a political society, concerned with the execution of plans which will retain that relationship. It is first a military group, and secondarily a governing group, with all the gradations of class and rank in a society fashioned to favor the king-idea. The theory of the State as something set apart, above and beyond the people, the divine right of kings, and the godlike quality of potentates have all been used to provoke submissiveness and fear in the masses. The control of the common people by those in power has meant almost universally an exploitation of them for state, imperial, or military,

[15] William James, *Memories and Studies*, New York, Holt, 1911, p. 287.

that is, for political purposes. Throughout the eighteenth and nineteenth centuries the increasing growth of nationalism as a form of political organization has tended to irresponsible empires, and yet, in the life of most modern nations, physical education has served the king. Thus, one is to read the history of German gymnastics in the light of Frederick's armies marching through the Germanies wasted by war, in the annals of the War of Liberation, and in the urgency created by the traditional enemy to the West. Physical education in Germany served the king. Its function as a disciplining, body-building activity goes back to such sources.

Even in democracies the importunate character of the military sanction for physical education is shown in the hysteria of legislation for military drill in public schools which follows the beginning of every war. The graph indicating the incidence of this disturbance approximates the one for national strife in America. The function of physical education as an agency not only for organic development and vitality, but also for happiness, richness of life and joy is not the view held by the average person. The warping of the possibilities of this educational agency is due to the pertinacity of the military idea, maintained as it has been with the argument of professional soldiers.

It should be clear that physical education is not pacifistic when it opposes military training of high school boys as a physical training measure. It is evident that strength, courage, stamina, and agility—important qualities in the soldier—are to be developed in youth through vigorous activities and not by means of the formalities of military drill. During World War II, bills were introduced in the Congress and in several state legislatures which would have required military drill of high school boys. Legislators are so uninformed in biological matters that considerable effort must be expended to prevent the imposition of such frauds upon the youth of the nation. The way to vigorous physique, strength, and courage is through strenuous, adventurous, and challenging exercise. There is no other way. This is a function of physical education and not of military drill.

During World War II, the proponents of military drill

urged that it should replace physical education in the schools. It required a letter from the Secretary of War to stop the agitation. Mr. Stimson's letter to the Commissioner of Education stated two important considerations:

> The amount of military drill which can be given in schools and colleges can also be given after induction into the Army, in a relatively short period of time, and under the most productive circumstances. A good physical condition, however, cannot be developed in so short space of time, and the physical condition of the soldier is of prime importance to the War Department. . . . The War Department does not therefore recommend that military drill take the place of physical education in the schools and colleges during the war period.[16]

Physical education should maintain programs of fitness without assuming or accepting responsibility for fitness for military service.

The figures of rejections in the draft are often misunderstood. The Act of 1917 called to service all males between 21 and 31 years of age. It selected about 60 per cent. Inasmuch as there is no comparable examination available of the young men of the nation at other periods, it is impossible to tell whether or not the situation was better or worse. Study of the rejections shows that the great majority of the defects listed are preventable; they are defects of environment and of development rather than heredity. They are in the main defects which require medical, surgical, and educational treatment.

The Act of 1940 followed a different procedure. Males between 21 and 36 years of age were called. Of this call four groups were exempted for a time at least: (1) college students, (2) medical and engineering students, (3) most married men with dependents, and (4) men in essential industries. It is obvious that college and professional students who have experienced quite generally physical education, hygiene, and health service programs in college and university are probably the fittest groups we have in America; that men who can marry and men who can

---

[16] The entire letter from the Secretary of War is reprinted in the *Journal of Health and Physical Education,* September, 1943, p. 368.

hold responsible jobs are also reasonably fit. In short, the Act of 1940 selected from the less fit part of our population. Nevertheless, of about 2 million registrants examined, about 50 per cent were found to be unqualified for general military service by local boards and Army induction stations. Of the million unfit, 900,000 were refused because of physical and mental defects and 100,000 because of educational deficiencies. Of the defects which disqualified, the items were: teeth (20.9 per cent), eye (13.7); cardiovascular (10.6); musculoskeletal (6.8); venereal disease (6.3); hernia (6.2); ear (4.6); feet (4); lungs (2.9); and miscellaneous (17.7) (Table 1).

In a preliminary report by the Selective Service System it was noted that of the 900,000 rejected because of physical and mental defects 200,000 could be completely rehabilitated.[17] In the Annual Report (1951) of the Director of Selective Service for the period October 1948 – June 1951, a very brief statement of the rejection problem was presented.[18] This showed a rejection percentage of 40 for the United States and Territories; it was 39.7 in Continental United States.

There was a variation in the rejection rate in the years from 1940 into 1945, explained largely by the administrative policies and procedures that prevailed from time to time. For example, rigid physical standards, and a ban on the induction of men with less than the equivalent of a fourth grade (English) education produced high rejection rates in 1940-1941; lower standards, including induction of some educationally deficient men and some with limited service defects, reduced rates of rejection during 1942-1943; and the scarcity of manpower, occasioned largely by previous enlistments of 17-year-old youths, tended to raise the rates during 1944-1945.

In 1944 the leading cause for rejection of white registrants was mental disease of which the principal diagnoses were, in order: psychoneurosis, emotional instability, and asocial and amoral trends.

[17] Selective Service System, Analysis of Reports of Physical Examination, Washington, D.C., Medical Statistics Bulletin, No. 1, 1941.
[18] Annual Report of the Director of Selective Service, 1951, Washington, D.C., Government Printing Office, January 3, 1952.

TABLE 1. FITNESS FOR WAR

DATA FROM WORLD WAR II Selective Service Act—1940				
MALE POPULATION—AGES 21–36 YEARS				
Exempted Groups	2,000,000 Registrants			
1. College students 2. Medical & engineering students 3. Married with dependents 4. Workers in essential industries	1,000,000 Accepted	1,000,000 Rejected		
		100,000	900,000	
		E d u c a t i o n a l D e f i c i e n c y	Defect % Teeth 20.9 Eye 13.7 Heart 10.6 Mus-skeletal 6.8 Venereal 6.3 Hernia 6.2 Ear 4.6 Feet 4.0 Lungs 2.9 Miscellaneous 17.7	200,000 Number who could be rehabili- tated by dental and medical service

Chart showing the fitness picture of American youth for war service in 1940. Figures in round numbers; percentages as reported by Selective Service.

It is apparent from the experience of both world wars that the disqualifications of youth for military service are the result, in part, of carelessness, ignorance, and neglect. Schools, local communities, and many parents have failed to visualize their functions. Schools teach dental hygiene to children, many of whom show gross dental defects, and for a variety of reasons, the defects are not corrected. Defects of eyes, ears, and teeth, and hernias and malnutrition in youth are often remediable, but neither their occurrence nor their correction is a responsibility of physical education.

Moreover, even the boys who pass the examinations are not vigorous enough, alert and strong enough for some of the special services. The three-month physical education program for the air arm of the Navy before technical instruction is given indicates the need for a greatly extended program of physical education in our schools.

The high rejection rate for mental disease in both white and colored registrants suggests that the health examination now given to school children and college students is grossly inadequate. It has been apparent for some time that the health examination of youths was partial and often perfunctory, but the experience of recent wars, as well as the increase of mental disease in the general population, shows that new methods and more comprehensive examinations are needed. Very few schools and colleges discover and use data from the adjustment record or data from the social (intergroup) relationship record. In general, examinations begin and end with physical defects, while abnormalities in the mental and emotional areas are neglected until the individual becomes a problem case. The extent and gravity of the situation demand far-reaching reforms in the scope and conduct of the health examination.

Bernard D. Karpinos of the Medical Statistics Division of the Army Surgeon General's Office reports on fitness of American youth for military service in the Korean War.[19] This report is abstracted in the *Research Quarterly* as follows:

[19] Bernard D. Karpinos, "Fitness of American Youth for Military Service," *Milbank Memorial Fund Quarterly*, July, 1960, p. 213.

Moral, mental, and medical criteria determine the individual's fitness for military service. The examinations and acceptance standards have been changed from time to time as manpower needs dictate. At the present, for instance, psychoneurosis of any degree is acceptable if it has not incapacitated the individual in civilian life.

During the Korean War 3,500,000 registrants underwent a preinduction examination, of whom 31.8 per cent were rejected. Of these, 0.8 per cent were rejected for administrative reasons (nearly all moral), 13.3 per cent for mental reasons, 3.3 per cent for combined mental and medical reasons, and 14.4 per cent for medical reasons only. These disqualifications rates are inflated by the fact that many youths entered military service other than through the Selective Service. Statistical adjustment for this indicates that 23.6 per cent of the applicants could not qualify for military service. Diseases and defects of the bones and organs of movement were the main cause of medical disqualification (20 per 1,000), followed by psychiatric disorders (18.6/1,000), circulatory system diseases (17.8/1,000), digestive system diseases (11.2/1,000), eye diseases and defects (9.8/1,000), and various lesser causes. Many were rejected for more than one reason. The main cause for rejection due to psychiatric reasons was character disorder.[20]

It is apparent from this study that many previous reports have misinterpreted the "physical fitness" of American youth. Karpinos states that 68 per cent of the American youths liable for military duty during recent years have qualified for service in the armed forces.

Physical education should have the responsibility for the leadership of its program in war as well as in peace.

During peace there is never any question about the fitness of physical education to give leadership to its many and varied programs. During World War II, important posts of leadership in physical education were given to persons totally unqualified by training and experience. The profession as a whole meekly accepted this arrangement under the mistaken plea of patriotism. The medical profession would have fought against the appointment of a drugless healer to leadership of the Medical Corps, and the nursing profession would have proudly refused to accept as head of the nurses anyone but a registered nurse.

[20] *Research Quarterly,* March, 1962, p. 150.

In an address before the International Council on Health, Physical Education, and Recreation, Oberteuffer said:

> We need protection in every land from quackery—from fraud, the charlatan, and the fool who, under the guise of physical education or health education, persuades the public that his "system" of exercises, his road to good health, or his brand of physical culture is a panacea for all the world's ills. We have these in every country, I presume. We are richly endowed with them here. We have ex-prize fighters, "diet" experts, lady contortionists, weight control specialists, faddists of all kinds who, through the media of press, television, radio, and personal contact, "sell" their wares to a gullible public.[21]

This failure of the leadership of the profession to demand professional competence in those who are to lead its programs can be repaired by forthright action when appointments are contemplated.

Physical education needs to abandon an apologetic attitude and to appraise properly its competence. There are hundreds of highly trained, experienced, and capable leaders, both men and women, who are thoroughly competent to fill high posts of leadership in any federal organization for physical education during war or peace.

Physical education should oppose fascistic influences in national life everywhere.

When political power is dispersed among local communities, the determination of policies and the financial support of policies are the responsibility of local government. The American public school system has grown and developed under this theory of democracy. Moreover, there is the principle that the schools belong to the people, not in general, but in particular communities which build school buildings, hire teachers, and fill the schools with children. Under this kind of political control, American public school education has looked to the states for leadership, and over the years, some centralization of power

[21] Delbert Oberteuffer, "Confederation and Mutual Assistance," *Report of the WCOTP Committee on Health, Physical Education, and Recreation, on the International Conference of ICHPER*, Washington, D.C., 1959, pp. 4-11.

over educational policy has shifted from the local community to the state. The state controls licenses for teachers, enacts compulsory attendance laws, and may set standards for school buildings, curricula, and credits. Even with centralization of power in the state, there remains in the local community the conviction that the schools belong to the people, that the boards elected or chosen to direct them are local representatives, and that the kind of school provided reflects the desires of the locality.

On this background of American public education, the proposal of the Federal Government to build school buildings seems very ill-advised. If this is done, the next step would be for the Federal Government to train teachers, and the next one to determine the curriculum. Moreover, the states have adequate resources for building schools. The states know what the problem is, and the states should solve it.

When the people tax themselves to build schools, the schools belong to the people. When the people abdicate to a dictator, the dictation from a central source determines educational policy in precisely the same way that it manages the currency, controls industry and agriculture, embarks upon war, and shapes the life of the nation. The youth movement of the German Republic became the Hitler Youth under National Socialism. The local initiative, freedom in method, and varying programs in Germany during the years 1918-1932 disappeared in the dictated policy of 1933.

Physical education is important in a democracy, or in a despotism, but the marching, the regimental drills, the formal discipline of the latter contrast sharply with the play, education for leisure, experimental method, emphasis upon initiative, leadership training, and similar objectives of the former. Americans can have the kind of physical education they want.

Physical education in its close cooperation with recreational forces should support the policy of developing recreation as a responsibility of education.

By law, education is a function of the State; by a reasonable interpretation of custom and history of American education, recreation is the proper concern of the State also. There is considerable agreement in the matter of the State's responsibility for recreation, but there are two opposing views regarding plans of organization. One position would organize recreation under a separate recreation commission; the other advocates the organization of recreation under the State Department of Education.[22] The arguments have considerable force on each side but the important principle to consider in determining policy is the necessity to move forward on a broad front, to avoid duplicating services and facilities, and to secure the reciprocal effects of recreation on education and of education on recreation.

In an analysis of the problem, it is clear that education and recreation have mutual interests and supports. Moreover, the basically related forces and structures in a community can be brought into a pattern of social organization that will allow movement forward on a broad front, in which the gains may be as marked for the school as an institution of society as for recreation as an activity of the people. If a recreational philosophy is accepted by the American people in any substantial fashion, its effect upon educational policies and curricula may produce tremendously needed changes in public school education. This in turn, would have the most salutary effects upon recreational practice. It is essential that we consider social institutions and services in their interrelationships and that we plan broadly for social progress. From these considerations, it is apparent that a broad attack can develop only by abandoning the policy of water-tight compartments, and in this instance, by making education in the State the responsible agent for serving both the vocational and avocational needs of people.

Physical education should support the policy of developing recreation as a state rather than a federal responsibility

Before 1932, the Federal Government manifested little concern with recreation. The tremendous unemployment problem of the depression with its enforced idleness — not leisure — of people, seemed adequate justification for Federal activity to provide recreational facilities, to promote recreational programs,

[22] Public Education in Washington, *Report of a Survey of Public Education in the State of Washington,* Olympia, 1946, p. 381.

and to sustain recreational leadership. Between 1932 and 1937 the Federal Government spent for recreational facilities and leadership about $1,500,000,000. This enormous expenditure reflected the growing appreciation of the need for recreational facilities. With respect to opportunities for recreation the American Council on Education[23] advised that nearly all youth should have opportunity to participate in sports, games and other outdoor activities; opportunity for creative experiences — to make things with the hands, to paint, to act, to build; opportunity for better social life; and opportunity for recreation at home.

The development of recreational facilities by the Federal Government is exemplified in the enlargement of our national forests, parks, parkways, and other recreational areas. The total area of these resources is 21,000,000 acres. Of this tremendous acreage only 11 per cent of public land is east of the Great Plains; the great centers of population are also east of the Great Plains. It costs more to visit the national parks and forests than the majority of the population can afford.

During the prewar years of the Roosevelt administrations, various federal agencies concerned themselves with recreation and spent millions of dollars on recreational projects. These contributions of the Federal Government to recreation are not to be viewed as simple emergency donations, but in the light of fundamental issues of government and democracy. Few of the political moves of the administration during this period were political planks on which the elections were fought; in these years the democratic process of discussion and enlightenment was lacking. Still, it is believed that promotion of recreation by the Federal Government was generally approved. Nevertheless, it now appears that the State Governments are awake to the recreational needs of the people and comprise much better agencies for meeting these needs than the Federal Government.

It is evident on every hand that the public schools do not

[23] C. G. Wren and D. L. Harley, *Time on Their Hands*, Washington, D.C., American Council on Education, 1941.

always meet the pressing needs of youth. The schools as social institutions have tried to do more than an academic curriculum demands, but their efforts have been partial and sporadic. Since the schools belong to the people, then perhaps we should say that American fathers and mothers have failed to understand the urgent needs of youth. With respect to recreation it is clear that if local and state groups do not attack the problem, then there is always the hazard that the Federal Government will act. Experience of recent years shows that recreation is a necessity in modern life, that communities must either provide or accept leadership, and that education is basic to participation in constructive recreation.

The general educator often philosophizes about a wider use of the school plant and an identity between the school and community. Progress in public school administration is spotty in this direction. In the area of recreation the situation is chaotic. It is not unusual to find public funds wasted because two community groups compete in recreation for the same purposes. It is not uncommon to find one set of recreational facilities constructed, equipped, and staffed for school children and another series of facilities prepared for nonschool persons of the same community. In some respects the Federal Government has added to the confusion. Recreation organized and conducted outside local control loses the opportunity to foster local responsibility and so weakens the democratic tradition.

Recreation is a community problem; it cannot be solved by remote control of the needs and interests of people. Group action at the local level is necessary to provide facilities and leadership. The organization of leisure is possible only on this basis of community interest and cooperation. The most important communal unit is the family and opportunity for family recreation is also a community problem. This proper emphasis upon the local group is even more apparent when the leisure and work life of the whole community is concerned. Hours of work, location of shops, and housing conditions bear sharply upon the uses of leisure, and hence must be considered along with other community problems such as play areas, gardens, woods and fields, streams and lakes, theaters, athletic clubs, schools, libraries, and other recreational features.

THE CONTINUED SEARCH FOR THE DEMOCRATIC WAY

Over the years the search for democratic principles and their applications to American life has continued. At times, interest in the matter lags; at other times, such as the present, the issues are acute and challenging. Jefferson in the Declaration of Independence wrote of "self-evident truths," Lincoln in the debates with Douglas declared: "In relation to the principle that all men are created equal, let it be as nearly reached as it can. If we cannot give freedom to every creature, let us do nothing that will impose slavery upon any other creature."[24] In our generation, Adams made the "American Dream" real and attractive,[25] Dewey stated it in educational terms,[26] Russell followed after Thomas Paine with a popular statement of the democratic heritage,[27] and the current literature of the topic is enormous.

QUESTIONS AND PROBLEMS FOR DISCUSSION

1. Why is democracy a moral rather than an economic system?
2. What kind of social system regards man as a person of real worth, in and of himself?
3. List the points at which Jefferson's self-evident truths conflict with the principles of despotic governments.
4. What is meant by the phrase "natural rights"?

[24] Carl Sandburg, *Abraham Lincoln*, New York, Harcourt, Brace, 1926, Vol. II, p. 131.
[25] James Truslow Adams, *The Epic of America*, Boston, Little, Brown, 1931.
[26] John Dewey, *Democracy and Education*, New York, Macmillan, 1922.
[27] William F. Russell, *The New "Common Sense,"* New York, Macmillan, 1941.

5. What is the basis for considering democracy a moral system?
6. If democracy is a moral system, why should economic questions appear to dominate current controversies?
7. What is necessary for the survival of democratic governments? What role must education play in the process?
8. Interpret Jefferson's phrase, "all men are created equal" in terms of biological equality and also equality of opportunity. What are the justifications for the position you take?
9. Consider the three applications of this principle of equality of opportunity as given in the text and suggest others.
10. What conditions should be met before public money is expended for the development of an athletic team?
11. What justification is there for placing upon the excellent individual large obligations of the citizen?
12. How does an élite behave?
13. Is it socially sound to expect individual return to match social expense?
14. What is the significance of the principle of personal worth in a democracy?
15. Is it good or bad physical education to use a player who is unfit in order to win a game? If so used, is he regarded as a means or an end?
16. Under what conditions is uniformity necessary and desirable?
17. What are some of the differences between the discipline of authority and self-discipline?
18. What is self-expression? What can the individual express? What has happened to the diver in "Paracelsus"?
19. What are "antecedent sensory stimuli"?
20. Is it unhygienic to repress oneself? Always? Ever?
21. What sort of activities give large opportunity for expression? Why is this so?
22. Why is individual responsibility required in persons for the perpetuation of a democracy? Can democracy persist if the responsibilities of citizens are assumed by government?
23. In what ways can the teacher of physical education promote the development of a sense of individual responsibility?
24. What are the limitations of a policy of pupil sharing in the determination of what shall be taught?
25. What is the meaning of the principle of self-achievement?
26. Why do commercial motives in sport jeopardize educational values?
27. How does competition in sport differ from competition in business? What items would you include in a code of sportsmanship?

28. Why is cooperation an essential element in competitive sport?
29. What are the origins of competition and cooperation? Can they be strengthened or weakened by the culture in which an individual lives? Illustrate.
30. Can these traits be modified by education and experience? Illustrate.
31. Should one feel humiliated when he loses? Do you? Should you teach your pupils to be right always and never to make mistakes? Does everyone make mistakes? What attitude should the player bring to the game he plays?
32. Discuss the impact of a totalitarian state upon personality.
33. Discuss the topic: There can be no public interest apart from the interest of the individuals of whom the public is composed.
34. Has physical education ever been used to develop docility in the masses? What do you know about the system of education in Imperial Germany?
35. Why is it difficult to practice democratic processes?
36. Read "The Moral Equivalent of War." Discuss the essay from the viewpoint of physical education.
37. What do you think of the proposal often made to substitute military drill for physical education? Formulate a reply to such proposal.
38. Would you approve the appointment of a famous athlete to be head of physical education in the Army or Navy? Explain your answer.
39. Why should physical education oppose fascism in American life? Why should it oppose communism? How do these two ideologies appear to be identical?
40. Discuss the proposal that recreation should be the responsibility of education.
41. What do you think of the suggestion that the Federal Government should be responsible for recreation?

REFERENCE READINGS

American Association for Health, Physical Education and Recreation. "The Contributions of Physical Activity to Human Well-Being." *Research Quarterly*, May, 1960, p. 263.
Bayles, Ernest Edward. *Democratic Educational Theory*. New York, Harper, 1960.

de Huszar, George B. *Practical Application of Democracy.* New York, Harper, 1945.

Djilas, Milovan. *The New Class.* New York, Praeger, 1957.

Farber, Seymour M., (Editor). *Control of the Mind, Man and Civilization.* New York, McGraw-Hill, 1961.

Knapp, Maud Lombard, and Todd, Frances. *Democratic Leadership in Physical Education.* Millbrae, Calif., National Press, 1952.

Labin, Suzanne. *The Anthill.* New York, Praeger, 1961.

MacIver, Robert M. *The Ramparts We Guard.* New York, Macmillan, 1950.

McCleary, Isabel S., and McDonough, Thomas D. "Competition and Cooperation." *The Physical Educator,* March, 1963, p. 9.

Nearing, Scott. *Freedom: Promise and Menace.* Harborside, Me., Social Science Institute, 1961.

CHAPTER FOUR

PHYSICAL EDUCATION IN A DEMOCRACY— ECONOMIC CONCEPTS

Luxury is clearly not a novelty; the satirists of ancient Rome had it as their subject matter. But material comfort and physical indulgence have probably never before been available to so many nor have they been before to so many a predominant obsession. Even in a palace, said Marcus Aurelius, it is possible to live well. But, as the ancient sage pointed out, it required a special effort under the circumstances.

Edman.

Prestige is by no means always conveyed by economic success; the quest for gain may at times bring reproof, and many of the positions that carry the highest status are bestowed on those who have removed themselves from the current economic competition. Nevertheless, the mainspring of the cultural institution of prestige-seeking seems intimately related to the quest for gain.

Murphy.

THE ECONOMY OF PRIMITIVE LIFE

There is an accumulated body of evidence to indicate that man has lived on the earth at least 500,000 years. This half-million years has seen little change, until recently, in man's manner of life, in his habits, and even in man himself. In his earliest period, characterized chiefly by the traits and reactions of an animal, the brain size was slightly less, the jaw was somewhat heavier, and the position of the heel bone and the shape of the little toe were somewhat different. From the Cro-Magnon man, a savage by modern standards, who lived 50,000 years ago, to the product of twentieth-century civilization, the evidence indicates little, if any, change in physical or mental resources.

Obviously, man's life as a primitive savage is very obscure. Nevertheless, on the basis of what is known it is fair statement to say that nothing in modern civilization is comparable to its poorness, brutishness, and filth. Even the slums of the cities are unable to produce anything as revolting. Primitive life contained nothing attractive in food, shelter, clothing, or safety. The modern camper who goes to the woods to be a savage again knows nothing of being without vessels to hold water, and never experiences the necessity to strike fire from flints, to eat insects, decayed fish, and putrid flesh.

One can only surmise the steps in that struggle upward from poor, brutish states to higher levels of power and achievement.[1] For long periods accustomed to small groups, hundreds of thousands of years must have elapsed before pastoral and agricultural life made large groups possible. With the coming together of many to form the tribe there developed the opportunity for leadership. The chief, the prince, or the king was he who had initiative. He ruled until another more powerful replaced him. There was always work to be done and laborious

[1] Melville Herskovitz, *Economics of Primitive People,* New York, Knopf, 1940.

hours were given to things that are simple and commonplace today. Fire, clothing, shelter, food, and safety demanded the efforts of the group, and required the labor of all. There could be no parasites, no leisure group, no nonproducers. Leisure then was not the problem for our primitive ancestors; all labored for long hours, but without hurry. In this respect, these ancestors of ours must have been something like the laborers of the Orient today.

Plagues, epidemics, and famine were the great calamities. The fear of disease that people have today goes back to racial experiences of man with calamities that came upon the group without knowledge of their causes and without knowing what to do.

Life was hard. Those who lived and survived to reproduce their kind were the strongest, the fittest. The death rate was appalling, as judged by modern standards; in some cases the defective were destroyed without compunction, in others they were allowed to live out their miserable existence and to propagate their kind. It would probably have been impossible to find any representatives of a tribe who could run as fast, jump as far, and throw as accurately as the members of the American Olympic team of any period since the revival of the Olympic games. Altogether primitive life offers nothing that one would wish to go back to, because its best elements, such as outdoor life, are possible in modern civilization to an increasing degree, as its joys and values become known.

THE ECONOMY OF MODERN INDUSTRIAL LIFE

The beginnings of civilization are marked by the triumph of man over the world of nature. Thousands of years passed between the invention of a wheel for drawing heavy loads and the printing press that made possible a continuous and easy record of man's accomplishments. To the middle of the nineteenth century, generation after generation lived in a simple, agricultural environment, with only a few cities that attracted the merchants and the ruling classes. The masses lived upon the land. In a remarkably short period of time, a few minutes in the life of the race, great numbers have been taken into sedentary occupations, collected into shops, stores, and business houses, forced by economic consideration to cluster in large groups in one locality.

Modern industrial life is primarily city life. The majority of people in the United States are living in urban communities. Great numbers of the American people, whose ancestors engaged in outdoor life or in work calling for muscular effort, are now indoors, and working day after day without enough exercise to put them into a perspiration.

The items in this industrialization are well known: the change from hand to machine work, from man power to steam, from home work to factory work, division of labor, aggregation of workers, women and children in industry. There are other items that grow out of the complex industrial picture such as serious problems of government, safety hazards incident to large aggregations of people in small space, and elaborate services demanded by the conditions that are created.

In spite of the many human advantages the city affords, its disadvantages are tremendous. The city magnifies the hazards of human existence; by concentrating them in small areas, it exaggerates a picture that in simple communities Nature softens and smooths away. To meet the persistent problems of mass aggregations and the services that conditions demand, complex governmental organizations appear. Thus, government in at least one of its several forms (municipal, town or township, county, state, federal) impinges upon the health, safety, education, recreation, employment, and welfare of citizens. The expansion of government and the increase in its functions do not necessarily give to the community the things it needs and wants; such service depends upon the political forces controlling government.

Moreover, the city in the industrial age has accentuated the problems of public safety. The automobile traveling at high speeds on streets designed for horse-drawn vehicles, fires in buildings packed closely together, and the general use of gas, electricity, and mechanical equipment have introduced hazards that did not formerly exist. Can the coordinations and rapid adjustments of man be developed sufficiently to save him from these dangers, or is the answer to be found in a radical reconstruction of our cities?

PROBLEMS OF THE MODERN ECONOMY FACING PHYSICAL EDUCATION

The change from simple, primitive conditions of life to the complex, industrial society of a modern nation presents a number of problems to physical education. While there are many features of modern life that have no particular bearing upon physical education, other aspects greatly affect man's growth and development in childhood and youth, and influence tremendously the way he lives over the years.

These economic conditions afford the source out of which certain principles of physical education arise; they are the scientific justifications for the selection of certain kinds of activities and the seeking of certain outcomes in the conduct of the program.

The most important economic conditions, pertinent to the program of physical education, are the following: immigration, urbanization of society, factory labor, mechanization of labor, mass production methods, women in industry, transportation, commercial amusements, leisure time, safety and world leadership. In the discussion of these, principles of physical education will be derived.

IMMIGRATION AND IDEAS

Between 1840 and 1860 the population of the United States increased naturally, but at the same time enormous numbers were added to the population by immigration. The years of

1845 and 1855 were marked by great waves of European immigration, consisting chiefly of Irish, Germans, and English. Of these groups, the Irish settled chiefly in the cities of the Atlantic seaboard; the Germans and English moved into the rural districts of the Middle West. By 1850 something over 2 million immigrants had come to the new world; in ten years more the total was considerably over 4 million.

This tremendous immigration up to the middle of 1914 brought many diverse elements. Unused to a democratic form of government, and retaining, as might be expected, the customs and traditions of the motherland, they frequently formed incongruous communities in America. Instead of a melting pot and ready assimilation, there arose "Little Italy," "A New World Bohemia," "German Cities," and other evidences of a transplanted people.

Many in these groups cast off their old-world allegiances and became both in war and in peace full citizens of the nation. All retained, in minor ways, the customs and viewpoints of their origin. Consequently we find educational practice in certain communities colored by the procedures of foreign schools, and particularly is this true in physical education. The native-born in the United States had been so busy with transportation, Indian fighting, the emigration to the West, that little time or attention was given to the physical education of the people. Consequently, immigrants from nations that had national systems of gymnastics not only furnished early leaders, but formed the nucleus around which gymnastic organizations were to cluster.

Physical education should evolve an American program sensitive to American needs and American aspirations.

Physical education is properly concerned with educating citizens of the American democracy. Its program should not only meet physiological needs of the individual but also reflect his cultural aspirations. It never occurred to the Germans and Swedes who had experienced in Europe highly developed systems of physical education that the aims and purposes, methods and materials of European peoples would be quite unsuited to the citizens of a New World democracy; that the values considered important in the training of the subject of a king might be quite out of place in the education of the citizens of a republic.

Since German and Swedish gymnastic systems are not prominent in the United States at the present time, it might be inferred that this principle was of little practical importance. On the contrary, it needs to be continually affirmed. Not many years ago, a strong effort was made to import a Danish system of gymnastics. Recent efforts to develop a fitness program based on tests made of Swiss children illustrates the need for a careful evaluation of foreign programs.

Physical education should give its full support to wise national measures that prevent weakening of the American population.

From time to time various proposals arise that claim national value. They need to be examined. The data on alien and native-born registrants[2] suggest that physical education should support the present policy of restricted immigration. But measures are not necessarily wise because they have national sponsorship. The parade of finely developed youth that passed from the palaestra into Greek life rested on a slave population. Greek infants without promise for the state perished from planned exposure on Hellenic hillsides.

In spite of valid evidence from the rejections of young Americans for military service, the claim continues that "brains" can save the nation, that "master minds" can formulate *plans* that will provide security for everyone from the cradle to the grave, and that physical education is a kind of "frill," perhaps concerned with vigor, vitality, endurance, skills, and certain social behaviors but, on the whole, not worth bothering about in an age of mechanical robots.

Recent German experience should be instructive. The German soldiers of Hitler's Reich, who ranged from Norway to Egypt and from the English Channel to the Caspian Sea, were the infants and children of the First World War generation and its aftermath of confusion, poverty, and despair. During child-

[2] Second Report of the Provost Marshal General to the Secretary of War, 1919, p. 160.

hood they lacked proper food, were malnourished, and suffered from widespread disease. When Hitler began his actual attack on the democracies, he had at his command an army of vigorous, alert, and competent youth. Something had happened during the intervening years.

When Hitler came to power he found youthful gangs and criminals roaming the cities, degenerate forms of social vice flourishing, and every evidence of human degeneration. With characteristic German thoroughness, the Germans set to work to strengthen the biological fiber of their youth. Science was enlisted with its knowledge; competence and experience were utilized.

They put young men into labor camps and while weaving around their procedure much foolish talk about racial purity, they carried out the simple process of having all young males engage in manual work out of doors. They set up standards of personal hygiene and inculcated attitudes of self-denial, self-discipline, and cooperative effort toward a greater Germany. We in the United States do and ought to disagree sharply with the final purpose of this devoted effort, with the cruelties, vile obscenities, and vicious crimes of the Nazi regime, but we should not be so stupid as to condemn everything achieved under the Nazi dictatorship nor so uninformed as to believe that we too must be ruthless, dictatorial, and imperialistic in order to build the biological resources of American life. Physical education should emphasize the need for an education of the whole man. Certainly the biological assets of the individual should be developed and maintained in good condition. This cannot be done without the support of educational leaders, who must envision their educational role as much larger than concentration on the verbal level.

URBANIZATION OF SOCIETY

The shift of population from the rural areas to urban centers is one of the striking social phenomena in America since

1830. Although this movement is social in its character, it is economic in causation. Gregariousness accounts in part for the shift, but the main factors are the economics of the factory system and transportation. The discovery of gold in California, and the consequent rush to the West in 1849, slowed down this flight from the land in the decade 1850-1860. The Civil War, in 1860-1864, further interrupted it, but by 1880 the movement was rapidly under way. In the decade 1930-1940, a period of great economic depression, the shift stops. The rural and urban percentages remain about the same, although when the rural is broken down into farm and nonfarm population, the farm shows an actual decrease in 1940 as compared with 1930. The nonfarm population includes those living in villages and suburbs. Over the next ten years, however, the rural population actually declined while the urban proportion increased markedly (Table 2).

TABLE 2.   URBAN AND RURAL POPULATION OF THE
UNITED STATES — 1910-1960

CLASS	1960*	1950	1940	1930	1920	1910
Total number ...	179,323,175	150,697,361	131,669,275	122,775,046	105,710,620	91,972,266
Urban ..	125,268,750	96,028,000	74,423,702	68,954,823	54,304,603	42,166,120
Rural ...	54,054,425	54,669,000	57,245,573	53,820,223	51,406,701	49,806,146
Total per cent ..	100	100	100	100	100	100
Urban ..	69.9	64.4	56.5	56.2	51.4	45.8
Rural ...	30.1	35.6	43.5	43.8	48.6	54.2

*Source: 1960 Census of Population, Supplementary Reports, Washington, D.C., Department of Commerce, June 9, 1961.

This movement of the population to cities has taken the ambitious, the ones with initiative and courage. It has frequently left the rural community depleted of enterprising and capable folk. In recent years there are distinct signs of movement in an opposite direction. New York City has lost many of its crowded millions to suburbs and rural areas, and gentlemen farmers are taking over many of the abandoned farms in New England.

While it has been popular belief that the country is healthier than the city, there are statements that people in the rural districts suffer from more disease than do city people. The explanation offered for these statements has several items. There are the improved methods in the city for securing sanitary water and food supplies, and the effort made by city people to compensate for the handicaps incident to urban life.

Physical education should gear its program to meet human needs that grow out of increasing urbanization.

This swing to the cities with its associated congestion in housing, limited play spaces, and decrease in natural types of recreation such as fishing, hunting, home parties, and picnics increases the demand on physical education for teaching skills and developing interests for recreation and for maintaining programs of vigorous outdoor activities.

Associated with the problem of congestion, but not limited to the cities, is the tremendously important lack of facilities. Many people have the skill and desire to engage in recreational activities for which there are no opportunities. Numerous studies have shown the need for both leadership and facilities; these shortages are factors in shaping physical education.

The environment may be impoverished and opportunities for the development of the individual so lacking that the usual child is weak, undersized, with no skills and no interests in recreation, unable to use purposefully the little leisure that he has. In some communities the shortages in facilities are very real. The practical person, who sees in such limitations the sole factors for the determination of programs, looks with disdain, if not contempt, upon one who is concerned with the kind of activities which all young persons ought to experience. There are programs that never get beyond the limitations of place. Of course, one cannot make a silk purse out of a sow's ear, but this proverbial wisdom too often endows an attitude which is quite unable to seek for more suitable materials.

The problem of education everywhere is to discover the kinds of experience which young persons need in order to develop the traits, interests, skills, and qualities which society

desires, and then to attempt, by every possible means, to establish the needed facilities. There is no other way for those who
see life as progress—a dynamism which continually evolves
new and better forms of living as it realizes the possibilities inherent in man and his environment. The need that people have
for vigor, for wholesome ways to use leisure, for functional motor
skills, and for democratic ideals is very great. Such need reflects
man's inner nature and is reinforced by the social scene in which
he lives. These two aspects of the problem comprise an imperative command to those who understand. The tragedy of human
life is always, "to little and too late." Too little understanding!
Too few playgrounds! Too little equipment! Too few teachers!
Too little time! These are the ceaseless complaints that well up
from schools and communities where the child is drilled in
stupid calisthenics because there is no opportunity to do anything else.

*Physical education should deal with sedentarianism as an
aspect of urban life.*

There are several significant problems for physical education that arise out of the shift of population from rural areas to
urban centers. Sedentarianism is one of the more important.
Whatever special virtues there are in physical work—and some
insist that they exist in real quantities—these are usually denied
the city child, and, in the opinion of some, are not made up in
the physiological returns of systematic physical education. Altogether, it seems clear that society has submitted to a pronounced change in distribution of population without feeling the
need for correction of errors, not having the confidence in its
ability adequately to compensate for the handicaps of urban
environment.

The hazards of the sedentary life run through the home,
school, and vocations. Provision for physical exercise of school
children is not enough. These children must learn skills and
acquire interests in physical activities which they will be disposed to continue after school days are over. Moreover, there
must be a great increase in recreational facilities such as golf
courses, tennis, squash, and handball courts, swimming pools,

skating rinks, walking paths, bowling greens, and playgrounds for young children. There is no other effective way.

Since development defects are prevalent among urban and rural youth, physical education should support preventive and curative programs of health service in schools.

Physical education has no direct responsibility for the prevention or correction of the major defects that occur in children and youth. Indirectly, through the development of vigorous organic functions, it may have a salutary effect in the prevention of certain abnormalities, but direct claims are not warranted. Since it is interested in the normal growth and development of children and youth, it should give support to those medical and dental agencies that are directly concerned. To be prepared to give such support, it is important to know the facts about the defects occurring in children and youth.

A distinctive feature of the defects in children and youth is the consistent picture over a number of years. Ordinarily, data that are fifteen years old are not significant at the present time but their consistency over the years reflects the failure to prevent their occurrence. Moreover, uncorrected defects in elementary children are likely to be the causes of rejection for military service ten to fifteen years later. It is important to understand this relationship and to examine the record of the past as well as that of more recent years.

The close correspondence over the years is shown by the tabulation of recorded defects reported by the Medical Inspection Bureau of New York State and that of the Philadelphia schools, the former in 1928-1929 and the latter in 1945-1946 and 1960-1961, as shown in Table 3. Note that the 1960-1961 percentages in the Philadelphia schools were lower than in 1945-1946 for all items except teeth.

The data in Table 3 show that in a large city school system the percentage of defects among school children were almost identical with that shown in New York State seventeen years before. The distressing fact is evident from many communities: we are not correcting the remediable defects of school children.

For more than thirty years studies and surveys have

TABLE 3.   PHYSICAL DEFECTS OF SCHOOL CHILDREN

DEFECT	PERCENTAGE OF SCHOOL CHILDREN WITH DEFECTS		
	NEW YORK STATE MEDICAL INSPECTION BUREAU, 1928-29	PHILADELPHIA SCHOOLS	
		1945-46	1960-61
Teeth	38.3	43.2	57.9
Vision	8.7	12.7	9.5
Hearing	1.6	1.1	0.7
Tonsils	18.6	13.8	4.8
Nasal obstruction	4.0	5.9	1.9
Malnutrition	9.2	15.0	10.7

shown high percentages of children with remediable defects. The most common physical defect in school children is carious teeth; this condition is due largely to faulty nutrition in the early years of life. Children with unsatisfactory diets will show from 5 to 24 per cent more dental defects than children with satisfactory diets.

The purpose of physical education to give support to health programs in schools should be widely accepted. It is a recognition that all aspects of public education have interrelationships. It is an expression of an understanding that the whole child does go to school. Physical education interested in the whole child need not fear neglect of its special techniques nor loss of respect for its particular services. Indeed, physical education has always advanced as it has broadened its understanding and has devoted itself to serving all the legitimate purposes of education.

FACTORY LABOR

The development of the factory system has significant lessons for physical education. Although proceeding at a more rapid rate at the beginning in England, it gained momentum in the United States after the Civil War. An indication of the tremendous growth in industry is given in the growth of manufactures.

Between 1850 and 1940 the population of the nation increased nearly six times but the products of manufacture gained more than fifty-six times. For nearly one hundred years there has been a steady growth in the total value of manufactured products. These data correspond generally with the swing to the city and portray the growing industrialism of the United States. Many other evidences could be cited.

The factory system changed the American home and the life of the American people. Industry was formerly carried on in the home, giving developmental and training activities to the young. The home presented innumerable opportunities for the development of initiative, leadership, and responsibility. It furnished unique physical activities in the work and play life of the child. The modern bungalow, with its narrow strip of lawn and backyard sufficient only for a clothesline and ash can, and the modern apartment house of the cities, are products of a kind of adult organization of society for economic gain through industry in shops and factories. They fail to provide the kind of opportunities required for the proper development of children. In less than one hundred and fifty years we have explored and exploited our natural resources, we have tilled and reclaimed the soil, we have stretched in all directions over 30,000 miles of railroads, we have built great cities, and housed there the teeming millions; we have recently taken a world position in international trade and international banking. But the biologic nature that has marked man for probably at least 50,000 years is not to be changed in fifteen decades. The demands of the organism for developmental physical activity persist, and the factory system and city life reinforce the need for physical education.

Machine labor has reduced the hours of work for man. Industry has been organized for production so that with fewer hours of work more goods are produced.   ,

The Fair Labor Standards Act (1938), usually known as the wage-hour act, provides for a five-day week and an eight-hour day. The argument for this legislation involves not only the welfare of the worker but also the economics of production. Industrialization has increased enormously the production of goods and now legislation increases materially the leisure of man. While the evils of the factory system with the accompanying herding of workers into slums near the plants have long been recognized as inimical to the health and vitality of man, the correctives achieved through socially wise legislation controlling hours, wages, housing, and working conditions may be adequate to protect against the more obvious hazards of the machine.

Physical education should teach the fundamental skills so that all labor will be more efficient and less fatiguing.

Formerly, in agricultural activities and in home industries the young learned many fundamental skills. The youth entering upon factory or clerical employment today engages in a very limited kind of work calling for a narrow range of movement. The advances in technology and automation in which more and more products are made by machines removes from industry the necessity for hand skills which formerly were essential — skills so highly developed that man could make very complicated things by the use of extremely simple tools. This coordination of eye, hand and mind represented "a degree of virtuosity," writes Aldous Huxley, "which is sometimes incredible."[3] It is evident that this training of the mind-body was a basic kind of education that needs to be continued and extended. The school child should acquire in school years a fine mastery of certain fundamental skills so that he can stand, walk, sit, and climb easily, without undue fatigue, and can lift and carry objects without strain.

MECHANIZATION OF LABOR

Some youths in some places in the world today grow into

[3] Aldous Huxley, "Human Potentialities," *Control of the Mind, Man and Civilization* (Seymour M. Farber, Editor), New York, McGraw-Hill, 1961, p. 68.

vigorous maturity without ever experiencing instruction in physical education. This happens in the Andes of South America, in China, in the Philippines, and in many parts of Africa. It happens also in some of the remote regions of the United States. These young people climb mountains, tend stock, and work with their hands using axe, shovel, loom, and other simple tools. But the vast majority of young people in the United States grow into adulthood without ever learning how to swing an axe or to thread a loom. A mechanical saw is used to fell trees, mills weave cloth, and machines dig ditches, plow, cultivate, and harvest the crops.

Physical education should provide childhood and youth with sufficient motor activity to insure development of vital organs and the learning of functional skills.

In general, physical education should comprise vigorous activities. Under certain conditions quiet activities are desirable but these will not provide for the development of the vital organs. Calisthenic exercises performed in the classroom are worth little more than a change from sitting still. Such physical education should be abandoned for more vigorous and functional movements.

The selection of games is very important. Games in which one child runs while the rest stand still are poor means for development of vitality.

In high school programs, change of clothing is desirable and showers are needed. In these years the strenuousness of the program is stepped up; every period should be vigorous enough to require a shower at the end. The size of classes often determines the kinds of activities that can be used. Classes should be small enough to permit the use of vigorous activities in which instruction can be given.

Richard H. Pohndorf, assistant professor of physical education, University of Illionois, reports:

> Roughly about 2 percent of our high school population has physical education about five times a week. Less than 50 per cent of our 12 million boys and girls in 30,000 high schools have physical education 2-3 times a week. Over 50 percent of the high school population has no physical education in the cur-

riculum. More than 80 percent of all physical skills, necessary for sports participation, which an individual develops during his lifetime, are acquired between the ages 7-17. These ten years are the "ten skill and fitness years" which are highly important and currently being neglected by school authorities.[4]

MASS PRODUCTION

The genius of American industry is mass production of goods. The ability to produce has increased wealth and raised the standard of living but these fine gains are accompanied by certain attitudes and ideals that impair the happiness and welfare of men.

The present American culture, developing rapidly out of a pioneer civilization, is frequently characterized by the foreign visitor as excessively devoted to work and the attainment of wealth. The good American life apparently is the very busy life in achieving a competence. Morals, which are properly concerned with health, efficiency, and happiness, conflict basically with a culture concerned with wealth. The average American's notion of work is thoroughly degenerate. The theory of man's essential laziness except under the lash of necessity led to the fiction of the economic man described by the political economy of the nineteenth century, and Alexander Hamilton's notion of state-building led to our present mood. The doctrines of modern business lead not to happiness but to more factories, not to beauty and efficiency but to more mills, not to health but to more wheat and cotton. What do we do with the money made from the manufacture of automobiles? Build more factories to make more automobiles. The achievements of business are lauded as signs of progress and the success of financial enterprise is set up as a goal for youth to aim at, while the increase in nervous and mental diseases cries aloud that our concepts of work and wealth confuse values. A supreme value in contem-

[4] Richard H. Pohndorf, "The Erosion of Physical Education in High Schools," *Physical Education Newsletter,* published by Croft Educational Services, June 12, 1961.

porary American culture is making a living, but the supreme moral achievement of man is living.

Of course, physical education must be concerned with these aspects of our culture, because health, efficiency, happiness and other moral values are involved. Many industrial workers are unhappy, disgruntled, selfish, and afraid. Their work fails to afford satisfaction; where can it be found?

"Production lacks criteria;" writes Dewey, "one thing is better than another if it can be made faster or in greater mass."[5] In this situation does physical education have a criterion? There seems to be one: **Stress at all times and everywhere the need of man for play, recreation, and wholesome leisure.** Beginning in the school years, all children must learn satisfying motor skills. The present emphasis upon a few athletes who perform for the crowd must be erased, and programs of play and recreation for all must be established. If the school population of this generation of Americans could become addicted to wholesome play and recreation, many of our present social ills relating to work would disappear.

Physical education should recognize the need to teach activities in which the individual can find joy and satisfaction.

The problems inherent in contemporary notions of work and wealth bear sharply upon the physical educator. They are real problems of the nation and demand his serious consideration. Modern factory work fails to offer opportunity for self-expression and self-realization in the activity itself. It is to be regretted that the joy in work which American craftsmen experienced two generations ago is not possible today. Today, too frequently, the industrial worker in shop and factory works only for the monetary return, and as soon as he is free from the demands of the schedule he is eager to get away and then for him, if possible, comes the chance to do something that provides satisfaction. He works to earn money with the hope that in some way he can buy happiness. He has never had a philosophy to help him understand that happiness cannot be bought,

[5] John Dewey, *Democracy and Education*, New York, Macmillan, 1922, p. 271.

for like beauty it comes from within and cannot be acquired from without. Stevenson is reported to have said, "One may travel over the whole world in the search for beauty and never find it unless he has it with him in his heart." Beauty and happiness are alike in this respect. Thus the happiness that the industrial worker finds is likely to be the kind catered to by professional and commercialized forms of recreation, and these, too frequently, have been associated with characteristic and lewd forms of vice.

To speak of joy of work when the whole process calling for imagination and creative impulse is the repetitive task of placing nuts on bolts, or throwing levers, or stacking trays, or watching for a thread to break in the rapid and phantasmagoric evolutions of a textile machine, is to call for that species of unbelief that greeted Dr. Eliot's address on the rights, duties, and privileges of the manual laborer. Cabot's analysis of the main features of this problem indicates clearly that the work of the industrial worker is lacking in those qualities so essential for self-expression and self-realization.[6]

Although recreation has health benefits to bestow upon those who share activity in its wholesome forms, it is important to develop positive and constructive approaches to play for its own sake. The relation that now exists between work and recreation is such that workers regard their occupations as necessary means of earning a living and their recreations as desirable or necessary so that the main business of life — namely work — may be pursued. Work and play constitute an antithesis for these persons. Truly creative people do not distinguish between work and play, however. Work ought to have some of the joy that it once enjoyed and play ought to be strengthening and recreating. In an international congress, one committee considering the problem reported as follows:

> For the attaining of this end a complete reordering of working conditions as well as of recreation activities is necessary. Accordingly, every opportunity must be cultivated whereby the

[6] Richard C. Cabot. *What Men Live By*, Boston, Houghton Mifflin, 1914, pp. 21-26.

masses of the people may be restored to a vital contact with nature, not in the sense of weak and maudlin sentiment, but in the sense of a vital struggle with the eternally destructive and eternally creative forces of nature. The promotion and cultivation of genuine folk-art is one of the most important means to the realization of this aim.[7]

This emphasis upon joy and satisfaction is certainly no plea for fun and pleasure as the ends of life or the objects of education. Nor should it give support to the practice, often seen in schools, of judging an activity by the sole criterion of enjoyment. Joy is the normal by-product of certain kinds of experience, the underlying purposes of which could be growth in the development of an excellent person, or mastery of significant skills, or expansion of enriching interests and superior appreciations. Too often such worthy ends are smothered by the sad and depressing atmosphere of a stuffy morality when in fact such goals can be sought and achieved gaily and with accompanying joy and satisfaction.

WOMEN IN INDUSTRY

Women have always assisted in the work of the home and, even when home industries flourished, they played a responsible part in the production of goods. While some aspects of such home labor are not commendable, since time immemorial spinning and weaving, and the fashioning of garments had been the peculiar task of the housewife. The advent of the factory system changed all that in most homes, and in the textile industry the women and children followed into the factory. Child labor and employment of women in industry have since been tremendous social problems, because the effects of factory life on these individuals have been especially harmful. In some industries, notably in the manufacture of cotton goods, hosiery, hats, caps, gloves, millinery, umbrellas, in the canneries, in textile factories, the women outnumber the men. The number of

[7] World Congress for Leisure Time and Recreation, Hamburg, July, 1936, p. 40.

women in industry, however, has fluctuated. With the advent of the First World War, and the call to military service of the able-bodied men, the women were naturally drawn into munition making and associated activities. During the depression the number decreased, but during World War II the number of women in war plants and other industrial enterprises exceeded all previous figures.

Strange as it may seem, efforts to protect women in industry are met by opposition from groups of women who are so interested in the principle of "equal rights" that they are willing to sacrifice their sex to establish a principle which makes the results of "equal" labor unequal.

The labor of certain women in industry impairs their procreative functions, and is distinctly dysgenic, opposed to all the biologic and social values of real significance to physical education. In general, it is distinctly bad for the race, although the experience of certain women may be cited to the contrary.

Programs of recreation are being developed by the labor unions, and naturally motor activities play a large part in the programs. The International Ladies' Garment Workers Union sponsors classes in music, dramatics, athletics, dancing, and gymnastics. The future of this movement is very promising.

Physical education should conduct programs for girls that will insure vigorous physique, skills, and interests in sport and dance.

Physical education, like other cultural forces, also has its traditions. At times, these have blocked programs of physical education for girls; at other times they have led to masculine type activities quite identical with those suited to boys. Over the years, however, the leadership of girls' physical education has promoted sound programs. With the purpose to conduct activities that would insure vigorous physique and that would arouse interests in sport and dance, three concepts are important.

The first is the concept that use develops and nonuse degenerates. This is a very old physiological truth. It is true for muscles; it is also true for interests, attitudes, and appreciations. To develop a girl's muscles they must be used; to develop her interests in the out-of-doors, in sport, in dance, there must be experiences in these forms. And nonuse degenerates.

The second is the understanding that strength of the skeletal muscles reflects deeper organic strength; this has been discussed previously.

The third is the recognition of important differences in the two sexes. The female organism is not strikingly a strength unit, and yet girls and women should be strong and vigorous in a feminine way. They are not to be asked to engage in weight-lifting, to perform masculine feats on apparatus, or to center their attention on the abdominal muscles and to forget interests, attitudes, minds, and emotions. The strength developed in modern dance is not only more suitable for girls and women than the strength acquired from stunts on heavy apparatus but also it will arrive sooner and stay longer. The strength developed in swimming, hockey, skating, and tennis is not only far preferable in type for girls and women than the strength acquired in weight-lifting but also more efficient and enduring.[8]

TRANSPORTATION

An economic development of far-reaching importance for physical education is motor transportation. The automobile has profoundly changed the usual experiences of growing youth. Before the automobile, most children walked several miles to and from school every school day, ran errands for the home, and secured in their daily chores a large amount of physical activity.

Today, children go to school either in the home car or on the school bus. The great danger to young children on the streets and highways has justified the use of the school bus. It should be noted, however, that in addition to the loss in exercise due to the use of the school bus there are other curtailments in activity. These occur because in many schools the bus leaves

[8] Jesse Feiring Williams, "Physiological Implications of Fitness in Women's Athletics," *Journal of Health and Physical Education,* November, 1943, p. 469.

at the end of the regular session, so that after-school activities of various kinds are missed by those children going on the bus.

Physical education should arrange with the administration for schedules that will allow for after-school participation by as many children as possible.

There would be many advantages for all concerned in a longer school day. For some pupils, assigned to physical education during the morning session, the late afternoon could be devoted to preparation of lessons so that home work would be unnecessary. Different schedules would allow other pupils to experience their physical education in the late afternoon. Persistence of the old pattern is nothing but a tradition that should be changed to allow for richer educational experiences. If adequate time is to become available for physical education, as well as for driver education, ROTC, band practice, and health education, the school day and school terms must be lengthened.

This alteration of the old school day would provide for more hours for physical education; in terms of the needs of children and youth this is highly desirable.

COMMERCIAL AMUSEMENTS

In Colonial America people made their own entertainment. Radio and television were unknown. Skating rinks were unnecessary because there was skating on the ponds and rivers. Harvesting of crops and the raising of barns and houses were occasions for neighbors to gather together to sing songs, dance, and engage in sports. Our modern world shrieks in a thousand ways for answers to the pressing problems of an industrial age; the usual proposal for modern man's boredom is some commercial amusement that he can look at but barely tolerate. While his problems in the area of self-expression arise out of the economic forces that play upon him, his basic needs are human. Listen to a portion of a letter written to the *Atlantic Monthly.*

Each and every morning, after an early and hurried breakfast, during which takes place a hectic discussion relative to the most satisfactory methods of transportation to our respective destinations, I conclude to walk (or run) to the station, while the children are motored in great haste to another station or direct to private schools. I take a seat in a train beside another business man and appear as happy, important, and conventional as possible while I read the morning paper. It is vital that I turn eagerly to the financial page, because everybody else does. I am then submerged in a seething mass of human protoplasms which presently scatters to every conceivable corner of this North American city. And the fight is on.

In a close, steam-heated office my day is given over to frantic pursuits which involve the dictation of letters, telephoning, calculations, and discussions. Both within the office and without, the noise is constant, the movement continual — and the fight eternal. When the formality of the day's routine is over, I rush homeward by another route, having learned by telephone that I am to entrain and be met, or extract a car from some distant garage, or linger on a windy street corner to be collected by my wife or someone. Finally I reach home. I am tired, nervous, depleted, almost unclean. It is difficult to be agreeable. Casual conversation irritates me. My remarks annoy the family. I am useless, a burden, a poor investment. Sometimes a bath or a cocktail or both revivify me for a time, but usually, with great effort, I pull myself together and go in to dinner, resorting to neither. If the evening is to be spent at home, it is sure to be a brief one. If we "go out," I pray for decided inspiration or wild excitement. And, in either case, tomorrow I pay. My home is bulging with dusty books; my musical instruments are stored in the attic; my pen is used to write checks; my garden is full of weeds, and the thrushes come and go before I know it. The world is too much with us.

His musical instruments are stored, his pen writes no sonnets, his garden is so full of weeds that flowers don't bloom there, and he never hears the thrush at evening. How could this man be satisfied with commercial amusements?

Physical education should strive consistently to promote the idea that play belongs in the good life.

In the light of conspicuous failures in living in our modern world, physical education must become even more interested than it has been in promoting play among all age groups. This conviction about the importance of play is not opposed to work, but it wishes to place work in proper relation to the whole of life, and to view it as only one aspect of living. It believes that such orientation will help to make work lose something of that quality that for many leads to drudgery. At all events, it is skeptical of the present mood that drives people to industrial, business, and commercial affairs, so preoccupied with the production of wealth that they have neither time nor temper to enjoy those things which are the sole reasons for acquiring riches.

It is apparent that the ideal of devotion to work must be altered and enriched by placing alongside another ideal although it may conflict with the development of the first. This other ideal would state that play belongs in the good life, that it requires no apologies from its followers, that its justifications are rooted deep in the basic nature of mankind and buttressed by the kind of world in which man lives today. C. A. Mace, professor of psychology, University of London, writes as follows: "Enjoyment of the activity for its own sake is what play has in common with the enjoyment of the arts. . . . Play ranks in all its forms — golf, baseball, cricket, and so forth — somewhere in the hierarchy at or near the apex of which we place music, sculpture, and poetry."[9]

LEISURE TIME

One admirable outcome of the economic development of the industrial age is the phenomenal increase in leisure time for all persons. The forty-hour work week frees millions of persons to engage in leisure-time pursuits. While education in general endorses recreational interests and skills, and while there are many fine forms of recreation, physical activity will remain always as a major interest in leisure time for those who are young enough to enjoy it. The contribution of physical education to leisure, however, will depend largely upon the purposes that dominate it.

[9] C. A. Mace, "Human Motivation in an Affluent Society," *Control of the Mind, Man and Civilization* (Seymour M. Farber, Editor), New York, McGraw-Hill, 1961, p. 152.

Physical education should select its activities for various purposes, but at all age levels it should be guided by the needs of individuals to acquire skill in activities that can function in free play or leisure time.

The imperative necessity of viewing physical education as concerned with something more than a substitutional activity, an exercise program, forces itself continually upon us. Physical education must deal with the whole of life, with all the problems that in any way bear upon this old and ever-present one, the adjustment of the individual to the environment and of the environment to the individual. It would appear that there are two aspects of the problem at once bearing upon the profession. One is the immediate recasting of the activity program to have some contribution to make in forming attitudes toward recreation and affording opportunities for habit formation in the acquirement of serviceable skills. Here, then, the whole school problem must get away from the common notion that physical education is a disciplinary or perspiratory or postural activity. It is clearly for the purpose of helping to make effective the purpose of general education in terms of abundant living. The other aspect concerns the intimate blending of the school and community programs of recreation. Physical education must give its active and thoroughgoing support to the efforts to enrich the community facilities for leisure time uses. On the side of adult recreation, this means athletic fields, recreation centers, evening gymnasiums, tennis courts, golf courses, facilities for hiking, swimming, camping, and all other things which make for an abundant life. It would mean more than that. It would mean opportunities for the extension of one's personal experience, opportunities for learning, in night schools, extension courses, and the whole gamut of adult education. It would mean opportunities for participation in and witnessing dramatics, musical contests, modern dance, and the whole range of allied movements.

It is, perhaps, not extravagant to say that the hunger for more abundant life, richer and fuller living, is opposed to the present idea of work that so widely prevails. Not that it is adverse to believing in work, but rather it resists mightily the idea of work that so overshadows life. Our language is spotted with phrases that deify work such as "the sweat of the brow," and this doctrine has been tied up to integrity, reliability, and fine personal qualities. But today such a saying is an anachronism in an industrialized society where 60 per cent of the population engages in occupations that never cause perspiration.

Some who are concerned about the social good are afraid of this new mood for play and enriched curricula in schools, because for them the old adage, "Satan finds some mischief still for idle hands to do," has a mysterious significance. They hope to get social good by tiring people out and like the poet, George Herbert, who wrote,

> If goodness lead him not, yet weariness
> May toss him to my breast,

they hope greatly from work, fatigue, and ennui.

What seems almost essential is the development of an attitude of good humor, an unwillingness to take things too seriously. "Life is real and life is earnest" sang the poet, but the seriousness of life is often nothing but the stupidity and dullness of grown-ups who mistake bile for seriousness and chronic indigestion for dignity and bearing. The puritanic tradition weighs heavily upon our emotional natures and presses down the gaiety that tends to crop out in all of us.

Those who are proposing enriched curricula in the schools and improved opportunities for recreation, on the other hand, wish life to be rich and full **now,** full of meaning **now,** abundant **now,** beautiful **now.** They are quite opposed to the doctrine that one should live a poor and mean life now so that in the future he may live a rich and full life. The old idea that one should work hard now so that he may enjoy the good life later is both hoary and venerable, but it is also a hoax upon life as shown by the thousands that have so lived. The newer view says in effect, "The only way to have abundant life in the future is to live abundantly now. The only way to enjoy beauty tomorrow is to enjoy beauty today. The only way to live at your fullest and best tomorrow, is to live that way today."

Part of our difficulty is due to our fear of play. We have been told since the early days of childhood not to let the golden moments slip by when it would have been the part of wisdom to understand, as Barrie suggests, that they are golden only when we let them slip. Without becoming lazy loafers we might learn that it is the slipping which makes them golden.

An episode of the home front during World War II illustrates sharply the notion of peoples that play is a kind of trifling, not to be considered when serious affairs are at hand. The appointment of a young dancer to the Office of Civilian Defense provoked a storm of criticism. Doubtless, some of the critics were inspired by political considerations, some were concerned with the desire to define more narrowly the function of civilian defense, but all showed a lack of understanding of the place of play in the life of a nation. Some persons seem unable to distinguish between the careless indifference of a Nero, fiddling while Rome burns, and wholesome play and dance in America while a small group of very gallant men fight for life in Bataan. The fear of play runs so deep in our culture that morale, like morals, is supposed to develop through the workings of an inner conscience and quite apart from the consistent realities of human experience — the everyday actions and reactions through which people live.

SAFETY

The hazards of modern life are so great that interest in safety education has grown enormously, and efforts to reduce accidents have affected markedly school curricula and procedures. Classes in the use of the automobile are now standard practice in city schools and safety instruction is often included in health courses. Increasing evidence shows that the driver's attitudes play a very important part in automobile safety.[10] Safety in physical education classes is important; several suggestions are appropriate.

[10] *Research Quarterly,* March 1962, p. 148.

Physical education should teach safety techniques.

Work that involves lifting, carrying, climbing, and judging the speed of moving objects is performed more efficiently by those who have learned in childhood proper motor coordinations. Correct movements in climbing stairs, in lifting weights, in opening windows, and in many other motor skills are indeed safety measures. Children should learn how to fall safely, how to jump and guard against injury, how to maintain balance, and how to judge the speed of moving objects.

Physical education, by instruction and supervision, should prevent needless accidents.

Children must be taught to think in terms of safety for the individual and for members of the group during participation in all motor activities. Good examples of safety procedures in the learning situation occur in a stunt program in which safety precautions are a necessary part of performance and in a softball game in which the method of handling the bat and the location of players waiting to bat can be taught.

Teachers should be alert to and aware of all that is going on in the entire playground group even while they are occupied with a single group. They must know what activities are being played, what apparatus is in use, and which supplies are in service. If an accident should occur, a definite procedure should be followed, such as: (1) giving first aid, (2) notification of parent, (3) securing expert assistance (nurse or doctor) if necessary, and (4) reporting the facts of the accident to the principal.

There should be as much freedom on the playground as children are able to use well. In general the atmosphere should be free rather than restrictive. In order to secure this desirable state of affairs it is necessary to teach three things: (1) how to use each piece of apparatus safely, (2) how to follow directions in group participation, and (3) how to cooperate in protecting others.

Attention must be given to the condition of equipment. Broken or faulty apparatus should be promptly repaired or removed from use until repairs are made. Broken chains, improperly set upright posts, loose horizontal bars, stumps, rocks, or hard surface beneath apparatus that requires a landing surface are the more common accident hazards.

The following safety suggestions are recommended:

1. Test the apparatus for rigidity, for loose nuts or bolts, or for broken parts.
2. Instruct children in safe ways to use apparatus.
3. Depending upon the size of the apparatus, control the number of children that may use it simultaneously.
4. See that children use both hands when grasping bars on the climbing apparatus.
5. Warn children that to climb with wet hands is dangerous.
6. See that pits beneath horizontal bars and slides are large enough so that children will not fall on the edges.
7. Have children ask for assistance of a teacher when they want to undertake new or difficult stunts on apparatus.
8. Discourage the swinging of traveling rings over the cross-bars.
9. Teach children to await their turn without pushing or going ahead of others in line.
10. Teach children the correct way to use the slide. Have them sit erect on the surface of the slide with the feet together.
11. Do not permit primary school children on high slides; there should be low slides for their use.
12. See that there are no cracks in the slides that could hold stones or splinters.
13. Have children use steps to reach the top of the slide, see that no one is on the slide before descending, and leave the foot of the slide by walking forward out of the pit.
14. Do not permit children to kneel or stand on swing seats.
15. Allow only one child at a time to use a swing.
16. Do not allow children to swing when wearing skates.
17. Teach children to decrease speed when desirous of leaving the swing.
18. Chain swings to the posts or together before leaving the playground.
19. Do not permit empty swings to be pushed or twisted.[11]

Physical education should always include vigorous and adventurous activities in its program.

[11] Winifred Van Hagen, Genevie Dexter, and Jesse Feiring Williams, *Physical Education in the Elementary School,* Sacramento, California State Department of Education, 1951, p 108.

In a recent school survey, it was discovered that the principal had removed from the school playground a horizontal bar because a child had fallen from the bar and broken his arm. Several years ago balance beams were removed from the gymnasium of another school because a girl had fallen and sprained her ankle. The idea of safety should never lead to such unwarranted and extreme action. Vigorous and adventurous activities are essential for the best development of growing boys and girls. It is the responsibility of the administrator of the school to acquaint parents with the important purposes of the physical education program. Instruction and careful supervision can and should prevent needless accidents, but many desirable qualities in physique and personality will be lost if children are restricted to quiet games. Ability to control the body in movement, to act quickly in motor emergencies, and to maintain balance in a precarious situation is worth the risk of sprains and even broken bones.

This emphasis upon vigorous and adventurous activities should not be misunderstood. There are some children who should be restricted. Those children recovering from infections, such as measles, whooping cough, scarlet fever, tonsillitis, influenza, diphtheria, and those who have had a recent operation should be restricted until their convalescence is complete.

WORLD LEADERSHIP

Finally, the economic influences in America flowing out of two world wars have their bearing on the problem. The United States is in a position of world leadership economically. The world struggle for oil, for coal, for rubber, the expansion of markets and the fight for commercial supremacy, the foreign loans and the commitments of international banking flow back into the industrial organizations of the nation to stimulate production, to eliminate waste, to lower production costs. These influences are directly pressor in type, speeding up the demands on the physical organism. Corporations, business houses, department stores, and similar large organizations are attempting to meet these hazards by welfare departments and recreational facilities. The economic loss in terms of sickness, inefficiency, and fatigue prompts the effort. It remains, of course, a pertinent question whether or not such attempts fully compensate for the strains, losses in vitality, and impaired national vigor. If they do not, the problem remains.

Physical education should help to establish the American Way of Life as a worthy ideal for all peoples.

It is essential that teachers of physical education have a proper perspective of America, recognize her greatness as a nation and also her weaknesses. We need to know her history, understand her struggles, appreciate her achievements, and correct her failures.

The winning of the West was a triumph of hardy, adventurous stock which tamed the wilderness. The first settlers were the pioneers, who hunted and fished to maintain themselves while a cabin was built, a piece of land was cleared, and some simple agriculture started. As others came, it soon became too crowded for these daring spirits who needed more "elbow room." So they moved on westward to work the same process over again.

Another wave followed and flowed over the simple, scattered settlements. The settlers of this group cleared the land for fields and crops appeared to reward their efforts. They built roads, school houses, and new homes.

A third group came to exploit the resources of the conquered land. Men of capital and enterprise soon organized the uncoordinated efforts of the community. Churches, colleges, and business districts were built and all the signs of thriving civilized life appeared.

Life in these developing communities was often significant for those who lived it. There is a certain blindness in people which prevents their discerning the meaning that others find in simple, rough, hard, and adventurous experience. Just as no social order is all bad, neither is it all good. The historian who recounts the glamorous events of the pioneer stage and the winning of the West should tell the whole story. By no means, therefore, should he omit the ominous facts that as city life developed, it brought with it jails, hospitals, clinics, reformatories, asylums, and other signs of man's efforts to care for human maladjustments in the march of civilization. The economic influences sufficiently deadened to the human and biologic needs of man court only a final disaster. The organism slowly adapted to sapient life through thousands of years may not be required too severely to adjust in 150 years. The wholesome life of a nation should not be put in jeopardy by a narrow view of economic values. Unless living becomes increasingly more worth while, happier, and kindlier, and unless man retains the power to enjoy, economic gains are hardly justified. To have wealth and not to know how to use it is a social loss; to have leisure and not to know how to use it is an individual and social disaster. Ever to interpret economic success as a measure of social worth or personal fitness is to assume a condition that is denied by history and invalidated by the experience of countless persons who have tried so to do. Obviously physical education must try to understand the profound influences of economic forces on human life and prepare itself to plan programs intelligently in relation to basic human needs.

Such planning will consider the lack of vigor and stamina in men and women, the prevalence of crime and delinquency in youth, and the tremendous increase in leisure time. In the face of these realities, physical education must plan for vigorous, adventurous, functional programs of activities. Games and sports of combat and contact type, contests of skill and alertness which will appeal to adventurous youth, and skills and interests which will carry over into leisure hours—these are the heart of the matter. The modern economy of the power age produces weakness, degeneracy, delinquency, and boredom in man who can be rescued from these dire results only by forms of living which are revitalizing, energizing, and motivating to wholesome behavior.

Without the traditions for holidays, the siesta, and other customs that favor play, rest, and recreation, and with the traditions of "the strenuous life" that grew up in a nation engaged for generations in conquering a continent, it will be necessary to carry on considerable educational efforts to teach and lead people in the use of leisure. Physical education must develop programs which will give skill in activities that are capable of use in leisure time, and must assist in the development of attitudes toward life, glorifying the wholesome use of leisure in recreative and expressive forms.

Physical education should provide needed personnel for the Peace Corps as a practical measure to increase understanding of American life and American people.

In the Peace Corps program physical education teachers are being trained for service in foreign lands: Tunisia, Ceylon, Venezuela, Iran, Thailand, Nigeria, Cameroun, Ethiopia, the Ivory Coast, Sierra Leone, the Philippines, and other countries.

QUESTIONS AND PROBLEMS FOR DISCUSSION

1. Describe briefly the economy of primitive life.
2. Contrast the economy of modern industrial life with primitive life.
3. What are the chief items that mark the industrialization of society in the United States?
4. What are some of the hazards of city life?
5. What are the ten conditions that characterize the modern economy of the United States?
6. Why should teachers of physical education be interested in problems of immigration?
7. Why is it not satisfactory to import foreign systems of gymnastics into the United States for the education of American boys and girls?
8. What is the record of alien in comparison with native-born registrants? Is it the same for persons born in this country of foreign parentage?
9. How can the young of a race be made strong? What were Hitler's methods? What are the advantages and disadvantages of his methods?
10. What is the general picture of population shifts in the United States?

11. Can teachers of physical education count on children engaging in a large amount of physical activity outside of school?

12. What answer would you give a farmer who wanted his boy excused from physical education because he got plenty of exercise on the farm?

13. What is sedentarianism? Why should it be a problem worth consideration by teachers of physical education?

14. Is the lack of physical education in schools responsible for the large number of young men rejected for military service? Justify your answer.

15. What is the significance to the nation as a whole of the uncorrected defects in elementary school children?

16. What is the nature of factory labor?

17. Why should fundamental skills be taught to all youth?

18. What effect has the mechanization of labor had upon youth?

19. What signs of organic activity could you recognize in children engaged in vigorous games? If the players perspired, what would that indicate? What would rapid breathing normally indicate?

20. If a period of physical education is not vigorous enough to require a shower by high school pupils, what rating would you give it? What other factors might change your rating?

21. What effect in general have mass production methods had on American life?

22. Why is it important to teach activities in which the participants find joy and satisfaction?

23. How useful is square dancing in a community? Justify your answer.

24. Why should girls develop vigorous physiques? Why should they acquire interest and skills in sport and dance?

25. Fifty years ago a boy would walk to school, come home to lunch, and cover about six to eight miles a day. Now he rides to school in a bus; sometimes in rural areas he leaves home before it is light and returns after it is dark. Does this raise the kind of question that teachers of physical education should study?

26. Contrast a commercial amusement with a group-initiated activity in which all participated. Would you favor a group of citizens using the gymnasium for folk dancing? Would you favor a group using the athletic field for a folk festival?

27. What are the implications of the statement: Play belongs in the good life?

28. If one has leisure time does it follow that he will use it wisely? What controls his decision?

29. What do you think of the attempt to make all play healthful or educational? Should one play golf for his health? In every instance?
30. Why is moral behavior related to the experiences of people rather than an expression of inner conscience? Out of what does one get inner conscience?
31. What are some of the common accident hazards of physical education? How may they be prevented?
32. What are the justifications for a vigorous and adventurous physical education?
33. What are the laws in your state under which parents may sue school officials in accident cases occurring on school grounds?
34. In what ways can physical education help to shape the American Way of Life?
35. Should our leadership in the Olympic Games be considered sufficient in the light of our world relations? Explain.

REFERENCE READINGS

Bloch, Herbert A., and Niederhoffer, Arthur. *The Gang: A Study in Adolescent Behavior.* New York, Philosophical Library, 1958.

Braibanti, Robert, and Spengler, Joseph J. *Tradition, Values, and Socio-Economic Development.* Durham, N.C., Duke, 1961.

Brightbill, Charles K. *Man and Leisure: A Philosophy of Recreation.* Englewood Cliffs, N.J., Prentice-Hall, 1960.

Bullis, H. E., and Kelly, Cordelia W. *Human Relations in Action.* New York, Putnam, 1954.

Cassidy, Rosalind. "The Contributions of Physical Education to Democratic Citizenship." *Journal of Health — Physical Education — Recreation,* April, 1950.

Cowell, Charles C., "The Contributions of Physical Activity to Social Development." *Research Quarterly,* May, 1960.

Duncan, Ethel M. *Democracy's Children.* New York, Hinds, Hayden & Eldredge, 1945.

Educational Policies Commission. *Learning the Ways to Democracy.* Washington, D.C., National Educational Association, 1940.

Hagman, Franklyn S. *Group Leadership and Democratic Action.* Boston, Houghton Mifflin, 1951.

Jersild, Arthur T. "Education in Motor Activities." *Child De-*

velopment and the Curriculum, Thirty-Eighth Yearbook of the National Society for the Study of Education. Bloomington, Ind., Public School Publishing, 1939, Part I.

Ross, M. G., and Hendry, Charles E. *New Understanding of Leadership.* New York, Association Press, 1957.

Russell, Claire, and Russell, W. M. S. *Human Behavior.* Boston, Little, Brown, 1961.

Sapora, Allan V., and Mitchell, Elmer D. *The Theory of Play and Recreation,* 4th Edition. New York, Ronald Press, 1961.

Scott, Harry A. *Competitive Sports in Schools and Colleges.* New York, Harper, 1951.

Sjoberg, Gideon. *The Preindustrial City.* New York, Free Press, 1960.

PHYSICAL EDUCATION IN A DEMOCRACY — SOCIAL CONCEPTS

PHYSICAL EDUCATION IN A DEMOCRACY— SOCIAL CONCEPTS

I would set a type of training which aims at the acquisition of skill, in one or other of its socially valuable forms, which are innumerable, contending that knowledge of any kind which fails to eventuate in skill is, at best, half-grown, and because half-grown, a source of cant, claptrap, insincerity, and shallowness, more likely to disqualify the possessor of it as a member of society and a citizen of the world.

Jacks.

Paradoxical as it may seem, it is the conservative functions of education that are most significant in a period of profound change. . . . The very time to avoid chaos in the schools is when something akin to chaos characterizes the social environment. The very time to emphasize in the schools the values that are relatively stable and certain is when the social environment is full of uncertainty and when standards are crumbling.

Bagley.

ORIGINAL NATURE AND CUSTOM

The continuity of man and the society of which he is a member prevails. Custom and established ways of behaving powerfully shape and fashion individuals. At one time original nature was believed to consist of certain definite qualities which provided sole and adequate explanations for man's behavior. Man did thus and so because he was angry. Merely giving a name to these qualities, such as fear, anger, sexual love, gregariousness, and sympathy exemplified the purpose to explain behavior in terms of their operation. To possess anger, for example, was sufficient explanation of any manifestation of anger.

The continuity of the individual and the group to which he belongs renders such a notion impossible. MacIver stresses this relationship when he writes:

> . . . our environment is not the world about us but rather that world, with all its aspects, as it comes into relation to our lives. The more complex the life the more complex must the environment be and the more complex the adjustment to this total environment.[1]

There are, of course, elements in human nature, and psychology has given names to them. The names, however, are nouns that follow verbs. Man acts or behaves in certain ways and later the action is given a name. Why he acts or behaves in a particular fashion is to be explained not only in terms of an inherent readiness but also with respect to an ever-present world in which he lives. This emphasis, then, upon interaction between the individual and various influences in the environment is not an attempt to deny that forces exist in and operate through the individual, but rather to refuse to assign to them a supremacy in human behavior. In similar fashion, more realistic views regarding heredity and environment are being phrased today. The hereditarians who flouted and denied the observa-

[1] Robert M. MacIver, *Society—A Textbook of Sociology*, New York, Farrar and Rinehart, 1937, p. 105.

tions of the environmentalists were met with a corresponding denial from the latter of the claims proposed by the former. The "all or none" principle of physiology by some strange propensity of nature or by some curious custom, or by both, seemed to phrase an essential approach for workers in these fields. But better understanding of the problem has forced saner and less exclusive views. The affirmative results from both fields contribute to an appreciation of what is often called "the total situation," a continuity of man and society, an interaction, action and reaction, between man and the forces which play upon him and to which he responds.

All human behavior represents interactions between elements of nature and the various forces of the environment. These elements are the stuff with which the individual reacts. They are real habits, real awarenesses, and real levels of responding, regardless of the difficulty in locating them in the organism or of describing all their variations.

At birth the infant is not yet a personality. His ideas, beliefs, tastes, interests, and fears are not yet formed; his occupation, his economic and social status is still to be shaped by experience. Sorokin compares him to a phonograph, as follows:

> He is like a phonograph, capable of playing any record. A well-constructed phonograph, to be sure, plays any record better than a poorly constructed phonograph. But what records it will play — whether a Beethoven symphony or jazz — does not depend upon the phonograph. Similarly a person born with a superior constitution may develop a better mind and play his "sociocultural records" better than one born with inferior hereditary endowments; but what "sociocultural records" he will play depends relatively little upon the organic or biological factors.[2]

What capacity the individual has at birth can be developed but what he has acquired later depends upon his experiences as well as upon his capacity. In the case of the famous twins, Johnny and Jimmy, Johnny was born lighter and weaker than Jimmy.[3]

[2] Pitirim A. Sorokin, *Society, Culture, and Personality,* New York, Harper, 1947, p. 5.

[3] M. B. McGraw, *Growth: A Study of Johnny and Jimmy,* New York, Appleton-Century-Crofts, 1935.

From birth, Johnny was encouraged in his motor activities and at the age of seven months he was taller and heavier than Jimmy. *Physical education should recognize that motor activity is never merely a physical exercise; it is also a social experience.* Whenever there is reaction and interaction between individuals the outcome is a change of some kind. A child bouncing a ball alone will show physiological reactions. When he plays catch with another he may have similar physiological results but to these are added a great number of reactions and meanings that arise out of how his playmate throws and catches and how he himself shares in the experience.

The forces that play upon the human materials of man are legion. They range from the diverse physical forces of climate, geography, wild animals and other men to the extremely complex habits and customs of the society in which he lives. Custom alone often explains behavior. When a golfer insists on counting as a stroke the movement of his ball that he inadvertently touches, he is manifesting the behavior of good sportsmen everywhere. Among such, this kind of behavior is socially approved and consistently maintained. Obviously, then, all the social elements of the experience are as much a part of what has happened to the individual as the contraction of his muscles and the circulation of his blood.

THE PERSISTENCE OF SOCIAL BEHAVIORS

The learnings of man with respect to behavior and especially moral behavior are embodied in institutions. Marriage, home, and family hold much of human experience and, in their best forms, are distillations and wise interpretations. Many forms of behavior, sure reflections of established ways of acting, are generalized conventions, **mores** that operate widely even among peoples whose institutions vary. These social learnings that the young acquire may be newly established ways of behaving or they may rest upon custom that is very old. Oldness rather than newness tends to prevail since customs change slowly. The child born today is the offspring not only of ancestors who lived in trees but also of ancestors who lived in the Middle Ages. In terms of present relative influence it is probably true that the social inheritance from the Middle Ages more intimately and more powerfully touches life as it is lived today than the biological inheritance of tree living.

Only with the greatest effort by individuals and after continuous experimentation by numerous persons does custom change. To break with authority challenges society that embodies it; to flout tradition opposes the institution that conserves it. Thus, individual behavior consists either of support of the social forces which play upon man or of attack upon them. When any particular custom has widespread social approval, acceptance or rejection by a single individual is of little moment; when this single person becomes a group, or gives expression to ideas held by many in unformed groups, then the conflict is real and the outcome uncertain.

In any case, newborn children are subject in turn to their world. The process is continuous. The continuity of man and society is evident. The society into which children are born may be stable and little changed from that which their parents entered or vastly changed in little more than a generation. Nevertheless, it is their world into which they have come, it is their world of which they must become aware, and it is their interaction with it that makes the lives that they must live.

Physical education should play a responsible part in the shaping of social practices, customs, and institutions.

Every experience of the individual has social significance. Physical education, concerned properly, although not exclusively, with biological outcomes, is now also compelled by the continuity of man and society to examine anew the kind of world it offers to the young. And this world is not an abstract affair but concrete experiences with teachers, costumes, playgrounds, locker rooms, contests, audiences, ideals, fears, and many other items of the social field. Moreover, the teacher stands at the center of the social learnings acquired by the pupil. His standards of behavior are the only ones he can teach. His behavior is the example given to the pupil, and what he says about sportsmanship counts for much less than his example when values are in conflict.

Physical education should continue its efforts to make games, sports, and dance real forces in the American culture.

The disposition to approve for children's education dull and uninteresting physical drills and to disapprove games and other activities enjoyed by children has its roots deep in the social tradition. The prejudices in these matters go back to old experiences of man in his attempts to escape from the drudgery of work. Man has always played, and to some extent the old forms remain in drinking and carousing, gambling, and sex activity. Commercialization of the play interest in the past has produced the saloon, various institutions for gambling, prostitution in the brothel or house of assignation. It is not strange, therefore, that play of the past has left marked prejudices behind, nor that even the play of children should at times be viewed critically by those who are moved to recite that life is real and life is earnest. In the light of this experience it is easy to understand the word and temper of the "**Methodist Discipline**" of 1792 outlining the policy at Cokesbury College toward play. It says:

> We prohibit play in the strongest terms. The students shall rise at five o'clock summer and winter. Their recreation shall be gardening, walking, riding and bathing without doors, and the carpenters', joiners', cabinet-makers' or turners' business within doors. The students shall be indulged in nothing which the world calls play. Let this rule be observed with the strictest necessity; for those who play when they are young will play when they are old.[4]

The Puritans feared emotions, largely because emotions and religious sin were frequently associated. This antipathy to emotions in general was felt against play in particular because all play has large emotional possibilities.

In these days, play and self-expression are respectable. The emotional life is recognized as a fact to be understood, and hence there is the responsibility to deal with it as such. Nowhere

[4] *Youth Leaders Digest,* December, 1938, p. 195.

are there greater problems in health or in education than in this field of the emotions, and yet there are certain antagonisms to physical education because of the play of emotions and the emphasis toward self-expression.

These are problems for directors of physical education: How can we use self-expression in physical education to secure worth-while educational results? How can the emotions be given opportunity for expression, and help in the development of the conscientious individualist? How can we organize activities to retain the joyousness and spontaneity of play without the hysteria, inefficiency, and emotionality which so often accompany our activities? How can we secure the benefits of self-expression and avoid the disadvantages?

Fear of emotions and sense activity arises out of the curious notions of spirit and body which prevailed in an ascetic period of life. The philosophy of asceticism has long ceased to exist as an active and powerful force, but the ideas of a time which saw the body as base and the supersensual as alone worthy, are reflected today in attitudes, conventional standards, customs and scales of values.

The pleasures of emotional experience and sense activity, however, have been identified with thrills, stimulations, and actions that have disregarded outcomes. They have stood therefore as evidence of dissipation and dissolute living. But if the test is to be results, then emotional activity and sense experiences are not to be condemned out of hand. A thing is good or bad, not by the name given to it, but by what flows from it.

The emotions and sense activity in games, art, song, dance, drama and nature may add fresh and significant meaning to life, deepen and mellow the personality, widen the sympathies and understandings.[5]

The dance has long been suspect, although it stems from religious ceremony; over the years, its association with the theater has given it a bad name. This attitude of antagonism to dance is so real that certain communities in the United States do not

[5] Erik H. Erickson, *Childhood and Society,* New York, Norton, 1950, p. 185.

permit dance to be taught in the schools—even folk dance is barred. Such restrictions extend particularly to social dance which is clearly romantic and may even be erotic. But again, giving an activity a name, pasting a label upon it, may do serious damage to the possibilities of experience. Young people will dance, will engage in romantic expression. This is inevitable. The school might, with a wisdom quite beyond usual expectation, recognize this fact and provide that kind of opportunity and leadership which educational and social understanding ought to give.

Such opportunity and leadership will need to consider some very real aspects of American life. Some may be listed here: the limitations of space in city life; the loss in effective opportunity for physical work, and the lack of intelligent substitution of other comparable activities; the need for education in use of leisure time; recognition of the growth and developmental needs of children; interpretation in programs and methods of the worthy, deeply ingrained traits of the people; direction of physical education in relation to recreational opportunities; improvement of facilities for recreation of the active, participating kind; orientation of the aims and objectives of physical education to express the best social customs of the day in the light of legitimate near and remote aspirations; and development of the program of activities to reflect good manners, to foster wholesome character and to maintain vigorous and dynamic individuals.

Physical education should maintain the moral significance of play.

The old proverb "The devil finds work for idle hands to do" expresses an old prejudice against play, leisure, and loafing. It glorifies work but is afraid of play. Generally the moralist regards the theater, artists, and those who play as exerting an immoral or at least an unmoral influence in society. It is heartening to read Dewey's comment upon this problem. He writes:

> When moralists have not regarded play and art with a censorious eye, they often have thought themselves carrying matters to the pitch of generosity by conceding that they may be morally indifferent or innocent. But in truth, they are moral

necessities. They are required to take care of the margin that exists between the total stock of impulses that demand outlet and the amount expended in regular action. They keep the balance that work cannot indefinitely maintain. They are required to introduce variety, flexibility and sensitiveness into disposition. Yet upon the whole, the humanizing capacities of sport in its varied forms, drama, fiction, music, poetry, newspapers have been neglected.[6]

And again, writing of play and art, he adds:

They both spring from failure of regular occupations to engage the full scope of impulses and instincts in an elastically balanced way. They both evince a surplusage of imagination over fact; a demand in imaginative activity for an outlet which is denied in overt activity. They both aim at reducing the domination of the prosaic; both are protests against the lowering of meanings attendant upon ordinary vocations. As a consequence, no rule can be laid down for discriminating by direct inspection between unwholesome stimulations and invaluable excursions into appreciative enhancement of life. Their difference lies in the way they work, the careers to which they commit us.[7]

Physical education should continue to enlarge the concept of what it means to be an educated person.

The most consistently hostile influence to physical education is the general educator devoted to the traditional school, its purposes and established curricula. Although he gives a superficial lip service to the objectives announced by his own colleagues, such as health, worthy use of leisure, and recreation, he is supinely indifferent to changes in the school curriculum by which the persistent problems of today can be solved. He cares nothing about stamina, strength, endurance, vitality, and physical courage; delinquency is to him a matter of heredity and the issue of leisure time is to be solved by reading and religion.

Traditional education is antagonistic to physical education in precisely the same way that the classics were opposed

[6] John Dewey, *Human Nature and Conduct*, New York, Holt, 1948, p. 160.
[7] *Ibid.*, p. 163.

to science coming into the curriculum. Vested interests, institutionalism, established values look with suspicion upon all new approaches, new goals, new activities. Often they support their position with the elevated and respectful regard for ancestors by observing what was good enough for father is good enough for son. On this basis, of course, the modern science of nutrition would have no contribution today, for son would then grow on the same diet of meat and potatoes that fed his father and the vitamins and minerals of the modern diet would be completely disregarded.

The academician is either antagonistic to or merely condescending about physical education. Perhaps it may be good for one's health, but this perspiring vigorous activity is not to be considered beside the contemplation of beauty or the facile verbalizations of an alert intellect. Muscles are necessary, but they are not in the same category with mind.

And yet in spite of the strength of the forces which oppose the humanizing and socializing science of a rationally conceived physical education, advances in appreciation and understanding occur. Play has a larger role today in the American culture, the emotions and sense educations draw fresh support daily from psychology and psychiatry, and the dance — especially in modern dance — is the most vital art found in American life. Antagonisms persist, but understandings increase.

The Second World War may in time result in new orientations, but it is too early to predict what the outcome will be. Some are inclined to believe that the colleges are slipping back into the old grooves, but others are optimistic about the possible influence of the veteran upon programs and teaching.

The continuing struggle in the field of secondary education is symptomatic of the conflict in values that runs through all of education and social life. Certainly, the issues are nowhere settled, and the conflict between an aristocratic educational philosophy and the pragmatic point of view persists.[8]

And yet, the old traditions are gradually breaking down.

[8] L. O. Katsoff, "Reaction in the Colleges," *Journal of Higher Education*, January, 1947, p. 28.

The recreation movement is spreading, and games, dances, camping, and various recreation programs are today a real part of industry and community groups that range from small villages and rural areas to great metropolitan centers. Moreover, the recreation movement, basically interrelated with physical education, has formulated principles for the conduct of recreation that promise progress in the play life of people.

But it is not to be supposed that physical education will have much influence in enlarging the concept of what it means to be an educated person unless its representatives are also broadly educated, persons with intellectual, artistic, and social interests as well as physical and emotional controls. It is persons who make a program work; it is persons who are the central core of any movement.[9]

NEGLECT OF BODY IN THE AMERICAN CULTURE

Throughout early periods of recorded history, **mind** and **body** have been regarded as separate entities. In recent years a new understanding of man's nature has become established. And yet in the thought and speech of many Americans today the dichotomy still prevails. Old patterns of thinking stem from centuries of belief that body was base while mind alone was capable of the highest good. From the fourth to the fourteenth centuries western European thought was dominated by the belief that mind alone was the true reality.

Although asceticism held the body in contempt, it is not philosophic asceticism that is responsible today for neglect of **body,** because that philosophy has few followers in this materialistic age. Nevertheless, the basic prejudices of that philosophy, traditional ways of thinking, and even habits of speech remain. Asceticism as a philosophy may be unknown or rejected, but the ascetic spirit remains.

It remains in the poor physiques, in the poor postures,

[9] Jesse Feiring Williams, "Persons in a Plan," *The Journal of Health and Physical Education,* June, 1942, p. 349.

and in the awkward movements of adult persons who could have been very different human beings if they had lived in a culture that valued highly physique and movement. Too few Americans appreciate the harmony that led Alexander Pope to write of "A faultless body and a blameless mind." And fewer still would understand what Edmund Spenser wrote in "An Hymne in Honour of Beautie":

> For of the soule the bodie forme doth take.
> For soule is forme, and doth the bodie make.

Physical education should regard its work as significant because it affords a proper emphasis upon the physical aspect of man.

The long account of the conflict over mind and body cannot be given here, but it is instructive to examine the Greek view of the matter. The achievements of the ancient Greeks in physical education lead us to inquire into the thinking of the Greek philosophers about this and related problems of physical education. Plato regarded body and mind as separate and disparate, and yet when he wrote of physical education, he insisted that the soul was the object of gymnastics as well as of music. It is apparent that in Plato's conception of education, body and mind are not simple opposites. For both Plato and Aristotle the aim of physical education was not the education of the physical alone but rather the development of personality qualities through the physical.

It is becoming increasingly clear that the words physical, mental, and social are aspects of a totality, a unity, a personality. It is now evident, as we follow the threads of investigation and teaching, that one may, for purposes of description, speak of physical effects, or mental qualities, or social values, but in reality these are only aspects of life which is single and absolute.

Physical education should maintain its emphasis upon the physical as an aspect of the total unified being.

The organic evolution of man produced the human hand as well as the human brain. The former is as much mind as the latter and indeed the development of the hand made possible the development of the brain. Of course, what is called "mind" represented something new in organic evolution.[10] One need not consent to the extremer forms of the doctrine of emergence to accept this view; nor does respect for scientific thinking demand that one remain hostile to the concept that mind is not a function of the brain alone. Patrick says:

> It [mind] is the characteristic activity of a unitary complex of an exceedingly high order. It is not a function of any organ or set of organs in the body but an activity of the individual as a whole in interaction with his physical and social environment.[11]

And Herrick, with convincing logic and evidence from comparative neurology, says we are **not** body and spirit. Indeed, for him the negative is not quite adequate. He writes in answer to the question, Is human nature body and spirit? "No, the unity of the normal personality is the most evident and incontrovertible thing in our experience."[12]

Moreover, this view should at once and for all time combat the pernicious and absurd contention that physical education is concerned with body-building, defect-correcting, and health-producing results and with these alone. Indeed, it is argued by some that physical education is not concerned with moral and social qualities at all, but only with physical ones, and that any attempt to postulate moral education on a games-and-play level is not only ridiculous but indeed positively charlatanistic.

Although man has a social inheritance, we should not forget that the social environment inherits man and transforms him after its own fashion. He may declare that he is master of his fate, but not one item of his language, local religion, or social organization "is carried in his germ cell."[13] Man's culture provides

---

[10] J. B. S. Haldane, *The Causes of Evolution*, New York, Harper, 1932, pp. 144-170.

[11] George T. W. Patrick, *What Is the Mind?* New York, Macmillan, 1929, p. 108.

[12] C. J. Herrick, *The Thinking Machine*, Chicago, University of Chicago, 1929, p. 334.

[13] Ruth Benedict, *Patterns of Culture*, Boston, Houghton Mifflin, 1934, pp. 12-14.

"the raw material out of which the individual makes his life. If it is meager, the individual suffers; if it is rich, the individual has a chance to rise to his opportunity."[14] Indeed, there is no way to ignore the social effect of all experience.

The emphasis upon unity increases the significance of mental and physical relationships. From many sources there are evidences of this.

From Germany comes the report of a study by Dr. Hermann Paull of 1400 children between the ages of 6 and 14 years who had failed at some time to be promoted. In each of sixteen age groups into which they were divided for the study, these repeaters were found to be inferior in weight and height to children who were nonrepeaters. Social study revealed that only a few were from very poor homes. In another study Dr. Paull divided 1500 school children into three groups according to their marks, and found that the group with the best marks contained the largest number of children with height and weight above the average, and that among those with the lowest marks the majority were below the average in these particulars. From these and earlier investigations, he concludes that there is a relationship between a child's physical development and his mental condition.

An American study[15] offers somewhat similar ammunition for school health campaigns. The investigators Nichols and Raubenheimer made an intensive study of 136 girls in a Los Angeles high school who were from 11 to 33 pounds underweight and suffered as well from other physical handicaps. A third of these carried the regular high school routine. A third were enrolled in a special nutrition class, with mid-morning milk, special instructions in nutrition, and a daily rest period, and were excused from all extraschool activities. The last third followed the same regimen, and in addition kept a voluntary daily health record covering a twenty-four-hour schedule. The investigators concluded from the records that even girls badly handicapped by serious structural or functional defects would

[14] *Ibid.*, pp. 251-252.
[15] *Journal of Juvenile Research*, Vol. 14, No. 2, p. 114.

gain in weight on a restricted high school routine thus supplemented; that there was a general tendency for scholarship to improve as weight increased and general health improved, a tendency more definite in the younger girls than the older; and that the group most handicapped physically showed the greatest number of failing grades, a poorer quality of scholarship, and the least improvement in scholarship.

Keal concludes that "physical condition is one of the greatest factors affecting school success and the duration of school life" and "the correction of defects constitutes one of the most important problems in education."[16]

According to a study of 1000 intellectually superior children made by Terman, "there is no shred of evidence to support the widespread opinion that typically the intellectually precocious child is weak, undersized, or nervously unstable."[17]

A study of the relation of physique of school children to their educational achievement was recently made in the city of Manchester, England. Only 2 out of 85 children of good scholarship were below the average in physique; while 68 out of 171 poor students, or nearly 40 per cent, were below the average in bodily measurements.

There is a great deal of evidence of the close relationship between mental and physical aspects of bodily function. Hebb writes:

> It is obvious that the growth of the mind and its later stability depend upon conditions which make for physical health, just as they depend upon the genetic endowment with which the organism begins its career, but it is now clear that mental function also depends essentially on sensory stimulation, upon the experience of the organism by way of smelling, hearing, feeling, tasting, and seeing.[18]

---

[16] *School and Society,* September 1, 1928.

[17] Lewis N. Terman, "The Discovery and Encouragement of Exceptional Talent," *American Psychologist,* June, 1954, p. 221.

[18] Donald O. Hebb, "The Role of Experience," *Control of the Mind, Man and Civilization* (Seymour M. Farber, Editor), New York, McGraw-Hill, 1961, p. 42.

Since all the pertinent scientific fields support the concept of organismic unity, it would appear that this idea would dominate educational practice. Such is far from true. Schools find it difficult to change traditional curricula and quite impossible to take a fresh start in a new direction. Although skills in a very wide variety of forms are tremendously needed today, there is more effort in schools to produce an able critic of life than to produce a skilled person. Skills in speech, in large body movements, in manual activities, in sport, in dance, in driving an automobile, in climbing stairs, in carrying bags, in walking, in manipulating cards in games, in public speaking, in singing, in playing musical instruments, and in numerous other forms are neglected or partially or badly taught because, although they comprise the great majority of life activities, they appear to be of the body. We continue in a scientific world the outworn practice of an ancient age, and like some recently westernized Chinese, we wear the garments of the Occident but keep our "pigtails" under our hats. It is evident that progress in all education rests, in part, upon the full application in schools and social institutions of the doctrine of unity of mind and body.

Physical education should identify at every opportunity the close relationship between the moral and the physical.

The cultural lag in all areas of human life is a common observation in social science. Neglect and disrespect of the physical over many generations have left their imprints, not only on the physique of modern man, but also upon many of his attitudes. Thus, inevitably, moral and physical are sharply contrasted; the former is supposed to operate in the field of conscience and sentiment, while the latter deals only with material affairs. And yet, some moral issues must depend for their solution upon such physical facts as housing, fatigue, and recreational opportunity. Again and again, the moral decisions are not to be made in "the unreal privacy of an unreal self," but in close contact with politics, industry, education, and social life generally.

It is the realization of such truths that make many aspects

of college athletics of great concern to those interested in moral values. What is happening to the system of moral values when the athletic situation teaches the student to receive payment for services not rendered? These young men will be setting the standards of business, politics, and the professions in the years ahead. What kind of leader do we get from a college that has made him a case of special privilege? What is the moral education given to amateur athletes who are taught to finance themselves both here and abroad out of expense accounts that are generously provided but meagerly reported? No, these and similar questions are not to be answered by conscience and sentiment but by a rigorous facing of the facts.

RESPONSIBILITY FOR TEACHING SOCIAL VALUES

Doubtless all persons agree that the schools have responsibilities to teach social values to the young. But are there certain teachers who are to do this? Can part of a staff be left free to concentrate upon perspiration, peristalsis, and vitamins? Can these special ones be free from responsibility for social outcomes?

It is obvious that the responsibility is plural; no one agency and no one group of teachers stands alone in this vital business. The home, the church, the school; the example of adults; the institutions of information and amusement; the acts of political authorities; the merchant in his store; the neighbor across the street—all the varied social forces of a complex industrial society have a share in what the young will think about human relations and how they will react to the problems which confront them. Because of time and opportunity, *all* teachers should be prepared to teach social values to the young.

Physical education should understand how social values are taught.

The most penetrating fact about the development of social values in school experiences is the realization that in such matters one teaches what one is. Recognition of this fact is sometimes a painful experience, and the pain comes when we look at ourselves with the eyes of a stranger who does not know what our hopes, ideals, and aspirations are but sees only our behavior. It seems almost degrading, certainly immodest to expose so much of our actual failure without at least a thin covering of some soft and silky material like ideals.

But the simple fact remains: he who would teach social values must himself possess them. The coach of an athletic team cannot teach sportsmanship if he himself lacks generosity and fairness. The teacher of health cannot lead pupils to face facts realistically if he himself rationalizes his own behavior and shows intellectual dishonesty in even the simple affairs of life. The teacher must be all of a piece of the values he would have his pupils acquire. The pupil properly assumes that the acquisition of what the teacher recommends will be borne out by every test to which he puts it. If there is a real connection between the teacher's code and the life he lives, the pupil will be doubly taught, by precept and example.

Physical education should not require that the teacher be perfect but only that he be sensitive to his own needs and to those of his pupils for achievement in personality.

Does this emphasis upon social values mean that the teacher must be the perfect personality? Well, no one is. Realization by the teacher that the best of us fail at times ought to provide a sympathy, generosity, and fairness in dealing with the pupil who also fails to meet the standards that he, too, learns about. The teacher who understands failure may be of more help to a pupil than he who never slips, who never has learned to pick himself up and, with renewed purpose, to push on. Boys and girls are looking for wisdom greater and stronger than they possess and all they have to guide them, at certain times, is the teacher's obvious possession of it.

The influence of example is paramount. We probably never improve our neighbor by talking to him, but a change occurs in him when we show him some particular excellence which he may wish to imitate. The social concepts and values we have are never as fine as they might have been, and the great tragedy is not our low attainment but our weak effort. More-over, the importance of personal effort in either success or failure is very large. This we often fail to admit. Generally we are willing to accept responsibility for successful outcomes. When by devoted effort we achieve our desired purpose, we are sure that we had some share in *that*. In such a moment we are unable to believe that the outcome was merely the inevitable result of genes or environment. When we accept responsibility for success, we cannot shed responsibility when we fail. We can-not eat our cake and have it too.

Physical education should gain increasing competence and expertness in guiding personality development.

In the process of personality development, certain norms of management seem well established. The young child needs to be loved and to feel secure but the security he needs is his mother's arms rather than old-age insurance. During the years of childhood and adolescence, the individual will be acquiring a sense of trust or distrust of those around him. But trust and confidence emerge from difficulties surmounted, and do not require an absence of conflict. Beware of trading adventure for safety; adventure achieves those things that are worth keeping safe. Nothing is quite so disappointing in youth as fear and ti-midity. As he grows older he gains some sense of personal inde-pendence. The desire for self-assertion needs to be guided and should not be destroyed. The sense of initiative and enter-prise should be encouraged. Proposals may outrun ability and imagination may need to be restrained at times, but the guiding principle for the development of a healthy personality requires that youth should not be made to feel guilty for having dared more than could be accomplished. Pupils should succeed in some tasks and a sense of real accomplishment should be pro-moted in order to avoid feelings of inferiority. This does not mean that pupils should never fail, but it does demand that failure should be understood for what it is and not be allowed to assume a place of undue prominence. The effort of some teachers to require that pupils be right always is destructive of that fine integrity which can meet both success and failure calmly and can recognize these two imposters for what they really are.

To build a set of social attitudes that are embodied in live convictions, the individual needs information that is pertinent to what he is doing and trying to do. He needs to know to what extent his desires can be realized, at what cost, and to what real advantage to him. In the tumultuous years of adolescence, when the approval of the crowd, or the class, or the clique seems to be more important than the advice of parent or teacher, how shall he know what information is pertinent? At what cost can he afford to break with the crowd and follow his ideals? What are the advantages of going it alone, of being different? It is not always a simple choice between the behavior of an intelligent human being and herd behavior. But still the issue of running with the herd or being true to oneself remains. In this circumstance of trying to decide between the herd and its rules and the desire of the individual to be true to himself, there is no doubt that the principle of excellence is without flaw— however imperfect its attainment may be. If one is to leave the herd and be true to himself, his only concern should be the kind of self to which he is giving allegiance. If he follows the tradition of excellence, of superior effort, rather than of mere novelty or uniqueness, his future is secure. The difficulty in such a course should not be ignored. We do no service to youth if we give the impression that excellence is easily come by, that there is no correspondence between ends and means, or that words can substitute for deeds. Youth should know that fine character does not come easily but rather that the great traditions of mankind are wrought out of struggle, sacrifice, and suffering. Personal effort and not circumstance produces the excellent man.

AUTHORITY AND SOCIAL ORDER

Americans in common with certain other national groups are undergoing a revolution with respect to tradition and authority. The most obvious evidence of this revolt is seen in the church. The conflict between those called modernists and those known as fundamentalists is real, sharply drawn, and highly instructive.

The same break with authority which marks religious circles has appeared in educational institutions, political parties, and labor unions. In education it is becoming increasingly popular to ask for facts upon which to base procedures. The movement has touched physical education too. And yet breathing exercises remain in programs. Posture is still regarded as only a matter of muscles, and many have failed to sense what the facts about the endocrine glands mean to physical education. Authority and not facts too often guide.

The authoritarian leader maintains order, but in a democracy, also, social control and stability are likewise important. The order will be less marked in the latter, uniformity of response will be lacking often, but the hope for success in an orderly democratic society lies in being true to democratic ideals, in having faith in democratic processes, however slow and halting they may be. Therefore, all educational agencies in a democracy should seek to promote democratic techniques, to achieve democratic processes in action, to foster democratic attitudes of shared decisions and independent judgments with responsibility for the effect of those decisions and judgments upon others.

Physical education rejects formal drill and authoritarian methods but nevertheless it should strive to promote social order.

Physical education in many of its activities contributes to order and social control through its socializing effects. But physical educators need to remember that mere membership in a group does not insure group reality in a social sense; more than mere proximity is required. When individuals, however, possess a common purpose and are interested enough in that purpose to regulate their behavior in relation to it, then a real community or group has been born. In that sort of group reality, sociability is always present.

The urge to go with your own kind, to stay with your own kind because it is more satisfying than to go with others who are strange to you, and who behave differently from the way you behave, leads to social amusement, play, games, dancing, and feasting. These very activities tend to widen the range of one's kind, and in turn foster friendly interest, spontaneous helpfulness, and a sense of solidarity, all of which are conducive to the maintenance of order. School principals know the value of this influence in the maintenance of order in the school, and it was precisely the recognition of this prestige of games that led de Coubertin to revive the Olympic games because of his interest in world peace.

With sociability physical education has much to do. The recreational activities of its program, its festivals, pageants, pantomimes, games, and dancing are distinctly contributive to sociability. The testimony of playground teachers and experts on this point is very clear. Gangs, sectional animosities, community quarrels have been dissipated in the social activities of the playground and community center. Again in promoting social control in a democratic state, physical education in its sports and games bulks large through its emphasis upon fair play.

When the players of a team believe that the decisions of a referee are fair, when the people of a community, state, or nation accept the decisions of judges and magistrates as fair and the acts of legislatures are just and wise, there exists in these groups a sense of justice. The sense of justice is an important attitude to develop in the maintenance of a democratic social order. It is an intellectual judgment learned from experience. The sense of justice has its beginning in the early training of the child under standards of conduct in the home, and its development continues through the schools.

The sense of fair play can be learned early; the home and school have no more important responsibility. The idea of fair play can be woven into the whole of the personality fabric. Although associated directly with games, it has implications in every human relationship. Of course, it is admirable to see children show fairness in games, but the idea must become generalized, so that fairness to other persons is a guiding principle of individual action. It is the clear duty of all teachers to help children apply the good standard of the game to other situations.

In proposing an educational program for the development of democracy in Germany, Walter Cerf stresses the sense of fairness. He writes:

> Fairness is a sense of justice and the rights of men even in fields where these rights have not been codified and where breaking the rules does not bring about punishment by society. The fair man voluntarily sticks to the rules and agreements of the game, gives his adversary the same rights he claims for himself, shows consideration for the weak, and accepts in good spirit the foibles and fortes of his teammates. Fairness brings about an instinctive appreciation of the rights of men, of the sacredness of mutual obligations, of justice and tolerance, and of the discipline of cooperation—all of them virtues basic to democracy. Storm troopers are impossible where fairness flourishes.
>
> The true habitat of fairness is competitive teamwork. Sports have always had the function of training men in fairness. There is no reason why the method of competitive teamwork should not be carried over from the playground to the classroom.[19]

As regards sense of justice, activities of physical education under capable leadership offer the richest opportunity in the school for education in forbearance, fairness, generosity, vital elements in this sense. What professional or occupational group has, even remotely, the influence to be exerted by the well-trained physical educator? The ideals of the ministry are directed too often toward the life to come, a matter so complicated with legalistic and ceremonial forms that it is not of immediate concern for group protection and special needs. The ideals of business are, quite generally, maximum production of wealth to the square mile. Trade unionism, concerned with economic rewards for its members, interprets social welfare, all too often, in terms of class warfare. The only group in the world concerned with teaching the basis of a sense of justice is that represented in

[19] Walter Cerf, "Sponsorship of Democracy," *Journal of Higher Education,* October, 1946, pp. 364-368.

physical education. In this field, under proper conditions, the teaching is continually "Play Fair," "Be Honest," "Be Square." The gymnasium and playground are laboratories where these standards may continually be illustrated in the face of the instinctive impulse to personal and selfish action.

SOCIAL MEANINGS IN ACTIVITIES

Over the years and through them, in countless generations, man has been played upon by two sets of forces. One comprises that complex group of influences represented in inner urges that drive the individual to engage in certain activities. The other is that highly varied group of agencies represented by the word "environment." These two forces are commonly designated as the biologic and social inheritance of man.

Whether in the realm of action or in the life of ideas, these forces ceaselessly operate. Moreover, their effects are distributed throughout the organism, although structure, and hence function, may be altered more in one area than another.

From this point of view, then, the life of ideas and the realm of activities are two ways in which the individual responds to the play of forces upon him. In many respects, the latter is more important than the former because some things can be known only through activity. Obviously, also, experience precedes all knowledge. Indeed, understanding and experience are so intertwined that for many years the dictum, **Learn by doing,** has had wide theoretical acceptance.

The full force of this view can be given in a simple illustration. One might read all that had ever been written about running, might talk with the best runners that live today, might have studied carefully postures of running form, but this simple activity would be essentially unknown in its unique and intrinsic qualities until one ran. The rhythmic flow of the muscles in producing the movement, the accelerated breathing, the heightened activity of all organic functions, the rapid locomotion, the kinesthesia—these are the essence of the experience and can never be acquired vicariously. In this sense, then, one can know man only by engaging in his activities.

The activities of man have accumulated, through the ages, highly complex and richly varied meanings. With respect to the biologic forces that have played upon him, these accumulations have universal character. Physiology knows no national boundary lines. Running has the same effects upon the Chinese as it has upon the European, and the Filipino boy has the same urge to run and throw, to jump and climb, to hang and lift, that impels an American child to do these things. Costume, custom, climate, diet, religion, and other influences — roughly classed as social — may alter the form of the running or place restrictions upon climbing or jumping, but throughout history the immemorial activities of man have appeared in some form among all races, in all climes, and under all conditions of life.

Physical education should interpret its program in terms of significant ideas.

Basically then, physical education in its various activities represents in part this biologic drive to engage in movement. Inevitably there accrue identical effects in growth and development as individuals engage in the same or similar movements. It would be complete failure to understand the influences wrought in human behavior by the play of social forces in man's activities if one were to regard movement as of no moment outside the boundaries of kinesiology or physiology. Some of the less significant social forces are revealed in the walk of the Bedouin, the carriage of the Polynesian woman, the posture of the American cowboy as they reflect the direct influence of costume, or occupation, or both, upon their movements. More significant social forces, however, are those leading to wars, to reorganizations of governments, to struggles for markets and raw materials, and to new interpretations of the relation of the individual to the state. Any attempt to examine the sociological foundations of these days must take cognizance of the tremendous forces now playing upon the biological materials of man. The effect of these upon physical education procedure is not always clear. Some important aspects, however, are apparent.

The beliefs of peoples regarding human relations, their fears of the unknown, their superstitions about the future and past, their marriage customs, their festival and carnival practices are swathed in movements of dance and pantomime. The Englishman playing golf at Repulse Bay in Hong Kong, the American teaching baseball to Igorot hillmen, the Scot promoting curling clubs in Canada and the United States—all reflect more than the urge to engage in sport. These effects are truly particular and lack the universal character of biologic agencies. Although the realm of movement and the life of ideas are closely related organically, they have their own particular domiciles in the particular groups in which they arise. Biologically all men are brothers; socially they are as unlike as their customs and beliefs make them. Blood pressure draws no national boundary lines, but the meaning of a dance to different national groups or the regard of some for a particular sport separates men whose muscles respond to the same kind of nerve impulse, whose glands produce identical secretions, and whose blood flows in arteries and veins. The universal character of man's biology and the particular quality of his social inheritance afford at once a challenge and an opportunity. Fortunately, the promotion of international good will is not dependent upon overcoming some strange arrangement of nature, but solely concerned with appreciation and understanding of the traits, needs, interests, and ideas of other peoples.

Physical education in the United States, however degenerate and inadequate it is at times, is nevertheless a vital aspect of biologic and social life. No one can understand a nation without knowing competently something of its play, dramatic, dance, and sport activities. In all lands, however, physical education goes back, for its biologic origins, to common sources. This is revealed in the vast series of changes that culminated in man's present form and function. The social setting, particular rather than universal in character, is far more recent, although still ancient. A real acquaintance with the ideas, purposes, and procedures that have marked physical education sends roots of sympathy deep into the history of many peoples. It may be truly said that organized physical education was born some twenty-three centuries ago in a civilization marked by intellect and understanding. There on the shores of the Aegean Sea it grew into a sturdy force to nourish the citizens of Greek city states. But its course was not to be one splendid series of progressive development. Fifteen centuries later students came from all parts of Europe to sit at the feet of Abelard. Physical education was forgotten in the spell of rhetoric and philosophy. These two periods carry their load of ideas, however. When we think of Athens, we think of the Parthenon, of Socrates, of Plato and Aristotle, and see in imagination finely educated youth parade from the palaestra into Greek life. When we think of Abelard, we think of the Middle Ages, of popes and emperors fighting for power, of feudalism, of peasants and poverty, and nothing that happened in Greece seems to have a place in the twelfth century in Europe. The fact is, of course, that a wholly different body of ideas swayed men's minds and what seemed vital to the guests of the palaestra counted for nothing in the contemplation of those in the monasteries. Each age has its own values, its own beacon lights set upon the hill, its own dreams and aspirations.

Ancient Greek life and the ascetic ideal express two periods in human history which have colored all of western civilization. Physical education has felt their full influence. Other forces also have shaped its present state. Physical education, ranging widely throughout the life of all peoples, bears the imprint of many cultures upon it. The examples of this are many. Everywhere, in all modern educational endeavors, Vittorino da Feltre lives today in the impulse to educate the whole child. Every gymnasium is a reflection of Nachtegall, who built the first one in modern times, and all sets of parallel bars, no matter how rejected and despised today, must lift themselves somewhat proudly because of the defense given to them by the great physiologist Du Bois-Reymond. Juvenal's famous phrase, **mens sana in corpore sano,** is only a little better known than Rousseau's aphorism "The weaker the body, the more it commands; the stronger it is, the better it obeys." Richard Mulcaster, working hard for little pay at the Merchant Taylor's School in London never founded a system of physical education, but he with others such as Mercurialis, Clias, Amoros, and Basedow helped to lift up educational endeavor from narrow concepts to larger ones. The great ones of the field, men such as Guts-Muths, Jahn, and Ling in Europe, and their fervid disciples who came to America, are never to be forgotten.

In actual practice the teaching of physical education in the schools develops the life of ideas through the activities carried on. There is, of course, real mental content in numerous motor activities. Much of this is technical in character, but for those interested in the promotion of international understanding, there will be found wide areas that yield appreciation of other peoples. It is not contended that teachers make full use of the materials available or that all teachers are competent to lead in development of appreciation and understanding of others. Social implications are not readily or widely taught. But the opportunity is inherent in the rich social background of physical education experience.

Physical education should continue to transmit the rich social inheritance of ideas in the folk dance.

Many persons believe that the dance offers the most outstanding material for portraying the customs, traits, and interests of other peoples. Among these, perhaps, Havelock Ellis most adequately expresses the opinion. He writes:

> If we are indifferent to the art of dancing, we have failed to understand not merely the supreme manifestations of physical life, but also the supreme symbol of spiritual life. . . .
>
> Dancing is the primitive expression alike of religion and of love . . . , is intimately entwined with all human tradition of war, of labor, of pleasure, of education. . . . For the solemn occasions of life, for bridals and for funerals, for seed-time and harvest, for war and for peace, for all these things there were fitting dances.[20]

When Cecil Sharp introduced English Country Dances in America and stimulated widely the interest in Sword Dances and Morris Dances, he helped American youth to learn more

---

[20] Havelock Ellis, *The Dance of Life*, Boston, Houghton Mifflin, 1923, pp. 36-37.

than steps. And yet it is in the steps that one gains what verbalization can never give. In these days of the "cold war," the "Merrie England" of Shakespeare seems strangely removed, but one who could be merry during the reign of Elizabeth found the secret, not in a philosophy of collectivism, nor in the harsh realities of earning a living, but doubtless in the Rigadoon or some dance where there was "set and turn single." Whatever resources Americans must employ to meet the challenges of these days, it is abundantly clear that they are not disposed to build "shelters" to protect themselves.[21] Their only real protections are inner resources of character, high levels of technical skills, and sincere devotion to national needs.

The Sword Dances of Scotland, danced years ago on the eve of battle, find their counterparts in Ireland, and even in the far-off Caucasus. In the latter the Lezginka is a solo dance of wild beauty. This sort of activity does not portray the character of a people as effectively as the Chumak (the Ukrainian Merchant), the Odzemok (the Slovakian Shepherd), or the Flip (the Dutch Fisherman), but, as in all character dances, attitudes toward life, interests and traits are shown. Something of the superficiality of court life and its effeminate and rococo character in the fifteenth and sixteenth centuries are revealed as one dances a Branle of Poitou, and then a Minuet that grew out of it.

The dances of love, courtship, and marriage dramatize not only sex but also ways of responding to romantic situations. The Daldans and the Vingakersdans of Sweden, the Zalman of Czechoslovakia, the Polstertanz of Austria present a manner of courtship that is quite foreign to American custom.

Grosse insists that it is the dance that socialized man. The Sequidilla of Spain, varying somewhat from province to province, remains nevertheless as truly national as the Hungarian Czardas, the English Hornpipe, the Polish Obertass, or the Russian Cossack dance.

The dance, whether brought to us from Sweden, Ireland, or Scotland, from Russia, Hungary, or Java, has its wealth of ideas, its ceremonials rich with meaning, its movement, music,

[21] Arthur I. Waskow, "The Shelter-Centered Society," *Scientific American*, May, 1962, p. 46.

and customs that tell a story of man's response to the forces that play upon him. Perhaps in dance more than in other activities, spectators may have significant vicarious experience. Havelock Ellis writes:

> Even if we are not ourselves dancers, but merely the spectators of the dance, we are still—according to that Lippsian doctrine of Einfühling or "empathy," by Groos termed the "play of inner imitation"—which here, at all events, we may accept as true—feeling ourselves in the dancer who is manifesting and expressing the latent impulses of our own being.[22]

Physical education should transmit the rich social inheritance of ideas in sports and games.

In sports and games the field of physical education is greatly indebted to foreign sources, particularly English. But early origins are Greek and Roman. The athletic aspects of the four great festivals—the Olympic held at Olympia, the Pythia at Delphi, the Nemea in Argolis, and the Isthmia at Corinth—have been revived in the modern Olympic games, but children in the grades engaged in the study of Greek civilization may have their own Olympic games in the gymnasium of the modern school; later in college years they may have a truly meaningful educational experience in the contest in music, poetry, dance, and athletics, such as that conducted annually by the freshman and sophomore classes of Barnard College.

Not even remotely, in the thoughtless opinion of some persons, are such experiences related to international understanding, but wherever there is a disposition to appreciate and to value the social practices of other peoples, worthwhile gains in this respect must accrue. There may well be some doubt about the gains for international peace that flow from the Olympic games as now conducted. The arguments about amateur status, the intense competition in events that have to be decided by human judgment, have been and are likely to continue, in the present state of affairs, to be foci around which collect rather readily expressions of national pride and acts revealing international animosities. The hope of de Coubertin seems lost

[22] Havelock Ellis, *op. cit.,* p. 66.

in the fierce desire to attain national supremacy, and the promising outcomes for the athletes themselves are placed in jeopardy by the strong nationalism that everywhere prevails. Little can be achieved in the promotion of international understanding through these games until there is a change in the mood and manner in which they are conducted. Like other activities, however, they reveal national traits and characteristics.

Physical education should recognize that camping is a potentially rich part of the physical education movement.

Physical activity out-of-doors is generally preferable to activity indoors, and physical experience in close contact with nature is always better than the civilized, conventional adaptation of the same thing. The development of camping, as an educational experience, is a recognition of values in outdoor life.

The growth of the camping movement is remarkable. There are innumerable private camps in all parts of the country; many organization camps, such as Boy Scouts, Girl Scouts, 4-H Clubs, and Welfare are everywhere. One of the striking developments in education is the school camp of a public school system.[23] School camping has passed beyond the theoretical stage in California. How to use camping as an integral part of the school curriculum has been well demonstrated by the San Diego and Long Beach public schools.[24]

The objectives of camping are in full harmony with the objectives of physical education. They include wholesome use of leisure, recreational skills, social adjustment, and physical experience in out-of-door activities.

HUMAN BEHAVIOR AND CALAMITIES

Fear has always been a powerful incentive in behavior. Fear of calamities, that came out of the unknown to make in-

[23] *Camping and Outdoor Experiences in the School Program,* Washington, D.C., U.S. Office of Education, 1947. Howard A. Ozmon, Jr., "College Experiment in the Out-of-Doors," *Journal of Health—Physical Education—Recreation,* April, 1962, p. 30.

[24] Winifred Van Hagen, Genevie Dexter, and Jesse Feiring Williams, *Physical Education in the Elementary School,* Sacramento, California State Department of Education, 1951, pp. 283-292.

tolerable or impossible life as it was lived, persists today in fear of some kinds of conduct, and hence disapproval of conduct that might invite calamity.

The experience of society with unknown forces led either to submission or to magical efforts at control. What is not understood cannot be managed successfully. Man dreaded calamity because he had no understanding of a plague that would cause death in a short time of whole communities, he dreaded famines that starved nations, storms and earthquakes that erased cities, and warring bands that descended upon peaceful peoples to kill, burn, ravage and destroy.

Knowledge has increased through science. Plagues and pestilences have come largely under control through knowledge of microorganisms, sewage disposal, and lines of transmission of disease. Today, it is difficult to appreciate the dread of calamity that prevailed in the seventeenth century about the Black Death, and yet something of that mood exists in the sense of helplessness and fear that arises among parents when war clouds gather. Famines are rare today and yet mankind in China and Russia knows famine. The wild vagaries of nature in the Ohio and Mississippi rivers in flood, San Francisco and Yokohama suffering earthquake, Mt. Pelée in eruption are near enough in time and place to capture in each generation something of the fear of calamity that in earlier times operated continuously and everywhere.

Man's experience with calamity and his complete ignorance of causal factors has led him over the years to be suspicious of many behaviors that might invite or precipitate a calamity. When the cause of a condition is not known the tendency persists to question many possible causes; the conservative mood prevails when the facts are not known. Hence, the superstitions about evil spirits and the attitude toward witches in Puritan New England reflect the fear that those called witches related to calamity in some way.

From this point of view, then, behavior of the individual has always been important to society. Although in many respects the family is the chief source from which individual behavior flows, the institutions established by society contribute profoundly to human conduct. Why do we have schools? Obviously not so that young persons may become alumni, nor only that they may acquire learning. Indeed, the slogan most heard in the battle for free public school education was "More schools, fewer police." Why do we attempt to teach the young? Why do we interfere with the actions of others? The answers go back to those early experiences of man with calamity.

Behavior of an individual which may produce calamity courts immediate disapproval. General condemnation of Japanese behavior in 1937 by Americans was not purely an expression of high regard for Chinese civilization, nor only a gesture to lofty humanitarian sentiment; it was also a manifestation of dread of that calamity which Japanese action did bring. Since behavior is the response of an individual to the varying forces that compose a situation for him, and since society is concerned with influencing this response, parents and teachers undertake the task of teaching the young certain acceptable responses. In addition, some persons study the forces that operate so that better responses may be made as the nature of the forces is understood. Behavior which is based upon facts in the situation is better than behavior based upon superstitious explanation of phenomena because, under the former interaction, guidance may be developed for attack upon similar problems; experience is thereby enriched by the verifiable data of action and reaction. Opposition to physical education arises at times out of a vague and mistaken fear that its activities will produce a calamity.

Physical education should educate citizens to accept its program as in harmony with the best American traits and characteristics.

The frontier in America has passed. The West has been won. From coast to coast highways link together lands which little more than a generation ago gave a home to the American Indian, herds of buffalo, elk, and wild horses. The frontier is indeed gone, but the spirit of the pioneer which developed and flourished in that scene remains in the present adventures into space. Independence, initiative, individuality, adventurousness, competitiveness — these are American traits that mark the American character.

It would appear, therefore, that physical education will do its best work in rugged, daring activities which call for independent judgment, exercise initiative, and promote competition. The safe and sane physical education of antiseptic calisthenic movements can never appeal to the American nature as long as this trait survives. Athletic games present many crudities and harbor many undesirable practices, and in comparison with English sports, they appear in many respects less admirable. They are typically American, however, and in the correction of mistakes and the elimination of undesirable forms, care should be taken to avoid sterilizing them.

It is often observed that we are a practical people. In education, as in business, industry, and technical fields, the criterion of utility is often raised. For years education has been demanding results which would function in the lives of people today. This has meant a reshaping of curricula from the kindergarten to the professional school with substantial modification of courses and offerings.

This movement for a functional education has also developed in physical education. The criterion of functional utility, if applied wisely to our activities, would rid our program of innumerable games, stunts, and movements whose only excuse for existence is the plea of variety. Any activity which has no other justification than variety is worthless in a modern program today.

And yet utility alone is not enough. It never is and never can be the one standard of worth. There are esthetics, leisure activities, and recreations which appear to have no practical slot in which to fall. Relative values must always be weighed.

People by nature do that which gives them pleasure and satisfaction. While it is urged that people should play, it is not always understood that physical illiterates are unable to play. They lack skill. Interest may be aroused by the recital of values that accrue, but without skills that yield satisfaction in achievement, participation lags. The extent to which modern life dwarfs and twists nature is suggested by the large number of persons who do not know how to play. A trait that practically all children possess — the ability to play — and that attains some development in many, is starved in the social life of an industrial world. The mechanical devices of commercial amusement further restrict the expressive powers of man. The radio and movie demand only simple sensory response; and the need for expressive, cooperative skill activity remains. The immediate need in schools is the education of all boys and girls in several motor activities that have recreative uses and that will yield satisfaction. When young persons have been **physically educated out of the dub class and into the enjoyment class,** the participation problem is on the way to solution.

Physical education should help parents to understand the nature of crime and juvenile delinquency.

Sickness, like famine, storm, and earthquake, has been regarded in the past as a calamity, and when calamity fell the gods have been invoked to relieve man from the full force of their displeasure. While in civilized lands scientific attitudes have largely replaced such superstitious practices, there remain forms of sickness which are treated after the pattern of seventeenth and eighteenth century witchcraft. Man, an organism, suffers from disturbances that attack the functions of his internal organs; these phenomena are called diseases, are diagnosed as to cause and treated as such by scientific medicine. But man, the organism, also suffers from disturbances in behavior and social relationships; these phenomena are called crimes, are often diagnosed as due to "evil nature," or similar mystical forces, and are treated commonly by placing the individual in a prison, which has been justified by the theory of punishment and protection of society. In diseases, the causes are micro-organisms, poisons, accidents, deficiencies in certain chemicals, malformation of parts, confusion between emotional and psychic factors, and new growths. The genius of scientific medicine is differential diagnosis and accurate prescription. The folly of placing all sick persons in the same kind of hospital and of providing the same treatment for all would be recognized today even by lay persons.

It is true also that the disturbances in behavior which characterize the social driftwood in prison arise from many causes. There is no one poison responsible, no social cancer that explains. Moreover, it follows that any social behavior which produces crime and results in imprisonment is a disturbance that calls for a modern scientific approach to the problem. Unfortunately, there is lacking techniques in diagnosis, the competent laboratory findings, the experience with varied therapies in the field of individual socialization that exist in medicine. Some techniques are available but progress in this direction is slow and halting. In some states authorities of penal and correctional institutions are leading in the development of a new attitude in which the purpose to punish for crime is being replaced by the purpose to rehabilitate the individual. This policy is often quite unrealistic. Although medicine seeks to restore the sick to normal, it is without illusions in the matter; some patients are too ill or have waited too long for medical skill to prevail. Experience with parolees shows that individuals without competent and socially needed skills, without a reasonable regard for others, and without an earned self-respect return again and again to the only practices they know.

Moreover, the analogy between disease and crime is not perfect. Today disease, although it may be communicable, is not permitted freely to invade the lives of others. Crime, however, is primarily an attack on the property or lives of other persons. It is this indifference to the welfare of others that accounts for the punitive and protective procedures of the law.

Crowell and Ismail report that boys in the 11 to 12 year age group who scored high on physical measures are likely to have leadership potentialities and to be well-adjusted socially.[25]

[25] Charles C. Cowell and A. H. Ismail, "Relationships Between Selected Social and Physical Factors," *Research Quarterly,* March, 1962, p. 40. Harold E. Jones, "Physical Ability as a Factor in Adjustment in Adolescence," *Journal of Educational Research,* December, 1946, p. 287.

It would seem to be true that efforts by parents and teachers to develop responsible behavior in youth would be far more promising than the present sentimental approach to delinquent behavior wherein rapists, kidnapers, and murderers are given light sentences or placed on probation.

Physical education should help to clarify the concept of continuity in experience.

The disposition of many persons today to regard the criminal as a person with "free will" ignores the influences and forces that have played upon his human materials. What a man is at any moment comprises a complex mosaic of his past, his present organic balances and equilibria, and the forces of his environment. To conceive of man as a body governed by a mind, or a will, or a spirit is as superstitious and uninformed as to regard him as bewitched or possessed of devils. Such ideas of his nature are on a par with spontaneous generation in biology, phlogiston in chemistry, horoscopes in astronomy, and forked sticks for finding oil or water in geology.

Man can only be understood and hence educated or rehabilitated as we interpret correctly the play of forces upon him over a long period of time. The boy who steals apples from a fruit stand when he is not hungry performs an incomprehensible act unless earlier racial experiences are examined.

It is important to stress the continuity of experience and the record left in each individual not only of what he does but of what his ancestors did. This point, stressed by Bergson, lays upon any understanding plan for education the necessity to see that what persons do is more important than what we say to them. The appeal of dramatic emotionalism unduly clutters up the hopes of those engaged in re-education or rehabilitation of human derelicts. Thus, to place humans in prison subject to a wide range of indignities and indecencies and to expect them later to emerge chastened in some miraculous way is naive at least.

A child born today comes into this machine age with certain organizations that enable him to live as an organism. There are respiratory center, circulatory center, sucking reflexes, and other mechanisms ready to operate in any appropriate situation.

He comes also with drives to engage in certain types of activity which played vital parts in persistence of the species. When his ancestors had to settle their differences and maintain their lives by physical struggle, there came into action certain dynamic and energizing forces of the organism. This selection of forces is described today in the researches in endocrinology, and the stimulation of adrenals with a corresponding inhibition of digestion in fighting situations is recognized as the patterns of racial memory in every child born today.

The preparation of youth by nature is suited to a by-gone age. The harsh realities of an industrial society call no more for courage in facing wild animals, speed in flight from other men, nor the capture of one's mate by force. Many communities are so industrialized that the only remnant in environment to meet this irrepressible urge of phylogeny is a moving picture in which youth vicariously is heroic or strong or victorious.

Thus, it appears that the individual prepared by nature over thousands of years for a life of physical struggle is catapulted into a society that scarcely knows what this means. The necessity of providing an equivalent has been recognized, however, and physical education exists as a great constructive social force to guarantee to youth the fulfillment of these early adaptations.

Physical education should emphasize the importance of functional defects in antisocial behavior.

The relationship of leisure to crime and deliquency has been frequently pointed out.

Austen McCormick says that 60 per cent of criminals have physical defects. It should not be assumed that correction of the defects will always change their behavior. These may be very important items in behavior, and yet by stressing such defects we may forget that they relate to structure. Delinquency is a behavior defect, however, that is a defect of function. Since all delinquents show 100 per cent defects in function with respect to social conduct, it is important to note that functional defects in play, dramatic expression, romantic love, hobbies, friendships, marriage, and family life comprise a most significant part of the delinquent's total picture as a psychophysical organism.

Such defects of function occurring in young persons may be more influential factors in causing delinquency than defects of teeth, tonsils, eyes, ears, and feet.

Physical education should offer opportunity for all youth to fulfill the wholesome urges of nature.

Unity of the individual implies that in situations which provoke fear in the organism, the functional systems open up the old switches and call into action the adrenals, heart, thyroid, and inhibit the digestive and procreative functions. This occurs even when no physical effort is involved so that today under modern conditions the whole organism may be raised to levels of great activity without any corresponding physical response. In this phenomenon every cell of the organism may be stimulated and the urge to find expression is correspondingly great. Most of the early crimes of youth are not sought as ends in themselves; they are sought as thrills and are the logical product of nature and nurture. The society that will not give youth a chance to make an end run, or tackle a charging back, or beat the runner to a base by a perfect throw, must of necessity take these into custody when they steal and run and hide.

It is obvious, of course, that all that we are socially reflects not only yesterday but a thousand yesterdays. Our ways of thinking, our emotional reactions, all that Sumner described as **mores**, mold our judgments of what is right and what is wrong.

Equally obvious to the scientist is the force of biological inheritance in each individual. Before the child of the twentieth century is born, he lives in a short time through countless ages of the past. To watch his development is to survey the whole panorama of man from the lower creatures that once he was, to see the possibilities in mental power and physical form become certainties, to see growth. Great areas of that past can only be guessed at, but its brief outlines are tremendously significant in understanding human behavior. The past that each child drags after him as he is born into a world also with a past, the past that clings to him—unescapable, as closely as a shadow and yet as clearly as substance—is himself: his muscles and bones, his spinal cord, his organs and numerous glands.

Physical education should offer wholesome activities as

substitutes for the unwholesome attractions of community life.
The principle of substitution is important. It is a well-recognized fact that the individual is continuously active when awake. There are always situations to which the organism is responding, internal and external receptors are continuously acting, and life flows as a stream of reactions. Moreover, it is also recognized that experiences shape what is called character, that complex congeries of reactions, reflexes, balances, ideas, habits, and predispositions; or, stated philosophically, it can be said that man builds his life out of the experiences he has. This view makes insistent demands upon educational and social policy because perforce he must live the life he makes. Any intent to rely upon revivalism stamps this purpose for what it is — ignorant and superstitious. Society must provide and guard the experiences of youth and by the principle of substitution offer those that are socially wholesome and constructive for those that result in antisocial behavior.

The role of physical education in the life of youth was indicated centuries ago when the chiefs introduced youth to the customs and practices of the tribe. Delinquents are the product of a society which has failed, sometimes in its biological controls, usually in its social program. The great social agencies such as the schools, the clubs, and playgrounds are man's organizations to develop youth. The literary emphasis in the schools directed at training the mind, the starvation of clubs and the pauperization of playgrounds — these shortages and others manifest themselves in rural as well as urban centers. The evident failures of these social agencies are the delinquents and criminals of today. To correct these failures society as yet has been unwilling to set up social institutions and provide a community life in which youth might succeed in development; but, moved either by sentimentality or fear, it has established jails, asylums, hospitals, and reformative institutions.

SOCIAL IDEALS OF THE TIME AND PLACE

The moment Andrew Jackson was elected President, in 1828, the advocates of European gymnastics had no chance of any nation-wide extension of systems of physical education. The social ideals constantly coming to the surface of our national life since that time have been embodied in such phrases as "the worth of the common man," "the rights of the common people." Lately, others have been expressed that further individualized the person, such as "respect for personality."

Moreover, new interpretations of the question "What is the chief end of man?" have been largely shaped by the prevailing social ideals. To an increasing degree, in the twentieth century, the biological answer to the question has been expounded. Fortified as it has been by the discoveries of science in many fields, the biologists' answer has been "to function." This answer meant clearly that the purpose of life was to live, to live completely, intensively, fully; to function in every aspect of one's being. This view not only failed to support the European concept of physical education as a military, drill-like, hospitalized routine, but, indeed, favored a view that physical education should be joyous, expansive, and developmental of all aspects of the individual.

Throughout all discussions of education the theme of equality has been sounded. The Declaration of Independence announced that all men are created free and equal, and although the notion of equality has expressed itself in absurd, inaccurate, and wholly indefensible ways, the effect of the idea has been to further the movement for American rather than European methods in physical education. It should be kept clear, in all discussions of physical education, that no confusion exists regarding political and biologic equality. Inequality exists among individuals in character, intelligence, courage, and personality. All that the social ideals of the day demand are opportunities to develop the maximum in the qualities possessed. To secure this equality of opportunity, society must be free from the "frozen strata" that mark European and Oriental life so sharply. Correspondingly, all forms of physical education must rely not upon the devices and methods of a class-bound civilization, but must devise ways and methods susceptible to free development of individual worth.

Physical education should devote itself to expressing the dominant ideas, needs, and purposes of the American people and should help them to acquire sounder ideas, to recognize more pertinent needs, and to hold higher purposes.

The tendency of physical education is to reflect the influences of social doctrines and ideas of the time. European physical education, developed in the United States in the nineteenth century, illustrated prevailing social ideals in Europe and, to the extent that such persist, it reveals today the sanctions of another century.

The European type of education was favored in America, largely because of economic influences. A system of gymnastics could be introduced into the classrooms of the school because it required no apparatus, because it aimed to correct physical defects, and because it did not require trained teachers, but it could not be extended and developed as a general form of physical education for the people unless its principles, as exemplified in methods and materials, were in harmony with fundamental social doctrines in American society.

The worth of any practice depends upon its service to the ideas, needs, and nature of the people of the time and place. In comparison with other efforts in other periods of time and by certain common standards, it may be superior or inferior but its supreme merit lies in the measures of fulfillment it gives to hopes, desires, and aspirations of human beings. Whether the contrast is made between home industries of a by-gone age and modern factory methods, between pastoral life with its flocks and herds and modern industrial life with its noise and haste, or between the wireless and pony express, airplane and stage coach, or daguerreotype and photograph, the excellence of each is relative to the ideas, needs, and nature of the people of the time and place.

But ideas change, needs are replaced with other ones, and purposes become enlarged. As an aspect of public education, physical education has the responsibility to clarify the ideas that affect its program, to awaken citizens to the imperative needs of children and youth for certain motor experiences, and to make attractive those higher purposes to which idealistic youth are always ready to devote themselves.

Charles C. Cowell writes: "We socialize our pupils or contribute to their social learnings when they learn the ways of the group, become functioning members of it, act according to its standards, accept its rules, and in turn become accepted by the group."[26]

QUESTIONS AND PROBLEMS FOR DISCUSSION

1. Why is it not sufficient to dismiss the pugnacious behavior of a boy on the playground with the remark, "He's angry"?
2. In addition to inner urges, what other forces explain behavior?
3. Discuss the topic: The continuity of the individual and the group.
4. What is the "all or none" principle in physiology? Why does it not describe the influence of heredity?
5. Why is an infant at birth not yet a personality? How may he be likened to a phonograph?
6. Explain what happened to Johnny.
7. Discuss the principle: Physical education is a social experience.
8. What understanding do you have of the influence of the Middle Ages upon present-day American thought? Why do social behaviors tend to persist?
9. Discuss the principle: Physical education should play a part in shaping social practices. What is the role of the teacher in influencing the behavior of others?
10. Discuss the change in popular opinion about play. Does this change imply that there are no more problems in the play area? Explain.
11. What is your understanding of the moral significance of play? Why is play a moral necessity?
12. To what "careers," in Dewey's words can good play "commit us"?
13. Discuss what it means to be an educated person. Why are persons always important in a plan?
14. Discuss fully the neglect of body in the American culture.

[26] Charles C. Cowell, "The Contributions of Physical Activity to Social Development," *Research Quarterly*, May, 1960, p. 286.

15. Does emphasis upon the body mean that one should devote himself to an education *of* the physical? Give some illustrations of persons who appear to have followed such a plan.
16. Discuss the ideas of Patrick and Herrick with respect to "mind."
17. What effect has physical condition upon school success?
18. Are highly intelligent children likely to have poor physiques? Explain.
19. Is the idea of organismic unity fully operative in public education? Explain.
20. What is the relationship between the moral and the physical?
21. Why should physical education understand how social values are taught?
22. How important is example in teaching social values?
23. Discuss the tradition of excellence.
24. What qualities of personality must a coach possess if he aspires to teach sportsmanship?
25. What is the relation of good thoughts to good behavior? What is the significance of human relations to behavior?
26. What proper interest should physical education have in a stable social order? Discuss fully the ways in which physical education can contribute to social order.
27. Why do physical activities have social meanings? Why must one run in order to understand what running really is?
28. What are some of the significant ideas in the experience of physical education?
29. Discuss the statement: "The weaker the body, the more it commands; the stronger it is, the better it obeys."
30. Discuss fully the social inheritance of ideas in the folk dance. Why is the dance a symbol of spiritual life?
31. What purpose did de Coubertin have in mind in the revival of the Olympic Games?
32. Explain the regard that people have for calamities. Why should they feel as they do?
33. Do some persons believe that physical education may lead to a calamity? What examples can you give of this in instances where children have hurt themselves on playgrounds?
34. What responsibility should physical education take in keeping adventurous and vigorous activities in the program?
35. Upon what does continued participation in physical education depend?

36. Is delinquency in a child a calamity? Discuss the nature of delinquency.
37. What equivalent can be provided for dynamic struggle of of early man with wild beasts? How important is it to give in youth such equivalents?
38. Discuss the difference in structural and functional defects as they affect delinquent behavior.
39. Are there differences in the rate of delinquency in states? In cities? In neighborhoods of the same city? How do you account for these differences?
40. What responsibility has physical education for the ideas and purposes of the American people?

REFERENCE READINGS

Anshen, Ruth N. *Moral Principles of Action: The Ethical Imperative*. New York, Harper, 1952.

Bandura, Albert, and Walter, Richard H. *Adolescent Aggression*. New York, Ronald Press, 1959.

Biesanz, John, and Biesanz, Mavis. *Modern Society*, 2nd Edition. Englewood Cliffs, N.J., Prentice-Hall, 1959.

Bogardus, Emory Stephen. *The Development of Social Thought*, 4th Edition. New York, Longmans, Green, 1960.

Bovet, L. *Psychiatric Aspects of Juvenile Delinquency*. New York, Columbia University, 1951.

Carr, L. J. *Delinquency Control*. New York, Harper, 1950.

Carr, William G. "How Can We Teach Moral and Spiritual Values in the Public Schools?" *National Education Association Journal*, March, 1951, p. 77.

Chinoy, Ely. *Society*. New York, Random House, 1961.

Cloward, Richard A., and Ohlin, Lloyd E. *Delinquency and Opportunity*. New York, Free Press, 1960.

Cohen, Frank J. *Children in Trouble*. New York, Norton, 1952.

Cressy, Donald R. *The Prison*. New York, Holt, Rinehart, & Winston, 1961.

Division of Girls and Women's Sports, American Association for Health, Physical Education and Recreation, and National Association for Physical Education of College Women. *Social Changes and Sports*. Washington, D.C., 1959.

Fraley, Lester M., Johnson, Warren R., and Massey Benjamin H. (Editors). *Physical Education and Healthful Living*. Englewood Cliffs, N.J., Prentice-Hall, 1954.

Gillham, Helen L. *Helping Children Accept Themselves and Others.* New York, Bureau of Publications, Teachers College, Columbia University, 1959.

Glueck, Sheldon (Editor). *The Problem of Delinquency.* Boston, Houghton Mifflin, 1959.

Gran, John M. *Why Children Become Delinquent.* Baltimore, Helicon Press, 1961.

Huizinga, Johan. *Homo Ludens—A Study of the Play Element in Culture.* Boston, Beacon Press, 1950.

Kaplan, Max. *Leisure in America: A Social Inquiry.* New York, Wiley, 1960.

Kvaraceus, William C., and Miller, Walter B., *et al. Delinquent Behavior.* Washington, D.C., National Education Association, Juvenile Delinquency Project, 1959.

Lantis, Margaret. "The R. Tait McKenzie Lecture: The Wholeness of American Behavior." *Journal of Health—Physical Education—Recreation,* October, 1961, Part 2, p. 73.

Larrabee, Eric, and Meyersohn, Rolf. *Mass Leisure.* New York, Free Press, 1958.

Layman, Emma (McCloy). *Mental Health Through Physical Education and Recreation.* Minneapolis, Burgess, 1955.

Lowry, Antoinette. "The Turbulent Years." *Journal of Health—Physical Education—Recreation,* February, 1961, p. 16.

National Society for the Study of Education. *Social Forces Influencing American Education.* 60th Yearbook, Part II. Chicago, University of Chicago, 1961.

Research Center of the New York School of Social Work, Columbia University. *Why the Swastika?—A Study of Young American Vandals.* New York, Institute of Human Relations, 1962.

Robison, Sophia (Moses). *Juvenile Delinquency, Its Nature and Control.* New York, Holt, 1960.

Steiner, Lee (Rabinowitz). *Understanding Juvenile Delinquency.* Philadelphia, Chilton, 1960.

Van Dalen, Deobold B. "Cultural Impact on Physical Education." *Journal of Health—Physical Education—Recreation,* December, 1961, p. 15.

CHAPTER SIX

THE NATURE OF MAN — HIS BIOLOGICAL FOUNDATIONS

Accustom him to everything, that he may not be a Sir Paris, a carpet-knight, but a sinewy, hardy, and vigorous young man.

Montaigne.

The impersonal wants, the cravings for truth, beauty, and justice, the zeal for competence in workmanship and the spirit of goodwill toward men which are the highest objects of life for man seem far removed from his original proclivities. They are remote in the sense that the forces in their favor have to work diligently and ingeniously in order to make them even partial aims for even a minority of men. But, in a deeper sense, they reside within man himself; and, apart from supernatural aids, the forces in their favor are simply all the good in men.

Thorndike.

"I love open air," said Professor Maturin, "but I hate what is usually called exercise."

Furst.

NATURE AND NURTURE

It has been customary for a long time to regard nature and nurture as mutually antagonistic and exclusive factors that determine the behavior of individuals. The inheritance of traits and the effect of environment have provided the battleground for long and heated arguments. With the advance of genetics as a science of inheritance, the exclusive character of one influence or the other has been seriously challenged and today, as Hogben says:

> . . . no statement about a genetic difference has any specific meaning unless it includes or implies a specification of the environment in which it manifests itself in a particular manner.[1]

Long accustomed to authoritarian views about nature, modern man retains in his beliefs, customs, and speech notions about nature of an exceedingly bizarre character. These range from the doctrine of man's inherent evil nature to the concept that nature is always right. The study of genetics has afforded the basis for new interpretations of nature. The failures of man to build a good world are due neither to his inherent evilness nor to his slavish devotion to and following of nature. On the contrary, the present incapacity to utilize constructively the forces of the environment and his own potential powers forms the problem. Society, rapidly changing under the force of man's inventiveness, science, and escape from the rule of authority and tradition, must now face the problem of human behavior. Thus, the crucial tasks we confront in physical education, as in medicine, education, and social life generally, are those of nurture rather than nature. We are learning slowly but surely that to get a better world to live in we must secure better living in the world rather than attempt to secure a transformation of nature.

There are, of course, many individuals with inheritable defects, and these incline us at times to expect reconstruction of

[1] L. T. Hogben, *Nature and Nurture,* New York, Norton, 1933.

society by means of reproductive controls. Such measures are important in particular cases but they have no general validity for all. We are confronted with the grim necessity of changing ourselves, devising new and better habits of life, and escaping thereby from degenerating practices and beliefs. Our parents endow us with genes rather than characters, and genes only partly determine the way in which we will use the organs and powers they provide. Strange as it may be, it is the science of genetics which has destroyed the notion of an all-powerful nature and has helped to substitute the double role of nature and nurture in human affairs.

This rejection of the idea that nature exerts an all-pervading influence in human life does not deny to nature a position of considerable importance. This influence, however, often relates to an earlier life of man. Man is still equipped by nature to live in an environment vastly different from the life that now is, as a result of science, art, reasoning, habit, language, tools, books, and various customs of his race. Hence, each new individual must unlearn much of his nature in order to live with others in the crowded, coordinated life of industrial society. By nature he cries from pain and fights for things he wants; he grabs and snatches from others. By nurture of particular kinds he learns to merit what he takes, and to earn or deserve the satisfaction of his wants.

The present understanding of nature rejects the notion that nature is always right or always wrong or half and half. It recognizes that the individual possesses drives, urges, and impulses to certain kinds of behavior and that these should be strengthened at times, weakened at times, and completely checked at times. Unless this is understood the nature of impulse may be improperly valued and the importance of wants and interests unduly praised. It is not an idle question in these days, when freedom and discipline are vital topics, to consider the views we hold regarding nature, freedom, and discipline.

Shall the individual be permitted to engage in all the activities he desires? Are his interests the only criteria for the selection of activities? If the answers to these questions are "No," does it follow that the desires and interests of an individual are of no major importance? Such questions should lead the student to study the suitability of the natural equipment of man for certain types of motor skills, the force and usefulness of natural impulses to activity in his various enterprises, and the needs that exist today for shaping and directing these skills and impulses toward legitimate social ends. These data are found, of course, in the biological and psychological foundations of human nature.

Physical education in the selection of activities should recognize that man is prepared by nature to engage in certain kinds of activity.

Many of the persistent problems in physical education today are clarified by reference to the facts of nature. For example, a program of physical education based upon natural motor movements which represent the racial motor activities of man, and a program based upon the artificial creations of "systems" of gymnastics are readily evaluated by reference to the facts of nature. Thus, the fact that man presents in the racial patterns of his nervous system certain underlying predispositions to function in well-defined motor activities characterized in type and quality by his motor experiences over thousands of years, that he is urged on by his very nature to exploit these established organizations, and that, under proper guidance, such expressions may be made to serve high causes and noble ends is of outstanding import.

It should be quite clear that this position does not require that the natural be always right. It admits that many natural tendencies in the use of the human body must be combated by directed physical education; its only requirement in such instances is that the materials or methods used avoid procedures that quantitatively or qualitatively ignore the nature of the human individual.*

Moreover, many activities today called natural are quite different from the original tendencies that they represent. The effects of nurture are present and the force of custom and tradition is very powerful.

---

* High jumping, swimming, and throwing are illustrations in modern performances of improvements on nature.

The so-called **natural** proclivities of man represent enormous changes from original traits. Learning and nurture in its various forms are represented in the liking of boys for fishing, sport, and adventure since nature knows nothing of canoes, rods and reels, footballs, guns, and sport records. Nature's tendencies may go as far as to enjoy throwing a small object and swinging a club-like thing, but the majority of the sports of youth are modifications and adaptations of these early proclivities. Such modifications are natural activities in their basic patterns but all reflect the influence of nurture.

Further analysis of the natural in terms of its purpose is important. The original is the material we have with which to work. If left to itself it will not by nature result in values of real worth. The material is not by nature good; neither is it by nature bad or evil. Original nature is the representation of the potentialities of the individual in need of direction, guidance, and experience which society seeks to give. This help, most often represented in the efforts of schools and colleges, should be of a kind that will be acceptable to society. For physical education the problem is so much clearer than for many other aspects of the educational process. The motor activities of man that are similar in type and quality to the movements that have been used by the race of men from early beginnings are the ones that today, by nature, provide satisfaction when employed, and discomfort when not. The importance of these original satisfiers and annoyers is well appreciated in the case of children. In adults, due to lack of opportunity in childhood for development of skills, or due to pressure of other interests in adult life, such as economic problems, absence of opportunity for these original forms may give discomfort. In fact, participation in any kind of motor activity for some adults may give discomfort.

What, then, is to be said of the efforts of certain persons to develop large and bulging muscles or to pursue certain odd skills that have no useful function in life? The satisfactions derived from such exercises serve only whimsical values such as exhibitionism; at times they are outlets for maladjusted personalities. For example, the yoga devotee may finally acquire unilateral control over the *rectus abdominis*, but the evidence is lacking that this has in any way deepened spirituality.

THE PERMANENCE OF THE PHYSICAL BASIS

One of the stupendous facts of modern civilization is the magnitude of the social inheritance that man has accumulated; he attempts to transmit this through tools, language, arts, laws, science, experience, and knowledge in varied lines of endeavor. This social inheritance is civilization. Since the early decades of the nineteenth century this inheritance has increased chiefly in the direction of sedentary activities and knowledge that makes, not for the employment of man's whole nature, but for exercise of his mental powers alone. The proposal has been made at times that the tendency and direction of evolution stimulated by the force of the social inheritance will produce increasingly a mental type of person so that as time goes on there will be less and less need for muscles.

Physical education should make clear to all the persistent needs of man for activity.

Physical strength, endurance, power, will always be needed as a basis for the operation of the nervous system. But more than that, the inheritance of man includes drives and urges for play, for chasing and fleeing, for a great variety of activities. Given the physical opportunity in childhood these inner urges will take care of the developmental needs of man on a physical basis. If the opportunity is denied, the results will be recorded increasingly in physical defects of development, lowered physical vitality, lessened power of observation and expression, stunted natures and stunted lives.

THE WHOLE MAN AND PRIORITIES

The study of man often leads to dissection; we learn about him by examining parts and single functions. The body is readily described by anatomy and physiology, but neither one nor both can give the complete picture. And it is not possible to ascertain the full truth by further details of his mental abilities, spiritual aspirations, and social relationships. The whole is more than the sum of its parts. And yet the only way to make clear how this whole is made and how it functions is to deal with the many particulars that define his structure and describe his functions.

This statement of the organismic wholeness of man made in earlier chapters is repeated here because of the discussion of certain biological details to follow. It is also made to suggest that since individuals are wholes, problems of physical education that appear very important to physical education teachers may seem quite insignificant to others who are greatly concerned about the atomic age, for example. In particular, the immense problems of atomic energy seem to baffle us and our steps falter — not knowing which direction to take. It is all so new; there is no experience to guide us. Atomic energy applied in war may actually destroy civilization, but adapted to peaceful pursuits it may give to human society new and better kinds of living for all men everywhere. So, in a time of crisis in world affairs, we stand confused.

In the face of our present doubts, there are nevertheless some certainties. These come from the immemorial experiences of man. We may wonder whether the energy of the atom can be harnessed to run our automobiles, but we should be certain that muscular energy will always be indispensable to man. We may hope that isolationism for the United States is dead and that our part in world affairs will become ever greater, but a weak people will fail in that larger arena where the demands on vigor and vitality are exacting. Amidst our confusion about strikes, free enterprise, and democratic processes, it is clear that weakness impairs life, that ignorance of bodily functions promotes disease, and that indifference about personal growth and development imperils the nation.

Physical education should insist upon the simple priorities of life.

Concerning unknown matters we must delay decisions. Much time is required to solve the complex problems of international relations, to mature the United States, to harmonize the sharp conflicts of national life, and to develop atomic energy for the kindly purposes of human societies. Concerning our certainties, however, it is stupid to delay. *The sure things of life are the simple priorities of everyday living.* We know now how to overcome weakness and acquire strength. We know now how to develop vigor and vitality in youth. We know now how to learn the essentials of healthful living. We know now that the strength of our nation is the sum total of the strength of the individuals who compose it. These are some of the everyday priorities of the atomic age—simple certainties in a confused world.

If we survive the atomic age, the leisure of people will be tremendously increased with a corresponding accentuation of problems in the use of leisure time. Now is the time to educate youth in those interests and skills that can make leisure a blessing rather than a bore. But there should be understanding of the size of the task. The problem of play and recreation spaces in our towns and cities, the adoption of budgets that are adequate for provision of recreational leadership, the correlation of the whole play and recreational life of the child with the instruction of the school—these are three of the urgent necessities of the atomic age. The wise community will organize its schools, plan its physical environment, and select its leaders with the view that education is life; and since the purpose of life is complete functioning of the whole nature of man, this community, also, must cease to think of physical education only in terms of posture, perspiration, and exercises.

Moreover, it is a grievous mistake to conceive as fixed any of the conditions of the present environment. The changes in the social environment that lie ahead are enormous. To think of modern conditions, scarcely over 100 years old, as set, leads at once to the offering of substitutes to make up for the defects of opportunity. The business of physical education is to establish the needs of boys and girls, needs that have existed for at least 50,000 years, and help to make clear the needs of happy, healthy adults. The increase in nervous and mental diseases should make us wish to provide a physical education that will strengthen the basal centers of the nervous system. An industrial era that produces a type of life in which man has no need to use judgment, thought, or skill in his vocation, is just the kind of culture that can be changed. Society can provide that kind of environment in which society believes. On the other hand, if conditions of the present are viewed as fixed and immutable, then physical education is brought forward as a great corrective, palliative, remedial agency, removing waste products, strengthening foot arches and abdominal muscles, enlarging chest capacity, and increasing strength of grip. Its failure in this direction has never been fully recognized, due to the everlasting promise of the enthusiastic proponents of the method.

It is a mistake, of course, to assume that the foot arches should not be strong, that adequate lung capacity is not necessary, or that a strong grip is not desirable. These values, however, should come as by-products of motor activity designed to serve more vital needs.

The other way is more difficult, but it presents a sounder view. It appears as an advocate of the essentials for a happy, healthy life. It proposes, quite indirectly, to combat sedentary living by educating boys and girls so thoroughly in enjoyable activities that they will be persuaded to continue them after school days are over; it proposes to secure more and abundant opportunities for recreation; it seeks to awaken in people to a far greater degree a love for the out-of-doors, and therefore includes in its program many activities that do not belong in the traditional systems; and, finally, in the selection of its activities, it recognizes the hazards of modern life, and seeks approval for those forms that will combat deleterious influences, that will supplement occupational deficiencies, and that will secure wholesome development.

These are the two roads. One leads to slavery to work, to factory, to office, to desk, chained to the oar of the business galley with the vain hope of buying happiness with the money that is earned, and with unwarranted emphasis upon special exercises to correct physical deficiencies. The other leads to play and recreation as a part of life, just as vital, just as worth while as work that is needed to be done, and that all wish to do. It is for physical education to help say which road shall be traveled by man in the incomparable experiences of life. The gates are open. The highway is ahead.

THE BIOLOGICAL BASIS OF LIFE

The account in Chapter 2 of the development of man's muscles, vital organs, and especially his nervous system is profoundly instructive to the student of physical education. Indeed, this knowledge of the biological basis of life, not merely as a general truth but also as a specific illustration of the way in which Nature proceeded, gives a cue to both program and method. All the details are not important, but the account worth remembering begins with the time that muscular tissue appeared in significant amount in evolution from rather simple organisms to more complex structures. At this level, typified by the lower flatworms, the muscles are arranged in circular and longitudinal fashion around the trunk of the worm and serve for locomotion.

The appearance of the muscular system increased the range of locomotor activity for the animals so endowed; it made possible a richer environment; but it required marked specialization of the body cells. In proportion as the muscle cell gained ability to do specialized work it lost ability to care for all the processes that are required in living tissue. This specialization of certain cells required that other cells take up the work of supplying the muscle cells with food and of removing the waste occasioned by their activity. Thus it is that special cells appeared to furnish the food and oxygen needed by the muscles, and other special cells took unto themselves the work of removing the waste. This is the beginning of the circulatory, respiratory, digestive, and excretory systems. The vital organs are being established, and they arise and develop in relation to the action of the large muscles of the trunk.

The contraction of muscle is dependent upon a stimulus that will cause it to act. In development, muscle cells required the addition of corresponding nerve fibers to the early type of nervous system. The increased power of locomotion brought the animal into new environment and new situations, and from here on through fishes, reptiles, lower mammals such as the cat and dog, and arboreal mammals such as the ape, up to man, the whole history of development is one of increase in complexity of structure and function of the nervous system. The brain, as the final and most complex structure to develop, presents an organ of wonderful usefulness to man. It exercises control over the other centers of the nervous system and hence over all the parts of the body. Part of this control goes on without the knowledge of its action on our part and irrespective of our will in the matter. It is impossible to make the heart stop beating by thinking or to make the liver secrete bile by reading about it. This control over the vital organs of life is automatic and involuntary, and although we know conditions that would modify the type of reaction that occurs we are limited greatly in an effort to guide the response. We have, however, immediate control over the skeletal muscles and hence we can increase the activity of the vital organs indirectly by making demands upon the large muscles which are developmentally related to them.

This emphasis upon the importance of the muscular system has been expressed by many physiologists and biologists. They have phrased in clear and scientific language what the ancient Greeks knew. We need to remember always that the muscles are controlled by nerve centers and that the centers in control of the muscles of the trunk are older, tougher, and have more endurance than the centers governing the extremities. To strengthen these older centers is an act of prime importance because they are the centers of that endurance which will enable us to withstand the strains of modern life. The toughness, endurance, and nervous poise of the individual who has experienced vigorous physical activity in youth are in striking contrast to the high-strung, easily fatigable, and weak children who are the product of a kind of living now widely practiced by our industrial, business, and professional classes.

Physical education should meet the biological needs of children and youth for vigorous activities, adequate time, and instruction in skills.

The foregoing would seem to indicate quite clearly the need for modification of some physical education programs. It appears obvious that calisthenic lessons in the classroom will not provide the activity essential for the child's development; such exercises are too restricted and the large muscles which stimulate the vital organs to action are not sufficiently employed. It is clear also that vigorous physical activity must be provided. Too much attention to safety may result in too little experience for boys in combat activities and in too many innocuous activities for both boys and girls. Individuals are sometimes stimulated to excessive effort in physical education, but in general most young persons are not getting enough vigorous physical experience. Moreover, vigor in activity can never be attained by the use of the small muscles of the arms and lower legs. Nor will the older centers of the cord and brain be developed by activities restricted to the conveniences of school rooms, or to the inconveniences of enormously large classes in the gymnasium.

It is pertinent to ask, can the school ever provide in its program of activities all that is needed by children for physical development? To answer this we need information concerning the time requirement. How many hours are essential? It is generally agreed that children in the elementary school need from four to six hours a day of large muscle activity. Obviously, not all of this time can be provided in the school schedule, but from one to two hours of the school day should include free locomotion, spontaneous play and games, dancing, and other large movements; this would necessitate that from three to four hours be provided for physical activity outside of school.

In spite of the rapid extension of physical education into the school curriculum, it seems clear that the school can never provide in its schedule of the regular session for all that children require for developmental purposes. The meaning of this then is that children must secure this development outside of school. Such being the case, then, the school program of physical education must be essentially a teaching program in activities that will be used in after-school play. The school period must be an instruction period to present play materials, to establish play standards, to foster play attitudes. To think of physical education in the public school as a corrective, disciplining day's order, designed to achieve "physical fitness," is to mistake the purpose of the period in relation to the developmental needs of boys and girls.

Physical education should be prepared to support and to participate in adult education.

Adult education today is a major instrument for improvement in community living; it is also an important means of education of adults in wholesome physical activities. Over 30 million American adults are now entered in adult education courses; these range from offerings by the agricultural and home economic extension service of the federal government to correspondence courses, public school programs, and extension services of college and university. About three million attend adult education programs of public schools. From a survey by the U.S. Office of Education it appears that about 5 per cent of the courses offered nationally are health and physical education classes.

The purpose of adult education is to serve the educational needs of the mature persons of a community. These needs vary but in every community the problem of keeping fit is often difficult for adults, especially for those without adequate motor skills in leisure activities. Physical education instruction for adults can increase personal efficiency and combat the degenerative effects of sedentary living.

THE SERIOUS NEGLECT OF THE BIOLOGICAL

All thoughtful persons are disturbed over man's failure to exert human control of the forces and resources of nature.

This failure is exemplified in three areas of human action.

The first failure is the reliance of man upon material and social culture, in the belief that knowledge of the academic curriculum plus some technical instruction in engineering and vocational subjects is sufficient for human happiness. The whole biological inheritance of man is practically ignored, and the simple fact that he is an animal organism is consistently forgotten. The developments of mind and the institutions of society can be effectively used only if he has a sound inheritance, only if he is well-nourished but not overnourished, only if he is properly exercised, and only if he is free from disease.

The second failure is the consistent effort to create a happy state of affairs by attention to economic policies alone. Any analysis of personal problems solely in terms of economic well-being forgets the nature of man and the sources of his common joys. Through all the years man has remained what he was and is, an individual finding joy in the senses, showing emotional, esthetic, social, and physical traits as well as intellectual ones. Was it intellectualism that enabled Nazi Germany to fight and nearly defeat the whole of Europe and America? The old German intellectualism of Berlin, Jena, Heidelberg, and Bonn played no part in the tremendous effort of that nation.

The stress upon economic welfare and the devotion to intellectual affairs are responsible for many of our problems. What puts so many of our people in hospitals for mental and nervous diseases? What is responsible for the sharp increase in the neuroses in contemporary life? What is the cause of the alarming rate of juvenile delinquency? Preoccupation with a particular end forces the adoption of particular means. Present emphasis upon the economic forces the employment of economic means. Hence other considerations are neglected.

The third failure is the assumption that ethical teaching alone can change an individual from a grasping, selfish, success-minded person to an altruistic, socially aware humanitarian. It is a hope as dubious as it is touching. Morals are a matter of the physical condition of the organism quite as much as they are reflections of high purpose. The whole man is involved in all behavior. Cowell recognizes this when he writes:

The essence of any physical education or recreation program is found in its values — its policies and its preferences, its moral commitments, its loyalties, its standards of excellence, its measures of success, its teachings by which students should live. For instance, one very urgent issue in athletic programs today is the creation, validity, and survival of values related to codes of conduct in line with the supposed educational purposes of athletics. This calls for planned, experience-centered, evaluative learning. Sportsmanship must be used functionally, not merely verbalized.[2]

Physical education should regard its activities as a continuing balance that can lessen the influence of excessive devotion to nervous and mental interests.

The evidence from many sources shows an increase in nervous and mental disease. Studies of the incidence of mental and nervous diseases in hospitals report that over half the beds in the hospitals of the United States are occupied by nervous and mental patients. As indicated earlier, mental disease was a prime cause for rejection of young men by the armed forces, and neuropsychiatric disturbance accounted for many casualties during the last war.

Many of those who comprise the statistics of nervous and mental disease are the wrecks from the two world wars; some are the product of economic stress during the depression; and some are the result of a competitive life that is too hard for them. Since other persons confront the same strains and stresses without loss of integration, it follows that those who fail to meet the conditions of modern life are, by that standard, inferior in a biological sense.

Cases of recorded insanity are also increasing, but it should be noted that there is also, in recent years, an increase in institutional treatment, with correspondingly more cases confined, and hence more available statistics. Almshouses for generations housed not only the poor in need of domiciliary care, but also vagrants, lying-in women, pensioners, imbeciles, and the insane. Today there are few insane in almshouses, and hence

---

[2] Charles C. Cowell, *The Growing Years*, 1962 Yearbook, American Association for Health, Physical Education and Recreation, p. 160.

more in the statistics from institutions for the insane. The change in attitude toward the insane also accounts for a recorded increase. Instead of viewing the insane person as possessed of the devil in need of exorcism, such a person is held to be sick and in need of special care. Scientific medical treatment of the insane keeps them alive longer, and hence increases the number reported at any one time. Keeping the insane alive longer may result in more children from such impaired stock.

With insanity physical education has no relationship. With nervous and mental disease of lesser severity than insanity, physical education is increasingly useful—not as exercise but as a way of return to play, to simple movements and coordinations, and to objective activity. To the extent that it promotes a philosophy of living that gives a balance to interests and an integration to persons, it may have large prophylactic values. The prevention of mental and nervous disease involves all the social forces that play upon man. Szasz writes:

> . . . to live, persons need to be interested in far more than just objects. *Man also needs games.* Interest in games—that is in being alive and living—may be variously expressed. Its main features are feelings of zestfulness and hope and an attitude of curious and hopeful expectation.[3]

Physical education, in cooperation with the anthropologist, sociologist, and medical physician, faces a tremendous problem that calls for the combined effort of those who recognize it.

Man can be no better than his animal organism. This is the basic fact upon which all decisions in education, in government, in public policy must rest.

THE DISADVANTAGES OF THE BIPED POSITION

There were not only great advantages but also great disadvantages in the evolutionary changes that brought animal

[3] Thomas S. Szasz, *The Myth of Mental Illness*, New York, Harper, 1961, p. 287.

life of the pre-man stage from the quadruped to the biped position. The liberation of the hands and their subsequent use, according to Sir Arthur Keith, developed the brain, but the disadvantages in other directions are no less real. Some of these have no particular meaning for physical education, but the difficulty of balance is at once apparent. Many of the postural problems that man encounters arise out of the attempt to balance his weight in a dynamic system where the forces to destroy balance are ever present. In the quadruped the trunk weight hangs from the horizontal spine supported at either end, but in the biped it is directed through a vertical line to a narrow and rather unstable base. Todd clearly describes the changes that are brought about as follows:

> In the first position, the weight of the spinal girder and of all the parts hanging upon it passes through the paired posterior facets on the articular processes of the vertebrae and rests upon the top of four shafts, the two humeri in front and the femora in the back. There is nowhere an accumulation of weight downward through a single axis, but instead side distribution through many short axes along the spine, with terminal distribution through the shoulder and pelvic girdles at either end. The lumbosacral connections of the posterior facets through which the weight passes from the spine to the pelvis are in alignment with the thigh-joints through which it passes from the pelvis to the femora. The supporting shafts of the femora are in alignment with the superior rami, or upper branches of the pubis as they curve forward into the ilia.
>
> In the erect position the forward supports are removed so that all weight is supported by the legs, which now have a different angle in relation to the spinal axis. The result is a change in the general direction of the weight-thrust throughout the structure, and in the particular parts of the vertebrae through which the weight passes. The facets, or articular surfaces, between the vertebrae being now in vertical alignment instead of horizontal, weight transfer is no longer directly through them, but the weight passes instead through the bodies of the vertebrae and the intervertebral discs.
>
> Next, we find that the direction of the weight-thrust from the spine to each leg is now oblique, from the lumbosacral joint forward to the heads of the femora. The springlike design of the

legs is also changed, since the femora are now in discontinuous alignment with the spine, and the lower bones of the leg and ankle are much more nearly vertical in their direction.[4]

It should be clear that in the biped position the viscera have a tendency to descend, to press upon one another, to impair by malposition the functions of the vessels that reach them through the mesentery, and to impede by pressure the circulation of the pelvic basin.

Physical education in the teaching of children and youth should give attention to the fundamental postures, such as sitting, standing, walking, and others.

The problem presented by the biped position is not to be solved by attempting to go back to the quadruped position but by skillful adjustment of the organism to the forces that operate in the erect individual. Obviously a strong trunk musculature is essential in childhood and youth for the development of vital organs and nerve centers; it is essential also in all ages for the maintenance of the viscera in proper position. In addition to the development of the musculature, an economical balance of body weights in different segments is essential for efficient use of the biped position. Man must learn to carry himself on his legs; there is no other way. It should be remembered that styles in clothing influence postures, that notions of body beauty do also, and that regard for certain traits of personality produce airs, mannerisms, and posings in which postures are the major means of expression.

THE FUNDAMENTAL MOVEMENTS OF MAN

An analysis of physical activities of the race would indicate the gulf between a natural primitive environment and present civilized conditions of life. Such an analysis in the anthropoid stage must necessarily be speculative. The physical

[4] M. E. Todd, *The Thinking Body*, New York, Hoeber, 1937, p. 69.

activities of primitive men were mainly hunting, with some use of the arms in manual tasks. It is likely that ground activities predominated rather than arboreal, so that running, jumping, lifting, carrying, and throwing are probably nearer modern man than climbing and hanging. Swimming was not natural even then, and is learned now with difficulty. The activities of man in the earliest periods probably determined and defined the lines of his motor evolution; his activities since then up to modern times have set that tendency.

The evidence shows or suggests that running, jumping, throwing, climbing, and hanging formed the basic patterns of motor movements throughout the life of man. As he passed from primitive to nomadic, to pastoral, to agricultural, to industrial life, he clung constantly to certain movements. These, therefore, are truly as much a part of his inheritance in function as are anatomical formations in structure; indeed, the persistence of these fundamental movements through the ages is dependent in part upon the conformation of his anatomy. His fundamental movements are truly racial.

Physical education should teach the fundamental skills and their modifications; in the latter stress on the fundamentals is important.

The development of play, games and sports, dances and festivals are only elaborations of immemorial racial activities. The highly organized motor activities of today are to be analyzed in terms of these racial types. Baseball is running and throwing; football is running, throwing, jumping, lifting and carrying; and basketball is running and throwing. Some activities involve special technique but depend for their attractiveness upon the basic relationship of these racial types.

Now physical education must consider seriously if it is wise to foster a program of physical education organized upon a basis other than this racial one. By what process of reasoning can it be justified? For developmental purposes it would appear that the children of man should engage in activities similar in type and quality to those immemorial racial forms which served so powerfully to fashion the frame and motor structure of man.

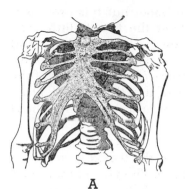
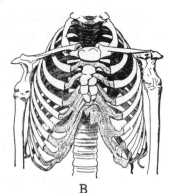

A   B

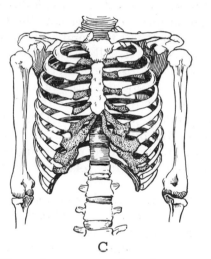

C

Figure 7. Ribs and sternum, to show the progressive ossification of the cartilage, which is indicated by stippling: A, Child at birth, reduced from life size. B, Child at 7 years, much reduced. C, Adult, 30 years, very much reduced, from life. From specimens in the Warren Museum of the Harvard Medical School. (From Minot.)

THE SKELETAL FRAME AND THE FUTURE FORM OF THE INDIVIDUAL

The skeleton varies greatly at different age levels, but it is at all times the frame of the human individual. Preformed in cartilage, it subsequently changes to bone; but this process is gradual and is incomplete until about the twenty-fifth year.

The skeleton of the infant shows a large proportion of cartilage and fibrous tissues. This fact explains the comparative softness of bone in the infant. In Figure 7, the skeletons of the newborn child, the child of seven years, and the adult of 30 are compared. The soft bones of the young child are readily subject to postural deformity and injury.

In the infant the thorax is nearly round; in the adult it is an ellipse. After the second year of life the thorax increases in diameter very much faster than the head. The greater transverse diameter of the thorax is indicated by the following proportions: At birth the anteroposterior diameter is to the transverse as 1 is to 1.5; at three years it is as 1 to 2; and in the adult it is as 1 to 3. In both infant and adult, it will be noted that the skeleton is formed of separate bones held together by bands of white connective tissue called ligaments, forming joints or articulations. In children the joints are more flexible than in adults. Range of movement tends to decrease with age. This difference is partly ligamentous; it is also due to the obstruction of joint movement by contiguous parts. The relatively large joints of children are to be contrasted with the relatively large, soft parts in adults.

Physical education should determine the skeletal pattern in each pupil and give attention to the prevention of defects.

In view of these anatomical relationships, physical education leadership should protect the young child from inactive school programs which result in the "school room stoop" and should provide competent supervision for vigorous play. The size and development of the chest are related to muscular components of the chest that increase in size and strength through strong use of the arms in swinging, climbing, pulling, pushing, and hanging movements, and to bony-ligamentous components of the thorax that expand and grow through increased respiratory need. Prolonged and heightened breathing arises in response to the demands of the muscles.

THE SPINE, A CENTRAL AXIS

At birth the child's spine is very flexible. It can be twisted in nearly every direction. This is due to the cartilaginous character of the vertebrae, which begin to ossify in the third year of life, and the softness of the ligaments and muscles surrounding the parts. The relative and absolute lengths of the cervical, thoracic, and lumbar segments vary. From infancy to adult life there is a relatively greater growth in the lumbar region than in either the cervical or thoracic; in fact the latter two regions show a relatively greater length in infancy than in adult life.

Physical education should protect the spine against distortion of its curves.

This transformation and greater mobility of the lumbar spine are highly suggestive of the need for integration of this region in all developmental activities. Such integration is achieved when the child learns to do a forward roll — as a ball with all parts, arms and legs — united as a whole in the act. Similar illustrations are to be found in broad jumping, climbing a ladder, and throwing a ball. Attention to postural patterns is important during the whole period of childhood and adolescence; increased lumbar curve, especially in girls, should be prevented through development of strong abdominal muscles, use of proper footwear, and suitable body mechanics of the lumbar region. In general, all movements in which the trunk is bent backward are undesirable.

SEX DIFFERENCES IN MALES AND FEMALES

The pelvis of the female is much broader after adolescence, which gives to the femur a marked obliquity. This mechanical disadvantage interferes with the running ability of the girl. In all movements of the lower extremities there is likely to be a marked lateral sway of the pelvis; the extent of this oscillation determines the speed of the individual in getting over the ground. Because of this one fact of body construction, the girl is unable to run so fast or so far as the boy of the same strength. The measurements of the male and female pelves are given in Table 4.

TABLE 4.   PELVIC MEASUREMENTS

DIAMETER	MALE			FEMALE		
	INLET, CM.	INTERME-DIATE, CM.	OUTLET, CM.	INLET, CM.	INTERME-DIATE, CM.	OUTLET, CM.
Anteroposterior...	10.25	11.5	8.52	10.25	12.75	11.5
Transverse........	12.75	12.0	9.00	13.25	12.75	12.0
Oblique..........	12.00	11.5	10.25	12.75	13.25	11.5

While there are anatomical and functional differences in the sexes, there is no evidence that, apart from training, the nervous system of the girl is different from that of the boy. In the measurements that have been made of instinctive, emotional, temperamental, and moral traits no significant differences have been found.

In muscle strength, however, the sexes show a marked difference. The female is weaker than the male in all muscle groups, and no amount of weight training is likely to make the female as muscular as the male. Heavy weight training of Soviet women caused menstrual problems.[5] With greater physical strength the male exhibits a pugnacity of spirit, and this doubtless explains the common notion that the male and female are different nervously. The average man has a strength grip of 81 pounds, the average woman 48 pounds. Women do not use their muscles so rapidly as men. Reaction time is longer. Tucker found that the average man took 70/100 of a second to apply the brakes

[5] A. McDonald, "Strength and the Female," *Physical Education,* July, 1960, p. 33.

of an automobile after seeing the "stop" signal. The average woman takes 87/100 of a second.

Physical education should distinguish in its activities for boys and for girls according to the stage of development in each sex.

It should be quite clear, however, that the profound changes in the pelvis require modification of the program in physical education for girls. What has been used with boys will not suffice for girls after the onset of puberty. Complete development of the pelvis in women does not occur until "well into the twenties," and this prolonged period of developmental change from 12 years to 25 suggests that girls be taught activities that will not make extreme muscular pull upon the pelvic region. This is of significance for maternity.

The emphasis upon competitive excellence in track and field that flows from the Olympic games and the tendency to select for professional preparation women of masculine type give an improper direction to physical education of girls and women. Skerlj reports upon the admission standards for women to the Warsaw Central Institute of Physical Education and observes that the tests used led to the selection of candidates, 79.95 per cent of whom had underdeveloped breasts, 60 per cent had flat and narrow pelves, and 65.3 per cent were leptosomatic (tall, thin, long, flat thoracic cavity). Obviously, types of physical education suited to the masculine type of girl are wholly unsuited to the feminine physique.

Since the arm strength of girls after puberty is small in relation to weight, their program should avoid activities which require support of the body weight by the arms. Hanging and swinging exercises on apparatus are usually unsuited to girls because of small arm strength on the one hand, and a low center of gravity of weight on the other. Many of the activities on the parallel bars, long horse, flying rings, traveling rings, and horizontal ladder, that girls can do equally as well as boys before puberty, become wholly undesirable for them afterward. It should be understood that this viewpoint is not an argument for physical weakness in women.

These statements relate to the ideal feminine physique (Fig. 9). Masculine type females may become very proficient on apparatus and excel other women in track and field events. George Q. Rich reports an interesting experiment on fatigue curves of boys and girls and concludes that "there are no sex differences in muscular fatigability, either absolute or relative, at age 8. As boys become older, they become stronger, but tend to fatigue to a greater extent and also somewhat more rapidly. In contrast, girls increase less in strength and in fatigability."[6]

GROWTH AND DEVELOPMENT

Technically, growth of an individual means increase in mass. It represents an accumulation of tissue. Development is the organization of that tissue into functional units or powers. Development of the child can be judged in part by growth, but growth may occur without a corresponding development. Nutrition and various hygienic factors condition growth and development. While physical education influences growth, its chief interest is in development. The chest measurement has been used frequently as an index of development.

From the first growth of the fertilized ovum until maturity of the individual is reached numerous forces determine growth. Some organs continue to grow even in old age. Heredity is a prominent factor. Certain races are small and never grow large individuals. In the same race, environment may operate, or the blood strains may explain differences. The small stature of the southern Chinese and the tallness of the Northern Chinese are interesting phenomena in one race. The agencies producing this variation may be climate, or what is more probable, strains from north of China in the one case and strains from India in the southern Chinese.

Environment has a pronounced influence, in which adequate diet, sunshine, care of the growing child, and adequate rest

[6] George Q. Rich, "Muscular Fatigue Curves of Boys and Girls," *Research Quarterly*, October, 1960, p. 497.

and play comprise the conspicuous items. Children exposed to a superior environment are taller and heavier, have greater lung capacity and lower blood pressure than the average for their age. The influence of nutrition upon growth in size is particularly prominent.

It is a commonly held idea that children show alternate periods of growth and nongrowth. It is believed that children grow tall in the summer and heavy in the winter. It is known, however, that infants grow regularly if the food is proper and there is no illness. It is probably acute illness, or other unfavorable factor, such as sedentary schooling, that causes the interruption to normal and constant gains in height and weight. Epidemic communicable disease in a school may interfere with growth. It is believed that serious disease in infancy not only checks growth at the time but acts as a future deterrent. The evidence is conflicting. Meredith and Knott in a study of 66 boys and 73 girls, ages 5 to 10 and 5 to 9 years respectively, report that frequent illness in these groups did not impair growth.[7]

Physical education should appraise all the factors that may locally affect the growth and development of individual children.

Important causes of growth disturbances are disease, food deficiencies, endocrine dysfunction, climate, lack of exercise, and various environmental hazards. In failure of development, lack of physical activity may be the prominent cause, especially in muscle, bone, and organic viscera.

CHRONOLOGICAL, ANATOMICAL, AND PHYSIOLOGICAL AGE

The age in years, months, and days of a child may not compare with the age of his development. Anatomical or physiological items in the individual may run ahead or lag behind in development for the normal age.

The ossification of bones indicates anatomical age. This may be determined by the x-ray.

[7] H. V. Meredith and V. B. Knott, "Illness History and Physical Growth," *American Journal of Diseases of Children,* February, 1962.

Physiological age represents a functional condition and in relation to chronological age may present marked variations. Chronological age is a poor measure of capacity in either boys or girls. Physiological maturity represented in sexual development may range over a period of four to five years. Maturity may come at 10½ years or not until 16½ years. The median age for this development is between 13½ and 14 years. Early maturity is not a sign of poor health. Tall girls mature generally earlier than short ones.

Physical education should take into account physiological age in the conduct of activities.

Physiological age has significance for physical education. Children tend to play with others of their same physiological age and they select activities suited to their stage of development. Girls are older physiologically than boys. Moreover, early or late maturity of youths may present adjustment problems of which the teacher should be aware. Large size in a girl often complicates the posture problem, and if the breasts are well developed, this sign of maturity may lead to a postural stoop and a marked decrease of interest in athletic activities. Small size in a boy is likewise contrary to the ideals of the culture and may produce emotional problems of compensatory character.

PHYSIQUE

Good physique is attained often as the result of exercise whether it comes as a by-product of life activities or from directed forms of education. Doubtless there are important influences in heredity, but the experience of Theodore Roosevelt in building up his physique is too well known for us to forget that developmental activity out of doors is the chief agent.

There are several classifications of body build. The terminology of Kretschmer gives three categories: asthenic, pyknic, and athletic.

1. The **asthenic.** These are tall and slender persons with flat chests and sloping shoulders. Functionally they are likely

to have great difficulty in digesting food due to their relaxed viscera. They have little energy.

2. The **pyknic.** These are short and thick-set persons with strong necks, barrel-shaped chests, and protruding abdomens. Functionally they enjoy food, eat large amounts, and digest it easily. They are likely to have abundant energy.

3. The **athletic.** These persons are intermediate between the other two. They are average in size, possess a strong musculature, have broad chests and large hands and feet.

Sheldon and his associates also define three types that parallel the Kretschmer pattern: ectomorph, endomorph, and mesomorph. In the ectomorph the trunk is short and thin, like the asthenic; in the endomorph the physique is large with massive viscera and much fat; and in the mesomorph the body is solid and hard with a tendency to prominence of bone and muscle (Fig. 8).

Most persons do not fit into these three categories; they are intermediates. To meet this situation Sheldon proposes a seven-point rating scale to define the degree to which any person expresses these three sets of attributes. Thus Kretschmer's pyknic or Sheldon's endomorph would be rated 7, 1, 1, and an asthenic or ectomorph would rate 1, 1, 7. A person of average build, halfway between these extremes, would be 4, 4, 4. By writing three numbers together, one has a code designation of

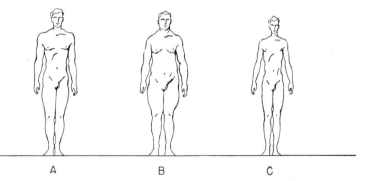

A   B   C

Figure 8. Three types of physique as classified by Sheldon: A, mesomorph; B, endomorph; and C, ectomorph.

the somatotype, as 711, 117, or 444. In a study of the population of male college freshmen, Sheldon reports 76 somatotypes.

The effort to classify individuals into types of physique creates more difficulties than it solves, since Sheldon himself shows 76 somatotypes in 200 college men. These types therefore serve very little purpose except in dealing with the extremes of a group. Although the types set up may describe the male, corresponding terms are not suitable for the female.

Physical education should study types of physique and correctly interpret activities in accordance with the findings.

In the cultural ideals of the United States, the typical male is broad shouldered, narrow hipped, strong in muscle, and skillful in movement. This would correspond with Kretschmer's athletic type, or Sheldon's mesomorph. The same culture, however, idealizes the female with broad hips, narrow shoulders, and little evident muscle. There are, of course, prominent women athletes whose physique is masculine in type, and individuals classed socially as males who show a feminine-type of build. Figure 9 shows these extremes and indicates how inadequate are present classifications to deal with the educational and cultural problems that such types of physique impose. Masculine type women athletes too often set, for the lay public and for uncritical professional workers as well, a standard of perform-

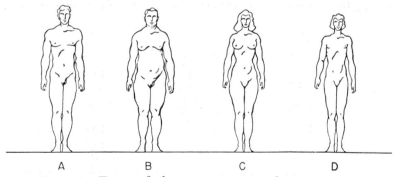

A   B   C   D

Figure 9. Types of physique in men and women: A, the ideal masculine physique; B, a male type with marked feminine characteristics; C, the ideal feminine physique; and D, a female physique with many male characteristics.

ance for women that is unreasonable and unsound. It is to be expected that both men and women teachers of physical education will give guidance in this problem of relating activity to physique.

Certain types of people tend to select certain activities. The asthenic individual will not play football; he may play tennis. The pyknic will not attempt the sprints but is likely to choose field events. This is desirable and usually salutary. The athletic type well suited for football may devote himself to that sport alone and limit his physical education.

There are advantages in being tall or short, light or heavy. Tallness is an asset in basketball and shortness an asset in tumbling and diving. Light weight is an advantage in sprints and heavy weight is an advantage in football line play. These favorable factors in physique are relative to the possession of other qualities, such as agility, speed of movement, and intelligence.

Physical education should be aware of various methods for determining physique and growth, for example, the Wetzel Grid.

The Wetzel Grid technique is designed to avoid the errors in estimating physical status and growth that are inherent in the ordinary height-weight tables. The age, height, and weight of the individual are determined in order to describe body size, body type (physique), and the direction and speed of change as he develops. The procedures involved in this kind of study are described in Wetzel's original papers.[8]

BODY STRUCTURE AND FUNCTION AS GUIDES

It is generally assumed by the physical educator that anatomy and physiology are essential studies for the student of this

[8] Norman C. Wetzel, "Physical Fitness in Terms of Physique, Development and Basal Metabolism," *Journal of the American Medical Association*, Vol. 116 (1941), p. 1187. Also *The Treatment of Growth Failure in Children*, NEA Service, Cleveland, 1948.

area of education. This rests upon the general acceptance that a worker should know the materials with which he works. There are values in appreciation and understanding which flow from such knowledge, but beyond these are the many procedures which must be referred always to the structure and function of the human organism for a final check. Practice based upon knowledge is clearly superior to practice based upon tradition, even if the tradition is obviously a popular one.

Physical education should teach the use of the foot in relation to the anatomical and physiological facts of this part.

The transverse and longitudinal arches of the foot are formed by the bones of the tarsus and metatarsus. They are maintained by ligaments and muscles. These arches carry the weight of the individual and react to the forces of weight and of use that operate. Use of the foot affects its form; in a remarkable degree the fusion of function and structure can be observed here.

In determination of the use of the foot, consideration should be given to the whole organism. It is not enough to consider the foot alone, important as that is. There appear, therefore, certain facts that may be examined.

In the foot, structure is more favorable for supporting the body weight on the lateral rather than the mesial aspect; the longitudinal arch is high on the mesial side; and the tendons of the ankle extensors pass to the toes and sole of the foot on the mesial aspect of the ankle joint. When the foot is placed straight forward, the superimposed weight may be transmitted from heel to toe over the lateral aspect of the foot and the longitudinal arch correspondingly protected. When the foot is turned outward, the weight in passing from heel toward the front part of the foot breaks over the mesial border, tending to impair the structure of the longitudinal arch.

When the whole mechanism is considered, the relation of the foot position to hip joint, pelvis, lumbar and thoracic curves, chest and head is important. When the feet are turned outward, the pull through the iliofemoral and ischiofemoral ligaments tilts the pelvis forward, increases the lumbar curve, and alters the position of the chest and head. Thus, the foot position is to be viewed not only in relation to the structure of the part itself, but also with respect to the entire correlated mechanism.

Tradition, authority or style may seek to establish a certain foot position. Exact and adequate knowledge should determine this matter.

Physical education should stress the development of a strong abdominal musculature.

The abdominal viscera are held in position against the pull of gravity by the floor of the pelvis, the muscles of the lower torso, and delicate bands of mesentery. Obviously the pelvic floor, a sloping shelf of no great size, plays a minor role here, and the mesentery is too fragile a structure to give much support. The responsibility for abdominal position of organs rests largely upon the musculature of the walls.

The significance of this anatomical fact for physical education is very great. Since so much of modern industrial life tends toward sedentary living, insurance against abdominal wall weakness must be taken by developing in youth strong abdominal muscles, by teaching postures that keep the abdominal muscles in tone, and by promoting interest in activities and ideals of physique that will maintain these primary muscles of the trunk in good condition. And yet, it must be understood that continued use of activities pointed solely toward physical outcomes, except in individually prescribed corrective exercises, is a deterrent to the acceptance of an intelligent physical education program.

Physical education should advocate the use of natural movements instead of artificial ones in warming up exercises.

Before engaging in strenuous activities the athlete should perform a number of natural movements in order to increase the circulation of blood through various parts and to step up the functional activity of the tissues involved. Baseball is an excellent example of using this technique. Players play catch, engage in batting and fielding, using the movements that are employed in the actual game. Golfers invariably try a number of practice swings before driving, and basketball players practice shooting, dribbling, passing and other movements used in the game.

A custom has grown up around football that sharply varies from this rational procedure. Players are made to go through what are called "grass drills" and often after they have been running, passing, and kicking for fifteen to twenty minutes. This sort of irrational use of exercise is a poor tradition and should be abandoned.

Physical education should give training directions to young athletes as essential to a top performance program.

In order to acquire an excellent state all the underlying conditions of best performance should be met. In addition to exercise in the activity, these include proper diet, adequate sleep and rest, nonuse of alcohol and tobacco, pleasant surroundings, and freedom from irritating and worrying emotions.

Physical education should watch the condition of athletes in order to detect staleness.

The signs of staleness or lack of condition may be shown in loss of weight after a norm has been established in training, failure of skin injuries to heal quickly, a "pinched" expression around the nose, lack of clearness and brightness in the eyes, and general signs of lack of energy.

Physical education should be prepared to answer as fully and as accurately as possible questions of the student about various conditions that arise in the course of activities.

Some of the questions asked by athletes cannot be answered with complete assurance. Some can be, and the teacher should be able to explain to the pupil the nature of "second wind,"[9] "pain in the side,"[10] "athletic heart,"[11] staleness,[12] fatigue,[13] and similar conditions associated with strenuous exercise.

[9] Edward C. Schneider, *Physiology of Muscular Activity,* Philadelphia, Saunders, 1939, p. 107.

[10] *Ibid.,* p. 96.

[11] Harry A. Scott, *Competitive Sports in Schools and Colleges,* New York, Harper, 1951, p. 167.

[12] Edward C. Schneider, *op. cit.,* p. 292.

[13] *Ibid.,* p. 279. Also James S. Plant, *The Envelope,* New York, Commonwealth Fund, 1950, p. 31.

Physical education should require an adequate medical examination of all participants.

While many structures and functions of the individual need appraisal before participating in vigorous exercise, the heart and circulation are especially important. The growth of the heart is rapid during adolescence. Lucas reports that the volume of the heart increases from 160 to 225 cubic centimeters during adolescence. In these years variations in the heart rhythm may occur, palpitation may develop; these are signs of the instability of the circulation in this period of rapid growth. A competent examination will reveal the condition, and a program can be arranged suitable to the needs of the individual.

Functional dilation may occur as the result of vigorous exercise. During rest the normal heart discharges from 4 to 9 liters of blood per minute. During strenuous exercise this may be increased four times—from 16 to 36 liters per minute. If the heart rate doubles in that time this would account for about half of this increased volume; the other half of the volume attained would come from increased force of the heart beat. This greater force of the heart contraction results from dilation of the heart which puts the heart fibers on greater tension. There is of course a limit to this process and if dilation continues, the force of the heart decreases. For full explanation of these phenomena the student should read a good book on the physiology of exercise.[14]

The conclusion is inevitable, however, that the only sound basis for deciding the fitness of an individual for vigorous activity is a medical examination. No lay person is competent to decide this question. It should be noted that many physicians today restrict the physical activity of their cardiac patients much less than was formerly the custom in such cases. There are other conditions than the heart for disqualification of the player. Among these are hyperthyroidism, tuberculosis of the lungs, weak abdominal surgical scar, hernia, and others.

Physical education should excuse an individual from activity during an infection.

The notion that athletic participation produces an en-

[14] Edward C. Schneider, *op. cit.*

largement of the heart which is injurious to health is very wide-spread. In recent years, however, a new view of the heart holds that such a conclusion is wrong.

Hearts of persons engaging in strenuous sports or hard physical work will enlarge in response to the effort made in order to maintain an active circulation. This enlargement of the heart corresponds to the enlargement of other muscles when actively exercised. Exercise also increases the tone of the heart muscle, so that strength and firmness result rather than mere increase of bulk.

When, however, the heart is used vigorously during periods of infection — often not recognized — then there may be injury which accounts doubtless for the observations made about exercise and heart injury. In all instances of infection, the individual should remain at rest.

Physical education should adjust its program for adults to the level of their physical ability.

The individual reaches his peak in motor efficiency in most activities by 30 years of age. In the less vigorous sports, high proficiency may be maintained for twenty years more, but by the time the half-century mark is reached, strenuous activity is not desirable. It is true that individuals vary greatly in these matters and much depends upon the kind of life lived by the individual under consideration. The hazard in vigorous effort for the older person is in the heart, blood vessels, and joints.

Teachers of recreational activities for adults should remember the limitations that may exist among members of a group and not expect all persons to engage in all activities. Simple dances may be enjoyed for a short time but fatigue will come early to some persons, and swimming, skating, and other sports should be adjusted in time and effort to the condition of the players.

RESPIRATION

The first act of the child at birth is an inspiratory one. Breathing takes place by the operation of a competent mechanism. During infancy and early childhood the respiration of the child goes on without disturbance, but on entering school it has been the custom for certain exponents of physical education to assume that the child did not know how to breathe properly, or was in need of oxygen, or for these or other reasons there was the necessity to teach the child some breathing exercises. This practice is purely traditional and comes with all the other unacceptable procedures from the so-called systems of gymnastics. It is important to examine some of the physiology involved in respiration in order to determine intelligent procedure.

1. **The respiratory mechanism easily provides sufficient oxygen from ordinary air for the body needs.** The interchange of oxygen and carbon dioxide in the lungs takes place through the alveolar membrane of the lungs. This area is so large that an enormous margin of safety exists. For example, the alveolar absorption area is over twenty times the area required in normal breathing. It is not always appreciated that we use only about 25 per cent of all the oxygen we take into the lungs. People are greatly interested in getting oxygen and believe that the lungs need enlargement for this purpose, but the lungs are normally more than adequate. To enlarge the lungs more is, in a physiological sense, like carrying coals to Newcastle. Delhez reports an experiment with thirty-two males, free from respiratory infection, ages 12 to 15 years, who were taught to perform forced breathing exercises three times a week for fifteen minutes over a three-month period. The frequency and ordinary volume of spontaneous respiration was not changed by the practice of these exercises.[15]

2. **Is the amount of oxygen used by the tissues conditioned by the needs of the cells, or by the supply of oxygen?**

The above discussion answers this question in part, but there is additional evidence to prove that the needs of the cells at any one time determine the combustion of oxygen that will take place.

This point was settled by the German physiologist Pflüger, and elaborated more fully by the English physiologist Barcroft.

[15] L. Delhez, "The Immediate Effects of Respiratory Exercises," *Revue Belgique de Thérapie Physique*, February, 1960, p. 23.

It has been demonstrated that the cell takes up oxygen only in relation to its needs. It takes up only what it can use, and rejects the rest.

The evidence is clear that breathing exercises are of no value in relation to getting oxygen to the body cells at times other than those moments when there is a demand from the organs for this particular gas. The evidence supports the contention that the circulation meets the need created by the increased activity of the cells. It is a common observation that both circulatory and respiratory systems respond to the emergency by speeding up their functions. That these changes are subsequent to activity, that in no instance do they precede it, are data of importance for those who are concerned with the initiation and direction of programs of physical education.

3. Breathing exercises disturb the normal balance of the chemical elements of the blood and artificially throw out of harmony a relationship which the organism tends to maintain at all times.

The facts show that breathing exercises disturb the normal balance of acid and base elements of the blood. If forced breathing occurs, as in breathing exercises, carbon dioxide normally present in the blood can be decreased in amount. Afterwards the rate and depth of respirations decrease because the lack of carbon dioxide is also a lack of stimulus to the respiratory center. When the breathing exercises are stopped, the carbon dioxide accumulates in the blood until it is normal again, at which time the respirations return to normal.

Physical education should not, in general, teach breathing exercises.

In instances of certain chest defects breathing exercises may be used to correct certain depressed conditions. It would appear then that, except for corrective purposes in selected cases, breathing exercises are unscientific and probably harmful.

RECIPROCAL INNERVATION

We are indebted to Sherrington for the clear facts regarding reciprocal innervation. When impulses are sent to a group of muscles to produce action, at the same time other impulses go to the antagonists to inhibit their action. Thus, when a nerve impulse passes to the biceps causing it to contract, at the same time an impulse passes to the triceps causing it to relax. The result is a smooth and harmonious movement. This is normal; this is physiological. It is called reciprocal innervation.

Now the use of exercises at times is made to violate this very clear fact. So-called "resistive exercises" are advocated in certain systems, and in so-called "educational exercises" the individual is asked to hold the active and antagonistic muscle groups in a state of contraction. Thus, these movements are stiff, rigid, and hence unphysiological.

A direct application of this principle is seen in the learning of new movements. In skating, for example, the beginner holds himself stiff, due to the fear of falling and some doubt concerning his own ability to execute the movement. This stiffness, awkwardness, or lack of what is commonly called grace, is due to the fact that he is contracting antagonistic muscle groups, that he is inhibiting normal inhibitory impulses. The awkwardness of many gymnasts in general is due to large muscle masses in part; also to the kind of movements they have been practicing. The value of relaxation of muscle groups in golf, tennis, and other athletic performances, attested to by experts, is practical evidence in support of the argument made.

Physical education should avoid developing tenseness in the pupil and should teach relaxation as the normal state.

In this connection, the full application of Sherrington's contribution to movement should be stated. Contrary to popular notions which emphasize tense muscles, and contrary to popular words which praise the "go-getter" type of attitude which so frequently provokes tension, the normal physiological state is one of relaxation. This normal condition will depend upon the operation of numerous factors, such as balancing of body weights and avoidance of psychological tension, which is reflected readily in hypertonus of muscle.

The notion that it is good to relax arises out of a false concept of what is normal and desirable. The relaxed state is the normal; the tense condition is the abnormal. Relaxation should not be interpreted as slumping with respect to postures, nor as lack of tone with respect to muscles.

NORMAL LOAD, CREST-LOAD, AND OVER-LOAD

Schneider describes these three conditions as follows:

> . . . a load is a normal load as long as the intake of oxygen is adequate to supply the need of the body at the time the work is being done, thus balancing the oxygen account; it is a crest-load when the intake of oxygen is still equal to the demand, but when the oxygen supplying mechanisms (the breathing, the circulation, and the unloading of oxygen) are all working at top-notch capacity and are unable to increase further the delivery of oxygen; and it is an over-load when the intake of oxygen is insufficient to meet the demand, the oxygen account is over-drawn, and the oxygen debt steadily increases as the work continues.
>
> The crest-load is increased by physical training and decreased by disease. It is increased by moderate daily exercise and again decreased by the neglect of physical exercise. Thus in the case of a young man who spent an hour a day for two months playing tennis or handball the crest-load, which was 6000 ft. lb. as determined on a bicycle ergometer prior to beginning training, advanced to 7000 ft. lb. during the first week of training, then more slowly to 8000 ft. lb. by the end of the fifth week, and finally to 9000 ft. lb. at the end of the seventh week. Then because of a Thanksgiving Day recess with complete neglect of exercise for four days and less regular indulgence in exercise thereafter, the crest-load dropped back to approximately 8000 ft. lb.[16]

Physical education should provide in its programs for youth some activities that call for supreme effort.

In the process of maturation, muscles gain in strength and in size as a normal manifestation of growth. This condition persists until maturity is reached. Aside from this force, exercise increases the strength and size of muscles under certain conditions. When an individual executes movements that he performs

[16] Edward C. Schneider, *Physiology and Muscular Activity*, Philadelphia, Saunders, 1939, p. 66.

regularly and habitually, the muscles remain in good tone but there is no gain in size and strength. In order for gains in these directions to be secured, the individual must make special efforts; he must of necessity struggle to lift the weight, to climb the height, to jump the hazard, or whatever it is that requires more effort than he is accustomed to use. In this sort of exercise the muscles and vital organs carry a crest-load in the sense that the load is greater than the usual and commonplace. The principle operates more frequently in the years before maturity is reached, probably because the crest-load type of activity is more frequently selected by younger persons. It is obvious from these facts that gains in functional strength to perform work come only when the activity is vigorous enough to make full demands upon the oxygen-supplying mechanisms. Soviet investigators report that the development of strength, speed, and endurance is most effective when excessive physical strains are not produced.[17]

FUNDAMENTAL TO ACCESSORY

The common notion regarding the use of big muscle activities rests on belief in the widely accepted theory that development takes place from the fundamental to the accessory muscles. This theory may be interpreted to mean that the larger, older, and central muscles and nerve centers play a major part in the voluntary control of muscles and should be developed before the accessory ones are brought into play.

The meaning of this theory for physical education is of course to emphasize the use of the large muscles of the body rather than the small ones, but this might conceivably be entertained if based only on the physiological returns from the activity. It emphasizes also the use of free, spontaneous move-

[17] N. V. Zimkin, "The Importance of Size of Load, in Rate of Performance and Duration of Exercises, and of the Intervals Between Sessions in Relation to Effective Muscular Training," *Sechenov Physiological Journal of the U.S.S.R.*, 46:1000-12, 1960. (Abstracted in *Research Quarterly*, March, 1962, p. 156.)

ments before the voluntary. This will involve the fundamental before the accessory.

Physical education should stress the use of the large muscles of the trunk and hip joints.

It would appear that in addition to the physiological aspects of the matter, the use of the trunk or fundamental muscles should precede that of the extremities, and be developed in early years prior to any emphasis on training of extremities, because of the significance of trunk control in motor movements and the order of use in those acts involving the entire neuromuscular mechanism. Thus, in dancing, it is important not to dance only with the arms and legs but to use the trunk as the center of expression; in throwing, the torso is the major agent and the arms and legs complete the act; in golf, the trunk and arms synchronize but the control is largely in the torso; and in many other acts it is the trunk muscles and mechanism that hold the center of attention and control. From these considerations, then, physical education should interpret fundamental to accessory in terms of physiological and developmental values, and also in the light of certain kinesiologic explanations.

THE CONFERENCE ON FITNESS

On July 2, 1956, President Eisenhower called a Conference on Youth Fitness. Following this Conference, the President appointed a Council on Youth Fitness. On September 12-15, 1956, one hundred delegates assembled in Washington, D.C., to consider the problem of fitness of American youth. These delegates represented the field of physical education. Back of all this interest and activity was the report that 56.6 per cent of American children failed the Kraus-Weber Test, as compared with 8.2 per cent of European youth.

The Kraus-Weber Test consists of six exercises:

1. Ability to sit up from a supine position with legs straight, hands behind the neck, subject's feet held down by the examiner.

2. Same as for (1), only with knees bent and heels kept close to the buttocks.

3. Ability to raise the legs 30 degrees and hold for ten seconds from a supine position while the hands are held behind the neck and the legs are extended.

4. Ability to raise the trunk and hold for ten seconds. The subject begins the exercise from the prone position with a blanket under the abdomen, and hands held behind the neck, while the examiner holds the feet down and in contact with the table.

5. Ability to raise the legs and hold them in a raised position for ten seconds. The subject begins the exercise from the prone position, with hands on the table, blanket under the abdomen, with the examiner holding the upper back down with the chest in contact with the table.

6. Ability to bend over slowly from an erect position and touch the finger tips to the floor without bending the knees.

These tests lack criteria. There is no evidence that the tests indicate fitness or lack of fitness, and the scoring method used — *pass* or *fail* — does not indicate levels of ability. Publication of the report that American children were less fit than Swiss, Austrian, and Italian boys and girls led to an unwarranted assumption. The test items lacked validity. For example, the ability to bend over and touch the finger tips to the floor without bending the knees is a kind of "stunt" flexibility. It is almost as abnormal as the ability to wiggle the ears; it is dangerous for many adults, and its use by them results often in sacroiliac sprain. Indeed, this sixth item, performed more readily by girls than boys, accounts for the greatest number of failures in the test at every age level and makes the girls appear to be more muscularly fit than boys.[18]

Moreover, the comparison of American children with European children is valueless without a comparable study of the kinds of physical activities practiced by each group. Perhaps the greatest mistake is to assume that practice in these six exercises, with an inevitable improvement in test scores, is indica-

---

[18] Glenn Kirchner and Don Glines, "Comparative Analysis of Eugene, Oregon, Elementary School Children Using the Kraus-Weber Test of Minimum Muscular Fitness," *Research Quarterly*, March, 1957, p. 16.

tive of improvement in fitness. For example, a group of 2281 boys and girls in an Eastern school system were given the K-W Tests. Forty-two per cent of the children failed to pass the test. After vigorous conditioning exercises the test was given again two months later and only 8 per cent failed. Were these boys and girls more fit? Yes, they were more fit for passing this test, but could they run better or faster, play games better, dance better, swim better, show more sustained interest in outdoor life, and react to difficult emotional situations with greater poise, fairness, tolerance, and generosity? These real fitness qualities are not developed by push-ups, pull-ups, sit-ups, or touching the floor with the finger tips.

The evidence regarding the fitness of American youth is contradictory. F. H. Adams, L. M. Linde, and H. Miyake report a study of Swedish and California children:

> Physical work-capacity, using the bicycle ergometer, was determined in 196 normal Swedish country and city school children, 10 to 12 years of age. Work-capacity increased with age, weight, surface area, heart volume, and degree of physical education. Boys had greater work-capacity than did girls of the same age, body size, and heart volume. *There was no significant difference between these results and those obtained from California school children.*[19]

The impression prevails that the fitness of youth today is much less than a generation and more ago. Anna S. Espenschade and Helen E. Meleney report a comparison study of motor performances of junior high school boys and girls in 1934-45 and 1958-59. The results are summarized as follows:

1. Boys and girls of today are taller and heavier than were those of the same age, grade, and school twenty-four years ago.
2. Girls of today are significantly superior in jump and reach and "pull," but inferior to the earlier comparable group in dash, broad jump, and "push."
3. Boys of today are significantly superior in jump and reach,

---

[19] F. H. Adams, L. M. Linde, and H. Miyake, "The Physical Working Capacity of Normal School Children," *Pediatrics*, July, 1961.

throw for distance, Brace, grip, and pull, but inferior in dash and broad jump.

The authors make two significant comments: (1) "The present day program does not include track, whereas the 1934-35 program did"; and (2) "Superiority of today's group in most other events may be related to size since height and weight have been shown to correlate positively with performances of boys of 13.5 years."[20]

Physical education should never assume that its program is adequate; it should examine critically all that is done and revise its selection of activities, if necessary, so that all children, able to do so, can engage in vigorous activities.

It should be apparent to every physical educator that the President's Council on Youth Fitness may stimulate many persons to pay more attention to physical education in the schools and even to their own physical condition. On the whole this may be salutary. But in this as in other technical problems, lay judgment is usually not competent to recommend. The trained personnel in physical education should examine their programs and eliminate activities which do not provide vigorous exercise for children.

This does not mean that sound programs should be replaced by stupid calisthenics, most of which are not vigorous at all; they may appear to be effective only because they require the individual to move in unnatural ways.

Since the Conference on Youth Fitness in 1956, numerous individuals and committees have been engaged in studying the problem. The American Association for Health, Physical Education and Recreation formed a national committee to devise a battery of tests that could, with reasonable accuracy, measure some of the qualities of fitness. The battery proposed comprised seven items as follows: (1) pull-ups for boys; modified pull-ups for girls; (2) sit-ups; (3) shuttle run; (4) standing broad jump; (5) softball throw for distance; (6) 50-yard dash; and (7) 600-yard

[20] Anna S. Espenschade and Helen E. Meleney, "Motor Performances of Adolescent Boys and Girls of Today in Comparison with Those of 24 Years Ago," *Research Quarterly*, May, 1961, p. 186.

run-walk. Standards of performance for these test items have been validated.[21]

An interesting report by Richard H. Pohndorf gives the results of a study of the performances of British and United States children in the AAHPER fitness tests.[22] These tests were administered to 8500 American children. In 1958-59 the same tests were administered to more than 10,000 boys and girls, ages 10 to 17, from urban, rural, public and private, boys and girls, and coeducational schools, in England, Scotland, Wales, and Cyprus. Since American and British youth have similar experiences in sports, games, and recreational activities, a comparison of their performances in these tests was a logical study. The results show that the British boys are far superior to the United States boys in all the tests except the softball throw. The British girls are also superior to the United States girls, exclusive of the softball throw in which the United States girls excelled slightly at ages 12 and 15. The graphs in Figure 10 give the actual performances.

These tests and comparisons are valuable in stimulating greater interest in physical education. To the extent that more time is given to physical activities, more vigorous programs are pursued, and better teaching is promoted the results are likely to be valuable. There are, however, severe limitations to this sort of promotion. These should be mentioned.

1. Fitness depends upon more than exercise. While one cannot become or remain fit without exercise, physical activity alone is not enough.

2. Fitness is maintained over the years only if motivation is continually present. The tests do not provide the basis for an enduring motive.

3. Fitness depends upon adequate health knowledge and health practices; these are vital elements in fitness.

[21] *Youth Physical Fitness*, President's Council on Youth Fitness, Washington, D.C., July, 1961, pp. 44-55.
[22] Richard H. Pohndorf, "Physical Fitness of British and United States Children," Athletic Institute, 1961, pp. 8-16.

4. Fitness is not a uniform condition but a highly variable standard. Fitness for heavy work demands far more strength and endurance than is either reasonable or desirable for persons engaged in light occupations.

5. Fitness should not be associated with unusual or stunt performances, such as a 50-mile hike, which when once completed is likely to leave the untrained person convinced that he is not interested in fitness.

6. Finally, fitness for living depends upon motor skills that give satisfaction in performance, interests in motor forms of recreation, and emotional controls and attitudes that favor enjoyment and continuance of physical activities.

Physical education should understand that a program of Youth Fitness depends not primarily upon a plan but upon the persons who operate it.[23]

There is an old story about a young poet at the Court of King Charles IV. The poet asked a courtier, "How can I write an immortal song?" The courtier replied, "Look into your heart and write." The poet was young, ambitious, and eager; he wanted to write an immortal song. He wanted the courtier to give him a plan.

According to the legend, this happened many years ago. It was before the day when it was popular to plan. The courtier knew little or nothing about planning, a planned economy, or a planned immortal song. So he answered, "Look into your heart and write."

We in this modern world live in a period of planning. It is popular to plan. Some years ago, Russia in the convulsive throes of a revolution announced the first of many five-year plans. Later Germany had a four-year plan, and since 1932 Washington has formulated innumerable plans.

In the summer and fall of 1941, the American Associa-

[23] Part of this section is abridged from an article by the author, "Persons in a Plan," in *The Journal of Health and Physical Education*, June, 1942, p. 349.

tion of Health, Physical Education and Recreation announced a plan to cooperate with the Office of Civilian Defense in a program of physical fitness. It should be helpful in these days to recall what happened to a program that had an Advisory Board of representatives from fourteen national organizations and hundreds of program coordinators. In a few short months, the program blew up and the profession was caught in the falling debris. A plan perished and physical education was pilloried from coast to coast in cartoons and editorials.

Now, more than twenty years later, another plan for Youth Fitness is developing. Will it repeat the previous debacle? It is always persons who are central in such matters. There are

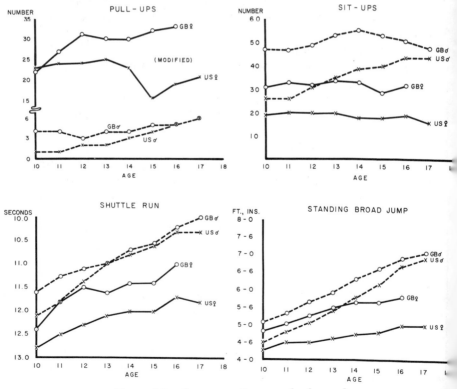

Figure 10.   See opposite page for legend.

four imperatives which ought to guide those who engage in this movement.

1. Be Fit Yourselves. You never improve your neighbor by talking to him—improve yourself. This is a fundamental principle, long recognized in human experience. Kant in his philosophy directed our attention to what he was pleased to call the *categorical imperative*. Every man has the obligation *to be* something. For us who sponsor an area of human behavior, Kant's imperative comes clearly—*be fit yourselves.*

It is not a cynical observation to report that the children of professors of education are often grossly neglected. Experience with human weakness led to the remark that the children of shoemakers go without shoes. It is easy to *be* for something

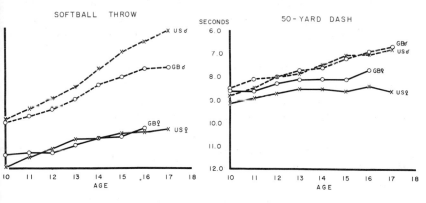

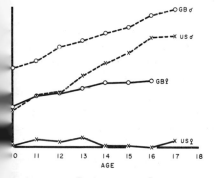

Figure 10. A comparison of the performance of 8500 boys and girls in the United States with that of 10,040 boys and girls in Great Britain on the AAHPER fitness tests. (Courtesy of Richard H. Pohndorf.)

in general; it is difficult to *be* for a particular line of action. No one of us speaks for fitness more eloquently than he who is fit. No song is more immortal than the one we sing each day as we take the hand of a friend, as we complete intelligently our daily regimen, and as we fulfill the responsibilities of every task which is ours. Our plan begins with ourselves. *Be fit.*

2. Know What You Mean by Fitness. It is always difficult to know what we mean. We will not agree always about the meaning of anything, we will probably not agree about the meaning of fitness, but know what *you* mean.

In reality there is no entity such as physical fitness. The persistence in our speech, customs, and traditions of old dualistic concepts of nature leads us to use phrases which we should have abandoned long ago. We hear about physical health, mental health, and physical fitness when we should be singing with Robert Browning, "Can soul help flesh more now than flesh helps soul?"

When we know what we mean by the term fitness, some of us will say that fitness is total, that how we think, how we feel, how we exercise, how we work, how we treat our friends — how we do all that comprises life — these determine our fitness.

It is obvious, of course, that every movement succeeds or fails, in part, because of the ideas behind it. When we believe that there is an entity — physical fitness — that we can develop in people by means of an exercise chart, we tie our hands behind our backs and stand mute and dumb before all that science says about organismic unity.

3. Examine Your Own Program. What kind of program are you promoting? Does it contribute to what you mean by the term fitness? Since national fitness is nothing more than the fitness of the people who compose the nation, your program is at the heart of the matter.

There is no better time than this to ask ourselves: Have we been riding a hobby? Have we been misled by some contagious enthusiasm? Have we promoted activities that failed to yield strength and tone of muscles, or generous behavior, or really functional skills, or purposes and interests which are excellent?

4. Stand on Your Own Feet. It is a common observation of anthropology that man has assumed over the years a biped position, which he retains with difficulty. Whether or not we remember that our ancestors lived in the Middle Ages, which accounted for many of our fears and superstitions, or that they lived in trees, which accounts for our ape-like characteristics, if we go back far enough, we have ancestors who were quadrupeds. Because of this fact and the bodily mechanics of the biped position, we must exert ourselves constantly to keep from slipping back into the primordial mud. We may recall that in one stage of our ancestral inheritance there is the flat worm, but that was very long ago. It means very little now. We must learn to stand on our own feet.

When some promoter tries to sell us a faulty program and to seek our support for an unsound plan using all the ballyhoo of patriotism and cooperation — *Stand on your own feet!*

When some "scientist" tries to capture your support for the exercise of touching the floor with the hands without bending the knees as a test of fitness — *Stand on your own feet!*

When some magazine seeks your endorsement of a "fitness costume" and tries to use your professional status for commercial purposes — *Stand on your own feet!*

Let not the great need for fitness of youth go unsatisfied — *Stand on your own feet!*

DEVELOPMENTAL HAZARDS OF NURSERY AND KINDERGARTEN CHILDREN

The early years of the child are given to pure growth. Gain in motor power and function is rapid and mass increases sharply. The child runs certain hazards of the communicable diseases, which may cause death, leave serious complications, or be relatively without significance. The death rate from such causes varies in different countries and in sections of any one country.

The child in this period is weak in self-control and nervous stability. Even allowing for the correction to be made in adult standards of judgment, the fact still remains that one of the serious hazards of development is the unstable nervous system. It is unwise to stimulate the child beyond the limits of his own free-play situation.

The instability of the nervous system which gives rise to neuroses, while more marked in children than in adults, is not to be regarded as characteristic of all children. Individual instability represents a hazard of development. Medical and educational help should be brought to bear upon such cases long before the child goes to school, and should be continued as needed in the years of school life. The neurotic child unguided is the forerunner of the adult neurasthenic.

By the time the child enters kindergarten he is either left- or right-handed. It is unwise to attempt to change this trait. He is a very active being but tires quickly; if not stimulated, he will rest when tired. If he is tired excessively, he is likely to be irritable.

During these years the death rate is decreasing and hazards of childhood are lessening somewhat. There still remain serious developmental chances of acquiring disease or defect, and hereditary deficiency may betray itself in the latter part of this period. Anemia, rickets, lack of energy, and skeletal defect are the outstanding dangers. The proper guidance and treatment for rickets is, of course, medical. It will consist of direct sunshine, cod liver oil, and diet. These children need the gentle stimulus of outdoor play.

The skeletal defects are mainly of the spine and feet. Some orthopedists regard all simple, at times called functional, deviations of the spine as the end-result of previous and unrecognized cases of anterior poliomyelitis. There is practically no scientific proof for this interpretation, but it should be kept in mind as a possibility when school sanitarians are inclined to place upon school seating, clothes, and habitual postures the onus for these lateral deviations of the spine. Within wide limits variations of the spine may be considered normal.

The importance of the defects of the feet is not to be overlooked in the enthusiasm for the more dramatic and apparently more serious deficiencies. Observation of the use made of the foot will reveal before entering school that there may be need for a lift of one heel, or a wedge on the inner aspect of the sole and heel to throw the weight to the other side. Kindergarten children should be carefully examined to determine these facts of use, and early correctional measures instituted. Candidates for army life, for industry, for insurance are examined at entrance, but children entering school are not always given the careful psychomedical examination they ought to have. The child entering school may be normal and ready for education; he may be handicapped and in need of special medical attention or educational adjustment. An adequate examination alone can determine this.

Physical education should advocate a medical examination for all nursery school and kindergarten children and a rational schedule of activity.

To determine the cases and their degree of defect is essential to right placement for school work and to their follow-up with appropriate treatment. For this work a school health service, comprising health examination and supervision, a psychological examination, and an educational analysis and placement are needed.

During this preschool period, the child is normally impelled to movement and activity. Care should be taken to prevent custom from interfering with this normal impulse and expression. Free games, a suitable diet, outdoor air, sunlight, and adequate rest are the essentials for normal development. For the normal child, given these essentials, no artificial method of exercise is required.

THE CHILD FROM 6 TO 10 YEARS OF AGE

The child in this period is rapidly gaining in strength, but it must be remembered that he still retains his infant characters.

The heart is still small. Its weight is about one-third of its adult weight, and yet it has to pump blood to a body that has two-thirds of its adult weight. There is at the same time a great increase in the desire for physical activity, and this, too, makes great demands on the heart. For these reasons there is imperative necessity that his activity be carefully guided and that undue demands in the form of vigorous competitive contests be avoided. Simple team games may be used but kept free from the stimulation to unusual activity occasioned by championship or other social pressures from a group. Some authorities call the later years of this period the fatigue years, and they may well be so regarded because of the slow development of the heart.

Physical education should pay attention especially to normal growth for children of this group.

This fact should point to the great need for out-of-door life and the right kind of food. So far as the program of physical education is concerned, here again the emphasis from scientific fact is on the out-of-door type of program rather than the traditional one of the school room. For the proper development of the child he cannot be out-of-doors too much. The emphasis in this period should be to secure normal growth.

During the early years of childhood, motor development interlocks with intellectual, social, and emotional development. Often motor development plays an important role as a vehicle for social development. Throughout childhood, and especially in the preschool and elementary school years, common motor activities are the ready means for a child's social contacts with his peers. Moreover, the child's motor development may bear directly upon emotional features of behavior. Thus, a child who is backward in motor development has occasion to be angry or afraid in the face of obstacles which the more skillful child will meet unemotionally.

The demands of sedentary school work are probably the most serious handicap to normal development in this period. Fatigue is a serious problem expressing itself in mobility, automatism, and dispersed and disordered movements. Studies of elementary children's weekly hours in class work in different countries show a range from the low of 15 hours in Switzerland to the high of 39 in Egypt. In the United States, the hours are 25 to 30. It is evident that a radical reorganization of the American school day is necessary before conditions for normal growth and development of all children can be established. Home work should be abolished for this age, diets must be improved, more outdoor life must be attained, and motor activity must be increased.

Boisterous games with much running and jumping are needed in this period. Form is not important, but incorrect patterns should be changed.

THE CHILD FROM 10 TO 14 YEARS OF AGE

This period is not sharply defined, and especially for the sexes there must be a certain latitude given in classification. Thus, we may well include here the girls from 9 to 14 and the boys from 10 to 15.

The child during this period is growing rapidly. This acceleration produces a marked increase of mass before the extensive developmental changes of adolescence. Heart irregularities are common, but these usually resolve into regular action. Curvature of the spine is frequent; strength is not yet developed, and supervision is at all times important.

The individual has a greater interest span and can profit from somewhat longer periods of motor activity. He desires group approval and shows growing interest in the opposite sex. Manifestly some interest in ideals and standard ways of behaving are acceptable.

Competition is keen and there is a feeling of respect for good sportsmanship. Prestige among his own classmates is more important than adult approval. Some children may show an unwholesome interest in their own health.

Physical education classes for boys and girls should be separated at the end of the fourth grade.

At the beginning of this period boys and girls prefer their

own kind of activity. It is a period of sex antagonism that is based on the efforts of each to find their own distinctive traits and qualities.

ADOLESCENCE

Puberty and adolescence are periods of dramatic change in the bodies, interests, abilities, and lives of boys and girls. It is a general principle that the faster the rate of change in human development, the greater the opportunity to influence the outcome.

The rapid growth of the adolescent is the popular sign of the profound changes taking place, but a less spectacular growth in height fails to conceal the mental and emotional shift characteristic of the period. The preadolescent spurt that marks puberty shows considerable variation in different children. This variation suggests that great restraint should be exercised in using tables of height and weight averages for this period; such tables have serious limitations when used as standards of nutrition for adolescents. In general, it is unwise to accept **mean** values of any of the descriptive items of this period.

During adolescence, boys become relatively broad shouldered in relation to hip width, while girls increase in hip width markedly. This is the approved cultural pattern as well as the factual picture, but many variations occur. Individuals may change in a few years from one physique to another. A boy who appears at 11 years of age to be an endomorph may at the age of 17 shows the athletic physique of the mesomorph. The understanding teacher will be aware of this fact of variation in both guidance and teaching.

The changes in the sex organs and the associated organic and personality transformations that accompany the maturation process are initiated by two hormones secreted by the anterior lobe of the pituitary gland. One of these is a growth hormone which stimulates in the healthy child normal growth for age. If the hormone is excessive in amount, then giantism of the pituitary type follows. The other hormone is gonadotrophic (gonad-stimulating). This hormone appears in the circulation just before the onset of puberty and is responsible for the development at that time of the ovaries and testes. The process continues and the male hormone initiates a series of changes in the voice, growth of hair, and muscle strength that characterize the male, while the female hormone produces changes in the breasts, mammary glands, skin, hips, and voice in the female.

There is usually nice coordination between these two hormones; one takes over where the other leaves off. At times, however, the balance is upset; if the growth hormone is dominated by the gonadotrophic one, children small in stature will show a precocious puberty, or if the action of the gonadotrophic hormone is delayed, the growth hormone produces a tall person who is quite immature.

The growth in organic systems may lag behind the growth in stature. The tall boy of 15 years of age may have not only undeveloped gonads but also immature respiratory, circulatory, and digestive systems. The boy or girl who matures early usually shows fewer organic disturbances and is much less of a problem in physical activities. An excellent summary of adolescence—changes and needs—is given in the 1962 Yearbook of the American Association for Health, Physical Education and Recreation.

Physical education should adjust the program of activities to the developmental status of the individual.

It is apparent that the maturation process with its individual differences requires sympathetic understanding by the teacher in all forms of physical education, and especially in sports where size may not indicate maturity and the pressures of the game may be excessive. Strength and physical ability are highly regarded by boys 13 to 15 years of age, and are more influential in determining popularity than other abilities. Athletic contests are suitable activities but they should occur in a natural social situation. Artificial stimulation by means of championships and record breaking should be avoided. These increase the competitive effort, and for boys under 18 years serious competitive effort is unwise. The rapid increase in weight, height, and size of internal organs demands high metabolic activity and generous supply of energy. Depletion of this by excessive activity is undesirable.

Work in school and elsewhere needs to be controlled with respect to other values. Rest, play, social dancing and recreation are essential. Holidays are not only social, they are also biological in effect.

The social adjustment of the adolescent to the adult culture of the industrial age is marked by considerable distress, not only of teachers and parents but also of the individual himself. In the age period 15 to 19, the death rate increases nearly 100 per cent, and in the period 10 to 14 years of age mental disorders increase tenfold. In addition to this deplorable loss, the social maladjustment is portrayed in the suicides, gangsters, vagrants, alcoholics, and drug addicts that come out of this period of stress. Health of the adolescent as in others is an achievement; it is not something lost in mysterious ways, but rather a fulfillment of the conditions of living, a meeting of the tasks and opportunities of life adequately and successfully. The failure of parents and teachers to appreciate the crucial character of the adolescent's problems often comes from the adult's inability to recall how important to **him** were such things as lack of height (boy) or excessive tallness (girl). When a defect is regarded by the individual as serious, then it may have marked effect upon the personality. An individual with marked defects is often made aware of his status quite early.

Physical education should adjust its program of vigorous activities to the climatic situation.

The American Medical Association's Committee on the Medical Aspects of Sports advises gradual adjustment of athletes to prevailing weather conditions in the following suggestions:

Require a careful medical history and checkup before the first practice.

Schedule workouts during cooler morning and early evening hours.

Acclimatize athletes in hot weather activity by carefully graduated practice schedules.

Provide rest periods of 15 to 30 minutes during workouts of an hour or more in hot weather.

Supply white clothing (to reflect heat) which is loose and comfortable (to permit heat escape) and permeable to moisture (to allow heat loss via sweat).

Furnish extra salt and water during hot weather.

Watch carefully for signs of trouble, particularly in determined athletes who may not report discomfort.

Remember that the temperature and humidity, not the sun, are the important factors. Heat exhaustion and heat stroke can occur in the shade.[24]

QUESTIONS AND PROBLEMS FOR DISCUSSION

1. What distinction do you make between nature and nurture? Which has more influence in the development of the individual?
2. How can we get a better world to live in? What can physical education do about it?
3. How may problems of physical education be clarified by referring them to the facts of nature?
4. Are the natural activities of man original in their present form? Explain.
5. Discuss the topic: The material of man is not by nature either good or bad.
6. With the increase of inventions and gadgets will the time ultimately come when man will have no need for muscles? Explain.
7. What is the meaning of the phrase The Whole Man? Discuss the implication of this concept with reference to the range of interests that a teacher of physical education might properly have.
8. Name and discuss some of the simple priorities of life with which physical education is concerned.
9. Discuss the statement that society can provide that kind of environment in which society believes.
10. What two roads representing ways of living does current life suggest? Which road appears to you more desirable? Is it worth recommending to all persons?
11. In the biological development of forms of life, what re-

[24] *AMA News*, September 2, 1963.

lation does the muscular system bear to the appearance of vital organs?

12. How can we increase indirectly the activity of the vital organs?

13. Why are calisthenic exercises in the classroom a poor kind of physical education? Are they any more suitable when performed in the gymnasium?

14. Can the school program provide all that elementary children need of activity? Explain. What implication follows from the position you take?

15. In what three respects is there failure in modern life to provide for the biological?

16. Discuss the statement that man is no better than his animal organism.

17. What are the disadvantages of the biped position? Why is it important to stress education in posturing? Why is the word posturing a better semantic choice than the word posture?

18. What are the fundamental movements of man? Why do they require teaching? Why should they still be stressed in their modifications?

19. What differences exist between the child's and adult's skeleton? What significance has this for physical education?

20. Why should the curves of the spine not be increased beyond normal? What does this mean in the choice of movements?

21. What sex differences are there in the pelves of men and women? Of what significance are these in running, jumping, hanging, and climbing?

22. What kinds of exercises are unsuitable for girls after adolescence? Why?

23. What is the difference between growth and development? Do children show a seasonal growth? Explain.

24. In what ways does physiological age indicate the development of a person? What significance has this for physical education?

25. What is Kretschmer's classification of body build? How does it compare with Sheldon's? What implications have physique types for physical education?

26. What is the Wetzel Grid?

27. What anatomical facts about the foot indicate the way the foot should be used?

28. What is the importance of a strong abdominal musculature?

29. What kind of exercises should be used in "warming up"? Why?
30. Why are training routines important in superior motor performance?
31. What is staleness? How may it be recognized?
32. Why should the athlete pass a medical examination before engaging in strenuous activities?
33. Would you allow a boy with a sore throat to play in a basketball contest? What would be your decision if he had a temperature above normal?
34. What kinds of physical activity would you recommend to a man of 50 years? 60 years?
35. Discuss the question of breathing exercises. Should breathing exercises ever be used? When?
36. What is reciprocal innervation? What are some of the causes of tenseness? Why should you promote relaxation?
37. What is the crest-load? Explain how the physiological load may be used to develop the powers of the individual.
38. Discuss the concept: fundamental to accessory. What are the reasons that indicate the importance of using the large muscles in the development of the individual?
39. What is the significance of criteria in evaluation of a test? What is the significance of the two comments made by Espenschade and Melency (p. 225)?
40. What specific activities would you list as vigorous for Elementary boys and girls? For Junior High pupils? For Senior High pupils?
41. What reasons can you suggest for the popular approval of touching the floor with the hands without bending the knees? Do persons in picking objects up from the ground generally move in that way? What are the limitations of the national physical fitness tests?
42. Discuss the developmental hazards in the life of the nursery school child and the kindergarten child.
43. Discuss the importance of the medical examination of children entering school and explain how uncorrected conditions at that time may affect the individual in later years.
44. Explain how lack of skill may affect the emotional behavior of a child. Discuss the following: "Where there's a skill, there's a way."
45. Why should boys and girls be separated in physical education classes?
46. Discuss the importance of adjustment of activities to the development of the individual in adolescence.

REFERENCE READINGS

American Medical Association. *The Wonderful Human Machine*. Chicago, 1961.

Bogert, L. Jean. *Nutrition and Physical Fitness*, 7th Edition. Philadelphia, Saunders, 1960.

Broer, Marion R. *Efficiency of Human Movement*. Philadelphia, Saunders, 1960.

Dauer, Victor P. *Fitness for Elementary School Children Through Physical Education*. Minneapolis, Burgess, 1962.

Davis, Elwood C., and Logan, Gene A. *Biophysical Values of Muscular Activity*. Dubuque, Iowa, Brown, 1961.

Hunsicker, Paul. "AAHPER Physical Fitness Test Battery." *Journal of Health—Physical Education—Recreation*, September, 1958, p. 24.

Hurlock, Elizabeth B. *Child Development*, 3rd Edition. New York, McGraw-Hill, 1956.

Hutt, Max L., and Gibby, Robert G. *The Child: Development and Adjustment*. Boston, Allyn & Bacon, 1959.

Karpovich, Peter V. *Physiology of Muscular Activity*, 5th Edition. Philadelphia, Saunders, 1959.

Lee, Murray J., and Lee, Dorris M. *The Child and His Development*. New York, Appleton-Century-Crofts, 1958.

Lentz, John L. "To Exercise or Not to Exercise." *Today's Health*, March, 1963.

Millard, Cecil Vernon. *Childhood Growth and Development in the Elementary School Years*, Revised Edition. Boston, Heath, 1958.

Partin, William C. "A Comparison of Three Approaches to Improving General Motor Ability." *Annual Proceedings of the College Physical Education Association*, 1961, p. 93.

President's Council on Youth Fitness. *Youth Physical Fitness*. Washington, D.C., Government Printing Office, 1961.

Tuttle, W. W., and Schottelius, Bryon A. *Textbook of Physiology*, 14th Edition. St. Louis, Mosby, 1961.

Van Huss, Wayne, et al. *Physical Activity in Modern Living*. Englewood Cliffs, N.J., Prentice-Hall, 1960.

THE NATURE OF MAN
—HIS PSYCHOLOGICAL
FOUNDATIONS

THE NATURE OF MAN —HIS PSYCHOLOGICAL FOUNDATIONS

The vitality of thought is in adventure.

Whitehead.

The sciences and arts arose by the impetus of wants, and continue in their service. They are the ultimate source of all values.

Thorndike.

To know in general is as easy as Aristotle indicated; but to know the when, the where, the wherefore, the where-unto, and the how much—this, as Aristotle concluded, is the final test of a wise man. An education which does not recognize this, and specifically provide for it, makes not wise men, but educated fools.

Gideonse.

If all mankind minus one were of one opinion, and only one person were of the contrary opinion, mankind would be no more justified in silencing that one person, than he, if he had the power, would be justified in silencing man-kind.

John Stuart Mill.

THE UNITY AND DIVERSITY OF MAN

The notions about **mind** and **body** held by man over the centuries have changed from time to time, and with these alterations, his ideas about education, its purposes, and methods have also changed. The concept of **mind** as a substance inhabiting the **body** prevailed long after the facts of organic unity were known, and it shaped the educational pattern of schools, which were conceived accordingly to be places for training the mind. This older notion that **mind** inhabited **body** and that **mind** and **body** existed quite independently as separate and disparate entities are, of course, not accepted today by modern psychologists. Among informed persons there is no respectable doubt concerning the unity of the organism. The concept of a unitary relationship between various functions is fully established. Thinking may be affected by the condition of the digestive tract, the amount of hemoglobin in the blood, and the secretions from various glands. It is from this point of view, then, that Herrick states that we do not think with the brain alone.[1] The old terms persist, however, but today the term mind is a name, not for a separate mental substance, but for a function of the individual.

Nevertheless, the organism shows not only relationships, but also diverse specializations. There are particular powers and these are dependent upon specific functional activity in particular organs. To declare that the whole child goes to school indicates that education should take into account all the significant functions of the living organism and should understand the relationships which exist. There is the danger, however, that this emphasis upon the whole child may lead to neglect of the particular.

We do not teach the whole child in general; we teach particular skills, we arouse particular interests, we present particu-

---

[1] C. J. Herrick, *The Thinking Machine*, Chicago, University of Chicago, 1929, p. 254.

lar concepts. It is the particular which we can grasp. The whole child may go to school, but his learning consists of such particulars as chinning himself, kicking a ball, writing words, adding numbers, and a countless number of specific things. The concept of relationships is helpful when it leads us to consider the various powers of the individual; it is hurtful when it leads to wishing for general good in the whole child. The concept of unity corrects the notion of separateness of **mind** and **body**, but the concept of diverse and specific functions provides the approach through which we teach.

The importance of particulars in relation to the concept of the whole child is stated in a recent school survey report as follows:

> But this emphasis upon the whole, as a general concept, should not lead to omission of the many particulars that enter into school experiences. Teachers are important particulars in the lives of children and the greatest care should be given to their selection and afterward to their guidance, conditions of work, and professional morale.
>
> Parents are particulars, and a very great extent of parental participation in all schools at all levels should contribute to more wholesome personality adjustment of children as parents learn, through guidance and proper programs, the functions of the school and the responsibilities of parents in the educational scheme.
>
> And other pupils are particulars. The spirit of a school is the reflection of the attitudes and behaviors of all the members of the school and constitutes a unifying and inspiriting force felt by every pupil. It is the prime business of teachers and administrators to promote industry in school work, enjoyment in play, self-discipline and self-reliance, willingness to face facts and to be guided by them; likewise, it is important to combat any disposition or action that represents the alibi, excuse in lieu of performance, rationalizations of failures, or undue stress upon success.[2]

THE SIGNIFICANCE OF INTEGRATION

For centuries the ideas of separate mind and body influenced education, legal concepts, and religious doctrines. In

[2] *Report of the Survey of the Pasadena City Schools*, 1951-1952, p. 382.

education these ideas led to plans for training the mind with little or no regard for the body. Today, the educational picture is considerably altered. Physical education is not conducted in order that mental training can go on but as a real part in itself of the educational process. And this change in attitude is not a concession to the insistent demands of physical education but a tardy, sometimes a partial, recognition of the basic facts of integration.

The concept of integration is growing also in physical education although there are individuals who are unable to alter their past convictions sufficiently to accept the principle of unity. If they were to examine not only the evidence from pertinent scientific fields but also their own experiences, the truth might dawn upon them. They would note that an athletic squad is a mere collection of athletes and that when these separate individuals coordinate their efforts in an integrated way, a team results. This simple illustration affords an example of how the individual personality operates. If man were muscles, bones, organs, nerves, emotions, ideas, and aspirations, all quite separate, the individual would be the abnormal psychotic being that results when integration is lacking. The normal person, on the other hand, is the integrated being. There is extensive evidence to support this conclusion.[3]

[3] The following works discuss this point:
Alvarez, W. C. *The Neuroses*. Philadelphia, Saunders, 1951.
Barton, Betsy. *And Now To Live Again*. New York, Appleton-Century-Crofts, 1944.
Cleckley, Hervey. *The Mask of Sanity*. St. Louis, Mosby, 1955.
Fetterman, J. L. "The Correlation of Psychic and Somatic Disorders." *Journal of the American Medical Association*, January, 1936.
Hartman, G. W. *Educational Psychology*. New York, American Book, 1941.
Johnson, Wendell. *People in Quandaries: The Semantics of Personal Adjustment*. New York, Harper, 1946.
Maier, N. R. F. *Frustration: The Study of Behavior Without a Goal*. New York, McGraw-Hill, 1948.
Pearson, G. H. J. *Emotional Disorders of Children*. New York, Norton, 1949.
Obertcuffer, Delbert. *Physical Education*. New York, Harper, 1962, pp. 49-65.
Sherrington, C. S. *The Integrative Action of the Nervous System*. New Haven, Yale University, 1906.

It is not to be supposed that integration of the personality is inherent in all experiences or that divisive forces do not exist that tend to cause disintegration. The contrary is true.

Physical education should accept the principle of integration and should use its services to prevent, so far as possible, disintegration of the person.

What is called mental is a manifestation of the whole; a person thinks with the thyroid gland, the tone of the muscles, the digestive process in addition to the brain. Also, what is called physical is a part of the whole; the hand is as much mind as body. The prime responsibility of physical education is to conceive of its work as related to all the reactions that participants experience, to be concerned for interests, moods, manners, morals, habits, and ideals as well as for strength, skill, agility, speed, safety, and endurance. The whole person participates; the whole person must be served.

Moreover, all teachers should be alert to recognize the divisive forces that tend to cause disintegration. The fat boy, the tall girl, the awkward adolescent, the many who are different from the average need thoughtful instruction and guidance. Young children are cruel in their franknesses to playmates and every group has ugly ducklings that need help. Oberteuffer gives numerous examples of disintegration that physical education can overcome.

PSYCHOLOGY AND INSTINCTS

Ideas about the existence and operation of instincts have changed. When two boys fought, this kind of behavior was explained formerly as due to the instinct of pugnacity which was an organization of force in the nervous system driving the young to engage in fighting. The term "instinct" defined a rather precise, specific, internal organization that operated, on the whole, remorselessly. The assignment of sex activity by Freud to a single, internal psychic force, called **libido,** is illustrative of this concept.

It has become increasingly apparent in recent years that

to name a behavior is not to explain it. The oversimplification, which results in the effort to classify, defeats the purpose of classification itself, which is to assist in thinking.

This denial of instincts as nervous entities which direct the individual to certain kinds of behavior does not reject as valid the observation that man tends to exhibit certain kinds of behavior. There is, then, acceptance of the notion of drives, impulses, and urges toward ends, but also greater emphasis upon the wide variety in which these may appear, the influence of organic bodily states upon their functioning, and the force of the environment in producing sweeping changes in the products of their activity.

The simple forms of animal life manifest impulses, drives and urges to action. They are not entirely quiescent, waiting only until something happens. The ameba puts out its pseudopodia. It needs something. It acts. There are urges of some kind. It is not possible to explain what they are, although the older psychology attempted to explain Napoleon, for example, in terms of will-to-power, ambition, cruelty, and similar terms for exact, specific and separate instincts.

If we regard man as an organism which over the years has had certain experiences, we can understand the persistence of urges to kinds of action as readily as we can the presence of skeletal, muscular, and organic patterns. Man is the product of the possibilities within the organism and the experiences which have occurred.

Physical education should recognize the principle of readiness of the individual to engage in certain kinds of movement.

The inner urges of an individual denote a readiness to act in certain ways. It is obvious that children are constructed not only of muscles and bones but also of urges to engage in certain motor activities, such as running, throwing, jumping, climbing, and hanging. Refusal to accept the doctrine that there is an instinct for running does not demand also the rejection of the idea of a readiness in structure to act in certain ways.

It is not possible to state where this readiness resides nor of what it does consist. The best guess of its location is the entire organism and doubtless its composition is glandular as well as nervous, bony as well as muscular, structural as well as functional.

Hence it appears that physical education begins with these impulses of children to engage in certain kinds of movement. Children are ready to run, to jump, to throw, to climb, and to hang. Moreover, they are not only ready, but are urged by this readiness to engage in the activity. In the face of this modern understanding of the organism, it would require rather overwhelming proof and most convincing argument that we should teach children invented arm, leg and trunk movements, severely different from those which the child is prepared by nature to do.

Eleanor Metheny gives an excellent statement of the readiness of man to engage in certain motor activities as follows:

> Why do intelligent people like us spend many hours in the hot sun batting a tennis ball back and forth across a net? Why do we walk miles on tired feet in pursuit of a golf ball? Why do we bounce on trampolines, circle high bars, dive from diving boards into cold water, and stretch our ligaments on the practice bar in a dance studio?
>
> Why do we do these things? To become physically fit? To develop our ability to learn by doing? To improve our human relationships? Certainly all of these things can and do result from these movement experiences—but even more certainly, these are not our basic motivations in seeking those experiences. We do them because we find these movement experiences meaningful in their own right.
>
> We play tennis for the same reason that men paint pictures, sing, play musical instruments, devise and solve algebraic equations, and fly airplanes. We play tennis because it satisfies our human need to use our human abilities, to experience ourselves as significant, creative, and, therefore, personalized beings in an impersonal world. We do these things to intensify, structure, and enhance the sensory perceptions that are our only direct source of information about ourselves and the world we live in; and these sensory perceptions are the source of the human meanings we find in our human lives.[4]

[4] Eleanor Metheny, "The Unique Meaning Inherent in Human Movement," *The Physical Educator*, March, 1961, p. 3.

Moreover, the readiness of the organism to engage in forms of behavior gives a clue to habit formation. In young persons impulses are the highly flexible focal points for widely diversified activities. Any impulse may become organized into one of several possible habits according to the situation in which it operates. As Dewey observes:

> Fear may become abject cowardice, prudent caution, reverence for superiors or respect for equals; an agency for credulous swallowing of absurd superstitions or for wary scepticism. A man may be chiefly afraid of the spirits of his ancestors, of officials, of arousing the disapproval of his associates, of being deceived, of fresh air, or of Bolshevism. The actual outcome depends upon how the impulse of fear is interwoven with other impulses. This depends in turn upon the outlets and inhibitions supplied by the social environment.[5]

This readiness of the organism, however, does not mean that any habit may accrue from any impulse. The impulse to run cannot be shaped by experience into the habit of erect posture. The old orthodox psychology isolated the individual from his surroundings. Modern psychology insists not only that behavior is an expression of the total situation — organism and environment — but also that impulses are the foci for the formation of habits, the materials out of which new habits arise. It would seem, therefore, but the simplest conclusion of common sense that teachers of physical education should take advantage of the impulses toward activity and seek to develop habits with respect to running easily and well, throwing accurately, jumping and landing with weight control rather than types of habituations which are foreign to the matrix of native impulse.

Finally, impulses for movement are relatively permanent. Bodily efficiency wanes early; the athlete is at his best in his twenties, and after 30 he has passed his peak. This is well illustrated in baseball and boxing. The urge for excellence is highest during adolescence, unless kept up by commercial rewards. But in spite of these fading bodily coordinations the impulses behind them persist and ask for activity.

[5] John Dewey, *Human Nature and Conduct*, New York, Holt, 1922, p. 95.

Physical education in methods and materials of instruction should reflect modern psychology.

Modern physical education in its scientific and theoretical views recognizes that it deals with activities which carry with them an inner urge to do the very thing that the competent leader of the activity desires to set going. There seems therefore to be little justification for him to use extrinsic incentives because he is working with organizations, already set up and running, which provide their own intrinsic drives. The leader, however, may wish to direct the activity toward ends which are not inherent in the activity when left to its own propulsions. This is always the true function of the teacher — to use native impulses of the young as the starting points for assimilation of the knowledge, acquirement of the skills, and development of the habits of the society into which youth comes. The accumulated power of society is transferred into the personal ability of the individual. This is the social meaning of growth and development.

Psychologically, then, man is not a "definite collection of primary instincts" which may be numbered, catalogued and exhaustively described one by one, but an individual — still with driving impulses to action — responding to the play of many forces upon him. The forces of environment differentiate among individuals, the responses of all 10-year-olds are not the same to an identical situation. Munn states that this differentiating influence of the environment becomes increasingly great as one goes from the lower animals to man and "the more complex the organism, the more susceptible it is to these differentiating effects."[6]

In the newer views, the organism manifests energy in unstable equilibrium. This equilibrium is continuously disturbed, and continual effort to restore the balance goes on. Illustrations of this from the field of physiology are numerous. The impulses (called by some strains or tensions) lead to activity to satisfy needs of the organism, and the very activity disturbs

[6] N. L. Munn, *Psychological Development*, Boston, Houghton Mifflin, 1938, p. 51.

some physiological equilibrium that in turn is restored by organic function. The dynamics of living organisms then are the continual efforts to maintain an equilibrium. The interaction between the organism and the environment is continual.

But this general statement does not deposit all persons in a single mold. Within this pattern of interacting organism and environment there is the uniqueness of impulses and habits of every person. Jennings writes in this connection,

> The most important contribution of biology: . . . human beings are endowed with diverse tastes, temperaments, aptitudes, diverse ways of responding to the same conditions. And that, therefore, as Davenport has well put it, there can be no **impersonal** science or art, of medicine, of hygiene, of education; of any matter that deals with human beings. Always the nature of the particular individual dealt with must be taken into consideration.[7]

HABITS

Experience is not a passive affair. In response to stimulation the organism projects itself actively into the situation, seeking the experience and even attempting to open up new areas of experience. This restless activity for food, for mates, for shelter, and other desirable ends leads to manifold activities marked by curiosity, invention, and discovery so that satisfactions may be more complete or more general or more lasting. The picture is not that of passive self-preservation but an exceedingly active effort at self-expression and self-realization.

This activity exhibits the impulses, urges, and drives of the organism in a wide variety of expressions, modified in a countless number of ways by the play of diverse environmental forces upon them. Out of this tremendous activity, however, ways of acting become established as habits. Habits then are secondary and acquired.

Physical education should take into account the facts

[7] H. S. Jennings, *The Biological Basis of Human Nature*, New York, Norton, 1930, p. 222.

about habit formation in its efforts to produce certain habit-uations.

Habits are ways of behaving in the environment. They are not independent of the environment but require rather co-operation of the organism and environment. The innumerable habitual reactions which a person makes are not his private possession but always adaptations of a pattern with the various forces playing upon a person. The habit quality in posture shows this dual relationship. The posture of a boy in school before the principal and that of the same boy on the athletic field reveal the varying quality of the pattern and suggest the influence of outside forces. This, of course, is contrary to the ideals of the posture enthusiasts. They want the boy, for example, to possess a habit which will always give the same pattern response. Habits may be acquired which are so rigid and inflexible that variation is rarely possible, and that even strong stimulations from without do nothing to alter. Only the utmost confidence in one's judgment of what is desirable would lead a teacher to secure such habituation. Nothing is left for improvement and nothing expected from adjustment. If the habit of brushing the teeth with up and down strokes of the brush, as taught a few years ago, had been formed as a rigid and inflexible routine, the emphasis of present-day vibratory technique would be futile indeed.

HOW MAN LEARNS

Gardner Murphy writes: "Most learning springs from struggle. The motivated individual strives, blindly or intelligently, to find the means of satisfaction. As he strives, he discovers things and activities that bring him into contact with the source of satisfaction. These things and activities come to elicit, in their own right, part (or sometimes all) of the responses made to the satisfier itself."[8]

When learning was supposed to depend upon mere rep-

[8] Gardner Murphy, *Personality*, New York, Harper, 1947, p. 192.

etition its explanation was easy. The problem, however, of how one learns is far more complex, and several conditions must be examined in order to understand the elements of the process.

It is a principle of psychology that motor functions appear at a rate commensurate with the maturation of those structures which are essential to performance of the functions. This is known as the structure-function principle. It is necessary, therefore, that various organs and tissues reach a certain structural stage before certain motor skills can be exercised. Tilney asserts that all bodily structures must "attain adequate differentiation before they are capable of highly specialized reactions."[9] Gesell confirms this principle that only when appropriate body structures mature sufficiently can the complicated motor functions of which the individual is capable be called into action.[10]

It is clear then that motor ability in the young advances as the individual matures. The young child should have every opportunity to exercise his muscles but should not be stimulated to attempt skills beyond his maturational level. Maturation and learning are not separate processes but rather are two aspects of an inseparable structure-function relationship. Structure must exist before function can operate and exercise of function promotes structural growth. *Motor learning is not a special kind of learning. It conforms in all essential respects to the same psychological principles which operate in all acquired reactions.*

The behavior of the individual reflects the demands that the environment makes upon him. In a backward community where knowledge is restricted to a few areas, learning is also restricted; the child acquires knowledge and skills over a wide area when these are essential in the realization of the goals that come out of his environment. The play of the various forces of

[9] Frederick Tilney, In foreword to *Growth: A Study of Johnny and Jimmy,* by Myrtle B. McGraw, New York, Appleton-Century-Crofts, 1935.

[10] Arnold Gesell, "Maturation and the Patterning of Behavior," *Handbook of Child Psychology,* Worcester, Mass., Clark University, 1933, p. 210.

the environment upon man is constant; he is shaped by them and learns from them. We get most of our notions of social behavior, many of our attitudes and appreciations out of the varied environmental demands of the home, school, church, and other social institutions of society.

The meaning of environmental learning has important implications for physical education. The environment varies and the learner must take into account changes in the environment; he must adjust means to reach his desired goal. Thus, the golfer adjusts his club to the incline of the ground, the kicker his punt to the direction of the wind, and the runner his stride to the condition of the ground. The social environment may stimulate the learner to fine sportsmanship or the opposite; it may influence not only the athletes who compete but also the learnings of those who belong to the school.

Virginia F. Harrison in a review of the experimental literature on motor learning reports that various investigators have found that there are emotional and temporal factors in motor learning and that mental practice of particular skills improves performance.[11] Ryan in his study of the effects of stress on motor performance and learning determined that increased tension impaired the performance of a difficult motor task but had no effect on the rate of learning.[12]

Physical education should take into account the psychology of readiness.

There is considerable evidence to show that readiness to learn is an important factor in acquiring knowledge and skill. The import of this is clear when young children are introduced to experiences for which they are not ready. In learning motor skills, maturity of sensory and kinesthetic mechanisms is doubtless important; in some instances muscle strength is a factor. But readiness may depend also upon stimulation and training. Teachers help children become ready by the way material is presented to them and by the success children achieve.

---

[11] Virginia F. Harrison, "A Review of the Neuromuscular Bases for Motor Learning," *Research Quarterly*, March, 1962, p. 59.

[12] E. Dean Ryan, "Effects of Stress on Motor Performance and Learning," *Research Quarterly*, March, 1962, p. 111.

This fact of readiness suggests that activities should not be either above or below the ability of the individual. Perhaps the former is more important; certainly for this and other reasons elementary school children should not engage in competitive contests in the pattern of high school athletics.

Physical education should take into account the psychology of intent or purpose.

When the individual intends to learn, the outcome is most favorable; now he has purpose directed toward an end. Pupils vary in ability to possess purpose, and those who have it vary in degree to which it operates. Little is known of the way to develop intent, but there is agreement that this attitude is influenced by the general atmosphere of the teaching situation. One readily intends to learn when a worthy goal appears and the thing to be learned has merit in the eyes of the learner.

In physical education conspicuous differences are noted in the attitudes of those who elect to participate in an activity of their own choosing and of those who meet a requirement. Learning is far more rapid in the former and probably depends upon the intention that the individual brings to the experience. The dynamic force of intent may be shown when one's progress in learning seems to be stalled and is recovered by an increase of purpose. When progress in learning a skill lags, it is wise to ask the question, "Am I as strongly impelled to make headway as I should be?"

Physical education should give attention to stimulating, guiding, and controlling motives in relation to activities.

Motive, somewhat like intent, gives to the learner a drive that energizes the individual in the experience. The motives of men are most varied, and the goals they seek are endless in number. Because they are personal, they cannot be imposed from without; they are dynamic inner drives from within.

When there is motive to engage in an activity, then the individual is energized for action. Marks, prizes, and awards are often employed to motivate a program, but such extrinsic motives soon lose their appeal; even when operative for a time, they are less worthy than an inner desire for the activity as experience.

Some of the motives to engage in physical activity appear to be innate, as in chasing and fleeing games; others appear to be acquired and to result from training and environmental opportunity. The distinction is not significant, since the urge to engage in movement, which provides an inner satisfaction to the participant, is present in the more complex and highly organized activities as well as in the simple fighting plays.

Motives make an individual select some activities over others. In some cases the selection is based upon the intrinsic qualities of the activity itself; in others the choice depends upon some extrinsic factor, such as social relationships, chance to succeed, or others.

Recognition of need by the learner motivates strongly. Now there is purpose that makes the visualized activity come within reach. At times, the teacher can help pupils to see needs, but to be effective for action they must be felt by the learner. Often boys will postpone learning the social dance until the need for the skill is felt; to teach it earlier may serve no useful purpose. To earn a place on an athletic team, to become eligible for membership in a club where the standards of admission are skill and not age, or to wear the school letter on a sweater may be powerful motives that drive the individual through long practices over long periods of time.

Many grown persons remain unskilled because they lack motive to develop their native capacities. They tolerate in themselves needless inefficiency. Learning, therefore, is dependent upon the attitude taken toward the activity, the set of the mind, and the motive behind the act. Mursell stresses the importance of an aggressive will toward the matter to be learned; this attitude contrasts with a wishful thinking response.[13] Much of the poor walking among adults is due to the lack of purpose to walk better, to discover the exact coordinations required, and to have a motive for improvement.

Motive is an incentive but many physical education activities carry their own incentives. Most boys are eager to play a game; often there is no incentive to play it excellently or to

[13] J. L. Mursell, *Streamline Your Mind*, Philadelphia, Lippincott, 1936.

master the basic skills of the game; in this situation the skillful teacher may arouse motive to improve by an encouraging word or a pertinent comment.

Physical education should offer activities that will afford satisfaction to the learner.

The Chinese philosopher Lin Yutang observes that all satisfactions imply want. It is common observation that individuals like to do certain things and dislike to do others. People spend their lives striving for certain situations and dodging other situations. This represents a fact of human nature and should be understood in its entirety and in relation to the learning process. Thorndike writes, "Civilized man is . . . set to attain certain results in a large fraction of his waking life, and what the environment offers him in the way of satisfiers is usually relevant to some one of the wants which are responsible for the activity of the period in question."[14]

Kilpatrick stresses the fact that one learns what one accepts, which is another way of saying what is satisfying.

The experience that the learner goes through produces effects upon the individual. If these are satisfying, then he tends to repeat the process and to learn those reactions which are accompanied or followed by satisfying states. In this view, then, the process of learning is modified by the consequences incurred; human experience testifies widely to the fact that behavior is modified by consequences.

Success and failure relate to states of satisfaction or annoyance that persons experience. Success is a stimulant and gives profound satisfaction; it strengthens performance, releases further energy, and promotes effort. Failure displeases; there is no want that is met by its presence. It may promote indifference to an activity when all that is needed to secure interest is some measure of success. Success and failure are related to the level of aspiration. If the goal is too high, failure is certain for some persons; often the measure of success is not the actual performance but the individual's level of aspiration. Some per-

[14] E. L. Thorndike, *The Psychology of Wants, Interests, and Attitudes,* New York, Appleton-Century-Crofts, 1935, p. 50.

sons can never make the varsity team, and can be satisfied with the scrubs; others suffer the vicious pangs of failure because the varsity alone is worthy.

Thorndike observes that satisfaction may be extrinsic to the experience and exist as rewards of various kinds. On this point, he writes as follows:

> Learning and work in homes, schools, and shops is, and perhaps always will be, loaded with many items which have little or no intrinsic interest to the learner or worker. He is induced, or induces himself, to learn them by appeals to pride, self-respect, love of parents, desire for approval, prudence, and the like.[15]

Learning produces changes in the individual. The precise character of the change is unknown, but the effects of use upon form are recognized by all. Since the whole person is involved in a learning situation, psychology agrees with the physiological concept of related and correlated functioning of all organs, and the integrative functioning of the nervous system. Major changes may occur in the nervous system but other structures are doubtless involved also.

Physical education should state its goals clearly.

It is important that the learner know precisely the nature and form of his objective. The first step in the teaching of skills is to give the pupil a clear idea of the end to be achieved. As he progresses in the experience, he tends to approximate the successful performance that he has in view. After each trial, the learner can judge his performance by the objective and so modify his next trial in the light of what he has accomplished and what he desires to attain.

In visualizing the objective, it is a mistake to attempt to concentrate on bodily sensations associated with successful performance of the movement. Subjective thought usually interferes with bodily function. There may be cautions considered or cues given, such as, "Keep your eye on the ball." They are enough in that direction. If one is trying to pitch a baseball

---

[15] E. L. Thorndike, *The Original Nature of Man*, New York, Teachers College, Columbia University, 1919, p. 108.

over the plate, he should look at the plate, go through the wind-up, and at the last moment before delivery look at the catcher's glove. If he has a fault to correct, he will during the windup pay attention to that, but when it no longer impedes his perform-ance, it is better to think no more about it. At the end of the act, he should pay attention to where the ball went; was the pitch successful, and if not, why not? In games of speed, such as basketball, the passing of the ball and the try for goal occur so rapidly that any attempt to concentrate on bodily sensations would defeat the tactics of play.

In some of the complex skills, for example, golf, the per-formance may at times be poor even after a considerable degree of skill has been attained. Often the player cannot diagnose the difficulty for himself and so requires the help of a capable golfer to discover the fault and to eliminate the troublesome reaction. The good teacher or coach has the ability to pick out the par-ticular difficulty that a learner faces, to discern why he misses certain balls, fails to block an opponent, or is slow off the mark.

Physical education should facilitate insight into a motor coordination by clear analysis of the problem.

Insight into the nature of the problem to be solved facili-tates learning. When the individual discerns the true features of a situation and understands it as a whole, he has insight; at that moment learning proceeds rapidly in contrast with the sit-uation in which the learner fails to comprehend exactly what is to be done.

The insight phenomenon probably appears in every form of motor learning. After long and relatively unsuccessful prac-tices, the skill may come very rapidly and quite suddenly. The comparative swiftness of the final stages of some motor skills suggests that some cellular organization within the body is nec-essary to the mastery of the skill. The old saying that we learn to swim in the winter and to skate in the summer is to be ex-plained in terms of this insight phenomenon. In this connection Hartman writes as follows:

> Differences in motivation, social and physical factors, and per-haps sheer maturation determine many details, but the broad picture is clear enough. A long period of little or no measurable

headway, then a sharp, quick rise followed by a slower and less spectacular gain in the learning curve—this is the type followed by skills that have an all-or-nothing character. The difference between swimming and nonswimming is usually apparent to an observer, although the nonswimming stage of effort appears to be necessary to prepare the ground.[16]

When insight comes, the individual is aware that progress is being made; this is a stimulant to further successes. In general it is better to consider the total response rather than to fix attention upon correct and incorrect parts of the whole. In skating, golf, tennis, football, and similar complex skills, correction of errors is essential, but this should never intrude enough to overshadow attention upon the total response.

Physical education should conduct its activities on the principle that the whole person is involved.

It is agreed that the whole person learns and not merely nerves or muscles. This "whole" concept is apparent in such an activity as broad jumping. In the act there are technical learnings, such as the approach, the take-off, the form in the air, and the landing; these involve the whole organism and not merely muscles and nerves. Moreover, other learning takes place. The jumper is learning attitudes about the activity, the teacher who instructs him, and his fellows who share the experience either as team mates or opponents. These concomitants cannot be excluded from the process; they are as inevitable as the ideas he acquires about training for the jump, the kind of shoe most suitable for the act, or the process of "warming up" before putting his muscles to the test.

The teacher of physical education may ignore these concomitants and center his attention solely upon the technical phases of the act, but they arise in the experience nevertheless. At this point, teachers become great or remain ordinary; the great teacher knows that he is teaching the whole person and therefore takes the whole person into account.

Physical education should use both the whole and part methods in teaching motor skills.

[16] G. W. Hartman, *Educational Psychology*, New York, American Book, 1941, p. 303.

There are many conclusions that the whole method is better than the piecemeal one. It is the accepted method in teaching swimming today.

Nevertheless, the whole-part problem is not a simple one. In the first place, it is important that the unit to be learned is a functional whole. The whole method is greatly superior to part learning when the material to be learned is "closely articulated internally and tightly knit in structure." Swinging a tennis racquet is a closely articulated and tightly knit structure; it illustrates what is meant by teaching a whole. Murphy gives some excellent suggestions for teaching tennis to beginners which illustrate several principles of learning. With respect to whole or part methods he advises as follows:

> A reasonable amount of proficiency in the basic strokes is a prerequisite to tennis play, and the drill-on-parts method is the most effective method of acquiring these and other necessary skills. . . . The whole method should be used only after the pupil has achieved a reasonable degree of success in the basic strokes.[17]

It is apparent that there can be considerable misunderstanding in employing the whole or part method until the unit is defined. Teachers of tennis will gain many helpful suggestions from Murphy's article.

It is always advisable to use the largest whole permitted by the material and the level of development of the learner. Putting various unrelated exercises into a lesson is not comparable to the wholeness in the act of swimming. The superiority of the whole method depends precisely upon this fact that in physical education much of the program consists of functional wholes, such as a game, a dance, a stunt, or some other complete act. In the second place, the value of the whole method rests upon the learner's comprehension of the whole pattern to be learned. In swimming instruction, for example, it is difficult for all learners to understand what the legs, arms, and head are to do in the whole act of keeping afloat and moving through the water. There-

[17] Chet Murphy, "Principles of Learning with Implications for Teaching Tennis," *Journal of Health—Physical Education—Recreation,* February, 1962, p. 26.

fore, when the skill is very complex so the pattern cannot be apprehended readily, then it is wise to break the whole into its functional parts.[18] Thus, the leg movements may be taught while the learner hangs on to the edge of the pool, the breathing may be taught while the swimmer stands in shallow water. These are functional wholes and should be integrated into the complete act as soon as possible. Another illustration will help to make the meaning clear. The kip-up on the high horizontal bar should be broken up for most learners into the forward swing with body arch, the back swing with feet elevated to the bar, and finally the thrust which completes the act. In such an analysis, it is important to keep in mind the relation of parts to the whole. In learning to juggle, Knapp and Dixon found the whole method superior.[19]

Physical education should not expect unrelated skills to transfer.

The old view held by some persons today who seek to speak for educational methods is that memory, discrimination, judgment, deliberation, reasoning, skill, attention, order and obedience are general powers of the mind and that they can be added to very much as you add to a pile of bricks by putting more bricks on the pile. Thus, the school is looked upon as the agency for the development of these general faculties. Typical of this view is the following:

> This is primarily the training of subjective motor control and incidentally of attention, will, and self-discipline. For developing the character and cultivating a wholesome temperament there is no discipline superior to athletics. Will power and attention are educated by gymnastics. The Battle of Waterloo was won on the playing fields of Eton.

Numerous experiments have been performed to determine the truth concerning the transfer of ability in one capacity to that

[18] John O. Lewellen, "A Comparative Study of Two Methods of Teaching Beginning Swimming," Doctoral Dissertation (unpublished), Stanford University. Abstract, *Fifty-fifth Annual Proceedings, College Physical Education Association,* 1952, p. 71.
[19] Clyde G. Knapp and W. Robert Dixon, "Learning to Juggle II. A Study of Whole and Part Methods," *Research Quarterly,* December, 1952, p. 398.

in another. James' first experiments in 1890 have been followed with numerous other ones. If transfer is to occur there must be identical components. Gates phrases this view as follows:

> The theory of identical components, then, would deny that practice in tennis would improve one's attention, will power or temperament for meeting all situations or dealing with all kinds of data equally but would affirm that certain skills, **procedures**, and **attitudes** such as judging the flight of a ball, remembering to keep one's eye on the ball, and to keep cool by thinking of the game instead of the spectators would carry over to another activity such as handball to the extent, roughly, that the two games and the general situations have important characteristics in common.[20]

It is evident that transfer of training does occur, but not in the form believed to be true some years ago. It is obvious that increased strength of leg muscles from bicycle riding may be useful in climbing mountains, and that increased strength of arms from rowing may help in chinning the horizontal bar. Therefore, wherever strength of muscle is involved and not skill of movement, then the power available can be used in situations other than those in which it was developed. Generally, however, skill is involved; strength then is useless without learned reactions in which it can be used.

Transfer is not automatic. The more meaning there is in an experience the more likely it is that something will be carried over. Development of an attitude of fair play may be so generalized by an individual that he tends to be fair in situations other than that in which it arose, but this is not likely to occur unless there is a deliberate attempt to interpret new situations in the light of past experience and to apply appropriately the meanings or methods previously learned.

Applied to the problems of physical education it would appear that there is no evidence for and considerable evidence against the notion that ability gained in arm swinging upward above the head will result in anything more than arm swinging upward above the head or something very similar to that, for

[20] A. I. Gates, A. T. Jersild, T. R. McConnell, and R. C. Challman, *Educational Psychology*, New York, Macmillan, 1942, p. 514.

example, arm thrusting upward above the head. The accuracy
and alertness so confidently written about leave the impression
that the participant in certain exercises acquires an increase in
accuracy as a capacity. It would be reasonable to expect if such
were the case that there would result greater accuracy in typewriting, in delivering messages, in citing dates and references in
books, and in numerous other ways from being accurate in response-command exercises. Such is not the case, however.
Elizabeth Rodgers' study on the learning of game skills supports
the theory of identical components.[21]

The evidence indicates that transfer may take place under
certain conditions. Allport holds that the equivalences and
resemblances we often see among objects that have no obvious
identity of components form the real basis for transfer. Moreover, the more meaningful the learning, the more likely it is
to transfer. Meaningless drills are sure to be disappointing.
When sportsmanship as an ideal remains restricted to the
specific sport situation, then transfer to other areas of experience
does not occur. When the essential relationships of the concept
are learned and generalized, then there can be application to
the whole of life.

Henry, in reporting on specificity versus generality in
learning motor skills, writes that the evidence is adequate to
conclude that transfer of improvement due to learning is specific
and not general.[22]

The teacher of physical education will recognize that
there are certain similarities and recurrent uses of familiar skills
in new patterns of response that can and should be stressed in
the teaching of motor skills. Some of these should be pointed
out to pupils; others may be consciously set up as problems for
pupils to discover for themselves. This attitude of self-discovery
by pupils should be one of the important learnings that the

[21] Elizabeth Rodgers, *The Teachings of Team Games*, New York, Teach-
        ers College, Columbia University, 1936.
[22] Franklin M. Henry, "Specificity vs. Generality in Learning Motor
        Skills," *Proceedings of the College Physical Education Asso-
        ciation*, 1958, p. 126.

teacher of physical education attempts to make transfer from skill to skill. This kind of generalization is similar to that which the teacher seeks to secure in teaching sportsmanship and fair play in games; both represent an effort on the part of the pupil to see important relationships between different activities and to find that the value in one experience is not restricted to the area of its origin but may operate quite generally.

As a part of the idea of transfer, inhibition is frequently made to appear as important and vital in the work in gymnastics. Thus, much of the posture work is based upon the conception that the individual is to inhibit the tendency to droop; or in the so-called "educational exercises" he is to learn inhibition through responding in a rigidly prescribed fashion to the command of the teacher. The view is that by inhibiting movement until the command of execution is given, he has thereby learned inhibition.

When one studies the numerous mechanisms involved in postures of the body, the enormous complexity of the structure appears. While these complex mechanisms may be brought into marvelous coordination and corresponding harmony, it is still a fact that posturing involves kinesthetic and vestibular pathways of the muscle sense and cerebellar functions, pyramidal pathways from the motor cortex, and other pathways such as the ocular tract. When these are considered in relation to attitudes, fatigue, habits, examples, and other forces, the problem is more difficult than at first appears.

Inhibition is a common phenomenon of the organism, particularly in the internal organs. Thus, the movements of the alimentary canal go on without the intervention of consciousness, and yet under certain conditions, largely emotional, they may be altered or completely checked. The striking case is that of the heart which responds to the stimulating action of the accelerator nerves and yet under the control of the vagus (involuntary) may be inhibited to a remarkable degree.

In the skeletal muscles over which we have conscious control the fact of inhibition is directly centered. When a muscle has been inhibited, it becomes readier for activity, and this phenomenon suggests that inhibition is something more than mere interruption of activity; it is, in a very real sense, preparation for activity. This change is a central affair and reflects significant alterations in the neurons rather than the muscles.

Inhibition should be regarded as a preparation in the body for movement; its effect is to reinforce the ability of the individual to move. This latter point emphasizes the necessity to consider the damage to the mechanism by asking or requiring it to keep from action when the preceding procedure has in the physiological economy made the individual more ready to act.

In short, that which is desirable in self-control, inhibition, and self-direction relates to a learning by the individual of the conditions under which he should act and the development of an attitude toward the whole experience which favors his acting in such fashion, that is, in relation to the conditions. The idea that response-command exercises have anything to contribute to this process in normal social life is without any supporting evidence whatsoever.

Physical education should take into account the effect of a plateau on learning progress.

The learning curve shows an interesting characteristic in the progress of learning. The process does not go on at a constant rate. There is marked success at the beginning. The unusual skill of the amateur when he first tries a new skill is well known. There follows as a rule in most learning, then, a period in which progress is delayed. This is known as the plateau. Plateaus may be caused by too rapid progress at the start, with lack of sound and thorough foundation in the preliminary skills so essential for the subsequent steps. Trying too hard may prevent learning. Plateaus are associated with external conditions, such as the proximity of vacations, depressing weather conditions, a change in the teacher, fatigue, and lack of condition. A plateau is a level or depression lasting for a long time, weeks or months. They are not common. They correspond in the learning process with the bodily condition known as staleness (Fig. 11). Temporary fluctuations in performance are not to be regarded as plateaus. Short up and down movements in the

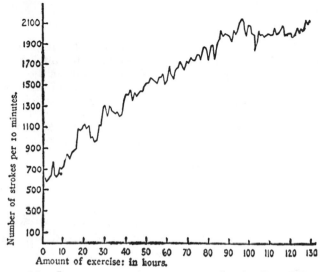

Figure 11. Improvement in typewriting by the "touch" method. Improvement is fairly uniform until the hundreth hour, where the curve flattens out. This is probably a "plateau" rather than the physiological limit. The highest speed attained is about 30 words per minute—not a high rate. (From Thorndike, *Educational Psychology*, vol. ii, p. 139, after Book.)

learning process are universal. Various studies indicate that there is no one curve of learning. The form of the curve depends upon many factors such as the skill to be learned, the maturity of the learner and his past experience, the length and distribution of practice periods, and the learner's ability to organize his responses into a more coordinated pattern. The appearance of plateaus may reflect habits, fatigue, interest, distractions and other temporary influences (Fig. 12).

It was once believed that a plateau was a constant element in all motor learning; this is most improbable. As indicated above the phenomenon may have many causes. None of these may be present and still progress falters. In such instances, the plateau may mark the present level of achievement in the light of the incentives that impel the learner. If the motive to improve is strengthened, the plateau is left behind. Or the plateau may rep-

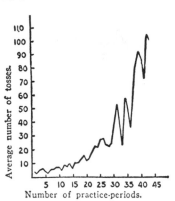

Average number of tosses.

5 10 15 20 25 30 35 40 45
Number of practice-periods.

Figure 12. Improvement in tossing and catching balls. The improvement is slow at the start, but becomes more rapid as the subject becomes more proficient. (From Thorndike, *Educational Psychology*, vol. ii, p. 120, after Swift.)

resent the level reached by a certain method of working; if the procedure is changed and better methods used, the plateau is excelled. Or the plateau may appear from concentration of the hard parts of the task at the beginning; when they are mastered the plateau disappears. Finally, some experiments show that if the learner deals with the whole experience as a unit, he tends to progress without a plateau regardless of the simplicity or complexity of the movements.

Physical education should apply the principle of over-learning in teaching skills.

Whenever a skill is learned, its retention depends upon the use and practice of it. If several days intervene between the learning of a skill and the performing of it again, about the same number of trials is necessary to perform the act successfully. However, if when the skill is learned there is also over-learning—that is, practice of the accomplishment—then it is easily repeated at some future time. There appears to be a ratio between the amount of overlearning and the length of interval that may elapse without loss of skill. Walking is an example of a skill in which much overlearning has occurred. Ice skating usually is well overlearned. When this is the case, many years after learning to skate, a person may again perform the skill successfully. It is apparent then that drill on an accomplished skill is important, but especially so on those skills that we desire to retain. Moreover, in instances of transfer continual reinforcement is necessary if the transferred ability is to persist.

Physical education should plan practice periods.

A practice period is an important instrument for learning skills. The period should be planned and used for particular purposes. The practice will be most productive of learning if pointed to particular skills; little progress can be expected otherwise. The teacher can help most by noting the action and indicating to the learner any improvement as it occurs. When old faults persist, a new demonstration or further analysis of the skill may be necessary. It is important not to assign a practice period as punishment; the period should be used to gain mastery over a skill and not as a disciplinary measure. Mental practice improves performance.

Physical education should use short practice periods.

Very little has been achieved in discovery of the best distribution of practice periods in the different motor activities. From the work that has been done it appears that practice for short periods and often is best. Distributed rather than concentrated practice is to be preferred. Fatigue makes long practice periods less preferable to short ones. Boredom and lack of interest decrease effort and these qualities may be more prominent in long periods.

Cozens in a study of college freshmen found that learning was more rapid if the practice of 100-yard dash, 120-yard low hurdle, half-mile run, running broad jump, 12-pound shot, and discus throw was spread out rather than concentrated.[23] It would appear then that short periods for a longer time are better than long periods for a shorter time, but the optimum is unknown. How short may the period be? How long may the interval be? These remain to be discovered.

Physical education should promote an attitude of confidence in the learner.

One learns better if the problem is attacked with con-

[23] F. W. Cozens, "A Comparative Study of Two Methods of Teaching Class Work in Track and Field Events," *Research Quarterly*, December, 1931, p. 75.

fidence than if fear and doubt prevail. Fear, timidity and doubt restrain the learner. In many skills one must "let go" in order to succeed. It requires confidence to "let go" in skating, in apparatus activity, in tackling, in numerous activities that require courage. Even in sports such as golf where courage is not required to perform the stroke, the ability to "let go" is tremendously important. Confidence in ability to accomplish a skill promotes relaxation and tends to overcome neuromuscular hypertension that prevents good movement.

Physical education should employ the principle of Learning by Doing.

Motor skills are learned best by attempting to perform them. It is a mistake for the teacher to spend a great deal of time in explanation. As the learning process proceeds, the teacher may help by clarifying the goals to be sought and improve insight by further analysis. Teachers should not discuss at length the values of the game or stress unduly the difficulties that will be met.

It should not be supposed that meanings and relationships are to be ignored. One of the richest aspects of folk dance is the folklore of the activity. This must be a part of the experience. In some instances this can be read to better advantage. Indeed, there should be a large increase in the reading assignments that are given to high school pupils and college students. As this is done the necessity for lectures during the activity periods disappears.

Physical education should use demonstration in appropriate situations to facilitate the learning.

All teachers should be able to do the thing they attempt to teach. Average performance is required. The champion performer may be a poor teacher because he is scarcely aware of the difficulty of the movement that he performs so easily. The art of demonstration is analysis. In throwing a baseball, what is the problem? What part does the leg take in the process? The back? The wrist? In all movements proper analysis with demonstration of the technique is important.

Demonstration should take into account not only the direct movement itself but also related bodily organizations that are important in the process. The use of peripheral vision in basketball, the feint in boxing, and others give some of the possibilities of demonstration.

QUESTIONS AND PROBLEMS FOR DISCUSSION

1. Discuss fully the concepts of **mind** and **body** which you hold. What is the meaning of the concept of unity of the organism?
2. How do unity and diversity relate to each other? Discuss integration fully and give examples of disintegrating experiences or conditions.
3. What is the difference between the concept of instinct and that of urge, drive, or impulse?
4. What is the meaning of readiness of an individual to engage in a motor activity?
5. Are the fundamental urges to engage in activity temporary or relatively permanent?
6. What are the efforts of an individual to maintain a psychological equilibrium?
7. How can physical education operate to influence the learning of habits?
8. Rigid habits may limit the individual. What examples of this can you give?
9. What are the environmental forces that play upon the materials of man? How do these affect learning?
10. How may readiness to learn depend upon stimulation and training?
11. What relation has a worthy goal to intent? How do you explain the difference in attitude of those in voluntary and required activities?
12. What is the difference between intrinsic and extrinsic motives? Which are more effective for learning? How can the teacher arouse motive to improve performance?
13. In what respect do physical activities carry their own incentives?
14. What are wants of people? How do they influence action? What influence has success or failure in learning? What happens when the goal is too high?
15. How important are goals in learning? In performing a difficult skill, should attention be directed toward bodily sensations of a well-executed movement? Explain your answer.

16. Do we learn to swim in the winter and to skate in the summer? Explain.
17. What are concomitants in learning? Do they always occur? Why?
18. What are whole and part methods?
19. What is meant by transfer of training? Will skill in roller skating help to learn ice skating, tennis, golf, or dance? Explain your answers.
20. What does the learning curve show? .
21. What is inhibition?
22. What is the influence of past experience in learning?
23. What is overlearning? Is it desirable?
24. What are some points regarding the distribution of practice periods?
25. What effect has confidence on learning?
26. What application of the principle of learning by doing should be made in the teaching of a new game? A new folk dance?
27. Why should teachers be able to do the skills they propose to teach to others? What is peripheral vision?

REFERENCE READINGS

Andrews, Michael F. (Editor). *Creativity and Psychological Health.* Syracuse, N.Y., Syracuse University Press, 1961.

Breckenridge, Marian E., and Vincent, E. Lee. *Child Development: Physical and Psychologic Growth Through Adolescence,* 4th Edition. Philadelphia, Saunders, 1960.

Delza, Sophia. *Body and Mind in Harmony.* New York, McKay, 1961.

Fulton, Ruth E. "Speed and Accuracy in Learning a Ballistic Movement." *Research Quarterly,* March, 1942.

Guilford, Joy Paul. *Personality.* New York, McGraw-Hill, 1959.

Guntrip, Henry James S. *Personality Structure and Human Interaction.* London, Hogarth Press, 1961.

Mussen, Paul H. and Conger, John J. *Child Development and Personality.* New York, Harper, 1956.

Strecker, Edward A., and Appel, Kenneth E. *Discovering Ourselves,* 3rd Edition. New York, Macmillan, 1958.

Zubek, John P., and Solberg, P. A. *Human Development.* New York, McGraw-Hill, 1954.

THE HISTORIC ROLE OF PHYSICAL EDUCATION IN THE PROBLEM OF ADJUSTMENT TO LIFE

CHAPTER EIGHT

THE HISTORIC ROLE OF PHYSICAL EDUCATION IN THE PROBLEM OF ADJUSTMENT TO LIFE

If I were talking to an athlete, I should say, show me your shoulders; and then he might say here are my Halteres. I reply, Slave, I am not inquiring about this, but how you exercise pursuit and avoidance, desire and aversion, how you design, and purpose, and prepare yourself, whether conformably to nature or not. If conformably, give me evidence of it, and I will say you are making progress.

The Discourses of Epictetus.

The real, sole and profound theme of the history of the world and man, the theme to which all others are subordinated, lies in the conflict between faith and disbelief. All the epochs in which faith dominates under any form whatever are splendid, encouraging and fruitful for contemporaries and for posterity; and, on the contrary, all the epochs in which disbelief in any form whatever wins a poor victory.

Goethe.

THE INFLUENCE OF THE EXPERIENCE OF OTHERS

In a broad sense, physical education in America arose out of the life of the people here. More narrowly, physical education in America reflected the experience of others, but the very poverty of American ideas in this field in the early years of the nineteenth century contributed to a rather heavy weighting of foreign programs and purposes.

In the field of general education, we are indebted to Europe for the pattern of a state school system with state oversight and control. The motives approving state education in Europe would be obviously quite different from the ones guiding the plan in America. The influence of Pestalozzi is hard to estimate, and yet everywhere he contributed both in method and subject matter. Impetus was given to the movement for professional training of teachers by the example set for us in Europe and this was outstanding not only in general education but also in the special field of physical education.

It is a desirable scientific trait to see what others have done before setting out upon any project.[1] Too frequently, wasted effort and futile undertakings result from failure to survey the field properly and to learn of the progress of others in similar lines. This may be carried to extremes; to ignore home values and look for excellence only in foreign places is undoubtedly a serious mistake. So commonly is this quality exhibited in human nature, however, that there has passed into the language the saying, "A prophet is not without honor except in his own country." The philosopher may explain this as a quality to be observed in young nations; it has been commonly commented upon among Americans prior to the First World War.

[1] Billy D. Wireman, "Role of History and Philosophy in Determining Future Directions of Physical Education," *Proceedings of the College Physical Education Association*, December, 1961, p. 27.

There are many illustrations of failure of people to explore and evaluate domestic resources. America is the land of the Indian scout, and yet with all the background in scouting and the rich lore available and the keen interest of Americans in Indian life, it remained for an Englishman, a hundred years after the material was available, to use Indian life and the scouting psychology in an educative way that would appeal to youth. The domestic resources in scouting as means for physical education of the American boy were not discovered because we were too much interested in imitating and paying homage to foreign physical education.

In physical education the Filipino people do not use the material that is available in their tribal and folkways. Their native sources in dances and games are particularly rich and suitable for the children of the Islands. But instead of seeing any of the native festival dances in the schools, an observer will notice these barefoot children of the Islands going through the movements of a Russian dance without any comprehension of its meaning and of course without the equipment that belongs to a dance in the north temperate zone where heavy leather boots are worn. Another failure to evaluate native sources.[2]

The American population is in origin a transplanted people. Even those whom we call native-born are at the most less than ten generations from the motherland, and most are less than five. It is quite natural, therefore, that in physical education the experience of the motherlands should have weight and bearing in determining the kind of physical education to be developed and carried on. Sentiment, however, must not be permitted to play too large a part. We should wish to arrive at a solution scientifically.

THE RELIABILITY OF THE EXPERIENCE OF OTHERS

How valuable is another's experience as a guide? To what extent can we learn by the experience of others? Mechanical

[2] Board of Educational Survey, *A Survey of the Educational System of the Philippine Islands, 1925*, Jesse Feiring Williams, Chapter V, Manila, Department of Public Instruction, p. 488.

things are readily transplanted; procedures in manufacture, technical skills, certain of the arts and crafts are easily learned. Wherever **things** as distinguished from **people** are dealt with, then it is quite easy to do as others do. In the organization of people as contrasted with the organization of things, there come into play ideas, customs, attitudes, and beliefs that color and shape the procedure in such fashion that, when taken over for another people, such educational projects may be completely changed. Failing to take into the account the underlying ideas, customs, and beliefs may hamper the transfer of a procedure in manufacture, as, for example, wood carving, rug weaving and basketry, but the influence of these factors is tremendously more effective in the matter of education, religion, and similar forms of culture.

Because some people are inclined to accept at times as reliable the experience of others is not sufficient basis for thinking that they were right in doing so. It is not uncommon to find people ready and willing to be guided by the experience of others, and especially is this true where there is ignorance of or doubt about the matter in question. Thus, in the feeding of children, in the treatment of disease, in the investment of money it is the rule rather than the exception to find people following, without discrimination, the experiences of others in the immediate environment. This is of course due to the general lack of knowledge prevailing among people concerning the proper way to feed children, the scientific treatment of disease, and the correct principles of investing money.

It would seem, therefore, that among the possible many, there are two conditions of experience that should always be considered.

Physical education should take into account all the pertinent conditions of the experience.

An illustration of the importance of this view is afforded by a discussion of the conditions that should be assessed when the rejection of American youth for military service is considered (see Chapter 3, pp. 84-88).

Physical education should recognize the psychic factors in experience and if possible evaluate them.

The ready assumption that two things coming together are therefore related is a common fallacy. *Post hoc, ergo propter hoc* is a common error in medicine, in education, in experience in general. For example, the West Point cadet is reported to show good postures in sitting, standing, and walking. While at West Point he learns what is known as West Point breathing. Instead of associating in cause and effect relationship such things as the West Point stance and the West Point breathing, the psychic factors of West Point life should also be given careful consideration.

EVALUATION OF THE EXPERIENCE IN TERMS OF RESULTS

The experience may be reliable and the inference sound; but there is more to the question than that. Is the experience desirable? Are the results desirable? The experience is valuable for what it does or does not do. By results one is not to be limited to such misleading terms as "practical," but the indirect and the more subtle effects are to be examined. Thus it would appear that several questions should be asked:

1. Are the results desirable? Are the results of Swedish gymnastics desirable? Desirable for whom? They are not necessarily desirable for people in general, although they may be desirable for the Swedish people. To affirm otherwise would be to ignore all that we know of people's ideals, ideas, customs, attitudes, beliefs.

2. Are the results lasting? Do they represent modification of conduct or are they of temporary nature and susceptible of change at an early date? The posture of the children in their physical education periods is a case in point. Before one decides to adopt a plan of posture training he should give careful consideration to the matter of posture out of school and the question of lasting effects. What should be his position if he learned that posture in the schools was a school posture to be discarded as soon as the children were set free from school?

Moreover, even very rigid systems of gymnastics change. Hackensmith writes:

During the past half century in Europe the monopolistic position of gymnastics (marching tactics, free exercises with and without apparatus and exercise on heavy apparatus) has been seriously challenged by a growing interest in games, sports, and recreation. Parallel with the social changes following the two great wars the peoples of European countries developed a more liberal attitude toward certain modifications in the educational curriculum. The addition of games and sports to the program of physical education in the school has been one of these changes which gained momentum after the close of World War I.[3]

3. Are the results contributing to the principles which are held? The results should be referred to principles and judged in relation to the basic beliefs surrounding the experience.

EXPERIENCE IN TERMS OF TRAITS AND CUSTOMS

Many of the notions and standards for individual and social life in America arose out of a life quite different from the present and with sanctions that would scarcely meet with approval today. Many of the moral virtues with which the physical educator deals most intimately arose out of the ideals of the warrior class. Thus, it happened that in an insecure society, the chief business would be fighting and not raising grain or breeding sheep or making steel rails. Warriors with serfs had found the way to make others work for them and fight for them. The virtues that were built up were the ones set forth by the powerful of the groups and show a curious mixture of good and evil. Honor, courage, loyalty, and chivalry come to be interpretations of the way people think of human relationships and not absolutes in themselves.

If we choose a man to some high office, we honor him and we select him because of qualities he possesses. Honor, then, means excellence in some quality which is admired by the group. It may mean one thing in one place and quite a different thing in another.

[3] C. W. Hackensmith, "International Development of Movement Education," *The Physical Educator*, May, 1962, p. 54.

In a nation where men are born to positions, and receive honor because they are subservient and true to the traditions of the class to which they were born, to their clan and its intimate associations, honor comes to have a very different meaning from that given to it where it comes as a reward of merit. In the former instance, it is not of great importance to have in the educational scheme plans for choosing leaders intelligently and on the basis of excellence in some quality admired by the group, supplemented by plans for educating the group to admire the things of greatest worth to the greatest number. Now in physical education, the necessity for games and training in leadership have, until more recently, never appeared as vital to certain nations because such traits were not required by their scheme of social organization. Therefore, it would appear that what people do in their social organization is an expression of the value of certain ideals and their recognition of the necessity of planning for securing them through education. Their practice is good or bad only in relation to the ideas of which it is an expression. It is clearly unwise to select for a people with one group of fundamental ideas a type of practice which illustrates another group of ideas, out of harmony and never to be accepted by the ones to whom the new practice is introduced.

The significance of the ideas which move people is given by an analysis of loyalty. This virtue arose out of the warrior's code and required that the serf, squire, follower, and retainers in general be true to some superior. There was thus developed through the centuries the notion that one must be loyal to a superior. Loyalty, as a quality of persons, has been the theme of some very interesting novels. Galsworthy's play *Loyalties* reveals the power in the topic as a theme for the dramatist. Now, among certain people to be loyal to the priesthood, the king, the overlord is of paramount importance, and although this type of loyalty is not so much in evidence today, still it played a rather prominent part in the life of people in the eighteenth and nineteenth centuries. On the contrary it may be said that in the United States the highest good is loyalty to truth as one sees it. Or take an illustration from the use of the word gentleman. To be a gentleman means one thing in London, another thing in Boston, and quite a different thing in the rural districts of the Middle West. To be a gentleman in China, in Jolo, in Java is altogether different from being a gentleman in Soviet Russia. Thus the notions which people have regarding virtues as well as many other things depend upon the whole hinterland of ideas shaping their judgment and are to be evaluated in terms of the sanctions of the society into which they are introduced.

It should be quite clear, therefore, that the type of physical education in any nation reflects the customs, the ideas, the beliefs, the attitudes, the conscious needs of the people. Also these characteristics are different for different peoples and they vary, especially, when the notions of human relationships vary greatly. We are never to be absolutely sure that we speak the language of the foreigner, even when we are able to carry on a conversation with him by using his own words and imitating successfully his inflections and pronunciations.

In the light of the foregoing, it would seem to be important to survey, even somewhat superficially, the social, political, economic, and military influences that shaped physical education in various countries.

GERMAN PHYSICAL EDUCATION

The origin of a national system of physical education in Germany began with the work of Friedrich Ludwig Jahn (1778-1852). With Jahn nationalism was a consuming passion and he devoted his energies not only in gymnastics but also in language and literature to a strengthening of national life.

There was need for it. "By 1808 all the Germanies were at the mercy of Napoleon. Prussia was shorn of half of her possessions and forced to obey the behests of her conqueror."[4] Jahn's popular gymnastics are to be viewed in the light of a nation's tragedy. The ideas of German teachers, leaders, and

[4] C. J. Hayes, *Political and Cultural History of Modern Europe*, New York, Macmillan, 1937, Vol. I, p. 667.

most of the peasants were by this fact of subjugation to France grouped around such central and pervasive motives as resisting the enemy to the West, development of national power, unification of all the Germanies, national consciousness as exhibited in language and literature, and German culture. The force of these ideas eventually led to a rehabilitated Germany.

The ideals and aspirations of Jahn were never realized. The motto of the German Turners, "Frisch, Frei, Frölich, Fromm," had to compete with a reactionary and feudalistic government. Jahn, brave and courageous spirit, rebelled from time to time against the limitations of the national life. In 1820, he and his Turners were suppressed and until 1850 reaction was the note in Germany. Even then, with a free press and free speech granted, the force of education aimed to standardize individuals for the king.

The liberal and forward-looking philosophy of Jahn should not be forgotten. Stecher in a stirring article interprets the meaning of the motto "Frisch, Frei, Frölich, Fromm." He writes:

> A free translation of this motto would be: Free, Cheerful, Intelligent, Dependable or Good. We might also ask: What were Jahn's ideals? A reading of his rugged writings can leave no doubt in anyone's mind that what he wanted to accomplish by means of "Turnen" was something entirely different from what, in recent years, is so often called "gymnastics."
>
> Jahn and his followers wanted to educate human beings. They were not interested primarily in the strong man nor in acrobats. Physical strength, it is true, was to them something worth striving for. But it was not an end in itself. It was a tool by means of which it was possible for a man to become free and healthy. To be weak meant that a person was at the mercy of all men, strength and freedom were linked together by them as something desirable for all human beings.
>
> Cheerfulness to them meant mental health; a sane outlook upon this world of ours with its "good" far outweighing the efforts of the things that are bad. Cheerfulness was a worth-while possession to be striven for, and gymnastics was the tool most useful to acquire this trait.
>
> Intelligence to them meant the utmost development of the natural mental endowment that is the precious possession of

all human beings. It meant the ability to understand, to comprehend, to analyze, to think constructively. Gymnastics was a tool by means of which dormant mental faculties were aroused, cultivated, and strengthened.

Dependability meant to them that human trait that in modern times be called morality. A person who could not be depended upon, who was not good, was immoral; he was not to be trusted; he was a social misfit. Gymnastics helped to train such persons into a higher type of human being.

An understanding, therefore, of what "Turnen" really means should show that it does not mean merely muscular work of great skill, but that it also means mental, social, and moral training and education. . . .

When Jahn took his boys out to the Hasenheide, to the great open spaces outside Berlin, his gymnastic lesson was a combination of the most informal type of work, or songs or games, and of inspirational talks. He looked upon gymnastics as an instrument by means of which he aroused in his pupils a greater patriotism.[5]

But Jahn's ideals and purposes were never realized in the national life of Imperial Germany. He helped to create a nation out of the struggling and warring principalities, only in the end to be thrown into prison, to see his liberal principles thwarted by the reactionary tactics of a landed aristocracy.

In the play of social forces, one gets an impression of the worth of human life, the value of human relationships, and the respect accorded to personality. Up to 1807, feudalism in Germany was the dominant social organization. Its lack of respect for personality and disregard for individual worth were finally understood by certain leaders, and in the six years following 1807, Baron von Stein and Chancellor Hardenberg put through the following reforms:

1. Von Stein's Edict of Emancipation, which abolished serfdom throughout Prussia, October 9, 1807. Free trade in land was established and ownership of land was permitted to peasants and bourgeois as well as nobles. The peasants thus became free, although they were still bound to make fixed payments to their lords in the form of rent.

[5] W. A. Stecher, "The Turners and Physical Education," *Mind and Body*, February, 1927, p. 419.

2. Grant of local self-government (November 19, 1808) to all Prussian towns of population of 800 and over.

3. Hardenberg continued these reforms in 1811, by making peasants absolute owners of part of their holdings.

4. Compulsory military service was introduced.

5. Formation of organizations, with governmental approval, that developed nationalism. In this respect the work of Jahn in the Turnverein and that of Fichte and Arndt in the Jugendbund are outstanding.

These are memorable achievements, but the type of physical education produced is to be viewed in the light of the prevailing social ideals, which were so constrictive to human personality. Legal enactments reflect public opinion, but the advances indicated above represented no great improvement in the social philosophy. The individual was still regarded as of little worth.

In Germany in the nineteenth century, the relation of the individual to the state reveals more accurately the ideas that molded practice. The King and subject relationship was strong. The Church and school maintained these bonds by preaching and teaching. The teacher-training institutions were tuned to patriotism as the central theme. In the regulations of a seminary at Pyritz, piety was to be shown, among other ways "by respect for the King, our sovereign, and by unshaken fidelity to our country." The reforms inaugurated by von Stein did not mean freedom and personal liberty as we in America understand the terms. For years a fierce conflict was carried on between conservative and liberal political opinion. And the rigid, formal, conservative view won. The naturalistic program of Jahn was not accepted by those in authority who gave their support to the more formal, rigid, and disciplinary materials and methods of Adolph Spiess (1810-1858) who developed the German system of school gymnastics.

King Frederick William III, who had decreed on January 2, 1820, that *Turnen* should absolutely cease throughout Prussia, stated his ideas of education, and political and social rights as follows: "We do not confer upon the individual or upon society any benefit when we educate him beyond the bounds of his social class and vocation, give him a cultivation which he cannot make use of, and awaken in him pretensions and needs which his lot in life does not allow him to satisfy."[6]

Physical education engaged in a procedure of handling human beings must use a method which conforms to prevailing ideas. The procedures and methods of a foreign system of gymnastics can never be acceptable in America unless we are willing to accept the ideas behind them. German physical education of the nineteenth century, admirable though it may have been in Germany, is without universal application because nations are social groupings with their own cultures. Foreign systems of physical education must give, without reservation, full service to the political, social, and military ideas of the time and place. If these ideas are quite repugnant to Americans, the practice that expresses and embodies these ideas is also unacceptable.

The physical education of Germany under National Socialism was vastly different from that before 1933. The greatest importance was assigned to physical education, with character education next, and intellectual training last. Through physical education the boy was to become a man, learning to obey so he may later be able to command. He was taught to take greater pride in a well-formed physique than in fine clothes. True to the principle of reflecting national ideas it developed with amazing rapidity new and interesting forms. The significance of these forms should be studied in relation to the prevailing ideas, customs, and standards in Germany.

The developments in physical education in Germany under National Socialism had far-reaching importance. In schools and universities, physical education occupied a place of major importance. In the latter, for example, no student could enter his fourth semester without having participated proficiently for eighteen months. The Ministry of Education defined physical education as premilitary training. Through

[6] E. H. Reisner, *Nationalism and Education since 1789*, New York, Macmillan, 1923, p. 144.

Geländesport, or open country sport, and **Wehrsport**, or military sport, the Germans laid the foundations for a well-trained body of youth for the national army.

In industry, in the army and navy, and among the general population, physical education was promoted in a variety of ways. The **Kraft durch Freude** organization sought not only to promote health, but also wholesome use of leisure time. National Socialism used physical education as one of the chief agencies for achievement of its program. Thus, through the school and university, in the youth movement, in the labor service, in the Reichswehr, and in civilian life, there was the clear obligation to keep fit, to be strong, to be ready to serve Germany. To attain such goals, extensive facilities were provided, leaders were prepared, and organizations worked constantly at the problem. The old nineteenth century intellectualism characteristic of Imperial Germany disappeared. The whole official emphasis was upon self-denial, not as a philosophic principle of asceticism, but to conserve supplies. Since the defeat of Germany, the occupation forces have not permitted continuance of the organizations that embodied the purposes of National Socialism.

EAST AND WEST GERMAN PHYSICAL EDUCATION

The development of physical education in East and in West Germany since the close of World War II is described in considerable detail by Wolfgang Karbe.[7] On page 282 of this chapter it was stated that ideas of the time and place determine what people do in education and in physical education. This is well demonstrated in East and West Germany today. In East Germany the leaders of a Communist society formulate the policies which are to govern physical education in the country. These policies reflect the ideas of dialectical materialism as expressed by Marx and Lenin, and are designed to give answers to all problems so that East German youth are conditioned to

[7] Wolfgang Karbe, "Physical Education and Sports in East and West Germany," *The Physical Educator*, October, 1962, p. 108.

serve the State. West Germany is a pluralistic, democratic society. The schools are organized and conducted so that youth can become free, happy, healthy, tolerant, just, and moral individuals. These aims correspond with the motto of Jahn: "Frisch, Frei, Frölich, Fromm" (page 284).

SWEDISH PHYSICAL EDUCATION

The history of Sweden in the eighteenth and nineteenth centuries is one of struggling nationalism. Up to the Battle of Waterloo her nationalism was scarcely recognized, the military and naval prowess of Russia, England, and France ever contributing to her deep humiliation.

In 1807, both Russia and Denmark suddenly invaded Sweden. The Finnish province and the Åland Islands were taken from her. Reverberations of this act of international piracy were heard in 1919 and 1920, after World War I. In 1809, Gustavus IV was compelled to abdicate in favor of Charles XIII, an infirm and childless old man. This weak and partitioned Sweden was the national heritage of Per Henrik Ling (1776-1839). Inspired by the same kind of ideals that moved Jahn, Ling saw in gymnastics national strength and unity. Thus, too, in Sweden physical education arose in relation to military needs. The military character of Swedish gymnastics for nearly a hundred years is illustrated not only by the development of military gymnastics as such, but particularly by the presence of military teachers of gymnastics in the secondary schools.

Much of the procedure and method in Swedish gymnastics is essentially drill-room technique, and this procedure is to be interpreted in terms of military needs.

Since the Napoleonic era, political and social movements have been marked by efforts of reform. Feudalism never secured a real hold in Sweden. The Church never attained much political power. Instead of an absolute king, there was created an absolute Riksdag, and under the constitution the nobles played the chief roles.

The peasantry were better situated politically than in Germany. Many owned their own lands, and the country has remained largely agricultural. But still the common man was so little valued throughout the nineteenth century that universal manhood suffrage was denied. The social history of this land takes on the coloring of all peoples ruled by king and nobles.

Explanation of the emphasis on corrective gymnastics in Ling's system and in the recent gymnastics of Bukh (Denmark) is suggested by the occupational life of the Swedish and Danish peasant. The boy or girl from rural districts, accustomed to heavy, manual labor, becomes well muscled, but set and rigid from occupational activities.

What Ling and Branting (1799-1881), his successor, did at the Royal Central Institute of Gymnastics is to be understood in relation to the military, political, and social ideas of their time and place. An extensive analysis of economic factors would doubtless reveal many interesting comparisons. Clearly, the reforms which were instituted were chiefly of an economic kind and of form more than content. So long as the education in the nation seeks to make the child docile, obedient to a superior, disciplined in a military sense, just so long will those in control permit unessential modifications in social or economic status. Swedish gymnastics in its insistence on precision of movement, response-command exercises, and rigid day's order was, together with similar educational experiences in school, church, and home, favorable to the perpetuation of the existing social order. But that social order has changed greatly; although the monarchy remains, the state is socialistic in its economy today. In 1955 the Swedish Board of Education published the primary school curriculum in physical education. This document stresses the importance of selecting exercises suited to the age and physical and mental development of the pupils. Initiative and individual activities are to be encouraged. Team work and respect for the rules of games and sports are to be taught in all grades.[8]

It is interesting that increasing democratization in the

[8] Education Abstracts, *Physical Education, Official Primary and Secondary Programmes*, UNESCO, February, 1959, p. 15.

nation is paralleled by the development of more functional programs in the schools. Physical education in Sweden has felt also the influence of Danish gymnastics. There is more emphasis today upon rhythmical movements. In the training centers, however, tradition and custom strongly prevail in the character of their gymnastics programs.

PHYSICAL EDUCATION IN OTHER SCANDINAVIAN COUNTRIES

In the other Scandinavian countries, Norway, Denmark, and Finland, physical education is also a regular part of the educational system. These four countries share similar viewpoints on material and method. Gray notes, "Gymnastics still serves as the basis of physical education but no longer does it constitute the total program. Leaders in these countries readily agree that gymnastics alone can never be justified as a complete system of physical education but that all sports are complementary to each other and all must have a place in a sound and rational program."[9] In addition to the school programs, sport organizations in each country promote sport activities through the medium of clubs.

Professor Howard G. Knuttgen of Copenhagen reports that Emanuel Hansen in his book *Sport in Denmark* holds to a view, long discarded in the United States but maintained by Danish educational specialists, that physical education can develop general qualities such as "courage, determination, initiative, self-control, consideration for others, team spirit."[10] However faulty such a notion is, apparently it does not impede the conduct of an active and vigorous physical education program for boys and girls in the schools or an enthusiastic membership in numerous sport clubs.

[9] Charles A. Gray, "Physical Education in Scandinavia," *The Physical Educator*, March, 1960, p. 31.
[10] Howard G. Knuttgen, "Physical Education in Denmark," *The Physical Educator*, May, 1961, p. 70.

FRENCH PHYSICAL EDUCATION

The nineteenth century revealed in France an Empire, a limited monarchy, the Second Republic, the Third Empire (an attempt at a commune in Paris, 1870), and finally the Third Republic. A long history of kings, nobles, and clergy, who strove for temporal power, and serfs at the mercy of their overlords precedes that. Many of the political conditions that confronted Germany and Sweden were at one time duplicated in France, but still no Frenchman arose to found a national system of gymnastics. Doubtless, asceticism, scholasticism, and dominance of the all-powerful medieval church are back of the Frenchman's characteristic disregard for gymnastics. During the Napoleonic era, for obvious reasons, there were no incentives for national gymnastics; but even in the dark days following the Franco-Prussian War (1870-1871) nothing of outstanding development took place in gymnastics. This is to be explained in relation to the ideas, values, and appreciations that in France as elsewhere determine practice.

The lack of genuine interest in physical education in France is to be traced to ideas regarding its function in society. First, it is historically associated with war. Disliking war, Frenchmen find the drill a necessity but not a pleasure. They associate drill in physical exercises with their period of military service, which they are very glad to have completed. Moreover, their originality and individuality are repressed by drill. Through the Revolution they gained their independence, and this is a precious thing to every Frenchman. Though of necessity they must give up some of this liberty while they train themselves to protect the nation, at the expiration of this period they return with joy to "la liberté," and are likely to associate all physical exercise with this less pleasing period of their life.

In the second place, the influence of the two great privileged classes, the clergy and the nobles, is important. Though without actual political power today, the ideas they represent are still pervasive. As a heritage from medieval times the modern Frenchman retains his contempt for education of the body.

The ascetic and scholastic philosophy touched deeply the life of the people. As early as 1580, Montaigne attacked the scholastic attitude in the following words, "It is not a soul, it is not a body that we are training up, but it is a man." Nearly two centuries later, Rousseau in his "Emile" (1762) again called attention to the defects of scholasticism. Following the humiliation of 1870, Swedish gymnastics were introduced in France, but it failed to become rooted in a country that politically was similar to the Sweden of 1808, but socially vastly different. The influence of scholasticism made arduous the labors of Baron Pierre de Coubertin to revive the Olympic games. So little regard exists for the education of man through physical activities that it is unusual to see in France a gymnasium class where there is real spontaneous interest in the work.

The nobility established in France the ideal of a refined and elegant existence which included brilliant conversation (a play of wit), the play of emotions (note Delsarte's contribution and that of the French pantomimists), the enjoyment of the presence of the opposite sex, a sincere appreciation and love of beauty and art. It is these things that the Frenchman enjoys; not in the same degree of refinement and elegance by all, but each according to his means and taste. The appearance of a heavily muscled athlete does not appeal to French taste. It is not beautiful. They associate this type quite naturally with gymnastics. Due to a lack of wholesome play in the schools, games seem dull and pointless to adult Frenchmen; even the supreme Lenglen and the debonair Carpentier aroused only a mild interest. To the bourgeoisie, an ideal of a conventional existence with aspirations to imitate the nobility is most influential; to the peasant play and games seem a waste of time because he has enough physical activity.

And yet there is physical education in France, but nothing as extensive as the popular gymnastics in Germany. It has seemed, doubtless, a necessary evil. Its early development was marked by application to utilitarian purposes. Physical education for firemen was something that could be understood, but for all persons, no, that was impossible. The truly French development of physical education by Lieutenant Georges Hébert reflects this same utilitarianism. It is based upon the idea of training soldiers rather than citizens, and it is considered in France to be preferable to Swedish gymnastics for this purpose.

The system developed by Lieutenant Hébert is based upon the natural activities of man, namely, running, jumping, climbing, combat, and so on. Lieutenant Hébert says, "Progress in physical education consists not in inventing movements of a special nature but in distinguishing by experience the best exercises to use in reaching the goal—physical perfection."[11]

It is interesting to note a growing tendency in all modern states to reduce rigid procedures in education and to encourage initiative in teachers. A governmental document (1952) recommends the following to French teachers: "to put an end to a system whereby teachers are all required to apply a uniform method; to stress the value of principles unanimously accepted by all physical training teachers, and to make it clear that, so long as principles are loyally adhered to, any teacher may, in the organization and conduct of his lessons, give free rein to his own personal ideas and initiative in order to obtain the best possible results."[12]

ITALIAN PHYSICAL EDUCATION

When Vittorino da Feltre established his school at Mantua in 1423 for the sons of Italian noblemen he called it "La Casa Giocosa." It was one of the first efforts to educate the whole man after the debacle of Greek and Roman civilization. Long years were to intervene before Italy again was to see an outstanding example of physical education at home. When Mussolini assumed the dictation of Italian national policy, he set a new pattern for Italy. La Casa Giocosa is forgotten and a "nation in arms" exploits to the limit the possibilities of physical education for

[11] G. Hébert, *Le Guide Pratique d'Education Physique*, Paris, Vuibert, 1916.

[12] Education Abstracts, *Physical Education, Official Primary and Secondary Programmes*, UNESCO, February, 1959, pp. 8-9.

the development of physique. He who would build a nation must develop the young and if that nation has military ideals, the education will have its own appropriate forms.

In Italy before World War II, physical education was promoted by a national organization outside the schools, called the "Opera Nazionale Balilla per l'Educazione Fisica." The purpose of the "Balilla Institute" was to develop the youth of the country, to promote sports, and to create a live and dynamic patriotism.

In pre-Fascist days physical education scarcely existed in Italy. A sterile intellectualism pervaded the schools which saw no need for anything in education but the systematic items of knowledge which constituted the curricula. The schools during the revolutionary period seemed quite unable to acquire quickly a new viewpoint, and, therefore, a special institute was created to conduct physical education. The "Balilla" served boys 8 to 14 years of age. After this, boys 14 to 18 years of age were trained in the "Avanguardisti," from which they went into the Fascist "Milizia." Similar organizations for girls were the "Piccolo" for little girls and the "Giovani Italiane" for older ones.

Pupils of elementary and secondary school age received instruction in physical education and military training in the "Balilla." Special attention was given to fencing, cycling, football, swimming, riding, and skiing. Since the war, all the property in playgrounds and buildings, and the direction of physical education in the schools have passed to a special organization called the "Commissariato per la Gioventù Italiana."

The "Accademia di Educazione Fisica e Giovanile" was a creation of the "Balilla" for the training of officers for youth organizations and leaders of physical education in the secondary schools. The academy was excellently equipped, not only to conduct the practical courses in activities but also to give the scientific, theoretical instruction. There were laboratories for anatomy, physiology, radiology, anthropometry, physiotherapy, psychology, and chemistry. Students for the academy were selected by examination. The course covered three years. There was a similar academy for girls. In Italy as in Germany, physical education served national ideals.

ITALIAN PHYSICAL EDUCATION TODAY

The Italian Information Center, 686 Park Avenue, New York 21, N.Y., has supplied the author with information regarding new aims and new methods in Italian schools today. The Central Service for Sport and Physical Education was formed in October, 1947, under the title Special Office for Physical Education. The Service has several functions. It is concerned with the teaching of physical education in schools of every grade, State and non-State, and in the programs of various gymnastic and sport clubs. It stresses corrective forms of physical education and aims to benefit youth physically and morally. The Service is also responsible for construction of gymnasiums and sport facilities. It sets standards for physical education instructors in the schools and administers the selection and appointment of teachers.

The quasi-military character of physical education under the former regime has been completely abandoned. Examinations of pupils of every grade are held and certificates are awarded that attest to the results of the tests. Besides physical education in the schools the Service gives special attention to the activities of numerous athletic clubs. During the period 1954-1955 there were 1905 sport groups with a total of 616,585 individuals engaged in sport activities.

ENGLISH PHYSICAL EDUCATION

Ever since 1215, with the signing of the Magna Charta, the English people had been gaining political control of their government. The seventeenth century saw the triumph of parliamentary government in England. In many ways during the eighteenth and nineteenth centuries, the English people exacted from their sovereigns written promises by which the crown surrendered certain powers. These were taken over by Parliament, making Great Britain a limited rather than an absolute monarchy. Taxes, law making, control of the courts, and the right to make war thus passed to the people in name only at first. Qualifications for voting depended upon estate holdings; Parliamentary bribery, and corruption in the eighteenth century served to retain the control in the hands of the nobles.

But reform movements headed by Fox and Pitt, later by Wilberforce and Clarkson, gradually succeeded in establishing a content for the phrase, "English liberty."

Socially, the eighteenth century in England gave little value to the individual human life. England held to overseas traffic in slaves up to 1807; in 1819 there were 223 capital offenses known to law. The industrial revolution in the first portion of the nineteenth century created deplorable conditions for the masses. In 1833, a fifth of the 200,000 persons working in cotton factories were under 14 years of age; considerably more than a third were under 18.

But the ideas of feudalism so marked in Germany, the tragic fatalism of Sweden, the asceticism, scholasticism, and estheticism of France, although represented in part, were never characteristic of the English people. The separation of the Church and State in England (1534), arrived at for ulterior purposes on the part of Henry VIII, contributed to a greater freedom in thought and action for the people as time went on.

Opposed to the distinctly unfavorable political and social factors in the life of the English people throughout the eighteenth and nineteenth centuries is the body of traits and national characteristics seeking freedom, liberty, and self-directed activity. Shearman remarks "that competitions in running, jumping, and hurling of heavy weights are not only indigenous to the land, but have been one of the chief characteristics of both town and country life in England as far back as chronicles will reach; and that athletic sports, though they have had their days of waxing and waning, have always been a feature of life in 'Merrie England.' "[13] Young Londoners in the reign of Henry II (1154-1189) practiced jumping, wrestling, casting the stone, and ball games. While gymnastics were being established in Germany and Sweden a wide variety of sports and organized games had become an established part of life in the English public schools and universities. Leonard writes of this development as follows:

> When Thomas Arnold's fourteen years as head master at Rugby Public School was ended by his death in June, 1842, cricket was the recognized summer sport at the English public schools and at Oxford and Cambridge universities; rowing was firmly established as a fall and spring exercise at Eton College, and the Oxford–Cambridge boat race was an annual affair; football was regularly played at Rugby and others of the public schools; and continuous records of the "big-side runs" of the Rugby School Hare and Hounds—forerunners of the later track and field athletics—were already five years old. By the time Thomas Hughes published his "Tom Brown's School Days," fifteen years later (April, 1857), all of the public schools had adopted football as the chief winter game, and the first steps looking toward organized track and field athletics as a recognized branch of public school and university sports had been taken. The annual track meets between Oxford and Cambridge date from 1864.[14]

But physical education in Great Britain was never restricted to school and university. Sports in some form were pastimes of the people who held competitions on Sundays, at Church festivals, and at the frequent county fairs. In describing these activities Leonard writes:

> Activities once practised as a necessary part of daily life survive in the sports of hunting, shooting, falconry or hawking, fishing with rod and line, and archery, and the same is true of walking, mountaineering, rowing and sailing, swimming, skat-

---

[13] Montague Shearman, *Athletics and Football*, Badminton Library of Sports and Pastimes, Boston, Little, Brown, 1885.
[14] Fred E. Leonard and George B. Affleck, *A Guide to the History of Physical Education*, Philadelphia, Lea & Febiger, 1947, p. 134.

ing and the like. The primeval joy of combat has been furnished by wrestling, boxing, fencing with foil and sabre, single-stick and quarter-staff. Man has matched himself against man in foot-races, broad and high jumping, weight throwing and putting the stone or shot, the hammer-throwing and caber-tossing of the Scottish highlands, and the pole-vaulting which probably had its origin in contests between messengers whose calling required them to cross ditches and hedges with the help of jumping-poles. The game of bowls has been traced back to the thirteenth century or farther, and curling has been popular in Scotland for three centuries or more. Skittles, quoits, and hockey or shinny (shinty) have been played time out of mind. Golf was a formidable rival of archery in Scotland as far back as the middle of the fifteenth century; but English interest in the sport is comparatively recent. Polo was not introduced from the East until about fifty years ago. Tennis and fives, racquets and squash racquets have long had their devotees, and lawn tennis is now added to the list. Cricket, while it existed in England as long ago as 1600, did not become widely popular until toward the middle of the next century; but football is undoubtedly the oldest of all English national sports.[15]

The Youth Hostel movement "grew out of a long established custom of walking and cycling," as Cassidy observed.[16] In contrast with a similar development in Germany, the English retained voluntary association and allowed the movement to grow in relation to typical English traditions of freedom.

Sport in various forms reflects the Englishman's ideas of life. The colonial in Hong Kong going to play golf at Repulse Bay and the army officer in India engaged in polo are illustrations of the same trait. Although the traits and characteristics of Englishmen are apparently best expressed and satisfied in the games, sports and athletics that have been their heritage since the earliest days of the British people, the contribution of Archibald MacLaren (1820-1884) should not be omitted. About 1860, MacLaren, who had established a gymnasium at Oxford, was asked to develop a system of physical education for the British Army. This was done and the system appeared in the

[15] *Ibid*, p. 201.
[16] Rosalind Cassidy, "Youth Hostels: England and Germany," *The Nation's Schools*, May, 1937.

publication *A Military System of Gymnastic Exercises for the Use of Instructors.* About two decades later the London School Board introduced the use of Swedish gymnastics in the London schools. In 1902, Swedish gymnastics were introduced into the British Navy and substituted in part for the MacLaren gymnastics in the British Army.

It will appear, therefore, that the type of physical education developed in any nation reflects the customs, ideas, beliefs, attitudes, and conscious needs of the people. It may be asked, then, what European nation more nearly approximates the ideas, customs, attitudes, and conscious needs of America? In addition to our ancestry (largely English), our language, our common law, it is the verdict of history that America most nearly resembles England in these fundamental qualities. This judgment will explain why the gymnastics of Sweden, Germany and Denmark, and the emotional posturings of Delsarte (France) never gained any wide acceptance in the United States. On the contrary, the sports, games, and athletics of England are the very heart of our physical education today.

After the 1936 Olympic games in Berlin, where the British team made a very poor showing, popular demand for improved health and physical education programs led to intensified effort to train teachers and to install programs. The National Fitness Council for England and Wales represented the interest of the Government in the matter, which was also expressed by the Physical Training and Recreation Act to provide grants-in-aid for improvement of facilities.

In a recent study of physical education in England, Richard H. Pohndorf reports in a personal communication that the English are doing a better job in physical education than we are. He visited more than fifty schools and found "no medical excuses, no driver education taking children out of classes, no cheerleaders, no ticket takers, no band, but plenty of participation by everyone. They have more fields per capita than we have. Our biggest gap in the fitness curves (Fig. 10, page 228) is in the elementary years. We have very little physical education in our elementary schools, yet in England the youngsters dress for the activity. In the United States a teacher is assigned to supervise recess in her silk dress and high heels while the others have their coffee break."

RUSSIAN PHYSICAL EDUCATION

In Russia physical education is used to promote Communist social theory, as indeed is all education. Physical education is never an end in itself but aims solely to serve the Soviet state. This view pervades Soviet literature on the subject. Panov writes:

> Proletarian physical culture in the U.S.S.R. should by no means be considered as an independent field of work, unconnected with the whole proletarian culture . . . ; [it] aims at the restoration of the health of the working masses and tries to combat the one-sidedness and often mutilating effects of implements; [it] should not only strengthen the health . . . and increase labor productivity . . . it should also train in them [workers] certain occupational habits and accustom them to distribute their energies regularly during the working day.[17]

Russian physical education is characterized by a deep seriousness of attitude. In the United States, it is not uncommon to hear criticisms of the serious attitudes of our athletes in championship competitions and of the drudgery that pervades the training and practice periods of so many of our games. The Russian seriousness, however, is of another sort. The athletes are preparing themselves for the class struggle and strong, healthy, and vigorous physiques are needed for that. They little knew, a few years ago, how well they were preparing themselves or how severely they would be tested for stamina and endurance in the years 1941-1942.

In the early days of the revolution, there was created a special Supreme Council of Physical Culture, headed by scholars and professors who were competent in the scientific and

[17] Quoted in Thomas Woody, *New Minds: New Men*, New York, Macmillan, 1932, p. 409.

practical aspects of the field. The dangers confronting the Soviet Union led them to value high such qualities as health, strength, dexterity, discipline, boldness, presence of mind, sturdiness, and alertness. They were realistic enough to understand that these were desirable qualities, not only in the men of the Red Army but also in all persons of the population.

Physical education (culture) in Russia is compulsory for all school students, and widely promoted for all adults. In the schools the program is centered in three groups; Octobrists, Pioneers, and Komsomols. The Octobrists include children 7 to 10 years of age, the Pioneers 10 to 17, and the Komsomols 18 to 25. These are organizations of the Communist Party, but all do not become members of the party nor are all youth in these groups. The Pioneers developed out of the Boy Scouts and Girl Scouts, which disappeared as organizations during the revolution. Hence, the Pioneers conduct many of the procedures of scouting. Older boys of the Komsomols serve as leaders of the Pioneers.

The Komsomol is the League of Communist Youth. It is actively political. The responsibility of these two groups for carrying on the program of physical education rather than their political status makes them of interest here.

In addition to the Pioneers and Komsomols, there are various athletic clubs, sports associations, physical education groups of labor unions, and other bodies which are concerned largely with adult needs and interests.

This movement in Russia is manifesting a real interest in national health problems. The anti-alcohol and anti-tobacco crusades are strongly supported by the Pioneers and Komsomols. They are also active in social hygiene education and seek to develop wholesome ideas and practices in sex life. Quackery in medicine and common superstitions are also attacked as a part of their effort to be scientific and socially useful.

But it should not be supposed that Soviet sport proceeds in a cultural atmosphere that is identical with that found in the United States. Sport is an expression of the culture, and the differences in the conduct of sport among the nations reflect the dominant ideas of the time and the place. It should be understood that sport in Russia is in accord with the social philosophy of the Soviet State in exactly the same way that American sport reflects the national scene. When Mussolini recalled an Italian soccer team from Austria because it lost a match, and when Hitler demanded victory rather than sportsmanship from German athletes, sport not only expressed cultural forces but also was used to shape and fashion them. In totalitarian states every social force is used to establish and maintain the principles upon which the government rests; it is not strange, therefore, that sport which strongly arouses the emotions of people should be actively employed to promote the social philosophy of the state.

All reviews of Russian physical education report the fact that physical education in the U.S.S.R. is an instrument of national policy and therefore is guided carefully by governmental officials. Esslinger writes, "A final purpose of physical education is to indoctrinate the participants with the communistic ideology."[18] McLendon discusses the Soviet effort to develop championship basketball. He writes:

> The determination on the part of the Soviets to defeat the United States in this particular sport is a serious one. In the early school grades, comparable to our sixth grade and up, basketball is required in the youth "Physical Culture" program. This is part of a long range plan. More immediately, and throughout Moscow and the various republics, especially Latvia, Estonia, Lithuania, the Ukraine, and Georgia, sports clubs, universities, colleges, and institutes emphasize the development of basketball as a major national athletic program with one main objective—to develop players skilled enough to be included on the Russian National Team No. 1 or the Russian National Team No. 2. These teams represent the Soviet Union in International tournaments, including the Olympic Games.[19]

[18] Arthur A. Esslinger, "Health, Physical Education, and Recreation Programs in the U.S.S.R." *Journal of Health—Physical Education—Recreation*, September, 1958, p. 33.

[19] John B. McLendon, Jr., "Russia's Future in Basketball," *Journal of Health—Physical Education—Recreation*, September, 1962, p. 31.

PHYSICAL EDUCATION IN OTHER LANDS

The magazine *The Physical Educator* has been reporting on physical education elsewhere in the world.[20] This excellent series of reports give a brief overview of what is going on in Iraq, South Africa, New Zealand, Yugoslavia, India, Holland, Switzerland, Thailand, Malaya, Colombia, and others. UNESCO, in *Education Abstracts*, gives a report of "Official Primary and Secondary Programmes in Physical Education" (February, 1959, Vol. XI, No. 2) in the following nations: Argentina, Australia, Austria, Belgium, Bolivia, Burma, Canada, Ceylon, Chile, Colombia, Costa Rica, Czechoslovakia, Denmark, Ecuador, El Salvador, Finland, France, Federal Republic of Germany, Ghana, Honduras, Hungary, India, Italy, Kenya, Korea, Libya, Malta and Gozo, the Netherlands, New Zealand, Nicaragua, Norway, Pakistan, Paraguay, Peru, the Philippines, Poland, Puerto Rico, Spain, Sweden, Switzerland, Tunisia, the U.S.S.R., the United Kingdom, the United States of America, Venezuela, and Yugoslavia. These sketches supplement the reports in *The Physical Educator*.

AMERICAN PHYSICAL EDUCATION

The third decade of the ninteenth century saw sporadic efforts at physical education in the work of Partridge with his military academies, the German refugees, Beck, Follen, and Lieber, the manual labor movement, and the calisthenics of Catherine Beecher. But the nation was engaged primarily in agriculture and its allied business. The energy of the population was poured out in wresting from nature a livelihood. It was a grim business and no time was left for leisure and little for education. The ideas of personal development and self-expression had little opportunity for realization.

With the industrial revolution came remarkable changes.

[20] *The Physical Educator:* October, 1956; March, 1957; May, 1957; September, 1958; September, 1959; December, 1959; May, 1960; March, 1961; May, 1962; and December, 1962.

New peoples coming into the cities found the church and the private and charity schools unable to meet the educational needs. "In 1833," says Cubberley, "it was estimated that one eighth of the total population of New York City was composed of public paupers and criminals, while the city had one saloon for every eighty men, women, and children in the total population."[21]

The strict moral code of the rural districts, living remnants of Puritanism, broke down in the cities, and the political ideals of those "fit to rule" fought in the open against the claims of the common man.

The industrial revolution after the Civil War opened new and varied economic opportunities which were eagerly grasped, with the result that in the latter half of the nineteenth century the distribution of the population in rural and urban communities was altered profoundly, and the factory, instead of the home, became the center of vocational life for many people.

These manifestations of human activity were in response to the ideas of the time and place. Political liberty, rich natural resources, opportunity for advancement in security, in prestige, in enjoyment of luxury, gave a different set of ideas to ferment in America than was possible in Europe in the same period. The need for a system of gymnastics which arose in Germany and in Sweden was never apparent in these early days in the United States.

But the factory system and urban life were not favorable for normal physical development, and many parents became concerned about the poor physique of their children. Foundation for this concern was laid earlier by the work of a number of German refugees who had introduced the Jahn gymnastics into America; it was strengthened by the lectures and writings of Dio Lewis and Catherine Beecher in the middle of the century, who vigorously assailed the physical weakness and physical defects of American boys and girls.

Consequently, at the sessions of the famous Physical Training Conference held in Boston in 1889, the outstanding

[21] E. P. Cubberley, *History of Public Education in the United States,* Boston, Houghton Mifflin, 1934, p. 107.

view regarding physical education was the corrective one. But the conference was not a meeting of specialists in physical education alone; it was also attended by educators, and these school people set up a number of conditions that reflected the ideas they had concerning the function of education. In effect, the schoolmen proposed that any physical training that was to be taken into the school must require very little time, must be inexpensive and not demand specially trained teachers, must conduct its activities in the classroom (activity carried on outside the school building could not be educative), and must not require apparatus.

Unfortunately, the experts in physical training of the time came forward and said in effect: We have just what you want. We propose systematic exercises that can be taught by the regular teacher in the classroom. No apparatus will be required, and the expense is very moderate. These exercises will correct the schoolroom stoop, provide relief for the mind, and bring health and vigor to the body. The antiseptic request of the schoolmen was accorded a sterilized program, vestiges of which remain today as "ten minutes a day of calisthenics."

Now, this in brief represents the beginning of physical education in the schools of the United States. No study was made of the kind of activities boys and girls need for developmental purposes, nor of the usages to which physical activities may be put in the setting up and acquirement of standards of conduct. The schoolroom stoop and physical weakness loomed large as the problems. A ready cure was proposed for a very complex disturbance with the usual unsatisfactory results when unscientific methods are proposed.

This type of physical training (for it was nothing more than a training procedure) never caught the imagination of boys and girls. They were asked to go through an innumerable number of stupid posturings when their whole being was calling for a kind of activity based in the neuron connections already set up and organized in their nervous systems. Consequently, from time to time, youth took into its own hands the business of physical education. In colleges and high schools, teams were organized for the playing of games, meets were held with other teams, and soon the institutions represented found themselves involved in disputes, financial arrangements, and real embarrassments. Not yet appreciating the place of physical education in the education of young people, schoolmen set up faculty advisers, or managers, to control an activity with which they had little sympathy and no understanding.

Thus, for more than three decades after 1889, examples of two types of physical education in the school could be found; one, composed of artificial exercises, arose in response to a group of ideas wholly foreign to the traits, characteristics, and needs of American boys and girls, and which were justified by those who proposed them on the grounds of correction of defects, acquirement of health, or promotion of discipline. That such exercises given en masse do not correct the defects which require accurate diagnosis and specific, individual treatment, that they are not conducive to health interpreted in the light of present-day available knowledge, and that the discipline they promote is that of the barracks, have not been understood sufficiently by educators.

The other was represented by the extreme development of competitive athletics which arose as a natural activity of youth, stimulated by the commercial and advertising values of games, and without the educational leadership which such an activity should attract. The early days of sport in America bear the marks of the gambler, pugilist, and plug-ugly. Some of its present-day manifestations reveal these early scars. But games have been continued in the school not so much because superintendents desired them as educative activities, but because they were helpless to prevent them, or saw in them an advertising asset. It has rarely occurred to schoolmen to use physical education for worthwhile educational goals. If one wished to teach children the value of international good will, one would not select as teacher a believer in war. If one desired to teach science in the schools, one would not place children under the guidance of an antivivisectionist or an antivaccinationist. However, in the teaching of school games, the teacher (coach) is selected frequently not on his educational qualifications but on his reputed ability to turn out a winning team. That he may be a cussing, raving, roaring type of bully makes little difference, because as yet, too frequently, the goals are commercial rather than educational.

Through these stormy years of developing a program around which the varied interests of the profession might rally, the work of Dudley Sargent and Amy Morris Homans in training teachers, the leadership of Joseph Lee in the playground movement, and the sure genius of Luther Gulick in many creative and artistic aspects of physical education, marked the scene. From the latter part of the nineteenth century through the early decades of the twentieth, these leaders were supported by the work of Seaver in anthropometry, Leonard in history, Bancroft with her games book and posture test, and many others in all sorts of institutions.

Recent Trends in America.   The most recent trend in physical education flows out of the wars, which have given an immense emphasis to physical fitness. But already, there are signs that schools and colleges are slipping back into the old grooves. The lessons in physical fitness of the Pre-Flight Schools for Naval Aviation candidates are nowhere being fully applied. More recently the fitness of American youth has been questioned by means of a very inadequate study which compared American with European children. This has been discussed in Chapter 6.

There continues a real emphasis upon recreational interests and skills. The need for desirable ways of living in longer leisure periods has been expressed by many in various professional fields. Education for leisure marks a proper emphasis in physical education today. Corecreational programs for boys and girls give large social promise in the years ahead.

The remarkable modern dance movement appears to be one of the most vital, thoroughly alive art forms in current American life. In some respects its development in the theater and in stage recitals goes beyond what seems desirable in schools. For example, the demands of art in the dance frequently conflict with the welfare of the individual performer. Notions of line design, rhythm pattern, and emphasis often lead to use of the foot in a weak, pronated position, to strong accent with the bare foot, to bending of the trunk backward, and similar distortions which injure the musculoskeletal mechanism. What the dance does in the theater may be interesting but it is often unacceptable as a criterion of what to do in schools.

The sport, game and athletic activities continue to appeal to both players and spectators. Many aspects of sport are very wholesome. The intramural sports program has been greatly extended in the schools and colleges, and is, in many instances, a better illustration of sport than that given by the varsity teams. Winter sports are developing rapidly, and are, in some areas, the most significant activities of young people during the winter months. In spite of many fine and wholesome developments in sport, the situation in the college area is particularly disturbing. The scandals in basketball revealed an aspect of collegiate athletic affairs that is deeply deplored by all. And yet that sort of outcome is a logical result of the commercial influence that has been rampant in football and basketball for years. It is not reasonable to suppose that these conditions can be changed without a new orientation of the purposes for which intercollegiate sport is conducted.

It is rather remarkable that the role of the spectator at music recitals, dance recitals and art exhibitions is socially approved, but that watching such intensely dramatic and human art as football and baseball contests is called "spectatoritis" and frowned upon. It should be granted that participation is desirable, and surely the pages of this book argue for that. It may also be observed that participation in music, dance, painting, drawing, and sculpturing is also admirable. But all cannot play football, nor baseball, nor compete in the Olympic games. There is a place for the dramatic festivals of sport and the modern American culture gives them a welcome. The role of the understanding spectator is not to be despised.

Swimming is increasingly popular. More and more pools

are being constructed, beaches reclaimed for use, and streams restored to their natural state. The woods and fields, camping, hunting and fishing claim their followers.

Table 5, based on a tabulation issued by WCOTP, the World Confederation of Organizations of the Teaching Profession, gives the time devoted to physical education during the school day by those nations responding to the inquiry (1960).

TABLE 5. TIME DEVOTED TO PHYSICAL EDUCATION DURING THE SCHOOL DAY

Minutes	For a Child of 7 years	For a Child of 11 years	For a Child of 15 years
20/day	Gambia (plus 1 period of 40 min. per week) Philippines		
25/day	United States	Philippines	Philippines
30/day	Italy Yugoslavia	Gambia (plus 1 period of 40 min. per week) United States	China
40/day			Gambia (plus 1 period of 40 min. per week)
60/week	Denmark India Sweden	Denmark India Ireland	India
75/week	Northern Ireland		
90/week	New Zealand	New Zealand Nyasaland	Nyasaland
120/week	Hong Kong Luxemburg West Germany	Hong Kong Italy Luxemburg Switzerland West Germany	Hong Kong Italy Luxemburg New Zealand West Germany
150/week	Ghana Netherlands Nyasaland Scotland	China Ghana Netherlands Scotland	Netherlands Scotland

TABLE 5 — (*Continued*)

Minutes	For a Child of 7 years	For a Child of 11 years	For a Child of 15 years
110-170/week	Korea	Korea	Korea
180/week	China Japan Netherlands Switzerland Thailand	Japan Sweden Thailand Yugoslavia	Denmark Ghana Japan Northern Ireland Sweden Switzerland United States Yugoslavia
No mention of time, but inclusion of curriculum for all ages	Belgium Canada England France (2-3½ hrs.) Malta Iran Panama		

THE RISE OF A PROFESSIONAL ASSOCIATION

The American Association for Health, Physical Education and Recreation is the national organization for these three areas. Its origin goes back to the year 1885 when the Association for the Advancement of Physical Education was formed. Later this pioneer society became the American Physical Education Association; still later, as health education and recreation developed in the schools and colleges, the Association expanded into the American Association for Health, Physical Education and Recreation. There are several other organizations concerned with sports and dance, but the American Association is the largest with a membership roll of 27,722.[22] It is the central body for the 50 state associations and the six district organizations.

The government of the American Association for Health,

[22] *Journal of Health—Physical Education—Recreation*, October, 1962, p. 28.

Physical Education and Recreation consists of two bodies: the Representative Assembly, and the Board of Directors. The Assembly is composed of representatives elected by the districts. The Board of Directors consists of the president of the Association, president-elect, past-president, six vice-presidents (who are in charge of six divisions, namely, health education, women's sports, men's athletics, physical education, safety education, and recreation), parliamentarian, and one elected person from each of the six districts. The Board of Directors determines policies; it receives recommendations from the Assembly.

The Association holds a national convention every year in each of the districts on a rotating basis upon invitation from the district. The Association publishes *The Journal of Health— Physical Education—Recreation,* and *The Research Quarterly.*

The stated purposes of the Association are to:

1. Promote professional growth and perspective.
2. Give unity to the professional group.
3. Enhance prestige among other organized professional groups.
4. Lend dignity to membership and activities of the profession.
5. Supply united support of worthy projects.
6. Give competition within the profession a spirit of cooperation.
7. Sponsor valuable research projects which would prove too expensive for small groups to undertake.
8. Provide a wider field of authority to serve in the solution of problems.

There are many members who feel that the purposes are not adequate and that the ones stated are not vigorously pursued. These conditions, if they are faults, can be cured by strong recommendations from the Assembly to the Board of Directors. Certainly there seems to be little excuse for the lack of editorial views on many of the persistent problems confronting the members of the Association.

THE PREPARATION OF PHYSICAL EDUCATION TEACHERS

The early efforts in America to prepare teachers of physical education followed the European pattern in which the curricula were limited to the technical aspects of physical exercise. The first professional schools were privately established and for many years privately conducted. As the relationship of physical education to the complete education of the child was understood, it became clear that a different setting was essential in order to secure a proper preparation of teachers of physical education. Gradually colleges and universities established professional curricula for the preparation of teachers of physical education, and today the private normal school of physical education has disappeared.

From this experience certain conclusions can be drawn although their full force is not yet appreciated in all schools engaged in preparing teachers. In the first place, the preparation of physical education teachers should be conducted in a broad educational atmosphere. There are many items of an educational atmosphere. The more obvious are: The opportunity to read books, to discuss personal and social problems, to hear good music and stimulating lectures, and to think about the great events in human history from the days of ancient Greece to the present. But atmosphere is created also by clothing, manners, and speech. To spend the school day in the costume suited to the gymnasium or athletic field tends to restrict the interests to the place for which one is dressed.

Secondly, an educational atmosphere is dependent upon the facilities and staff that can arouse the student to breadth in learning. Students of physical education should read many books outside their area of specialization. History, philosophy, sociology, poetry, and religion can contribute a great deal to the preparation of a good teacher of physical education. One who has read little or nothing except the technical literature of his field will be a narrow specialist without understanding either of his colleagues or of the world of affairs around him.

Thirdly, preparation of the physical education teacher should be based on principles and not limited to materials and methods. At this point, many minors are faulty. The principal of a New York City high school recently asked: "Why is it that teachers of physical education have no interests outside the gymnasium and are unable to contribute to discussions in staff meetings when basic school problems are considered?" It is from principles that one gets a foundation for decisions.

And finally, the way students and teachers refer to their field sets the tone of the department. Dignity of a field is not attained through careless use of undignified terms. When major students use the terms, "Phys. Ed." and "P.E." to designate their field, they begin to destroy the respect of others for a professional area whose sponsors hold it so lightly. This point of view may appear to some to be a trifling matter, but its importance is apparent when one observes how colleagues in other fields refer to their professional interests. Colleagues in physics use the word "physics" and not "phys."; those in chemistry do not say "chem."; and even those with compound words to designate their fields do not resort to "Eng. Lit.," "Comp. An.," and "Ab. Psych." for English Literature, Comparative Anatomy, and Abnormal Psychology.

QUESTIONS AND PROBLEMS FOR DISCUSSION

1. Has European experience influenced physical education in the United States? Is the experience of others always of great value?
2. Why do peoples tend not to use their own indigenous resources?
3. How reliable is another's experience for you? Is this always, seldom, or rarely true?
4. Why is it important to know all the conditions of an experience?
5. What is the significance of the psychic factors in a cultural experience?
6. How can you evaluate the experience of others?
7. How do you distinguish between social customs as experience and biological findings as experience?

8. What were the cultural and political ideas in Germany which gave a background for Jahn's work?
9. What was the meaning of the motto of the Turners?
10. Why did Jahn's work not achieve success in his lifetime?
11. What significant changes in physical education were produced by National Socialism? Explain the differences in objectives of physical education in East and West Germany.
12. What was the political and cultural background in which Ling developed physical education in Sweden?
13. How has Swedish physical education changed in recent years? Is this change limited to Sweden?
14. Why have the French never produced a national system of physical education?
15. What was the dominant note in Italian physical education? How was it organized to accomplish its purpose?
16. What are the traits, customs, and characteristics of English culture out of which physical education developed?
17. What are the purposes of Russian physical education?
18. How did the Physical Training Conference of 1889 influence physical education in the United States?
19. What is the athletic influence in the United States?
20. What are recent trends in physical education in the United States?
21. Write an editorial for *The Journal* that deals with some important problem in the field.
22. Why should a teacher of physical education be as well-educated as his colleagues in other fields?

REFERENCE READINGS

Ainsworth, Dorothy S. *A History of Physical Education in Colleges for Women*. New York, Barnes, 1930.

Duncan, Margaret M., and Johnson, Ralph H. *Introduction to Physical Education, Health Education and Recreation*. Englewood Cliffs, N.J., Prentice-Hall, 1954.

Duncan, Ray O., and Watson, Helen B. *Introduction to Physical Education*. New York, Ronald Press, 1960.

Dzenowagis, Joseph G. "Professional Laboratory Experiences for Prospective Physical Educators." *The Physical Educator*, December, 1961, p. 139.

Fraser, Ellen D., *et al.* *The Child and Physical Education*. Englewood Cliffs, N.J., Prentice-Hall, 1956.

Jenny, John H. *Physical Education, Health Education and*

Recreation: Introduction to Professional Preparation for Leadership. New York, Macmillan, 1961.

Leonard, Fred E., and Affleck, George B. *A Guide to the History of Physical Education,* 3rd Edition. Philadelphia, Lea & Febiger, 1947.

Ley, Katherine, and Jernigan, Sara S. "The Roots and the Tree." *Journal of Health—Physical Education—Recreation,* September, 1962, p. 34.

Murray, Ruth L., and Hussey, Delia P. *From Student to Teacher in Physical Education.* Englewood Cliffs, N.J., Prentice-Hall, 1959.

Nash, Jay B. *Opportunities in Physical Education and Health Education,* Revised Edition. New York, Vocational Guidance Manuals, 1960.

Nixon, Eugene W., and Cozens, Frederick W. *An Introduction to Physical Education,* 5th Edition, Revised by Eugene W. Nixon and Florence S. Frederickson. Philadelphia, Saunders, 1959.

Oberteuffer, Delbert. *Physical Education: A Textbook of Principles for Professional Students,* Revised Edition. New York, Harper, 1962.

Rice, Emmett A., *et al. A Brief History of Physical Education,* 4th Edition. New York, Ronald Press, 1958.

Schwendener, Norma S. *A History of Physical Education in the United States.* New York, Barnes, 1942.

Scott, Harry A. *Competitive Sports in Schools and Colleges.* New York, Harper, 1951.

Smith, Hope M., and Clifton, Marguerite A. *Physical Education: Exploring Your Future.* Englewood Cliffs, N.J., Prentice-Hall, 1962.

Snyder, Raymond A., and Scott, Harry A. *Professional Preparation in Health, Physical Education, and Recreation.* New York, McGraw-Hill, 1954.

Van Dalen, Deobold B., *et al. A World History of Physical Education.* Englewood Cliffs, N.J., Prentice-Hall, 1953.

Voltmer, C. D. *A Brief History of the Intercollegiate Conference of Faculty Representatives.* New York, Bureau of Publications, Teachers College, Columbia University, 1935.

Weston, Arthur. *The Making of American Physical Education.* New York, Appleton-Century-Crofts, 1962.

Williams, Jesse Feiring. "Training Teachers of Health and Physical Education." *Teachers' College Record,* December, 1944.

THE CURRICULUM

THE CURRICULUM

Men shoot and throw. At first this is done as an "instinctive" or natural reaction to some situation. The result, when it is observed, gives a new meaning to the activity. Henceforth men in throwing and shooting think of it in terms of its outcome; they act intelligently or have an end (objective). Liking the activity in its acquired meaning, they not only "take aim" when they throw, instead of throwing at random, but they find or make targets at which to aim. This is the origin and nature of "goals" of action. They are ways of defining and deepening the meaning of activity. Having an end or aim is thus a characteristic of present activity. It is the means by which an activity becomes adapted. . . . Men do not shoot because targets exist, but they set up targets in order that throwing and shooting may be more effective and significant.

Dewey.

Physical education is for the sake of mental and moral culture and not an end in itself. It is to make the intellect, feelings, and will more vigorous, sane, supple, and resourceful.

G. Stanley Hall.

WHAT IS THE CURRICULUM?

The term curriculum is variously used. In high school it may designate a group of courses that are called the "college preparatory curriculum." These courses have a sequential character and meet certain time requirements. It is this orderly arrangement of planned experiences that fulfills the concept of a curriculum in this instance. Likewise a group of planned experiences in physical education in sequences and in time allotments may be a curriculum whereas a number of unrelated physical activities conducted according to the caprice of the principal would not be a curriculum.

This restricted character of curriculum, in a time and sequential arrangement, omitted from the curriculum a large number of after-school experiences that, for many years, were called "extracurricular activities." Over the years, it was recognized that many of these experiences contributed to the objectives of the curriculum. Gradually, the term curriculum has been defined to include these experiences as well. Hence, in physical education it is now acceptable to include both intramural and extramural athletics, dance clubs, and other after-school activities within the planned experiences of the curriculum.

The place held by any educational interest in the curriculum depends upon several factors. The understanding and ability of the leadership of the area are powerful forces in determining the opportunity that any interest will enjoy. Facilities condition what can be done but reliance upon this factor as the sole means of program selection is a policy of despair since facilities can be changed and opportunity made available if there are desire and will to do so. Probably the most important single factor in determining the place of physical education in the curriculum is the body of ideas that support it, the philosophic justifications that surround it, and the avowed purposes to which it is devoted.

WHAT IS THE COURSE OF STUDY?

Curriculum materials arranged for instruction in a particular field are called a course of study. These provided definite outlines and were rigid in form. Today, it is the better practice to offer for the use of teachers curricular materials as guides, enriched with resource materials of various kinds. This new use of curricular materials supports and facilitates a school program adjusted to the different needs of each community, its schools, and the children.[1]

Moreover, this shift from rigid outlines presented by some "authority" to a flexible type of material leads to a more democratic procedure in determining what children shall be taught. The conviction that public education is the proper concern of the community and that a democratic method is essential in securing the judgment and interest of parents conforms with the extension of democracy in other areas of social life. In this book there will be no attempt to present a course of study but rather to suggest curricular materials, to indicate how these may be selected for particular purposes, and to place upon the individual teacher responsibility for what he chooses, what outcomes he seeks, and what results he achieves.

STEPS IN PREPARATION OF A CURRICULUM

Some years ago when physical education was to be introduced into a school, it was customary to make an inquiry concerning the current practice in other schools where physical education was taught, and to adopt, often rather uncritically, one of the programs in use. The faults in such a procedure are obvious. Another approach to the problem was to discover what some "authority" recommended. If his influence was sufficiently great or if his particular bias coincided with the bias of the investigator, then his proposal was followed. The faults in this procedure are equally obvious.

[1] *Elementary Education in California at the Midcentury*, Bulletin California State Department of Education, Vol. XX, No. 2, December, 1951.

As education became more scientific in its procedures of organization, it became clear that what is offered as instruction to children should be selected with respect to certain considerations. These considerations suggest five essential steps in the development of a curriculum in physical education. These steps are: (1) analysis of the situation; (2) appraisal of the characteristics of the individuals to be educated; (3) statement of an aim for the program; (4) statement of the objectives to be sought; and (5) selection of the activities in relation to the situation, characteristics of pupils, aim, and objectives.

THE SITUATION

Whether one is entering upon a new position or continuing an old one, whether one is a novice teacher or an experienced workman, the features of the local situation should be learned and from time to time reviewed. A teacher may have high ambitions to develop a swimming program but a situation without pools or natural water facilities will make his hopes impossible of realization at that time. The state law may set requirements that must be met, the climate may prevent outdoor activities for several months each year, the religious character of the community may condemn dance of all kinds; these and other realities must be taken into account in planning the curriculum.

In almost every situation there are some lacks. The ideal and the real are far apart in some places, nearer together in others. Nevertheless, one works with what one has. Part of what one has is the deficiency, the lack of opportunity, the prejudice, the law, or whatnot. An impoverished situation is just the kind that can be improved. Deficiency in facility or equipment may be responsible for an inadequate program; at that point the chief problem in curriculum construction is the improvement of the situation. For many years calisthenics in the classroom were the main part of the physical education program. They existed in part, although not entirely, because there were no playrooms, no playgrounds, no pools, no athletic fields, no gymnasiums. But they continued long after opportunities were available due to the failure of leaders in physical education to see a correspondence between the situation and the curriculum. When one changes, the other should also be modified.

Every deficiency in a situation that is subject to change should be a continuous challenge to the end that a worthwhile and truly educational program can be conducted.

Physical education in curriculum construction should examine and take into account all the pertinent facts of the local situation.

In studying a local situation, the teacher of physical education will find it helpful to read several reports of school surveys and references on survey methods.[2]

THE INDIVIDUAL TO BE EDUCATED

The next step in the planning of a curriculum is to study and appraise the individuals who are to be educated. What are they like? What are their characteristics? What are their individual differences? What is their nutritional status? What is their level of skill? Some of the answers to these questions will be found in the records of a good health examination. Others can be assessed from the data on the growth and development, the characteristics, and the needs of boys and girls as collected from research materials. In general the teacher will learn that boys and girls after a certain age desire different activities, that a first grade class can be taught better in a circle than in a line formation, that bodily contact is hazardous for girls after puberty, and that certain precautions are necessary in the use of apparatus. Some of these things can be learned by reading books;[3] others will come from experience.

[2] American Association for Health, Physical Education and Recreation (Research Section), *Research Methods Applied to Health, Physical Education and Recreation,* Washington, D.C., 1949, pp. 315-352.

[3] American Association for Health, Physical Education and Recreation, *Developing Democratic Human Relations,* Washington, D.C., 1951, pp. 39-50.

Physical education in curriculum construction should study and appraise all the pertinent facts with respect to the characteristics of the individuals to be educated.

In the study of pupil characteristics the teacher will find Chapters 6 and 7 helpful. It should be noted, however, that individual children will vary from the general characteristics of groups and that exceptions are necessary in dealing with specific cases.

THE AIM OF PHYSICAL EDUCATION

It is a matter of considerable responsibility to declare to others what the aim of any area of education ought to be. No one who attempts to do so can assume to describe anything more than the goal that is so clear to him. In such effort there are several considerations that may serve as guides in formulating an aim of physical education.

The formulation of a theory of physical education ought to grow out of a practice that is continually checked by principles. Theory and practice should be subjected to a constant correction, the one by the other, affording a reciprocal and necessary modification. The effort should always be made to provide actual activities to illustrate the principles presented and to find acceptable principles to justify the practice.

This is the test that the practical person should set himself in working with a program of physical education. There is no reason for pride in a position or a type of work which is maintained on any other basis. The person who can teach a program and still have a very little understanding of the legitimate objectives and no concern about the relation of the immediate professional interest to other programs and other human effort is making a questionable contribution to the work of the world. Such teaching makes the person a slave to a system or method; hence he loses the inspiration that comes from work that has meaning.

This relationship of theory to practice and of practice to theory illustrates what is meant by the frequent admonition of thinkers that one should keep an open mind. The one thing that should be remembered by physical educators is that no discussion of physical education represents a final statement. The most elaborate dance technique is just the kind of method and material which is most susceptible to interpretation, modification, and, at times, complete rejection. It is always a vain thing to attempt to force the living into set molds. All the molds crack. They are too constricted and too rigid for what we try to put into them. The physical education of the human race cannot be resolved into a system or into a method for all time. At any one period, the best thought can be brought to bear upon the problems confronting the profession and the most practical solution offered. Succeeding generations will of necessity feel free to discard much that we have done, and to meet the problems of their day with new ideas, different organizations, and more abundant opportunities. For the present, the chief business is to find truth, to build sanely and with justifications; there will be more then to salvage in the future.

Students of physical education should remember that the doctrines taught them in their professional school are not necessarily true. To too great an extent students have the foolish habit of accepting fully the dicta of professors without going through the process of really making the conclusions of the professor their own. Even those whose judgment we respect and concerning whose integrity we have no doubt are liable to error and frequently make mistakes. The essential problem before the student or teacher of physical education is to arrive at a point of view that he can live with, acquire an attitude that he can support and, if necessary, defend. Authorities or experts in one's own field may be quoted, but only believed to the point where there can be essential agreement with the position stated. In a field outside one's own, one selects and follows an expert implicitly; to do so in instances where one should exercise one's own judgment is to stultify one's self.

An aim indicates direction, point of view, or goal. It is general in nature. As Dewey suggests, an aim is not really conceived unless the means are visualized and organized for the end in view. Objectives, on the other hand, are precise, definite, and limited statements of steps in the procedure of realization of the aim. Between aim and objectives there arises the need for statement of purposes which are not general enough to be an aim and not precise enough to be objectives. These declarations may be called platforms, purposes, and similar terms,[4] thus avoiding confusion in terminology. With these considerations in mind the following aim of physical education is proposed:

Physical education should aim to provide skilled leadership and adequate facilities which will afford an opportunity for the individual or group to act in situations which are physically wholesome, mentally stimulating and satisfying, and socially sound.

These terms require some elaboration. This will be given by stating what is meant and also what is not covered by the term.

By "physically wholesome" it is meant in general that situation that is good for a man as determined by scientific experiment or that can be inferred from available scientific knowledge, or that is shown clearly by experience. This will mean control of the environment as regards sanitary matters, such as air, dust, cleanliness, communicable disease, and so on. Moreover, since the subject is physical education the activity must produce the physiological results of exercise. The evidence is clear that a considerable amount of physical education is soft, not nearly vigorous enough to secure a high development of organic systems. Frequently insufficient time is devoted to the program. In order to secure "physically wholesome" outcomes, adequate time is essential. Often, however, significant time is fritted away in poorly selected activities. It is always important

[4] The American Association for Health, Physical Education and Recreation through its various sections and divisions has set forth platforms and policy statements. There are: A Platform for Physical Education (*Journal*, March, 1950), A Recreation Policy Statement (*Journal*, September, 1950), Camping and Outdoor Education Policy (mimeographed), Platform for Adapted Physical Education in Elementary and Secondary Schools and Colleges (Therapeutic Section), and others.

that activity should have reference to the condition of the individual. At times the most physically wholesome thing for the person is complete rest. There exists considerable unwholesome physical education in the schools and colleges which arises out of insufficient diagnosis and lack of proper classification of boys and girls for activity.

It is important to judge all activities by this criterion, "physically wholesome." In this connection mention is made of Marathon races, underwater swimming, and the boy's game of basketball played by girls; games in which one is active while other players stand around, and similar activities not "physically wholesome."

By "mentally stimulating and satisfying" reference is made to situations which provide necessity for thinking in relation to the activity, and which give satisfaction as the end-result of the activity that has been going on. Clearly then one must seek to secure from the participants a state of satisfaction from proper impulses and reactions and dissatisfactions from improper ones. One of the main concerns is to provide opportunity for satisfaction of the fundamental racial impulses which serve a useful purpose today in society. The chasing and fleeing games and numerous self-testing activities afford opportunity of a desirable sort. It should be clear also that in the final analysis the situation that is mentally stimulating and satisfying will secure the intellectual control and sanction over the emotional ones. Society is so organized today that the person controlled by the emotions rather than by the intellect suffers greatly and is distinctly less efficient.

It is important to point out that mental gymnastics are of limited power to stimulate, and are likely, if continued past the period of novelty, to be distinctly dissatisfying. Response-command exercises fall in this category. To develop an approving attitude toward physical activity, to acquire a point of view which favors its continuance, are vital to the pupil so far as his physical education is concerned. Physical education is an activity which should be based on the nature of the individual, and be conducted to increase interest as well as skills. Graduates of high school frequently come to college seeking to be excused from physical education because of dissatisfying experience in physical education. At times the experience is not satisfying because of administrative arrangements, such as crowded locker rooms, lack of towels, too little time for dressing, and similar inadequacies. Faulty aims and traditional teaching result at times in a positive dislike for an activity which is largely justified in education on the basis that it will be continued throughout life.

The problem in movement is always the individual pupil's or student's own problem, however. The realization that the individual has a problem, related as it is to an inner urge to solve it, opens the way for thought and favors thinking about it.

It is precisely at this point that we find the weakest link in all types of physical education, although the formal, traditional type fails utterly here. We need to remind ourselves continually of the need to give the child a situation where mental activity can go on. It will go on actively whenever the individual has a goal in view, plans to achieve it, and makes an intelligent effort to do so. This is sound psychology and should guide all teachers. In attempting to develop this situation, however, some teachers err by complete withdrawal from the scene, leaving the individual without help in formulating a goal, without assistance in planning to achieve it, and without appropriate stimulus that could provoke high effort. It requires high competence in a teacher to know how much or how little to direct the process of learning.[5]

An experimental procedure to determine how to use physical education as a learning medium in the development of language arts concepts in third grade children is reported by James H. Humphrey.[6] This is the sort of imaginative research that is greatly needed today. As more data are acquired in this

[5] Boyd H. Bode, *How We Learn*, Boston, Heath, 1940.
[6] James H. Humphrey, "A Pilot Study of the Use of Physical Education as a Learning Medium in the Development of Language Arts Concepts in Third Grade Children," *Research Quarterly*, March, 1962, p. 136.

area of education, the contribution of body movement in development of the perceptive and sensory functions will be enlarged. Aldous Huxley stresses the importance of training perception and enlarging the sensory experiences, which are the sure source of whatever awareness an individual possesses.[7]

By "socially sound" it is meant that physical education should make adequate provision for the appearance and development of moral and social values. This provision is secured largely through the teaching and directing staff in charge of the activities. The values to be taught must be possessed by the teacher, and should have such meaning that one would be willing to work for them. In teaching social and moral values one has to deal with building proper attitudes and general appreciation, so that the response secured in relation to physical education will be thought of as typical of the kind of response which should always be made. Honesty in play is of some importance in itself, but its chief value lies in the opportunity given to the teacher to develop an attitude which will favor honesty as a quality desirable for one to express at all times.

There are those who would wish the schools to build a new social order, and would therefore use the schools to teach social and moral doctrines not now acceptable to those who support and sustain the schools. Thus, the concept, "socially sound," has tight relationships with the teacher's view of the school as a reflector or creator of society. It is important to remember that society builds and maintains schools to provide a firm basis for itself. Society changes and the schools reflect this in accordance with the desire of those who are responsible for or the inheritors of the changes that have taken place.

What is accepted as "socially sound" by one generation may be discarded by another. Over a long period of time there has been established a number of qualities which are generally accepted today, and, in all probability, will be continued as worthy because of the contribution they make to social control

[7] Aldous Huxley, "Human Potentialities," *Control of the Mind, Man and Civilization* (Seymour M. Farber, Editor), New York, McGraw-Hill, 1961, p. 69.

and human happiness. These qualities are: truthfulness, honesty, fair dealing, the give-and-take spirit, loyalty, modesty, courtesy, submission to group opinion, self-restraint, self-discipline, gentleness, courage, generosity.

Moreover, in the grim realities of these days democratic ideals are not on trial. The United States of America is a republic consecrated in its Constitution to certain democratic ideals. The nation is not to be maintained by troops but by ideas and attitudes, however often it must defend itself against foreign enemies or however many must perish in that effort. The ideas and attitudes supporting the nation are taught largely by teachers, and therefore, physical education teachers together with all other teachers have a clear responsibility to interpret "socially sound" in terms of democratic ideals. Whenever they are unable to do so they should resign their posts. The valuable concept of academic freedom should operate in and report upon all areas of human inquiry, but its first loyalty is to the Republic of the United States of America, its first duty is to the nation that permits free inquiry, its first devotion is to national traditions and ideals.

Physical education in curriculum construction should state clearly its aim, the general direction in which it proposes to go.

In the formulation of an aim for physical education, it will be helpful to agree upon an aim for education in general. When this is done, the aim for physical education should be in agreement with the aim for education.

THE OBJECTIVES OF PHYSICAL EDUCATION

The term "objective" is used by the author to mean a precise, exact, and realizable end, and hence is not synonymous with aim. Popularized during World War I, and indicating a certain geographical position or tactical maneuver, it will help to clear the confusion caused by the more general term aim, and in practice should lead to a definite distinction between the two terms. In military terms, an aim may be to win the war; an objective to win a particular battle, to repulse an enemy assault, or to sink a particular ship. In educational terms, an aim may be to develop the human personality; an objective, to have a child criticize his own performance, to gain 5 pounds, or to walk with his toes pointing forward.

Aim is used, then, to denote the direction, general purpose; objective marks out the specific points along the way, all of which contribute to the realization of the aim. The moment an aim is achieved it becomes an objective in the action that goes on. Another and more remote aim appears to chart the continuing course. In this sense then, the aim is never realized, and only the objectives are within the bounds of practical accomplishment. In Browning's lines,

> Ah, but a man's reach should exceed his grasp,
> Or what's a Heaven for?

there is suggested this ideal character of aim. On the contrary, an objective is of the most practical sort. In fact, only as it can be realized and recognized as an accomplished fact, perhaps measured, is it a legitimate objective.

This distinction between aim and objective partakes somewhat of the quality associated with any philosophical discussion of ends. The realization of an end only prepares the way for a take-off in the accomplishment of other and more distant ends. In similar vein an objective represents one step along the way to fulfillment of the aim.

The objective, then, is concrete. One should be able to tell when it has been reached, but this measurable quality does not exclude statements of objectives that for the present cannot be measured. Some of the objectives to be presently set forth are of this tentative character. Nevertheless their indeterminate nature is due not to the quality of the objective, but more frequently to the lack of means of measurement. This feature will be cleared up as soon as the necessary research work is done.

Objectives may be classified in different ways. One may think of objectives as immediate or remote; the former are to be achieved shortly and the latter at some future time. In Figure 13, it will be noted that objectives are classified as technical, associated, and concomitant; such objectives are intimately related to methods and will be discussed fully in the next chapter. It is apparent that some activities serve more readily certain

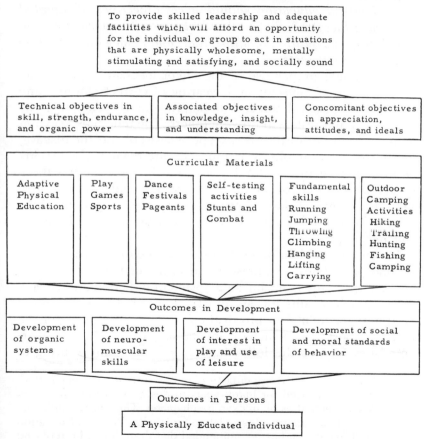

THE AIM OF PHYSICAL EDUCATION

To provide skilled leadership and adequate facilities which will afford an opportunity for the individual or group to act in situations that are physically wholesome, mentally stimulating and satisfying, and socially sound

| Technical objectives in skill, strength, endurance, and organic power | Associated objectives in knowledge, insight, and understanding | Concomitant objectives in appreciation, attitudes, and ideals |

Curricular Materials

| Adaptive Physical Education | Play Games Sports | Dance Festivals Pageants | Self-testing activities Stunts and Combat | Fundamental skills Running Jumping Throwing Climbing Hanging Lifting Carrying | Outdoor Camping Activities Hiking Trailing Hunting Fishing Camping |

Outcomes in Development

| Development of organic systems | Development of neuro-muscular skills | Development of interest in play and use of leisure | Development of social and moral standards of behavior |

Outcomes in Persons

A Physically Educated Individual

Figure 13. A diagram to suggest that an aim of physical education in harmony with its objectives operates through the activities of a program to secure certain outcomes that can eventuate in a physically educated individual.

objectives than do others. Moreover, activities that are similar in type and quality may have similar or identical objectives, for example, folk dances and national dances, handball and racquets, football and soccer; in this section the kind of objective that seems to be pertinent to the activity will be indicated. The teacher of physical education should formulate his own objectives for the activities he selects to teach.

Physical education should select objectives of adapted physical education* that will reflect preventive measures and will justify expenditure of effort, time, and money on correction of remediable defects.

Through proper use of the motor mechanism, adequate nutrition, strong muscles and wearing of correct clothing and shoes, some postural defects can be prevented. Mental hygiene and normal interests will prevent others. The tendency to assign a single factor as a cause is, except in cases of specific disease, a mistake. For example, strong muscles are regarded by experts as insurance against postural defect, but in some studies there is no relationship between muscular strength and good postures. Defects resulting from disease, such as anterior poliomyelitis, tuberculosis of the spine, and rickets, may be prevented in some but not in all cases.

In the problem of good postures,† the objectives involve a concept of body relationships in terms of readiness to act. By good postures is meant **an adjustment of body parts to each other which results in an erect, alert whole, representing readiness for mental or physical effort.** This broadening of the concept "posture" to include mental as well as physical characteristics implies the following: (1) selection and wearing of

---

* The terms "corrective gymnastics" and "individual gymnastics" have been used for many years to designate a program of remedial activities of an exercise character. The Therapeutic Section of the American Association for Health, Physical Education and Recreation has recommended that these terms be replaced with the term "adapted physical education."

† The term "postures" is used to indicate that there are many good postures, not one. The term posturing might be better since what we seek is a dynamic adjustment, not a structural goal.

clothing that favors readiness; (2) facial expression, indicative of an emotional control that favors readiness; (3) objective rather than a subjective manner, as favorable to readiness.

The emphasis on the psychological in relation to postures is in line with the experience of teachers, and also conforms to experimental evidence from neurology.[8]

In this corrective phase of the objective for adapted physical education we are concerned with complete correction or maximum amelioration of the defect. The procedure for this objective is well stated by many specialists in this field.

In the discussion of principles Miss Todd stresses the importance of three factors: (1) balance of weight of pelvis, thorax, and skull; (2) position of shoulders and sternum; and (3) position of the fifth lumbar vertebra.[9]

Physical education must study the human motor mechanism with reference to body control, strains, and expenditure of energy. It is a mistake to regard parts of the body as isolated and unrelated mechanisms. Integration of the entire mechanism as a mechanical instrument is just as important for success in correction of defect or education in use, as integration with reference to physical, mental, and social aspects of life.[10]

Much of the so-called corrective work is not acceptable. Common errors are the attempt to correct individual defects of a large group in class work, the neglect of important elements in personality, and the failure to recognize the need for integration of the entire individual.

Physical education should select objectives in games, athletics, sports, aquatics, and equitation that will seek development of vital organs, insure functional skills for leisure time, stimulate interest in play, and set high standards of behavior.

Activities in this group should be vigorous enough to

[8] C. T. Morgan, *Physiological Psychology*, New York, McGraw-Hill, 1943, pp. 316-329.

[9] M.E. Todd, *The Thinking Body*, New York, Harper, 1937.

[10] John R. Schoon, "Some Psychological Factors in Motivating Handicapped Students in Adapted Physical Education," *The Physical Educator*, December, 1962, p. 138.

stimulate the development of the vital systems. This is essential.

In this group, it is to be desired that skill in and love for an activity be established to the end that the activity will go on. The goal here is continuation of the activity. To secure this there must be acquired sufficient skill which will rank the individual above the novice class for his stage of development, and sufficient love for the activity to afford an incentive to participate even when the conditions are not favorable. The close relation between love for play and skill in play establishes the justification for reasonable perfection in the activity.

The precise games, athletics, sports, or aquatics one should be skilled in, and the exact degree of skill to be required, cannot be stated, since individuals differ in their preferences, and there is no possible agreement among experts. Nor is it known, in all instances, what particular modifications are necessary for age and sex differences. How many games should one know? How well should one be able to play? These are questions to which answers are most variable, and even extended study is not likely to produce acceptable objectives. Of the many activities in this group two, equitation and swimming, have quite definite objectives.

For the former, it would seem reasonable to propose that for certain persons who have an opportunity to ride horses the following obtain:

1. Ability to ride a "broken" horse with pleasure and profit to the rider and without harm to the horse. The number of gaits to be mastered is a matter of individual preference.

2. Ability to care for a horse, to feed, water, and bed down a horse.

3. Ability to enjoy the out-of-doors rather than the sawdust ring.

For swimming, there are a number of objectives set by departments of physical education. These vary greatly, but most departments agree in requiring some specific proficiency. The following are commonly held objectives:

1. Ability to swim any stroke the length of the pool (60 feet) and to execute a plain front dive.

2. Ability to keep up in the water for a period of three minutes.

3. Ability to swim, to float, and to turn from a front to a back position in the water and vice versa.

4. Ability to swim different distances. Obviously every soldier and sailor should be able to swim.

Swimming lends itself to precise statement of objectives, and objectives may be used to stimulate performance in the activity.

With respect to the development of interest in play it can be assumed that individuals who gain skill enough to enjoy an activity will have interest enough to continue it. With respect to standards of behavior the teacher is the example; that is enough comment.

Physical education should select objectives of dance that aim at vigorous activity, certain skills and controls in poise and movement, appreciation of music, line, rhythm, and design.

Dance in its various forms has become a recognized part of physical education during the past thirty years. But only for the last ten years have many persons stopped to ask the reason for its increasingly wide acceptance and the magnitude of the place it fills in our educational program. Before that we heard that dance was good exercise — but so were Swedish gymnastics; or that dance was pretty and graceful — but so was "Hearts and Flowers," rendered gracefully as a parlor accomplishment. Neither of these reasons is sufficient to justify the place dance occupies today in physical education.

During the past fertile twenty-year period definite objectives have been formulated which serve as a basis for the selection of the types of dance activities which are best suited to the desired ends.

Dance activity is a broad term which should include folk, national, tap, social, modern dance and their basic techniques as well as the singing and dramatic games, the pantomimic rhythms of the kindergarten and primary grades. No one type of dance is adequate to meet the varying needs of individuals, old and young, tall and squat, literal and imaginative.

Modern physical education is concerned with the development of the whole individual. Dance from time immemorial has been an expression of the most fundamental impulses of mankind, his desires and aspirations, his needs and hungers. Until recently, the veneer of civilization has blocked any dance expression that could possibly satisfy the whole child or the whole man. Modern dance, vital, controversial and dynamic, has gradually evolved to resolve this difficulty, to satisfy the whole thinking, feeling and acting person. To project meanings through rhythmic movements is a challenge that can be met only by the whole personality.

Any well-ordered program will include relaxation and coordination that involves considerable tension or contraction. So far as dance is concerned, the power to relax consciously is valuable only as a foundation upon which to build movements of varying degrees of tension. It is important that a student should acquire those motor skills which are essential to a satisfying performance of all types of dance. This will necessarily include locomotor movements—walking, running, leaping, hopping, skipping, sliding, galloping, and combinations of those: the polka, waltz, mazurka, and schottische. This will also include a broad experience in nonlocomotor or axial movement —swinging, sustained, sharply accented—or percussive movement. If no one type of movement is overemphasized, a wide movement repertory will be gained and harmful muscle patterns will not be set.

With the majority of people only the legs are used in walking, with perhaps a swing of the forearm. Women, especially those past their first youth, tend to walk with little action in the upper leg or thigh. If the hips are used at all, it is usually with a tilting motion from side to side. The back is held rigid, or is carried as a load, not as a part of the mechanism; the foot is used as though made of one solid bone. In such a walk the accent is down and the result is heavy and unlovely.

When the body is rhythmically coordinated, the spine is flexible, the leg swings from the hip, knees are slightly bent and there is a push-off from the toe of the rear foot. With each step there is a slight forward-upward tilt of the pelvis. The arms swing slightly from the shoulder, not the elbow. There is an effect of "upness" that reacts on the spirit and the whole walk gains in resilience and efficiency.

In addition to the objectives in motor techniques, there are specific ends in adjustment of the individual to the group. A sense of belonging to a working group is valuable to every personality. It comes from planning and working together for a common purpose, a goal that is recognized and accepted as valuable and desirable. The necessity for adapting one's own movement to synchronize with that of others and of conforming to a particular design carries with it a strong feeling of responsibility to the group.

The achievement of this objective necessarily leads to the acquisition of poise. A person who is absorbed in rhythmically coordinated movement necessarily loses self-consciousness. Self-consciousness is a form of fear—a fear that the individual may not convey to the group the impression his mind thinks he should make, a fear that his inadequacy of expression may make him ridiculous in the eyes of others. This self-consciousness is inhibitory, and consequently destructive. Much of the lack of poise in persons is due to lack of skill. In young children fears and self-consciousness in various situations have been lessened by an increase of motor skill. Where there is a skill, suggests Jersild, there is a way.

To remove self-consciousness it is frequently necessary only to change the attitude of an individual toward his own performance. There are many who believe that only those who are graceful should dance. These persons should be brought to realize that it is for the value of the experience itself and not for the polished perfection of the results that dance is worth while in the physical education program. As Walter Pater remarked, "It is experience we want, not the fruits of experience."

When movement is regarded from an esthetic point of view, the unique and distinctive elements in dance are considered. These include beauty of line, scope of movement possible for the human body, and consciousness of power in the control of a responsive body.

Ability to appreciate music is important. This ability is manifest in recognition of and response to those elements in music that are basic to good dance composition and that pay attention to dynamics, expressive quality, form or design and rhythmic elements, such as primary rhythm or meter, secondary rhythm or note-pattern, phrasing, tempo, and syncopation.

Ability to make one's own rhythm, not merely to respond to the accurate accompaniment of a good accompanist, is an important objective.

Appreciation of good design in movement will consider floor pattern and body contour.

There are important by-products of dance. The power to relax carries with it the means of improving postures. The appreciation of beauty in movement is a strong motivation for good postures. A dance that calls for extension and elevation of the whole body is far more stimulating than the catch phrases "stand tall" and "stretch up." The latter is purely physical in its application, while the former carries an emotional appeal that is undeniably more effective. The technique of modern dance aims to develop an expressive body, flexible and well coordinated. In detail, such a body will exhibit a flexible spine with normal dorsal and lumbar curves; strong, flexible feet; well-developed waist muscles; a strong contracted abdominal wall; a head carried high, but without tension in neck, shoulders, and chest. These points sought in the name of artistic expression bring with them the beauty of ideal postures and bearing.

Another by-product of dance is an increased appreciation of the other arts; music, painting, sculpture, stage and costume design. This does not come about as the result of direct teaching but from comments made by the skillful teacher upon the associated arts as they relate to any dance project.

In general, the objectives pertaining to neuromuscular skills and organic stimulation have been emphasized to a much greater degree than the esthetic objectives. All objectives should be constantly in the mind of the teacher. The student, on the other hand, should want to participate because it is interesting to build dances, just as it is interesting to write poems, sing tunes or paint pictures; because it is fun to move well and expressively, to skip, to jump, to sway and to run.

Dance is the art side of physical education. In folk dance, the social element, and in tap dance the rhythmic and play elements predominate, but in modern dance it is clearly recognized that artistic execution by the individual and the group is the ultimate goal.

Physical education should select objectives in self-testing activities, stunts on apparatus, and personal combat activities that serve the aim of physical education.

The objectives of self-testing activities need to be determined in many areas and more exactly than at present. Should all boys be able to chin themselves? How many times? Should all boys learn the handspring, cartwheel, forward and backward rolls, handstand, and snap-up? Which ones should girls learn? The objectives in stunts may have wide application. For example, how high should one be able to vault? Is rope climbing an essential skill? What utilities have these in war? The objectives in this group seem to be well accepted. They are:

1. Acquiring skill and ability likely to be of value in everyday life.

2. Development of athletic skills in terms of some obstacle.

3. Ability to handle the body through increase of physical efficiency by development of neuromuscular skills in relation to some object to be surmounted by the body as a whole.

4. Afford opportunity to increase self-assurance and courage in face of physical danger. To make possible such work in artificial surroundings and with artificial equipment. The woods and fields offer the ideal situation to be used as much as possible.

5. Ability to attack and defend with many and varied means, for the defeating of an opponent or for defending one's self. This is valuable in society for all young males.

In seeking the objectives of this group, it is important not to lose the essential purpose through devotion to traditional forms. Thus, in stunts on apparatus, it is desirable to consider the apparatus as an obstacle to mount or to get over easily, or as soon as possible; to avoid forms which constrict the chest, make breathing difficult and postures stooped.

Physical education should select objectives in hiking, camping, fishing and hunting that lead to skill in these activities and a real love for the out of doors.

The objectives in hiking, camping, fishing, and hunting have distinct national value in preparation for modern warfare. They are equally valuable for normal life. The proposed objectives given below are tentative.

Hiking:

    (*a*) Ability in the adult to hike 15 to 20 miles a day with pack (one rest in every seven days, U.S. Army standard[11]) without undue fatigue. This should be scaled for different ages; also stated without pack.

Camping:

    (*a*) Ability to build a fire.
    (*b*) Ability to build a bough bed.
    (*c*) Ability to swing an axe and cut wood.
    (*d*) Ability to cook food in vessels by boiling, in pans by frying, in pans by baking or roasting, and on a stick.
    (*e*) Ability to make a blanket roll.
    (*f*) Ability to pitch a lean-to or tent, etc.
    (*g*) Ability to tie rope knots.

Fishing:

    (*a*) Ability to bait a hook correctly.
    (*b*) Ability to cast a fly correctly.
    (*c*) Ability to clean and prepare fish for cooking.

[11] Formerly, this was the U.S. Army standard for hiking. Under the current intensified training program the standard has been abandoned; there is relatively little hiking in the training program.

Hunting:

(a) Ability to recognize animal signs, such as tracks, marks on trees, etc.

(b) Ability to follow animals, based upon a knowledge of their characteristic ways of acting.

Physical education should select objectives for the fundamental skills that will conform to the basic facts about movement.

These skills comprise in related and associated forms, or in direct copy, all of the techniques of the four preceding groups. They are movements that are common to all men everywhere. In type and quality they differ from invented exercises. Since they have arisen in human experience as natural products of the developing organism, they are fundamental. Consequently, they belong to every man quite as definitely as his own bones and muscles. The objectives of the particular fundamental skills may be stated as follows:

Walking:

(a) Ability to move with feet parallel, the weight on the outer side, the heel striking first, and pushing the body with the rear foot so that the weight is transferred from heel to ball of foot. This illustrates opposition and the energy-activity ratio (pages 344-347).

(b) Ability to swing the arms alternately with the legs.

(c) Ability to walk at a rate of 4 miles per hour (adult). We need standards for individuals of different ages.

(d) Ability to walk two miles a day without undue fatigue, and on extraordinary occasions to walk 15 to 20 miles.

Running:

(a) Ability to run in recognized form. To determine good form apply the principle of opposition and the energy-activity ratio.

(b) Ability to run certain distances without undue fatigue. These are not determined yet, but there is great need for them.

(*c*) Ability to run certain distances in certain time. These are not determined.

(*d*) Shall the scout pace be an objective for boys and girls between 12 and 16 years? For what distances? Various performance standards in different events have been proposed. Books on practical conduct of athletics give many types of standards.

Jumping:

(*a*) Ability to propel the body into the air. Distance not fully determined. One phase may be represented in Sargent's physical test of man. Another is represented by standard performances in jumping.

(*b*) Ability to land easily and to fall forward toward the hands. Contrast this form with the usual gymnastic jump and landing.

Leaping:

(*a*) Ability to propel the body into the air and over the ground, taking off from one foot and landing on the other with continued motion.

(*b*) Distances are not yet determined fully. Various standards have been proposed.

Throwing:

(*a*) Ability to use opposition and energy-activity ratio.

(*b*) Ability to throw with accuracy.
Various standards have been proposed in tests and rating schemes.

(*c*) Ability to throw certain distances.
Various standards have been proposed in group and individual records.

Hanging:

(*a*) Ability to support oneself by the arms in a hanging

position. Age and sex differences are not clearly established.

(*b*) Ability to hang strongly so as to mount an obstacle. Age and sex differences are not clearly established.

Climbing:

(*a*) Ability to climb a ladder. How high or how fast is not determined.

(*b*) Ability to climb a rope or pole. This is included in numerous physical efficiency tests.

(*c*) Ability to climb a tree, a fence, a wall. How high an obstacle and age-sex differences are not clearly established.

(*d*) Ability to climb stairs without undue fatigue. This needs more specific statement in terms of one's weight.

Lifting:

(*a*) Ability to lift an object lighter than one's weight, back straight and lifting with the legs. This may be illustrated with window, table, chair, or other common object.

(*b*) Ability to lift a weight ½, ¾, and 1 times one's weight. The exact relation here is not known.

(*c*) Ability to pick up objects with proper attention to the principle of energy-activity ratio.

Carrying:

(*a*) Ability to carry one's own weight in balance and control.

(*b*) Ability to carry ½, ¾, and 1 times one's weight. How far and age-sex differences are not known.

(*c*) Ability to carry 30, 40, 50, 60 pounds for a distance of 5, 10, 15, 20 miles. The precise weights and distances for age and sex have not been determined.

Physical education should exemplify in all activities the principles of movement.

There are six well-known principles of movement. These are derived from an analysis of human structure and observation of persons who are able to perform very successful movements. They have their roots in racial patterns and bear a direct relationship to the anatomy, physiology and kinesiology of man.

The Principle of Opposition. This principle, with few exceptions, is seen in all movements. A motion picture investigation of stair climbing of twelve infants, one to three years old, shows the child placing his left foot on the first stair and then advancing the left hand and right foot simultaneously.[12] The movement continues in opposition of right foot and left hand, left foot and right hand. A first-grade child, when asked to climb a ladder, will, if not instructed differently, show opposition in arm and leg movements.

Pictures showing primitive and savage peoples in action always illustrate this principle, so that we can say that many natural, untrained, and spontaneous movements show opposition. It is impossible, at the present time, to say that all do; it is likely that a very large percentage will be found.

Opposition may be defined as a natural selection by man of a method in movement of arms, legs, and trunk, caused by the nature of man's environment, by the character of his body structure, and by the success attendant upon the selection made. Examination of the way in which body structure is involved in locomotor movement will explain the principle. When the left leg, for example, strides forward, the trunk tends to twist to the left. To keep the individual facing in the direction of the forward movement the right arm is swung forward. This compensatory arm movement keeps the trunk oriented in the forward direction. It is this opposition between left leg and right arm, inherent in body structure, that illustrates the principle. The selection made

[12] Louise B. Ames, "Some Relationships Between Stair Climbing and Prone Progression," *Journal of Genetic Psychology*, 54:313-325, 1939. Also Arnold Gesell and Henry M. Halverson, "The Daily Maturation of Infant Behavior: A Cinema Study of Postures, Movements, and Laterality," *Journal of Genetic Psychology*, 61:3-32, 1942.

provides the use of opposite parts of the body in the synthesis of a movement. In the crouch start, right-handed runners invariable place the left foot forward, and left-handed ones the right foot.

In all throwing, climbing, walking, and running movements, where the feet and arms are used in succession, the opposition is between arms and legs on opposite sides of the body.

Right-handed boys show on anthropometric examination a larger left leg than right. This fact supports the coaching view that jumpers who are right-handed should take off always from the left foot. (This corroborating testimony to opposition justifies the method, although its reason is referable to the brain rather than to the skeletal structure of the body.)

There are several athletic events which fail to show opposition, and, in one instance, or two possibly, evince nonopposition. These are, in the main, position movements, and do not require moving the body over the ground or over an obstacle. These forms are exceptions, in order to achieve some value peculiar to the movement. For example:

1. Fencing—This necessitates the turning of the side of the body, in order to present only as small a front as possible to the opponent.

2. Shot-put—This violates the fact of opposition in the preparation. It fulfills it in the put in the simple forms. The modern complex form, with the turn, does not conform in the put.

3. Shooting an arrow—The bow and arrow as an instrument necessitates a nonopposition position.

It is interesting that fencing as an activity is not very popular today. It has gradually lost its place among sports. This may be due in part to the decadence of the feudal spirit, but it may also be due to the fact that as an activity it violates a natural principle, and hence it fails to give organic satisfaction.

The shot-put, it might be noticed, is the one event in track athletics that is not very popular. It secures the interest in a very imperfect way, and is not especially worth while as an event. It keeps its place in intercollegiate athletics largely because of tradition.

In archery, a very popular sport, it might be declared that the opposition is between the two arms, and not between arms and legs.

There are other matters to be considered in this discussion. When the body is supported in the water, the principles may be present in some strokes and absent in others. A study of the various forms should be made with this declaration in mind.

Now if this is a true principle, and if it can be applied to all forms of physical education, what will it mean for gymnastic practice?

1. It will eliminate all movements that in action show nonopposition, and will select those having opposition.

2. It will require that all climbing, vaulting, hanging, and other obstacle practice consider opposition in determination of form.

In athletics it will continually emphasize opposition, and in "form" events it will determine good form to be that form which is natural, i.e., the form which would be used if speed, skill, and endurance were the elements tested. Thus, hurdling for form will not be judged by esthetic considerations, but practical ones.

In dance, it will dominate movement, as movement is considered for the purpose of expression of mood or idea, and it will be most useful here, because it is not studied technique, totally unrelated to the movement.

The Principle of Energy-Activity Ratio. The second principle we may call the energy-activity ratio. It may be defined as that correlation of parts of the body for the purpose of securing the result sought with the least expenditure of energy, and with the most favorable adjustment of the body at all times. This is motor efficiency in precisely the same terms used by the engineer in speaking of efficiency. In particular, it recognizes that balance and control mean economical use of force, selecting appropriate muscle groups and inhibiting antagonists. This principle is supported by the scientific work of Sherrington;[13] it reveals the absurdities of Swoboda's resistive exercises.

[13] C. S. Sherrington, *The Integrative Action of the Nervous System,* New Haven, Yale University, 1906.

This principle may be illustrated by reference to movements that are called graceful or well-coordinated, and to those called awkward. In well-coordinated movement, only enough energy is used in order to produce the movement in the pattern of speed or force desired; the graceful person gives the impression of not trying. In awkward movements, more muscles are used and more strength employed than are needed to perform the acts; the individual appears to be making great effort.

This principle rules out movements that are used because they make balancing difficult per se, or the coordination difficult, or to satisfy some esthetic form without natural sanction. This would mean that no movement that is untrue and insincere can be natural, and especially that all movements making for inefficiency and waste of energy are false.

For example, there are numerous instances of practices in the gymnasium which violate this principle of energy-activity ratio. When understood, their occurrence will be less frequent. Examples are: (1) Relay race with basketball, and passing the ball behind the back while running; (2) relay race with basketball, and passing the ball between the legs while running; (3) numerous formal gymnastic movements, such as deep knee bending, trunk forward bending with straight knees, fundamental gymnastic positions with excessive expenditure of energy, and others.

Examples of movement in which the proper correlation of parts employs a desirable energy-activity ratio may be seen in walking, running, throwing, and others. Good form in these activities requires an economical use of force. When movements are judged with respect to this principle, the criterion is clear: Does the movement make an efficient and economical use of the motor mechanism?

The Principle of Qualitative Adjustment. The two previous principles dealt mainly with the form of the movement; the third involves the quality of a movement. Qualitative adjustment is the application of force or speed to a movement at the proper time. Speed, strength, and endurance are qualities that may be added to movements after the form has been determined. These additions are for the purpose of securing better results in the defeat of an opponent, the improvement of a record, and an increase in efficiency.

The Principle of Follow-through. The fourth principle of movement is widely recognized in all throwing, striking, swinging, and kicking movements. This principle requires that the individual continue the moving part in the line of motion at the time of impact, as after the ball has left the hand, or the object has been hit. In such continued motion, not only more force has been brought to bear but also the direction of the moving part remains true to the design with which the movement began. The follow-through in the golf swing, in batting a baseball, in tennis and badminton strokes are well-known cues. This principle is considered as basic for good performance.

The Principle of Objective Focus. This principle denotes the focus of attention upon the immediate objective rather than upon subjective sensations. In athletic sports this principle is often expressed in the advice "Keep the eye on the ball." There is involved in this principle more than a close attention to a moving ball; the ball is important because it is the immediate objective. Hence in shooting a basket, the ball is not the objective, whereas the goal is; hence the focus centers in the goal. It is essential for the performer to discern the immediate goal and not to confuse that with one that is more distant. The matter will be clear with an illustration. In bunting a baseball, the batter will sometimes start to run before he has hit the ball because the idea of reaching first base is the immediate objective for him. Of course, he is mistaken in this; bunting the ball is the immediate objective and reaching first base is the secondary objective. The same confusion of objective is seen in infielders who throw the ball before they have fielded it. It is important to keep in mind the objective at the moment, to take up the next objective in the series, and of course to change from one to the next in order as the occasion demands.

The principle of objective focus corrects the mistakes of those who center upon themselves. It does not require that the performer ignore the position of the feet, the way the arm is used, or the disposition of the weight. These are preliminaries of considerable importance to the beginner. When these matters have been attended to, then attention should come to rest upon the objective whether it is a pocket in pool, a cup in golf, or a bird in flight.

The Principle of Total Assembly. The sixth principle denotes the fact that good movement involves the whole body and not merely a moving part. Total assembly is the complete bringing together of all the muscular forces involved in a movement so that the objective is attained effectively. In efficient movement the whole neuromuscular organism is activated to an end; the uninitiated may erroneously believe that only parts are involved. Thus in good running, the arms and trunk run as well as the legs, and pitching a baseball involves proper use of the feet and trunk as well as the arms. The teacher of sports pays attention to all factors that make for good movement, and so will emphasize total assembly of the muscular forces in movement.

Physical education should recognize the effect of certain mechanical principles upon motor performance.

Dorothy R. Mohr, State University of Iowa, and Mildred E. Barrett, College of William and Mary, report an interesting experiment in applying knowledge of mechanical principles to swimming performance.[14] Through the courtesy of Miss Mohr, the following mechanical principles are presented below:

1. Once a force acts upon a body to put the body in motion, it will remain in motion unless acted upon by external forces, such as waves or water resistance. (Newton's Law of Inertia.)
2. When a certain amount of force is applied to a body to move it through water, the speed of the body will gradually increase until it reaches a certain point at which the resistance due to friction is equal to the applied forces. After this point, speed will remain the same as long as the same force is applied. (Newton's Law of Acceleration.)
3. To every action there is an equal and opposite reaction. (Newton's Third Law.) When you push against the water you move in the opposite direction.
4. Maximum force is attained by presenting as broad a surface

[14] Dorothy R. Mohr and Mildred E. Barrett, "Effect of Knowledge of Mechanical Principles in Learning to Perform Intermediate Swimming Skills," *Research Quarterly,* December, 1962, p. 574.

as possible in the propulsive movements of the limbs and by exerting backward pressure through as great a distance as possible, provided that undesirable forces are not introduced.

5. To exert the most effective force against the water, the larger muscle groups should be used to start the arm stroke and the kick. The small muscles only follow up and continue the motion.

6. To obtain the most effective force possible, the arms when stroking, and the legs when kicking, should be in an extended and relaxed position. The longer the lever (arm or leg) the greater is the amount of force exerted.

7. A rapidly moving body in water leaves a low pressure area immediately behind it. This is external resistance.

8. Resistance in the water is also caused by fear and tenseness that produce jerky or sudden movements causing waves and eddies. This resistance is internal.

9. Buoyancy is the lifting force of a liquid on a body immersed in it. This lifting force is equal to the weight of water displaced by the object.

In addition to the statement of the above mechanical principles, Miss Mohr has given numerous examples as applied to swimming. A valuable exposition of the mechanical principles involved in postures and in all movements is given by Mabel Ellsworth Todd.[15]

THE CURRICULAR MATERIALS OF PHYSICAL EDUCATION

Having surveyed the local situation where physical education is to be taught, studied the characteristics of the individuals in the various groups, formulated an aim that is in harmony with educational purpose in general, listed the objectives to be sought, the selection of curricular materials can then be made.

When one goes to a store to buy a hat, for example, several questions arise at once. The clerk asks, "What kind of hat do you want?" "What color?" "What size do you wear?" "What price do you wish to pay?" Answers to all of these questions lead to the selection of a hat.

There are also questions to be answered before one se-

[15] M. E. Todd, *The Thinking Body*, New York, Hoeber, 1937, pp. 45-77.

lects an activity for the curriculum. In addition to the principles discussed above there are other considerations to be taken into account. These are called criteria. In the case of the hat one criterion might have been "felt," another "black," another "7½," and another "$10." Therefore, in addition to consideration of the situation, pupil characteristics, aim, and objectives, the following criteria will guide in the selection of materials:

1. *The criterion of relative worth.* Several activities may meet all the conditions but one may do so better than others.

2. *The criterion of interest.* The activity should be within the interest level of the participant.

3. *The criterion of functional utility.* The activity should carry over into the life of the individual.

4. *The criterion of maturity.* The activity should be suitable to the developmental stage of the individual.

5. *The criterion of experience.* The activity should be preceded by proper "lead-up" activities.

6. *The criterion of safety.* The activity should not be hazardous beyond the ability of the supervisor to guard against needless injury.

7. *The criterion of achievement.* The activity should contribute to the realization of the objectives sought and be in harmony with the aim.

Behind all of these technical steps the philosophy of the teacher bends decisions in one direction or another.

These criteria are practical guides for the selection of activities. Suppose that after full consideration of the local situation, aim, objectives, and characteristics of pupils it is found that a choice must be made for a particular group between volleyball, handball, and tumbling. One activity could be taught but not all three. Which one shall be selected? In this kind of situation the above criteria could be used. The decision may be made that one of the three is relatively of more value than the others, that one yields greater interest, or that one is more suitable for the maturity level of the group. From this kind of analysis, a decision is made.

SOURCES OF CURRICULAR MATERIALS

Physical education is a form of education. It is life and living. Its activities are to be engaged in because of the satisfactions they offer to him who participates. To him who enters the lists of its activities there should come as by-products health, skills, good postures, strength, endurance, and the many results so frequently sought as direct ends and so rarely gained. Physical education is fundamentally an attitude, a way of living, a point of view; incidentally it is a technique, a performance, a particular skill. Given the former fundamentals, the latter incidentals are acquired; without the former, the latter are only rarely secured or fall early into disuse.

It is important to eliminate from the program all purely muscle-centered activities in favor of a program of functional activities, as illustrated by sports, games, dance, tumbling, self-testing sports, and similar natural movements, individualized where necessary and possible. The program should be taught with the purpose of utilizing the rich potential of such activities for the development of desirable social skills and wholesome interests as well as organic power.

If the program meets with approval and the body of ideas which lies back of it is sanctioned, then every one who so approves is obligated to secure the means to put the program into operation to the limit of his ability. That person is not a safe mentor who finds himself in agreement with a body of ideas but explains his lack of outward support by the remark, "I don't believe they will work." If the natural program is the one which should be developed everywhere, then those who accept the dictates of its truths are obligated to put them into operation.

The following six types of activities are the chief sources for curricular materials in physical education.

1. ADAPTED ACTIVITIES

Many individuals have defects which are remediable by means of the therapy of exercise. This is the function of adapted activities. In this program activities are prescribed for individual persons after an individual examination. To prescribe the same activities to a large group is like treating a group in the clinic with the same medicine. This is not only incorrect from the standpoint of kinesiology and individual pathology, but in effect it is also charlatanistic because such procedure blinds school people to the real necessity of provision in a scientific way for the growth and the correction of developmental defects of children. If adapted activities are to be used, a clinic should be established and the children in need of correction should practice their prescriptions under the eye of the expert in that field. In the college field some interesting work has been done in the correction of defects by assigning restricted exercise of a natural play type to appropriate cases. Moreover, as Stafford suggests, there are additional benefits, because through such activities the individual is not deprived of a natural physical education, but on the other hand is distinctly improved along the lines of his physical education and his ability to have at command activities for use in leisure time.[16]

2. GAMES, SPORTS, ATHLETICS, PLAY, EQUITATION, AQUATICS

In this group are included all the forms of play. Several types have been named to indicate that the entire range of play is involved. Wherever possible these activities should be carried on out-of-doors. In recess and recreational periods, direct supervision is not required if pupils have achieved self-direction and self-control. Just enough supervision should be given to prevent the play from disintegrating into rough house, and losing the values which are to be achieved through this activity. At other times, instruction in skills is important and the whole behavior of the individual is the proper concern of the teacher.

These activities for normal young persons are pursued because of the inner urge which arises out of the nature of boys and girls. For the former there will always be the stronger urge

[16] G. E. Stafford, *Sports for the Handicapped*, New York, Prentice-Hall, 1939.

to engage in play and games, but the present judgment may have to be recast in the future as more and more girls are given an opportunity in youth to participate in sports. These activities are at the very root of organic development for those who are prepared to enter. For those who are physically under par there is need for careful supervision, avoiding overdoing, tenseness, and strain associated with competitive enterprises. As the physically weaker ones gain in power they should be led into games gradually. No child can be considered educated unless he has acquired in childhood and youth familiarity and skill in a large number of games and sports which give satisfaction and lead to their pursuit in recreational ways out of school.

The individual who is physically educated in natural forms has an ability to use the body in ways to prevent strain; there is in such physical education an element of safety education. Skilled in the judgment of a moving object, such a person is less liable to accident. Sport, through its vigorous activities and its conditioning regimen, tends to keep all organic parts at a high level of function.

Finally, it is in the laboratory of play and games that standards are learned. One may talk about good sportsmanship, fair play, loyalty, honesty, and kindred virtues, but the play field is the only place in the school that provides the situations where the individual is under pressure to meet the standards set up. It is through standards and the acceptance of them that sport teaches a person how to adjust to others, how to compete, how to win, and how to face failure. Sport offers one sure way for the young to learn to appreciate other persons, to meet them in common experiences that prevent shyness, timidity, and psychological withdrawal. Thus, sport is one of nature's best ways of preventing introversion and introspection.

It is important not to underrate the effects that games, sports, and similar motor activities produce in persons. Of course, they provide valuable exercise. That we know. They also soften the rigidities within us which so often come from the tense times in which we live. They help us to find poise and balance. They refresh our spirit and renew the inner springs of our faith and courage. To keep the eyes fixed on the larger values and to remain true to significant causes require that we come to our daily tasks refreshed and strengthened. It is in this sense that all good play has moral significance and that wholesome recreation is vital for the morale of a people.

3. DANCE

The dance program should include folk, national, social, tap, and modern dance. It has no place for esthetic or classical dance, those forms which flourished in education when the ballet and the romantic dance of Isadora Duncan were supreme in the concert field. Esthetic dance—a distorted step-sister of the ballet, was not even a creditable imitation, for it perpetuated only the insipidness and preserved none of the beauty of that great art. Romantic dance too suffered abuses in its educational idiom, classical dance. There was meaningless scampering about with balloon and scarf, vitiated flittings and floatings into the realm of sweetness and light with no thought of significant form or intelligible content. But in the hands of the sensitive expert it possessed beauty, sincerity and real worth as an educative tool. The exclusion of classical dance from the present program is made entirely on the basis of timeliness. It served admirably its age. Neither esthetic nor classical dance possesses validity or integrity in the present decade of the twentieth century. By the inevitable process of evolution they have been supplanted by modern dance.

Dance in education should be an expression of a mood, feeling, emotion, or idea, and the outward forms should be determined by the content and arise out of the inner urges of the dancer rather than be determined beforehand by esthetic considerations. This is **not** to say that dance is self-expression, that it is a purely subjective projection of the joys, griefs, hopes and fears of a single individual. It is rather the objective comment of that individual personality upon the outward causes of those experiences; a comment upon the realities of life. To dance significantly one must really know life. This holds true for every type of dance worthy of inclusion in a progressive program of physical education. Evelyn Lohoefer makes a critical comment upon modern dance as it is taught by some teachers. She writes:

> Many teachers don't teach dance. They do teach technique. There is little if any instruction in the art of dance or music, in the history of dance, its aims, its wealth of meaning, its relation to other arts and subjects. Many advanced students have had classes for months or years without ever really dancing or knowing about the leaders then and now of modern dance. They do exercises and learn that "this is a Weidman study, or a Graham movement, or a Cunningham approach."[17]

There is relatively little controversy, as evidenced by current practice, concerning the educational fitness of folk, national, tap and some form of creative or modern dance. But social dance should also be taught by the school. Essentially a romantic form and of large social implications, it must be conducted to preserve the best standards of society. If the school does not elect to do this and says in effect that there will be no dancing in the high school, boys and girls will go elsewhere to dance. Instead of the dancing at the school where there could be wholesome influences at work to set desirable standards, there will be dancing at the public hall where the influences for wholesome standards are absent. Young people are not to be shut up in a box, as many adults are realizing today; but if they are not helped to appreciate and enjoy romantic things in a fine way, they will carry on their love-making in primitive fashion.

4. SELF-TESTING COMBAT AND SELF-DEFENSE ACTIVITIES

Many games are self-testing. Playing tag is testing the runners as well as the "it." But of more direct bearing is the

[17] Evelyn Lohoefer, "A View from the Corner," *Journal of Health—Physical Education—Recreation*, May-June, 1962, p. 69.

meaning of this term upon those stunts that are directly ways of testing one's ability. In general, tumbling and stunts, on and off apparatus, are included here. The usual apparatus work will have to be modified if it is to be acceptable in this classification. Much of the artificial form bears no relation to the actual doing of the stunt at all and is merely a form of window-dressing comparable to much in military tactics.

The combat and defense activities for boys are boxing and wrestling, and for both boys and girls hand wrestling and similar stunts.

5. FUNDAMENTAL SKILLS

It is a curious fact that one may observe many lessons in physical education without finding much intelligent instruction in the fundamental activities in which man engages every day. Games, stunts, and dance are frequently directed with little regard for technique of the activities. The reason for this condition lies in the unwarranted notion that the chief purpose of the period of physical education is to give exercise or to promote health. Walking, running, climbing, throwing, hanging, jumping, leaping, and carrying comprise the fundamentals of all natural activities, and their execution in proper form is important for the continuation of the activity of which they are a part. One likes to do what one does well and excellence in motor activity resides largely in proper performance of fundamental technique. Instead of working for exercise or health as immediate objectives of physical activity, the teacher should remember that, with proper selection of the situation and skilled direction of the activity, these popular values will accrue. The chief purpose on the technical side is to secure quality of performance. There are tests for measuring the achievement of elementary children in some of the fundamental skills.[18]

[18] Robert D. Johnson, "Measurements of Achievement in Fundamental Skills of Elementary School Children," *Research Quarterly*, March, 1962, p. 94.

A scientific program and methods of physical education should be viewed as means in the education of children and older persons. Because the means are physical, exercise will result from the activities. To be physically educated, then, will mean, on the technical side, ability to walk, run, jump, climb, throw, and hang with control, ease, speed, and strength. Walking, climbing stairs, throwing, hanging, climbing ladders, jumping, leaping, carrying—these and others comprise a great mass of technique that must be learned correctly or humans will continue to handle their bodies as if they were sticks, wholly devoid of balance, poise, and control.

Fundamental skills applied correctly to the acts of daily life should improve efficiency and conserve power and energy. Picking up objects, reaching for objects on shelves, lifting and carrying suitcases, making beds, raising windows, moving tables and chairs are a few of the common motor problems that men and women meet every day. There is a correct and an incorrect way to do these and other movements. Physical education should not assume that ability to do a folk dance will guarantee ease and control in carrying ashes from the basement or in raising a window in the bedroom. There must be specified training in the fundamental motor controls through identical or similar procedures and explanation of the principles involved.

Important points in the teaching of this phase of the program are illustrated by the five samples below:

1. In raising windows, stand close to the window and keep trunk straight.

2. In lifting heavy weights from the ground, bend knees, keep back erect, and throw effort on the large muscles of the legs.

3. In carrying objects in each hand, such as suitcases, bend the arms slightly at the elbows.

4. In moving oil cans, barrels, trunks, and similar objects, keep close to the weight to be moved.

5. In work in a sitting posture, where one must reach forward as in typewriting, keep the back straight and bend at the hip joints.

6. OUT-OF-DOOR ACTIVITIES OF THE CAMP

Whether or not it is the automobile that is responsible for taking people to the country, the fact remains that more and more persons are learning anew the joys of out-of-doors. This is a most salutary thing and promises much for the coming generation. Every school should encourage the Boy Scout and Girl Scout programs and do everything possible to further and extend the work that these organizations are trying to do.

To hunt animals with the camera, or by trail marking, to carry on treasure hunts, to fish and cook out-of-doors, are some of the legitimate educational measures to be used in the education of boys and girls. Recreational clubs that meet on Saturday afternoons for hikes into the country, picnics and excursions, something of the idea exemplified in the Wanderlust Clubs developed by Mr. Stecher in the Philadelphia schools—these are a legitimate part of the program of physical education.

One of the recent developments in education is the school camp. The movement is spreading slowly and shows great promise for a neglected phase of physical education.

WHAT PART HAS GYMNASTICS IN THE CURRICULUM?

Gymnastics has no responsible part at all if by gymnastics is meant the old formal exercises done to response-commands or in drill forms by imitation. There will always be a place for gymnastic practice of a natural kind because all of the preceding activities have a technique that must be learned in relation to the whole activity that goes on. The realization of a difficulty presents an opportunity for drill. Thus, practice in the difficulties arises out of doing the real thing.

Frequently mimetic exercises that in a poor way imitate natural activities are offered as a substitute for the more artificial exercises of German or Swedish origin. Such exercises are worth very little as training in the technique of the activity which they are supposed to represent; in some cases they do a great deal of harm. It should be perfectly clear that the place for drill arises when the individual or group has difficulty and when there is conscious need for perfecting some part of the movement before the whole thing can go on as the participants would wish to have it go.

If reliance for teaching of a program must be placed upon untrained teachers, then formal calisthenics will constitute a large part of the program. To conduct successfully a natural program requires intelligence, thorough training, and understanding of principles. Formal exercises which can be learned from a syllabus are about as useful as other things gained in such a way.

Clerks, business men and women, and other sedentary workers, who are frequently physically illiterate, employ setting-up exercises in their own homes or various programs of calisthenics, labeled by such alliterative catch-names as Daily Dozen. Such exercises are just valuable enough to mislead these unfortunates, and without an adequate appreciation of physical education they are unable to distinguish between the real and the counterfeit. In the adult world this view is illustrated by the organized instruction given by television for certain types who lack the vision, will, or opportunity to carry on effectively the complete business of living. Relief exercises for children in school and television exercises for adults at home are typical absurdities in an age that often forgets normal human needs, human possibilities in living a good life, and the place of joy and happiness in all of life.

Some teachers of physical education recommend a routine of calisthenic exercises that can be used when other, more functional activities are not feasible. There can be no serious objection to this as a substitute for the real thing. It should be remembered, however, that such exercises are temporary substitutes.

The fact that those who pursue economic goals solely can continue their business on half-hour, tri-weekly periods of sweat-exercises in the gymnasium is no criterion for the whole of physical education. This should be well understood. Even less so will the physical needs of these persons serve as standards in time, type, or quality for the physical education of children.

THE PLACE OF DRILL IN THE CURRICULUM

The simple play and dramatic activities of the first four grades present adequate developmental and educational opportunity without many technical difficulties. But with the more complex activities as illustrated in the games of higher organization, and in modern dance, an increasing skill is required for the satisfactory performance of the activities. These activities are desirable because of the range of satisfactions offered and the repertoire of plays provided. They add to the richness of life and help in avoiding that narrowness that comes when one does not know how or what to play.

But in teaching groups and particularly large groups, facility is provided by being able to analyze the motor difficulty to the end of better performance, and working on the difficulty and in relation to the activity from which it arose. Thus, natural activities have technical problems in movement which require practice of the fundamental elements inherent in them. For example, in teaching basketball to novices one would present the activity as a game, in the course of which it would readily be observed by the teacher and even the players themselves that a certain skill in the game was lacking, due to certain motor inabilities. This is the source and justification for drill in relation to basketball. In similar fashion practice in the technique of other activities grows out of the activities themselves. The essential condition of this situation demands that drill be presented only in relation to the activity which it represents. Therefore, the analyzed motor elements cannot be organized into a system of movements planned for and taught as exercise. They are not capable of reduction to "day's orders" or of use in syllabi except as illustration.

Finally, it should be noted that the real activity itself is

always superior to the practice of its parts. Practice of the
elements should never be made a substitute for the real thing.
The drill in sprint starting can never equal the actual practice
in that activity in its normal environment. Games, dance, stunts,
and camping should comprise the core of the program; drill
in parts is supplemental as a teaching method to facilitate the
acquirement of the real activities themselves.

Tennis teachers suggest a number of ball-handling
skills that might be called "lead-up" drills to tennis. In this
respect they are like "lead-up" games, and may be in themselves interesting techniques to the pupil, even though he has
at that time no interest in tennis.[19]

WHEN IS A PERSON PHYSICALLY EDUCATED?

To be physically educated includes more than a proficiency in a variety of skills. The medium is physical activity,
but the whole person is involved. Hence, it will include, also,
interests and attitudes, appreciations, understandings, and
knowledges. To be able to play a game well is important, but
to have such an attitude toward life that sport has a place is
equally so. To have some sportsmanlike attitudes about play,
to know significant items in conditioning oneself for activity,
and to recognize good play in others—these are imperative in a
physically educated person. And rhythm belongs, and the out-
of-doors; fishing and hunting—the vital touch with nature in
her creative powers—capture for modern man old responses
that light new fires and give new strengths.

Moreover, the place of skill and satisfaction is never

[19] Harry C. Leighton, "Introducing Tennis to Youngsters," *Journal of
Health—Physical Education—Recreation,* February, 1962,
p. 29. William E. Murphy and William G. Helms, "Developing
Simple Tennis Skills through Relays," *ibid.,* p. 30. Anne M.
Pittman and Sara Staff Jernigan, "The Fantastic Way to Tennis,"
ibid., p. 32. John W. Hendrix, "Teaching in the Gymnasium,"
ibid., p. 34. Judy Barta, Mary Donnalley, and Harrison Row-
botham, "Teaching Aids," *ibid.,* p. 36.

to be neglected. These are basic. The surest sign that one may possess an abiding interest in an activity is the possession of skill in it above the dub or novice class. There may well be criticism of efforts to develop champions and record breakers for these may yield limited social returns for the human energy and wealth expended, but there can never be a question of the social value of persons who have acquired levels of skill which help to make them interested in play, dance, and the world of the out-of-doors.

This concept of a physically educated person differs sharply with views that would make physical education a body-building, disciplinary, obedience-developing function in the schools. It maintains that we do not exercise muscles to strengthen them, but we educate individuals through motor activities which incidentally strengthen muscles. **The focus of the individual should be in society, and not in his muscles.** It is obvious that techniques will be learned and better learned in this approach, but the techniques are only means and never ends.[20]

In judging whether a person is physically educated, motor ability will always be a prime consideration but never an exclusive one. As physical education becomes increasingly accepted in educational institutions, ever higher levels of education in teachers will be required. In addition to competence in motor skills, familiarity with the literature of the field will be expected.

Forty-five years ago there were less than a dozen books dealing with the problems of American physical education; today the number is in the hundreds. At that time, doctors' and masters' theses in the field were nonexistent; today the product is so large that it is difficult to keep up with the publications.

The many references in this book illustrate the scope of the field and the intellectual activity of its sponsors. Another example of this literature "explosion" is given in a Basic Book

[20] Arthur S. Daniels, "Some Critical Issues in Physical Education," *Proceedings of the College Physical Education Association*, 1958, p. 1.

List on Physical Education for the College Library, by Jacob Mirviss. This excellent list appears in the *Journal of Health — Physical Education — Recreation*, January, 1963, pages 30-36.

QUESTIONS AND PROBLEMS FOR DISCUSSION

1. What is the curriculum? What is most important in determining the place of physical education in the curriculum?
2. What is a course of study? What is the trend today with respect to formulating courses of study?
3. What are the faults in the procedure that determines the curriculum by reference to current practice? What are the faults in following the advice of an authority?
4. What are five principles which indicate the steps in preparation of a curriculum?
5. Discuss the importance of the situation in determining content of the curriculum.
6. In an eastern city a very rigid system of formal gymnastics was developed in the public schools and defended as a sound and scientific system. Later when new schools were built containing pools and gymnasiums, the old system of drill remained unchanged. Discuss why.
7. Why is it important to know the characteristics of children?
8. Why is there a large responsibility in formulating an aim for physical education? What do you think of the aim given in the text? Compare it with other aims.
9. Discuss the significance of "physically wholesome," "mentally stimulating and satisfying," and "socially sound."
10. What is your attitude about academic freedom?
11. What is an objective? State an objective for physical education. How does it agree with the aim of physical education that you hold?
12. Discuss the principle proposed for the selection of the objectives of adapted physical education. Why is a verb better than a noun to denote stance?
13. Discuss the principle proposed for the selection of objectives of games. Of dance. What are some of the by-products of dance? Discuss the concept that dance is an art form.
14. What is a good objective for self-testing activities? Why?
15. What do you think of the suggested objectives of the fundamental skills?

16. Discuss the objectives suggested for out-of-door activities.
17. Discuss the principle of opposition. Give several illustrations of this principle.
18. Explain the principle of energy-activity ratio. Illustrate.
19. What is the principle of qualitative adjustment? Give examples.
20. What is the principle of follow-through? Give ten examples.
21. What is the principle of objective focus? In what activities is this important?
22. Discuss the principle of total assembly.
23. What are criteria? Name seven of use in determining curricular materials in physical education. Could they be used in home economics? In history?
24. Why does one's philosophy influence the application of a criterion?
25. Discuss the six types of physical education suitable for inclusion in a curriculum. What are some of the immediate and remote results of these activities? Do you have a personal preference for any one of these activities? Should that influence your judgment? Does it?
26. Why should corrective gymnastics be individualized?
27. What leads children to engage in games?
28. What should be a standard of education for boys and girls?
29. What should the dance program include? Why must one know life in order to dance significantly? Is this true for other arts?
30. What is the function of the social dance in high school? Why?
31. What are self-testing and self-defense activities? Why are they valuable?
32. What are the fundamental skills?
33. Why are activities of the field, trail, and camp a part of the program of physical education?
34. What part has gymnastics in the program? What part drill?
35. When is a person physically educated?

REFERENCE READINGS

American Association for Health, Physical Education and Recreation. *Physical Education for High School Students.* Washington, D.C., 1960.

Andrews, Gladys. *Creative Rhythmic Movement for Children.* Prentice-Hall, Englewood Cliffs, N.J., 1954.

Andrews, Gladys, *et al. Physical Education for Today's Girls and Boys.* Boston, Allyn & Bacon, 1960.

Cassidy, Rosalind F. *Curriculum Development in Physical Education.* New York, Harper, 1954.

Cowell, Charles C., and Hazelton, Helen W. *Curriculum Designs in Physical Education.* Englewood Cliffs, N.J., Prentice-Hall, 1955.

Dayton, Oliver W. *Athletic Training and Conditioning.* New York, Ronald Press, 1960.

Educational Leadership. Values: Their Impact on Curriculum. Association for Supervision and Curriculum Development, May, 1961.

Halsey, Elizabeth, and Porter, Lorena. *Physical Education for Children: A Developmental Program.* New York, Dryden Press, 1958.

Kleemeier, Robert W. (Editor). *Aging and Leisure.* New York, Oxford University Press, 1961.

La Porte, W. R. *The Physical Education Curriculum.* Los Angeles, University of Southern California, 1949.

Larson, Leonard A., and Hill, Lucille F. *Physical Education in the Elementary Schools.* New York, Holt, 1957.

Miller, Arthur G. "Physical Education in the Integrated Curriculum." *Journal of Health — Physical Education — Recreation,* March, 1960, p. 20.

National Education Association. *Those First School Years.* Washington, D.C., 1960.

Rathbone, Josephine Langworthy. *Corrective Physical Education,* 6th Edition. Philadelphia, Saunders, 1959.

Rucker, W. Ray. *Curriculum Development in the Elementary School.* New York, Harper, 1960.

Smalley, Jeannette. *Physical Education Activities for the Elementary School.* Millbrae, California, National Press, 1956.

Trump, J. Lloyd. "An Image of a Future Secondary School Health, Physical Education and Recreation Program." *Journal of Health — Physical Education — Recreation,* January, 1961, p. 15.

Van Hagen, Winifred, Dexter, Genevie, and Williams, Jesse Feiring. *Physical Education in the Elementary School.* Sacramento, California State Department of Education, 1951.

PRINCIPLES OF METHOD

PRINCIPLES OF METHOD

What really should be studied by those who are preparing themselves to teach and to direct the work of education is the aim of the educational process, its most useful subject-matter, its philosophic basis, and the history of its development. Very little time should be spent upon methods of teaching. Methods of teaching are purely personal, and are the effective application by an individual of the controlling principles upon which his work is based. Excessive devotion to the study of method quickly develops an educational self-consciousness that is destructive either of true effectiveness or of a correct relationship between teacher and taught. Given the possession of sound principles of education, the teacher should then be left with the least possible direction to give full expression to his own personality in his method of teaching.

Butler.

The primary function of democratic education is the cultivation of "the habit of relying on the foresight of consequences rather than on authority in the guidance of conduct."

Bode.

The range of our faculties for enjoyment is enormous and has been explored hardly beyond a fringe.

Whitehead.

SCIENTIFIC METHOD

It is a commonplace to say that we live in an age of science. But this is only partially true. Science dominates many of our human activities and yet in a countless number of ways we continue traditional and superstitious practices. We of this century are more scientific than our ancestors ten centuries ago, but unwarranted practices still prevail.

In educational practice, scientific methods are not everywhere pursued. Many old procedures persist in spite of newly discovered improvements. The basis of scientific method is very simple. It consists of careful observation of phenomena, accurate reporting of the data, and interpretation and presentation of the results for criticism and review by others. There is in scientific method no plea for special interpretation based upon an individual's unique powers or experience, no police authority to compel acceptance of the conclusion, and no disposition to keep the process of discovery secret.

Historically, teaching has been considered an art. Art and science pursue different paths, their methods contrast. Science is fundamentally analytical. It breaks things up, seeks details, and searches for causes and conditions. Art is ever engaged in giving meaning to experience. It puts things together. It is synthesis rather than analysis.

Science and Art in Teaching. It is sometimes said, "The good teacher is born, not made." Teaching requires imagination, facility in seeing relationships, perspective, and creative skill. These are essentially the qualities of the artist rather than the scientist. Moreover, it is argued, these qualities are inborn, and hence training of teachers is only wish-fulfillment, "like dreams in the Freudian theory."

But in any art, spontaneity, perspective, creative skill are dependent upon technique. The imagination is never free to operate when technique interferes. It is not the untrained who are spontaneous, vital, and free, but those to whom technical skill has become second nature.

369

When teaching is regarded as a science, it often assumes mechanical aspects. In this kind of teaching the techniques of standard tests, achievement scores, and examinations are prominent, and correspondingly, there is likely to be neglect of concomitant values and disregard of personality adjustment problems. The athletic coach is frequently forced by the practical realities of his job to win games or to lose his post. In such a situation he is quite unable to consider the more subtle problems concerning the effect of particular experiences in individual athletes. So, conditions force a mechanical approach to the problem.

When, on the other hand, teaching is regarded as an art, the dominant spirit is concerned with creative purposes which can be developed in students, with the doors of the mind which can be opened. This mood is not limited to appreciation courses but can operate fully in systematic science courses, such as anatomy, mathematics, and practical activities.

The outcomes in students are not easily measured nor are they the ready-made answers of the text or syllabus. This does not mean, however, that skills will not be learned, or that exact knowledge of a field will not be mastered. Indeed, the good teacher will always be a master of his own field and will lead his students to seek a similar excellence.

METHODS AND OBJECTIVES

It is a vital principle of teaching to consider methods in relation to objectives. What is the outcome desired? To secure this outcome, a particular method is selected. The close relationship therefore of method to objective forces the thoughtful teacher to examine the two together. Devotion to a method as a procedure that is unrelated to objectives ignores a vital principle in teaching.

Illustrations of a close correspondence between method and objective are numerous. In Germany in the nineteenth century the relation of the individual to the state reveals more accurately the ideas that molded practice. The king and subject relationship was strong. The church and school maintained these bonds by preaching and teaching. The teacher-training institutions were tuned to patriotism as the central theme. In the regulations of a seminary at Pyretz, piety was to be shown, among other ways, by "respect for the king, our sovereign, and by unshaken fidelity to our country."

The method of nineteenth century German education was directed at objectives. The Germany of National Socialism was equally realistic. The following statements are reported by Kandel from the *Allgemeine Deutsche Lehrerzeitung:*

> The taste for militarism must be inculcated in children; they must be told this at every opportunity that every man of noble birth must be a soldier. — Frederick the Great; in the issue for September 2, 1933.
> Rigorous discipline is desirable at a given time. . . . The same discipline imparts the qualities needed by the soldier and the scholar; in fact there is no competent scholar who does not possess the instincts of a good soldier. What should a rigorous school teach? — Obedience and command. — Nietzsche; in the issue for September 23, 1933.
> I know that we Germans will be victorious in the next war; it is the will and the way of God. Simply because it is our turn, no one can resist our health within and our young strength. . . . But such a nation whose hour sounds, must arm itself within and without . . . in such a way that it will lead us to victory and to power. Who could then be the heart and head of Europe? — Gustav Frenssen; in the issue for October 14, 1933.[1]

In these days of economic, political, and social disturbance it is important that Americans recognize the relationship between method and objectives. Those who wish to see the perpetuation of democratic institutions and processes in the United States need to be concerned about the objectives held for education. Is there a place for initiative, resourcefulness, independence of judgment, freedom of expression, individual leadership or are the goals docility, submissiveness, and mass discipline?

[1] I. L. Kandel, *The Making of Nazis*, New York, Teachers College, Columbia University, 1935, p. 75.

Method of one kind can be employed to secure the kind of objectives desired, but its opposite will fail. Educational method which requires uncritical obedience, acceptance of authoritarian statements, and external discipline is not focused upon the objectives of the historic American democracy.

On May 18, 1937, Stanley Baldwin addressed the youth of the British Empire. The following is an excerpt from that address: "The Christian State proclaims human personality to be supreme; the servile State denies this. . . . Use men as ends and never merely as means."

Education in England and in Germany in the third decade of the twentieth century used different methods. Precisely! Method is chosen to serve the objectives sought.

THE RANGE OF OBJECTIVES

The teacher may focus attention very properly upon a single and immediate objective. One cannot teach in general; one teaches particulars. Particular learnings have specificity; they occur in time and space. While this is true in teaching, it is important, however, for all teachers to recognize that learnings in one experience may be many. A teacher may be intent upon teaching how to pitch a baseball, but he should be aware of the fact that the pupil learning the skill is also acquiring other learnings. The wide range of teaching objectives should be indicated therefore. They may be discussed under three types of learning:

Technical Learnings. The obvious results of technical learnings are the particular skills taught. For example, the technical learnings in baseball are how to throw, bat, catch, and run. In learning how to bat, this is broken down into the stance at the plate, how to hold the bat, the position of the arms in the swing, timing the stroke, how to judge good balls, and similar points. Often persons believe that these comprise all that the player learns. They are only a portion, however. Other learnings take place also.

Associated Learnings. The body of ideas associated with an activity may be large or small, significant or trivial. Ideas of how to train for an activity, how to overcome fear of the water, how to acquire neuromuscular relaxation, how to maintain a high level of energy, how to use strength in lifting, how to play a game according to set rules—these may be important learnings and illustrate aspects of mental content in the motor field. Too frequently method focuses upon the technical alone and neglects the associated learnings.

Francis Stroup shows a clear understanding of the material available in associated learnings as follows:

> Despite the contributions made by knowledge and skills, it is through understanding that man achieves the ultimate in liberation. And through his personal involvement in a variety of circumstances and through the opportunities which he has to observe and compare, the student of physical education activities acquires understandings.
>
> Where, for instance, might a student get a more thorough understanding of Archimedes' principle than in a swimming pool with his own body as part of the experiment? Where will the problems related to center of gravity and equilibrium stimulate more personal involvement and ultimate understanding than in a tumbling class? The laws of motion, of acceleration and of resistance are as operative in the physical education laboratory as in the physics laboratory. Observations in an activity class frequently make the understanding of these laws more complete and more permanent.[2]

Concomitant Learnings. Technical and associated learnings do not exhaust the field. Other important learnings occur.

In the performance of any motor activity, one learns attitudes toward the activity and toward others engaged in the activity. It is clear that these attitudes may have no relation to the excellence with which the other learnings are acquired. Thus, one may become most proficient in swimming and be a thoroughly poor sport, or one may be only moderately skillful in motor skills and still be a generous, kindly, and fair player. Some

[2] Francis Stroup, "Physical Education and the Liberal Arts," *The Physical Educator*, December, 1959, p. 129.

of the concomitant learnings which are often sought are: giving the best that is in one, finishing the task begun, accuracy in completing assignments, integrity as respecting the rights of others, generosity to opponents and faithfulness to associates.

The relationship of method to concomitant learnings is peculiarly important. Consider what are those learnings when a physical activity is presented by a teacher who is a rigid formalist, a strict disciplinarian, believing in the objectives of docility, submissiveness, and obedience.

What does the boy or girl think about physical education under such methods? Why do some boys and girls come to college seeking to be excused from required physical education? What do they think of play? Is it mere fooling that leads nowhere? What are their ideas of self-expression in relation to honesty and excellence? Do they think of their bodies as splendid means for expression or as machines for the manufacture of perspiration? How do they feel toward authority? Do they chafe under it? Do they get any idea of what self-discipline means? What do they think about self-discipline in relationship to friends, to the school, to the nation? How far and to what extent are they cooperative toward ends that they know about, have helped to set up, and are willing to work for? Surely no partisan of formal discipline in physical education can neglect to answer such questions.

Moreover, it is the validity of concomitant learnings which makes the theory of interest so attractive to so many serious and dedicated workers. The appreciations, the ideas, and the attitudes developed, and the extent of their usefulness in a democracy such as ours depend upon the judgment we give in this trial of interest and effort.

MANY METHODS, AND ONE IS BEST

The best method is the one that accomplishes the desired objective. It is best only in relation to its objective. If individual and group welfare is important, the method that meets the situation with greatest advantage to the individual and to the group is the best method. With the goal of the highest individual development in relation to social welfare uppermost, it ought to be clear that the teacher must stand ready to meet situations rather than give allegiance only to a theory of action. There are times when play breaks down due to disturbing individuals. There are individuals who have never learned any self-direction at all. To give such persons unlimited freedom without opportunity to learn what liberty means, and how it is attained, is a serious mistake in method. The teacher must be ready to help out in the management of an activity. The teacher, as a member of the group, is therefore a responsible leader as well as a thoughtful follower upon occasion. Moreover, it is a plain truth of the matter that a formal method may be required, not for any special virtues to accrue from its use, but because it offers a way to meet a situation with greater profit to the individual and to the group.

It is with this reservation in mind that the student should examine all methods. One may become convinced that the interest of the individual is the greatest force for worthwhile, continuing activity. This conviction then takes a prominent place in shaping method. One may become convinced also that interests are not always wholesome, that some individuals are not cooperative members of a group. This appreciation stimulates the teacher to discover ways to keep desirable activities going while he seeks means of fostering wholesome interests; to devise methods of protecting group activity while dealing with a recalcitrant member or members.

With this fact established, the principles underlying methods may be discussed with reference to the three types of learning that take place. It is obvious that technical learnings are not isolated from associated or concomitant ones, and that method in one area has applications in others. Nevertheless some principles have more direct application in one learning situation than another. It is merely a matter of emphasis.

PRINCIPLES OF METHOD IN TECHNICAL LEARNINGS

There are many principles of teaching that relate directly to how an activity should be handled in order that children may learn it. These have meaning for method. In the following discussion the principle will be stated and its relation to method indicated.

Physical education should be conducted vigorously in order to insure organic development.

Organic vitality is developed by exercise. The only agency available for the development of the vital organs is exercise. Heredity and nutrition influence this development, but it is exercise that secures development.

Method will be employed therefore to provide vigorous physical activity presenting increasing physiological demands on organic functions up to optimum levels. In general, excessively severe activities are rarely found in school programs. These programs are probably not vigorous enough. On the other hand, in highly specialized sport and in modern dance projected toward the stage, there are numerous examples of improper and excessive demands upon the organism.

Physical education should promote growth.

Growth requires activity. This is especially true during adolescence. In this period of rapid growth, motor skills appear often to be lost. The individual is awkward. Things are knocked over, broken, or spilled. Conscious attention to these imperfect performances confuses.

Generous but not too strenuous participation in sports and rhythmic activities is required. Activity and time restore the old skills and even improve them. Method will avoid punishment, ridicule, and such cruel approaches. Encouragement, rewards, approval, a generous amount of activity, and patience — these are the cues.

Physical education should proceed from the known to the desired unknown.

The known is familiar ground. The use of "lead-up" games in teaching sports is an illustration of the principle applied to method. In such progression the teacher will proceed in relation to the individual's motor sense and kinesthesia. This means teaching activities within the range of the pupil's motor experience. An exercise in baseball would not be appropriate for a first-grade child. New activities to be experienced should be interpreted in terms of old activities that have meaning.

Physical education should stress rewards rather than punishment.

Reward gives a greater gain in learning than punishment.[3] The best method is to reward the correct response rather than to punish the incorrect. The best results in the use of punishment are obtained when the annoyance then and there encourages or causes the operation of the right connection and the accompanying satisfaction.

Persons learn better when a situation possesses its own intrinsic value rather than an extrinsic one. Mere repetition is wasteful. The value of repetition in learning resides in the after-effects of the process.

Fear of punishment may act as a motivation and hence lack of punishment may become in effect a reward. In the use of punishment, Thorndike suggests that there are five important guides to keep in mind.

1. Make sure that the punishment used is related to the act.

2. Forestall the punishment where the want that caused the offense can be satisfied innocently.

3. Shift the emphasis from the discomfort of one situation to the relief, security, and comfort of the correct situation.

4. Arouse confirming reactions by attaching relevant satisfiers to the connections desired in place of the wrong connections for which punishment might be required.

5. Make punishment rational and reasonable when they still remain important means of control.

Physical education should analyze a pupil's difficulty in movement and suggest the cue that will lead to improvement.

[3] E. L. Thorndike, *The Psychology of Wants, Interests and Attitudes,* New York, Appleton-Century-Crofts, 1935.

Learning is facilitated when the teacher can analyze the fault or difficulty and suggest the cue which will secure the correct response. This requires expertness in a wide range of skills. If the teacher is competent, there is much help that can be given. In directing the learning of a motor skill, the teacher should know: (1) the best form for performance of the motor act, and (2) how to analyze the act to discover what the pupil should do in order to learn the skill. Correct form is essential and early practice should be based upon this. After early attention is given to form, then attention should be directed toward results rather than form. Focus of attention on form interferes with the ability to "let go." Timing and coordination are dependent upon relaxation, objective attitudes; these are impaired when form is the focus.

Physical education should use drill intelligently.

Drill is important in fixing the skill learned, in perfecting its form, and in acquiring satisfaction in the experience. Mere repetition may yield nothing in learning. Drill must relate to outcomes that the pupil cares about; they must appreciate the relation of drill in parts to the accomplishment of the whole. Elizabeth Rodgers' study on the learning of game skills is important in this connection.[4] Some persons never experience much satisfaction in motor activities because they remain dubs, ever unskilled performers. If they had drilled enough in youth to do well an activity the reality of satisfaction would have appeared. It seems to be true that participation relates to proficiency. Drill is important in proficiency.

Physical education should set levels of performance in relation to the individual's development.

Levels of accomplishment should relate to development of the individual. It is a mistake to seek high accomplishment at the higher levels of performance too early. The following roughly outlines the age levels at which emphases may be made.

Age 6–11 — period of generalized activity.

Age 10–12 — period of beginning technique.

[4] Elizabeth Rodgers, *The Teaching of Team Games*, New York, Teachers College, Columbia University, 1936.

Age 12–15—period of team play.

Age 16 and on—period of speed and skill.

For the beginner in any motor activity it is always a mistake to seek speed before technique is acquired. This is recognized also in the teaching of handwriting, piano-playing, and typewriting. (Some activities proceed better when performed rapidly rather than slowly, notably balance activities.) This view supports Poppelreuter's law of practice that requires, for optimum results, retardation of speed of movement in the early stages of practice until high accuracy is attained and then increase of speed gradually.[5]

While the view expressed above is generally held, R. E. Fulton in her experimental work demonstrates that early emphasis upon speed in learning movements is advantageous in both ballistic and nonballistic movements.[6] She concludes that tennis strokes, golf strokes, and similar movements in which the accumulation of momentum is essential are affected adversely by early emphasis on accuracy.

PRINCIPLES OF METHOD IN ASSOCIATED LEARNINGS

The fundamental problem in teaching is to extend the learnings that children acquire. For example, it is not sufficient to teach correct spelling; it is imperative to have this skill extend into reading and writing. There is a kind of reciprocity in such matters. A teacher may teach a boy how to run a 100-yard dash, but if this learning extends into how to condition oneself and reading about great sprinters, there are not only these associated learnings that are valuable in themselves, but reciprocal emphasis upon the technical skills also. There are several principles that bear directly upon associated learnings.

[5] J. A. McGeoch, "The Acquisition of Skill," *Psychological Bulletin*, August, 1929, p. 470.

[6] R. E. Fulton, "Speed and Accuracy in Learning Movements," *Archives Psychology*, No. 300, 1946.

Physical education should teach activities that are inherently interesting.

Interest in an activity provides the drive to engage in it, insures more rapid learning, and is a factor in satisfying experience. The brief for interest in physical education claims an identity between the activity and participant; a relationship which is the sole guarantee of unified response. It notes that a child may be put through a set of exercises, but claims that there is no assurance that cooperation is present, because there may be the nearly perfect outward performance, and at the same time definite inward rebellion. It claims for the theory of interest a reality between activity and participant which precludes divided attention. Moreover, the brief for interest in physical education sets forth that over and beyond the effects of any period of exercise there must be recognition of the necessity for a continuing action; there must be developed a love for and a skill in some form of wholesome physical activity that will continue after school days are over. It contends that interest in the exercise is the only guarantee of such future participation.

Other positive claims are brought forward to present the case for interest in physical education; the relations of interest to the laws of learning, to the achievement of hygienic effects in exercise, and even to the correction of physical defects and deformities are prominent ones. But its brief also includes criticism of the theory of effort. It finds that any task carried on under compulsion, as it needs must be when it comes as a task, is rejected as soon as the pressure to do it is relieved. In writing of intellectual activity Hebb says, "He [man] objects to work when it is imposed from without, when it is not of his own choosing, and especially when it is in any way monotonous."[7] In effort situations, then, there is no provision for a continuing activity. Moreover, in the theory of effort there is reliance upon the fundamentals of interest, only the interest is an ignoble one, an appeal to fear, or a sentimental one, an appeal to love of

[7] Donald O. Hebb, "The Role of Experience," *Control of the Mind, Man and Civilization* (Seymour M. Farber, Editor), New York, McGraw-Hill, 1961, p. 50.

teacher. Instead of unified activity due to the identity between activity and participant, there is divided activity whenever the theory of effort is in force.

The product of the theory of effort is not the desirable citizen so often put forward to justify its practice. In the main the application of the effort philosophy results in rebellion of many individuals against authority. The history of nations in bondage, the tragic breaks in homes, the desertion of the school by many children, indicate the rebellion to this theory of effort. Those who survive the process are either narrow, obstinate, dictatorial, made in the likeness of their masters, or are dull, spineless, broken, submissive creatures, obedient and docile because the "vital juice of spontaneous interest has been squeezed out."

When a boy throws an object he gets satisfaction in the act because he is ready to be exercised in precisely that kind of thing. The boy is interested in activities which involve throwing, because the exercise or organic arrangements involved provide satisfaction. In similar fashion, climbing, hanging, leaping, running, and associated movements are of interest because they exercise organizations already present and ready to function. These organizations are just as real as the boy's bones or muscles; although they cannot be described in detail, their performance is governed by certain laws on the whole better formulated than those relating to muscular contraction. It is important to understand that the human individual is organized to take interest in and enjoy a wide variety of physical activities which relate to his social life.

Study of the psychology of interest reveals the identity of the individual with the object. There is a connection between the actor and the act; an indissoluble bond between the two. To take interest in an activity is to have the appropriate organizations concerned in a state of readiness to act. All is prepared in the body's organization to bring the desired result about. In such a situation the mind is set toward the end to be achieved, and the whole organism is ready for the experience. Thus, the presence of the appropriate object or situation calls forth the appropriate response, and in thus responding the individual shows interest. We are dealing, therefore, with a scientific fact, not a mere sentimentality. The preparation of this chapter took hours of time, required the reading, digesting, and annotating of many books, journals, and papers, and led to several conferences. But it was not a task; the mind was set toward an end; interest was there as a fact.

It is at this point that we need to comprehend the fallacy that shows in the dictum "that one should make the work interesting." Frequently, indeed, one hears this advice when a program is criticized for its lack of interesting material. This idea that artificial exercises are to be made interesting suffers from two pernicious errors. In one case it bases the selection of subject matter not upon native capacity, desire, or need, but upon certain artificial criteria of political or social sanction at the time. In the second case, it is confronted with the necessity of devising external and artificial procedures in method for dressing up an unrelated and meaningless activity so that it will attract some attention. The spectacle of children in school going through a calisthenic drill in artificial movements, moved either by love of teacher or fear of teacher, when never of themselves would you see them voluntarily engage in such activity, is a common illustration.

Such presentation of the theory of interest frequently brings out the question, "Do you mean to say that children should do everything that they please to do?" There is no need to jump to such an extreme position by either the most ardent advocate of interest or the most carping critic. The implication is perfectly clear; activities should be selected in physical education in relation to the child's experience, drives, needs, and capacities. Not all impulses are of equal worth; nature is not always right. At times the relevancy of acceptable material must be brought to the consciousness of the child, but in relation always to the things which already are appreciated, have meaning, and are of interest. Children are not to be permitted to do everything which interests them, but things that they are led to do must be in their very nature interesting. It is mistaken zeal and poor teaching to attempt to make unrelated material interesting.

Such implies at the very outset that it does not possess the quality of giving satisfaction, but must be dressed up.

Ultimately, of course, one's reaction to this view is determined by what one is trying to do. Is there any desire to build up an enduring activity which will, under proper guidance, provide health, motor skills, and growth values as by-products, or does one seek to develop unrelated and frequently useless skills as ends in themselves? Is there a purpose to cultivate joyous appreciation of wholesome activities which will continue after school days are over, or is there a puritanic dislike of joy and an academic disregard for play?

Consider the practice so stoutly defended by those who follow the theory of effort which permits and encourages children to work for years with the stilted, artificial, and deadening movements outlined in the syllabi of many cities and states. Consider the practice in so-called school gymnastics aimed at the correction of postural defects by ten minutes of exercise daily in the classroom, ignoring the physiological and psychological factors in postures. The posture problem in our schools is in part tied up with the domineering type of teacher who cows her pupils, who relies on fear as a motive, and who gets not only submissiveness of mind and spirit, but also of body. The question of posture must be viewed not merely as a problem in body mechanics, but also in its relation to fatigue, to nutritional and emotional states.

Physical education should follow psychological progression.

Interest in an activity rests upon psychological rather than logical grounds. The moment one has an interest in an activity, there is a drive ready to set it going. This contrasts with the orderly and logical arrangement of learning that adults have often proposed for children.

The old method of progression in school subjects was the **logical.** In teaching reading, for example, the procedure was to teach the alphabet, then words of two, three, four, and five letters, etc. Now in observing children it has been found that the first words they might desire to learn to spell or read were not those in the logical order. Thus, even before the alphabet is learned, a child may wish to spell "candy," "dog," or "rocking horse." The new approach to progression is to teach and give opportunity to learn according to the awakening interests of the child. This method of progression is **psychological** and not **logical.**

A similar situation exists in physical education. The systems brought to this country and perpetuated as formal gymnastics were extremely logical. Men had certain muscles and certain parts; they were to be exercised in order and sequence. Arm, leg, and trunk exercises were to follow in **logical** progression. Now the psychological approach in physical education considers the nature of the child and proceeds in line with the individual's impulses and organic urges. The third-grade child is interested in climbing; the sixth-grade child in team games. These are characteristic traits of the period. They become the guide for the progression—the guide is psychological.

Procedure along the psychological line would mean that the motor problems were to be raised to consciousness as problems of the children. The teacher is not to exercise the class; in working to gain certain power over pertinent motor problems, and important social (team) problems, the class will get exercise as a by-product of an activity that goes on because it is worth while to the individual or the group.

Physical education should promote activities that carry over because of inherent interest.

Interest in an activity promotes retention of the learnings acquired; the guarantee of carry-over resides in both the nature of the activity and in the interest developed in it. The doctrine of interest should never be viewed as opposed to true effort, because true effort finds its clearest illustrations, if necessary, in relation to interest. Life does present difficulties, obligations that we would wish away if we could, duties that knock upon the door of interest and time. And in the face of difficulties, of obligations, of duties, we want to see developed a real persistency in attack, and a thoroughgoing continuity of activity begun. Effort merely as increased strain is not the goal, but true effort toward the fulfillment of a growing and expanding activity. It is important to state, therefore, that what is wanted is not effort for its own sake, as the formalist would ask for, nor for some distant, unappreciated value, but true endeavor in relation to an end that is worth the energy put forth. Further analysis of this type of effort points to two considerations:

1. With such endeavor in mind let us think about one engaged in an activity which is not successful because of an impending obstacle. A condition of mental stress occurs; the end of the activity calls him to continue; the obstacle bids him give it up. As a mental experience, therefore, there is a combination of conflicting urges away from and toward dislike and longing.

2. Up to this point activity has been blocked of its end. The difficulty should lead one to stop and think. Is the end worth pursuing? The two-miler is hopelessly outclassed. Shall he give it up as a bad job? Is there a better course available? Even if the decision is to give up, the whole situation is different from giving up because of mere weakness of will. If the giving up is decided, it may be "quite consistent with tenacity" of purpose. Or, instead of giving up, it may mean that a new course of action has been decided upon. The problem has been taken out of the field of unintelligent effort and vain struggle, and has entered into the realm of consciousness and thought. Energy has been transferred from blind struggle and diverted to thinking. This not only makes him more conscious of his end, and increases interest, but through reflective thought he comes to make more intelligent effort in the rapidly expanding activity.

Hence we are to distinguish between effort at a task which has no meaning, no interest, that is wholly alien and uncongenial, which is kept up only by fear or other prods from the teacher, and true endeavor which leads from an activity with interest and meaning to reflective thought concerning the obstacle encountered, culminating in frank abandonment of the project, or in the discovery of new ways for continuing the activity which in itself is a growing and expanding one full of thoroughgoing purpose.

This view predicts a different approach in teaching physical education. Instead of the teacher being a dynamo for arousing energy in a class, he becomes a leader for the direction of energy already available. It is with this method that we must study the teaching of all activities. Here is a program involving a great many valuable and essential skills and body controls. Instead of the teacher leading the class in the formal way, with a conscious purpose to get uniformity of response, the teacher might introduce the class to a number of motor problems related to real interests. The individual makes the effort, for the problem is an individual or team problem for the individual to work out. The newer methods in the teaching of swimming make use of this same approach, and the difficulties of the stroke, of balance, of breathing, are brought to consciousness, to reflective thought. Here, through this method, we have the richest opportunity for the development of thinking, a real educational basis for physical education, at once a challenge and an opportunity.

Physical education should make clear the objectives of the activity.

Awareness by the learner of the objectives of an activity aids the learning. These precise ends become targets at which to aim; this helps the shooting. This is true for all types of learnings, but it is particularly important for the associated outcomes. The athlete may well become aware of a number of objectives in addition to the technical gains and as these are accepted as legitimate goals, the stage is set for learning them.

The use of achievement levels in motor skills and of knowledge tests of rules and training is illustrative of modern methods in helping pupils to become aware of objectives.

Physical education should practice learning by doing.

Learning results from doing. Activity in which the pupil becomes a responsible agent rather than a tool manipulated by the teacher is typical of learning by doing. Education for many years and in some schools today places reliance upon a procedure of learning by discipline rather than learning by doing. This view is represented by the theory of formal discipline and has enjoyed acceptance from time to time in physical education.

The spread of dictatorial methods of government with their corresponding control over national educations challenges all teachers to understand the full implications of the discipline.

The above position is increasingly appreciated, but some physical educators, unable to accept the conclusions of a logical process of reasoning, are driven into the position where they claim that formal gymnastics are suited to the needs of the schools as they are equipped, staffed, and administered today. This is a very plausible position, until you examine it carefully. It ought to be clear at the outset, in considering such a question, that any program which is justified because of inadequate physical equipment, teacher shortage, or other handicap loses its validity the moment these conditions cease to exist. The very weakness of the position is shown by the fact that schools are being built and organized today to carry on a modern, progressive program of physical education; it is tradition alone that forces on the same old program.

Any program in America which fails to recognize the nature of the individual, and the needs of a democratic society, but proceeds rather upon a basis of physical limitations, is pursuing bankrupt methods, and will fail to pay dividends. With regard to responsibility in this matter, it should be clear that school administrators are to be held accountable equally with specialists in physical education. Moreover, the superintendent of schools cannot with justification say, "I know nothing about this; that's the reason we have an expert to determine the program." It may be granted that he need not become familiar with the detailed procedures, but with the general aim, character, and nature of these activities he must be conversant or jeopardize his right to leadership in the education of children.

Finally, it should be noted that, where argument will not convince, the final test is the well-controlled experiment. In all respects, this is the preferred method of conviction. To give different and typical programs to different but equal groups, and to measure the results, would seem to be the sensible thing to do. This has been done and should be repeated by numerous other workers.

Formality in method is employed whenever several persons are brought under the direction of one leader. A teacher with only two children will set up some systematic ways of doing certain things. Any teaching of groups requires some formality. The real question at issue is whether the formality is a necessary means, used purposely for organization, or a device for securing certain disciplinary objectives. Apart from the necessity for organization whenever a group is taught, the formal method in physical education is advocated usually for values supposed to reside in the method itself. Here then are contrasting points of view: one holds that formal procedure is necessary to the extent that is required by the legitimate goals and sanctioned objectives of the activities; the other contends that the formality is an end in itself and should be employed because it is good for children to be disciplined under such procedure. These two positions are presented in the following discussion of interest and effort in physical education.

The theories of effort and formal discipline are essentially one. They base their claim for attention upon a belief that by doing an unpleasant thing one gains a kind of useful power. They frequently lead by the sheer logic of the case to absurd ends, as when Emerson, in his lecture on Compensation, argues that if one will be good (goodness consisting in doing what is uninteresting) one may have, at some future time, a great many interesting activities—that is, may then be bad.

In viewing formal discipline, it should be remembered that historically it has been profitable for king, lord, and ecclesiastical powers to foster obedience to authority; to cultivate docility and submissiveness in general.

Undoubtedly the extreme cultivation of submissiveness in the masses restrained progress. Men who have perpetuated submission rather than experimentation, curiosity, and kindliness have hurt mankind. The cultivation of submissiveness in the masses may be made to serve different purposes, religious, economic, or political. In the hands of aggressive, war-minded leaders great control over the masses may readily lead to war.

Hitler, Mussolini, and the war party in Japan never could have made their play for world power without mass submissiveness.

There are other aspects to this theory of effort and formal discipline. We need to consider the group of related attitudes which grow out of any activity in which one participates. In physical education of the formal type, there is seen a practice which gives outward obedience with inward rejection. An experience which outwardly yields while inwardly rejecting is significant particularly, because of the related attitudes, the concomitant learnings. It is important to investigate this point more at length.

PRINCIPLES OF METHOD IN CONCOMITANT LEARNINGS

Technical learnings yield skills, associated learnings yield knowledge, concomitant learnings yield attitudes and appreciations. There are no watertight compartments around these; attitudes influence the learning of skills, and skill enriches appreciation. But the importance of concomitant learnings should never be denied or neglected. The principles underlying method in these matters are presented in the following discussion.

Physical education should recognize individual differences.

Human behavior is dependent upon a multiplicity of factors, elements, and influences both within and outside the organism. This complex variation is accountable for the fact that every person differs from every other person. The principle of individual differences is rich in its suggestions for method. All children cannot be held for standard or norm performances. Goals must be set for groups in which individuals have membership because they fall within the specifications of the classification. Similarly all pupils will not gain identical associated and concomitant learnings. Indeed a teacher may teach all children in a class the same dance, but because of individual differences they will vary not only in their motor performance but far more markedly in the other learnings.

Knowledge must serve some drive before it influences conduct. Bacon's dictum that "knowledge is power" cannot mean always power in good behavior.

Thought is personal, belonging to the individual who has or expresses it. When the correct act gives satisfaction, this works backward to strengthen the connection.

Physical education should seek outcomes in excellent character.

The influence of participation in physical education activities in producing or modifying human responses in habitual behavior affects what is called personality and character. Alfred C. Werner reports an interesting study of cadets at the U. S. Military Academy on the relationship of participation in physical education and leadership profiles.[8] The relationship between tests of character and tests of strength of grip is practically zero, and that existing between health and character tests has very little correlation. It is becoming increasingly clear that what is recognized as desirable character comes out of experiences which are constructively wholesome, stimulating to effort, helping toward distant but recognizable goals. Indeed, so complicated is the problem that once and for all physical education must abandon its usual practice of claiming character education in general.

Character may be defined as that way of behaving which takes into account the remote implications and consequences of action. Character, as so defined, is the product of environment and heredity, of both nature and nurture; it results inevitably from the play of various forces in nurture upon the biological materials of man.

In the area of character education there are many forces

[8] Alfred C. Werner, "Physical Education and the Development of Leadership Characteristics of Cadets at the U.S. Military Academy," *Annual Proceedings of the College Physical Education Association,* 1961, p. 100.

at work creating the varied situations in which and to which the individual responds. A situation exists and the individual reacts. This is experience and out of this the individual builds his life. The character resulting flows from the experiences he has. The only test of importance is to what extent young persons are taking part in wholesome, constructive, and worthy experiences.

No place is more important for formative effects upon individual lives than the home. It rarely realizes its opportunity. Parents devoted to business, gossip, amusement, or even worthy community enterprise fail conspicuously to deal adequately with the only reality of importance in the home — the particular child or children in the home. Some strange vagary of human nature leads parents, otherwise well disposed toward social gains, to neglect the immediate practical problems of their own children. Recognition of this failure of the home leads the school to take over the responsibility with teachers who themselves have little understanding of the problem. The school devoted to its traditional program of transmitting the social inheritance neglects the biological needs of children and pays scant attention to avocational interests which are called extracurricular activities. When the school has concerned itself with character education, it has too often resorted to precepts, punishment, and procedures of like form and content.

If character education is to be undertaken by the school, it must consider methods of getting boys and girls to plunge into worthy enterprises, working with others to make high purpose and fine vision come true. In physical education there are many opportunities to help boys and girls arrive at a point of view about life, to acquire principles by which they live, and to understand their experiences in terms of the goals they have for themselves. Illustrations of the process in a variety of situations follow.

It is widely accepted that boys and girls should acquire the attitude of giving their best. This needs examination. One's best is frequently not given because, in the first place, the situation is without interest or meaning. One gives one's best when the activity has worth in one's judgment. This attitude is not to be confused with effort as a theory of action.

Secondly, someone else has not done something. "Mary didn't do it," is a frequent response. Lack of performance is never justified in unrelated instances on someone else's failure. Wherever you find excuse for lack of performance, this will be a common one.

Thirdly, contrary attitudes have been learned. The following of any attitude is not evidence that justice has been done. The right act and one's judgment of the right act are not the same thing necessarily. They may coincide, but they are not bound to do so. Appeal to conscience does not bring freedom from injury to the individual or group. Regardless of the motive, or the regrets, or the excuse brought forward, the act is done and its effect on others is a real thing.

A football coach some years ago saw this situation clearly, and taught the lesson that all should learn. A player who had been absent from practice the day before would be asked by the coach concerning his absence. All sorts of explanations are available for lack of performance. Some are valid reasons for failure; others are excuses that seek to relieve the individual of the responsibility for failure. In the latter instance, the coach would point out that the player was missed, that harm was done to the team since every member of the squad has responsibilities that affect all other members, and that an excuse never substitutes for the actual performance.

The effort to present an excuse for accomplishment is not surprising, as it is probably true that this player, as many others also, had been taught zealously from youth that when something is wrong he must do something and get it right. Beyond this he will have been told that, if he is conscientious, he will always try to be right and not wrong. This desire to be right becomes an obsession along with his purpose to satisfy his conscience that he is right.

On analysis it is seen that one's insistence on satisfying conscience is merely an attempt to unload responsibility. He has been taught by precept and example to deal with difficulties by excuses. He wishes to satisfy his conscience when the greatest need is to put into operation his reasoning intelligence. If intelligence could break through the fog of conscience and wanting to be right, it would reveal that the chief difficulty was in the high feeling coming from the criticism for which he develops a defense reaction in the form of an excuse. This salves his conscience by appearing to himself as justified, as right. He will grow, of course, only as he is ready to accept that he is wrong.

This same perversion is seen in numerous activities in physical education, although not here alone. A student learning a new stunt on an apparatus may approach the apparatus, and before trying the stunt remark "I can't do it." This is getting an alibi ready beforehand, so that, when urged to try, the probable failure may be minimized by the remark, "There, I was right; I told you I couldn't do it." Such a situation should be met at the start by the teacher not permitting the attempt until the student can say, "I can do it." If then the student fails of success, the teacher should help the student to understand that it is not essential that he succeed. The only essential is that he do his best. These are the facts for the student to face; and teaching should help students to face facts. The facts are the football player did not fulfill his assignment; the student in the gymnasium missed the vault. The individual should face the facts and not try to excuse himself.

The individual who is continually late, absent frequently, or failing in assignments and reports, throws into clear light the chaotic condition of individual programs at times, and the corresponding lack in fulfilled duties. Too many little side shows, too many unredeemed pledges, too many unfulfilled responsibilities! Excuses for these persons fan the flames that destroy effective personality.

Other standards taught by parents are frequently narrow and selfish. Frequently a generous, social view in giving one's self is smothered by the admonition to save yourself. Too often the narrow view is defended on the basis of love; the parent loves the child so much that he does not wish the child to do anything that may not appear at the moment pleasing to the child (again this is not to be confused with the theory of interest). Rabbi Wise once said: "Children should love their parents more and honor them less, and parents should love their children less and respect them more."

One may not give one's best because the conditions are not known. The standard performance that represents "best" is not understood. There may be an attitude of willingness to give the best, but he does not know how to do so. Effective teaching supplies such lacks.

Physical education should promote socialization.

Socialization is an important outcome in physical education activities. Civilized human relationships and expressions are learned reactions. An illustration of the problem is given in a discussion of courtesy. The attitude of courtesy is not expressed because, first, there are strong, instinctive impulses to get what one wants without thought of others. The development of courtesy is not to lead to weakness in personality, but to strength. In no sense is sympathy to be confused with courtesy. The sympathy that weakens one's courage, that seeks absolution for failure, is well contrasted in Guitry's great play *Pasteur*, with worthy sympathy for a worthy situation. Girls who receive physical injuries need to be carefully handled or the impairment of the moral fiber will be more damaging than injury to muscle, bone, or connective tissue. Epithelium for purposes of development of character should never compete with the nervous system.

Secondly, man has difficulty in being courteous because his social development has been with small groups, and large groups are relatively a new thing. He is courteous to friends, but not to the public.

In the third place, fatigue and ill health may be related causes.

Lastly, other standards may be operative. Thus one may be courteous when it pays, but real courtesy is without reference to returns. Or traditional standards may be operative, e.g., one may be courteous to business associates, but not to his wife and family.

One or more of these conditions may exist, and analysis of the situation by the teacher should assist him to help the student obtain the desired response.

Physical education should give opportunity for the expression of attitudes in several situations.

Opportunity to manifest an attitude in several situations is helpful in learning. Wide use favors habit. There are two attitudes which illustrate the principle here. One is finishing the task begun; the other, accuracy and thoroughness in work. The work is not completed frequently because of two reasons. In the first place, it fails to provide an incentive. A difficulty is met, there is mental stress between going on and giving up. Such is an intellectual problem. Shall one go on? How may the difficulty be overcome? If an incentive is lacking to go on, the difficulty is sufficient reason for stopping. It may be unwise to go on when a two-mile race, for example, is the task proposed. However, the essence of this attitude is to be achieved in relation to an activity of interest, and even then it may be undesirable to complete even that project of tremendous interest.

In the second place, this attitude is not developed because of a distorted view of one's place and importance in the scheme of things. This is illustrated by the player who quits the squad because he fails to secure a varsity berth, or teacher who stays one year in a place and then gives it up because of difficulties. This is the kind of person who would stop running to base because he was sure he would be put out, and would give up trying to guard an opponent because he was sure he would make a goal.

Accuracy and thoroughness are not present often because it requires diligence to be accurate. The lazy person is accurate only by accident. Failure to know the rules is a common illustration of lack of thoroughness and accuracy. Here is an enviable teaching situation: exact knowledge and a precise practical situation to give it expression.

Teachers and parents too readily accept inaccurate and general statements when accurate, specific ones are called for. Too frequently general statements are accepted with the assumption that the student knows, but cannot express the idea.

The fact is the student does not **know**. He may have a general, hazy idea, but he does not know. This is seen at times in grading examination papers when credit is given for part of the answer being right. It is ridiculous to credit as correct the addition, or division, or multiplication, if in the final process the subtraction is wrong and answer wrong. It would never be safe to build bridges with such engineering methods. This point should not be confused with imaginative activity in a young child.

The development of attitudes must consider appropriateness of time, place, and condition for their appearance. The question, "Should fourth-grade children be expected to show thoroughness in gymnastic work?" may be answered by saying that attitudes and responses are to be expected when the work which is suited to the characteristics of the group call for those responses. The propulsion for attitudes is to come from the work done, and the work selected to be done must be selected on a **psychological** and not on a **logical** basis. Thus, whenever it is physiologically and psychologically desirable for children to compete in competitive athletic events, it is desirable to expect that the response of "giving one's best" will be seen.

"GROUP PROCESS" AS A METHOD

Group consideration of a problem is an American democratic heritage. The New England town meeting was a method of solving problems that confronted the early settlers of that area; it has continued to this day in numerous New England communities. Class discussions in schools, and public forums on community problems and issues are common experiences of children and adults everywhere in America today.

Although group discussion of common problems is a widespread social phenomenon, it is not always democratically conducted and it is not always profitable in outcomes. Aware of these shortages, numerous students of education and social life have been interested to discover techniques of procedure which would insure democratic participation in the solution of problems and which would provide processes that would aid in making the discussion effective. Moreover, there is the expectation that the use of group process in solving problems will provide a way by which the resources of individuals in a group may be revealed, how individuals act in group settings may be discovered, and what can be done to facilitate cooperative effort in the solution of common problems may be discerned.

It is apparent that the presentation, analysis and solution of problems of immediate concern to groups is essential in a democratic society. Although the American government is republican in form and constitutes a pattern in which representatives selected by the people make the laws, there are countless numbers of questions upon which citizens must make decisions, not for themselves only but also for the group to which they belong and through which they act. This is not only a method of determining social policy by which the representatives of the people may be guided but also a process by means of which responsible citizenship may be developed. With respect to the latter value it is evident that group discussion may improve the ability of an individual to express himself in public, may increase his knowledge through the reported experiences of others, may enlarge his tolerance for the views of others, and may sharpen his awareness of the fact that there are many aspects to an issue and many sides to simple problems.

There is a considerable body of literature on this topic; some of the more helpful titles are given below.

Association for Supervision and Curriculum Development. *Group Process in Supervision*. Washington, D.C., National Education Association, 1948.

Baxter, B., and Cassidy, Rosalind. *Group Experience, The Democratic Way*. New York, Harper, 1943.

Benne, K. *A Conception of Authority*. New York, Teachers College, Columbia University, 1945.

Bennett, Bruce L. "Physical Education and Social Learnings in the Secondary School." *Journal American Association for Health—Physical Education—Recreation*, September, 1949.

Cassidy, Rosalind, and Kozman, Hilda. *Counseling Girls in a Changing Society.* New York, McGraw-Hill, 1947.

Cooper, A. M. *How to Conduct Conferences.* New York, McGraw-Hill, 1942.

Deane, Martha B. *Group Dynamics Research.* American Academy of Physical Education, Professional Contributions No. 1, November, 1951.

Deitz, Dorothea, Strasser, Rose, and Thompson, Harry C. *Methods,* Chapter XI in *Developing Democratic Human Relations.* Washington, D.C., American Association for Health, Physical Education and Recreation, 1951.

Educational Policy Commission. *Learning the Ways of Democracy.* Washington, D.C., National Education Association, 1940.

Everett, S. *School and Community Meet.* New York, Hinds, 1948.

Frank, L. K. *Society as the Patient.* New Brunswick, N.J., Rutgers, 1948.

Garland, J. V., and Phillips, C. F. *Discussion Methods, Explained and Illustrated.* New York, Wilson, 1940.

Golden, C. S., and Ruttenberg, H. J. *The Dynamics of Industrial Democracy.* New York, Harper, 1942.

Gunderson, R. G. "This Group Dynamics Furor." *School and Society,* August 18, 1951, p. 97.

Hopkins, L. T. *Interaction—The Democratic Process.* Boston, Heath, 1941.

Jennings, Helen Hall. *Leadership or Isolation.* New York, Longmans, Green, 1943.

John Dewey Society. *Intercultural Attitudes in the Making.* New York, Harper, 1947.

Lewin, Kurt. *Resolving Social Conflicts.* New York, Harper, 1948.

Lewin, Kurt, and Lippitt, R. *The Research Center for Group Dynamics.* New York, Beacon House, 1947.

Mumford, Lewis. *Faith for Living.* New York, Harcourt, Brace, 1940.

Roethlisberger, F. J. *Management and Morale.* Cambridge, Harvard University, 1946.

Skubic, Elvera. "A Study in Acquaintanceship and Social Status in Physical Education Classes." *Research Quarterly,* March, 1949.

Staff of the Physical Education Department, University of California at Los Angeles. *Group Process in Physical Education.* New York, Harper, 1951.

Whyte, William H., Jr. "Groupthink." *Fortune,* March, 1952, p. 114.

Whyte, William H., Jr. *Is Anybody Listening?* New York, Simon & Schuster, 1952.

Physical education leadership should be aware of the assumptions that underlie group process as a method.

The use of the abilities of all the individuals of a group is not easily accomplished. The purpose to do so depends in part upon the philosophy of the leader. Support for such a purpose can be found in the following basic assumptions:

1. Assumption by the leader that each individual has a contribution to make to the group. This may be contrary to fact and often a group will contain individuals who can make no contribution at the time; but the assumption is important as a means of protecting those whose contribution may be hard to elicit or for other reasons not easily expressed.

2. Assumption that a group representing a wide diversity of background, viewpoint, temperament, and ability can work on a problem common to all, can define the problem, and can agree concerning its solution. This assumption is often contrary to fact but as an approach to the process it has some value.

3. Assumption that progress in group consciousness and awareness of a problem can be promoted by securing early participation of each individual in the preliminary examination of various aspects of the problem.

4. Assumption that psychological blocks to participation can be removed by informality of the leader and by a friendly atmosphere developed by appropriate techniques.

5. Assumption that certain physical conditions may favor participation, such as circle or table arrangements, and provision for recess periods in long sessions.

6. Assumption that progress in agreement can be achieved when the goals sought are the goals of the group rather than the private goals of the leader.

7. Assumption that progress in agreement can be made by a timely summary of points on which agreement exists and therefore concentration upon those points still to be discussed.

8. Assumption that group solution means participation by all; it avoids domination of the group by either the leader or other individuals.

9. Assumption that some problems must at times be deferred for further study, that tentative agreement is acceptable and can be taken without prejudice to further examination of the problem.

10. Assumption that friendliness, mutual trust and respect, poise and sincerity of purpose shown by the leader are contagious and will promote the manifestation of similar or like attitudes in the group.

11. Assumption that opposing viewpoints may require some *give* by each in order to reach an agreement *at the time,* and the further assumption that no problem is settled *forever* and that any viewpoint represented may at some later time receive approval.

12. Assumption that the contribution of any individual is significant on its own terms rather than because it is the expression of a "leading citizen." When expertness is required in the solution of a problem, such resource should be used. The resource person or expert is a contributor in terms of his unique expertness on the one hand and his membership in the group on the other.

13. Assumption that individuals in a group will vary in speed with which a problem is recognized and a solution appreciated. Progress should not be so rapid that agreement fails from inability of such individuals to apprehend rather than inability to agree.

Physical education leadership should learn how to conduct group discussions in a democratic manner.

The following is a check list which may be used to evaluate a person's leadership of a group discussion:

1. Was there evidence that the discussion leader knew what he was trying to accomplish?

2. Was the leader clear in his presentation of the problem?

3. Did the leader analyze the problem so that the issues were clear to the members of the group?

4. Did the leader dominate the group and try to force his views upon it?

5. Was the leader willing to let the group talk and examine the issues from various viewpoints?

6. Was time given to the group to think through the relationships involved in the issues?

7. Did the leader allow hasty decision before all the facts pertinent to the issues were presented?

8. Did the leader help the group to keep the discussion focused upon the central problem which the group had selected or was extraneous comment allowed to confuse the issue?

9. Did the leader try to answer all the questions raised or did he try to get answers from the group?

10. Was the discussion general in which all participated or was it dominated by a single or few persons?

11. Was the leader able to keep control of the group?

12. Was the leader aware of the crucial issues that developed in the discussion and did he direct attention to consideration of these issues?

Physical education leadership should be alert to recognize procedures that may be used to exploit a group.

The ideal of group discussion is to arrive at an accord given by all members of the group. This is called a consensus. Traditional group procedure in America, when consensus is not possible, is decision by a majority. This is a practical way of arriving at a decision and is employed in elections and in all instances when a vote is necessary to decide questions. Its weakness is a minority, either dissident or complacent, rebellious or disillusioned. In an effort to secure a consensus, meetings may be unduly prolonged and the opposition forced by fatigue or disgust to retire. This procedure is reported from some of the meetings of labor groups dominated by communist leadership.

At times, either by design or from failure to plan carefully, important questions are delayed until previous commitments force many of a group to retire from the meeting. A notable instance of this arose at a recent meeting of the National Collegiate Athletic Association at which the decision was made to abandon the two-platoon system of football. At the start of the session over 300 ballots were cast in the votes upon various motions, but at the end of a long session this highly debatable question of two-platoon football was decided by a vote of 45 ballots.

It is important to note that the group process may be used to exert undue pressure upon individuals in order to secure conformity. Effort to secure group consensus is never justified if personal independence is lost. The book *Brain Washing in Red China* by Hunter describes a group process by which non-Communists are indoctrinated into acceptance of Communist policy.[9] In this process, so like the procedures used by some groups in America, there are observer, recorder, resource person, leader, and discussion. Similar to the procedure for securing a consensus, this Chinese Communist process takes no vote to determine majority opinion but continues to hold meetings until complete accord is achieved.

Every effort to get before the group relevant facts and to withhold decision until the issue is understood should be made; in some instances several meetings may be required. But after these safeguards against uninformed decision have been taken, then majority rule should operate. It should be the function of all members of democratic discussion groups to recognize when individuals are being manipulated to serve hidden purposes and when discussion techniques are subverted to other than truly democratic purposes.

UNIFYING LEARNING EXPERIENCES

For some years now teachers have been developing lesson plans which would provide related learning experiences. This kind of curricular effort enriches physical education

[9] Edward Hunter, *Brain Washing in Red China*, New York, Vanguard Press, 1951.

activities, broadens understanding, and deepens interest. For example, instead of teaching correct standing postures as an isolated skill, the relationships to all of living can be clarified, and hence postures can be related in a meaningful way to personality, appearance, and efficiency. There is a considerable amount of literature that describes in detail how to develop unified plans, what procedures to follow, and how to evaluate outcomes.[10] While this broad approach has many enriching experiences, successful use of this method requires more rather than less time in the schedule. The small amount of time now given to physical activity must not be curtailed.

QUESTIONS AND PROBLEMS FOR DISCUSSION

1. Why should the aim of the educational process be studied by teachers?
2. How do you distinguish between the science and the art of teaching?
3. Why must the teacher be a master of his field?
4. How is method related to objective? Illustrate this from Nazi Germany.
5. What democratic viewpoints are affecting method?
6. What are the distinctions between technical, associated, and concomitant learnings? Do all occur inevitably?
7. Can method aid in teaching a technical learning? Explain. Is method of value in other learning? Explain.

[10] Association for Supervision and Curriculum Development. *Action for Curriculum Movement.* Washington, D.C., National Education Association, 1952.

Cassidy, Rosalind. *Curriculum Development in Physical Education.* New York, Harper, 1954.

Cassidy, Rosalind, and Jackson, C. O. *Methods in Physical Education.* Philadelphia, Saunders, 1952.

Founce, R. C., and Bossing, N. L. *Developing the Core Curriculum.* New York, Prentice-Hall, 1951.

McCoy, Mary E. "Planning for the Physical Education Core Curriculum." *Journal of Health—Physical Education—Recreation,* December, 1954.

Tyler, R. W. "The Core Curriculum." *National Education Association Journal,* December, 1953.

8. What is the best method to use in physical education? Why is this so?
9. How does method relate to the development of organic vitality?
10. Why should we proceed from the known to the unknown?
11. Why are rewards superior to punishments in learning?
12. What is analysis in teaching?
13. What is the function of drill in learning?
14. How do levels of development relate to method?
15. What is the value of interest in promoting learning?
16. Should one try to make a lesson interesting? What are the limitations of your answer?
17. Should individuals always do everything in which they are interested? Why?
18. Should individuals be interested in what they do? Why?
19. What is logical progression? Psychological progression?
20. How does interest promote retention of learning?
21. Why should the individual be aware of the objective of the activity? How can this awareness be aided?
22. What is learning by doing?
23. What is formality in method? When is it used? What are its functions?
24. What is formal discipline? How does it relate to learning?
25. How do individual differences affect method?
26. How do we learn attitudes?
27. How do we learn socialization?
28. How do we acquire a sense of justice?
29. Why is it necessary to manifest an attitude in many different situations in order to learn it?
30. What is generalization?
31. Discuss fully the "group process."

REFERENCE READINGS

American Association for Health, Physical Education and Recreation. *Teachers Guide: For Physical Education for High School Students*. Washington, D.C., 1962.

Bucher, Charles Augustus, *et al. Methods and Materials for Secondary School Physical Education*. St. Louis, Mosby, 1961.

Clarke, H. Leonard, and Starr, Irving S. *Secondary School Teaching Methods*. New York, Macmillan, 1959.

Cowell, Charles C., and Schwehn, Hilda M. *Modern Principles and Methods in High School Physical Education.* Boston, Allyn & Bacon, 1958.

Davis, Elwood C., and Wallis, Earl L. *Toward Better Teaching in Physical Education.* Englewood Cliffs, N.J., Prentice-Hall, 1961.

Kozman, Hilda C., *et al. Methods in Physical Education, 3rd Edition.* Philadelphia, Saunders, 1958.

Rhoda, William P. "Student Attitudes Toward the University Service Course for Men." *Proceedings of the College Physical Education Association,* 1958.

Salt, Benton, *et al. Teaching Physical Education in the Elementary School,* 2nd Edition. New York, Ronald Press, 1960.

Sehon, Elizabeth L., Marian H. Anderson, Winifred W. Hodgins, and Gladys R. Van Fossen. *Physical Education Methods for Elementary Schools.* 2nd Ed. Philadelphia, Saunders, 1953.

Vannier, Maryhelen, and Foster, Mildred. *Teaching Physical Education in Elementary Schools,* 2nd Edition. Philadelphia, Saunders, 1963.

Vannier, Maryhelen, and Fait, Hollis F. *Teaching Physical Education in Secondary Schools.* Philadelphia, Saunders, 1957.

CHAPTER ELEVEN

PRINCIPLES OF GUIDANCE

In a time of crisis the individual likely to become a leader is he who senses the prevalent needs and knows how to structure the solution. Many kinds of leadership, however, are possible. If leadership that will enrich personality and satisfy its many potentialities is what we want, we must begin schooling the leaders early in life; if they are to lead effectively as adults, in competition with leaders who embrace authoritarian methods and appeals, they need democratic experience, and in particular experience in democratic leadership. The more there are of these potential leaders, the more competent they are and the more deeply they love their task, the greater the likelihood that at the points of choice in the coming years they will guide the pent-up energies of a confused people in the direction of genuine self-realization.

Murphy.

Where there is nothing to cling to or lovingly to brood upon, a restlessness of spirit is induced and a restlessness of body follows.

Edman.

WHAT IS GUIDANCE?

Guidance is a process of helping every pupil to discover and develop his full potentialities for personal happiness and social usefulness. Guidance is sometimes erroneously conceived; it is not a procedure for giving "advice" to pupils. The concept of the teacher giving advice to young people is not only fallacious; it can also be dangerous. The pupil who has problems in adjustment must be made aware of his own capabilities and inadequacies in order that he can help himself. The teacher has a twofold responsibility. The first is to know the pupil well, to see him in many different kinds of situations, to observe his manner of getting along with others, to understand his health status, and to know about his home life; the second is to bring all these into focus *with the pupil* in relationship to his problems.

Guidance consists of mobilizing the resources of the school in such a way that the pupil will be stimulated and assisted in using the powers he has for his development as a person and as a member of society. The pupil, usually, does not see the possibilities of his contribution to society, however, until he has made some progress in solving his own problems as a person.

In guidance, as in so many other areas of education, we come back to the first principle discussed in this text: The function of education is to develop the individual *and* the citizen. If the school accepts this principle, then every teacher has some responsibility for guidance of pupils. No one teacher can supply all the needs that pupils have for guidance; some will be more helpful than others. The fact that all pupils do not react in the same way to all teachers will not disturb the mature members of a staff; the teacher must be prepared to wear the crown that he deserves. These facts should be understood and made use of by the entire faculty of a school.

Guidance has grown and developed into a special area in

education and must now be recognized as an important function of the educational program. It is of particular significance that teachers, generally, are not prepared as experts in guidance, and yet they are the ones who come into daily contact with the problems of youth. Teachers must, however, be cognizant of the kinds of superficial problems which they can talk over with a pupil, and the kinds of deep-seated problems which should be referred to experts. These experts may be in the school itself or may be located in a central administrative office.

REASONS FOR GUIDANCE

The reasons for guidance arise out of the fact that pupils face tremendous problems–tremendous to them. And, of course, the size and scope of any problem are delineated by those who confront it. Locomotion is not a problem to the able, but it is to the lame. Vision and hearing are problems only to those who lack acuteness in these senses. Problems of personal adjustment are important only to those who have difficulty in "fitting into the group."

It is not very helpful to classify problems theoretically. People, and their reactions and their development, are the common denominators; nothing else matters quite so much. Strang describes the reasons for guidance in her analysis of the process. She writes as follows:

> First, it is a *process* involving a relationship between persons; it does not consist merely in solving pupils' personal problems or making out their programs. Though it is possible to "get" results, i.e., an immediate problem solved, a quick decision made — this approach seldom produces much real development of the pupil.
>
> Second, it is a process of helping each person to help himself —to think things out for himself and use the resources within himself.
>
> Third, guidance is concerned with every individual, whether he possesses 1 talent or 10 talents; it helps the gifted as well as those who present obvious, insistent problems. Gifted chil-

dren are often neglected; they receive no stimulus or opportunity to develop their special talents; consequently they lapse into mediocrity. On the other hand, children with only one talent are too often taught with the hopeless attitude: We can't expect anything better of Johnny.

Fourth, through guidance, by means of observation, interviews, tests, and other techniques, every pupil is helped to discover his potentialities—his abilities, interests, and needs. Guidance is a talent search—a search for every child's special gifts.

Fifth, guidance aims to develop these potentialities by providing the child with a "lush environment"—meaningful classroom experiences in which he can succeed, opportunities for creative activities, extra-class social experiences, educational part-time work experiences, wholesome recreation at home and in the neighborhood.

Sixth, in this process of personal development, guidance tries to develop self-discipline, self-direction, and attitudes of social service and social responsibility.[1]

It can be seen, then, that guidance *is* an aspect of the educational process for which all teachers must take some responsibility.

APPLICATION OF GUIDANCE TO PHYSICAL EDUCATION

Every person, no matter whether he is a youth or a mature individual, has the need for feeling that he belongs, that he is accomplishing something worthwhile, and that he has the approval of his elders and his contemporaries. These needs provide a basis for the teacher to help each pupil toward an understanding of himself and the problems he confronts.

If the six phases of guidance as given by Strang are examined in relation to the opportunities and abilities of the teacher of physical education, six principles become apparent. *Physical education should adopt the view of guidance as a process in which pupil-teacher relationship is the central fact.*

[1] *Report of a Survey of the Public Schools of the District of Columbia,* Washington, D.C., Government Printing Office, 1949, p. 697.

Regard for guidance as a *process* and pupil-teacher relationships as the media through which the process occurs indicate that the personality of the teacher determines whether the process works or not, and the kind of pupil-teacher relationships that develop. The characteristics of a teacher who is willing to assume his part in the guidance process are similar to those which are important for any good teacher to possess. He must understand young people, be neat and as attractive as possible in his appearance, be interested in his community, possess health and energy, know his subject matter, and manifest self-control and good judgment. This by no means comprises a complete list of qualities which a good teacher of physical education should have, but these qualities are requisite. They are the qualities that should evoke pupil respect and confidence in the teacher.

The teacher must be able to accept the pupil for what he is, and to work out plans for the pupil's improvement according to the pupil's desires in making this improvement. So often, teachers formulate rigid ideas about how pupils should behave. They may expect the same kinds of patterns of behavior from all of their pupils and may become extremely irritated with those who do not conform to these standards. The respect for personality of another does not imply approval, endorsement, or admiration, but it does demand recognition of the individual as a person who is not to be dragooned into anything, however admirable it may appear to be to the teacher. And this respect for the personality of the pupil means, of course, that "crushes" would not be allowed to develop. Homosexuality is too serious an abnormality to run the risk of its promotion by allowing such emotional relationships to exist.[2] The beginnings of such emotional dependence may be observed in the actions of a physical education teacher who also happens to be the coach in a certain high school. He is constantly looking for good players for his teams in his physical education classes. He would like all of the boys in his school to play well, and cannot understand why

²A. J. Rosanoff, *Manual of Psychiatry and Mental Hygiene*, New York, Wiley, 1938, p. 162.

they do not. When they make errors in playing, he becomes impatient. This same teacher has selected certain boys to be his "squad leaders." They are the ones who always run his errands; they take care of the equipment; they play on all the teams, and receive most of the attention of the coach because of their skill in playing.

This kind of situation can lead only to poor pupil-teacher relationships. It causes those who are not selected as the leaders to become frustrated and disinterested, and it causes those who are obviously the teacher's favorites to develop an exaggerated opinion of their own importance.

Physical education should help the pupil to take charge of himself.

Physical education has suffered more than other areas of education from the authority complex and consequently finds it more difficult to appreciate that the individual should discover his own resources, realize his own powers, and take charge of his own life. The influence of "response-command" exercises, although gradually growing less, still works its evil upon many teachers of physical education. The attitude of the coach who orders players around reflects not only poor teaching but also destroys any opportunity he might have had for guidance.

The ability to take charge of one's life may be restricted by a number of factors. In addition to home patterns of control, regimentation may arise from governmental powers. When governments give up the purpose to develop an intelligent, responsible citizen for the making of a German, a Russian, an Italian, or an American, the individual will find it difficult to take charge of his life, to determine personal goals, and to follow individual preferences. In the United States, although large grants of power have passed in recent years to the federal government, the opportunity for individual decision, now greatly impaired, still remains as an ideal, a hope, and in some areas (education, religion, choice of a vocation) as a reality.

When there is large individual freedom of action but little acceptance of the role of duty and social responsibility, then there is sharp criticism of a society in which many show greedy, selfish, and antisocial behaviors. This leads to pressures to limit freedom and to increase regimentation. Certainly a free people should make every effort to develop in their children and to show in their own behaviors that taking charge of their lives results in kinds of living that are good both for the individual and the nation.

The achievement of a youth in taking charge of himself is a challenge to physical education as a part of the total education program. To the high school boy who looks upon his coach as a "superman," the teacher has a great responsibility. For him to swear, for him to become angry if all does not go well, for him to hit boys who make mistakes in a game, can mean only that the coach has not learned how to take charge of himself, and therefore cannot share in the achievement of teaching the pupils under his tutelage to become independent, thinking, fine, controlled individuals.

Physical education should serve all pupils, giving adequate opportunity to those who need physical education the most, and proper opportunity to those with gifted powers and superior physique.

If guidance is concerned "with *every* individual, whether he possesses one talent or ten talents," it becomes obvious that physical education has ample opportunity to implement this principle. The chance in physical education for seeing pupils in various situations, for building wholesome attitudes, has been indicated clearly by all those who have written about the contribution which physical education makes to education. Yet, many young men and women who, at first, may be timid or who may seem uncoordinated because of lack of experience in an activity have been relegated to the locker room, the back row or the sidelines because of an overzealous coach or teacher. The author knows of one school where any boy in the school may play on any of the interscholastic teams. True, the teams are not championship ones, but the boys are deriving the real benefits which are inherent in competitive play. The reader may very well say, "Yes, but the coach will not last in this school because he does not produce championship teams." This teacher has held this same position for twenty years. He has the admiration of not only the boys but their parents and his colleagues as well. And he is giving young people who might never have been able to play an opportunity to improve their skill, and to take their place among their peers. This same teacher has seen the importance of organizing many different kinds of teams: golf, swimming, fencing, and tennis in addition to the usual football, basketball, baseball, and track. Adherence to this principle implies that the teacher must be ever watchful for the so-called "motor-moron" as well as for the highly skilled individual. He must give each a chance to develop his skills, and must know when and how to guide them so that they may have some success in the activity of their choice.

Physical education provides a "natural" proving ground for one aspect of this principle, for those who have special abilities do have great opportunities to display them. We fail, many times, on the other hand, to give attention to those who do not have these obvious abilities.

Physical education should, by means of techniques available, serve to discover each pupil's special abilities.

Again, in the atmosphere of a physical education class, it is possible to discover the abilities of boys and girls. The techniques of observation and interviews can be utilized in helping to determine these. Physical education has not developed the tests and other techniques for this purpose to the extent that other areas in education have. We have available numerous strength, agility, and endurance tests, and we have some special skill tests at our disposal, but these are not in general use and will not become a part of the program until teachers are more firmly convinced that they help in their search for each pupil's special gifts.

Another obstacle confronting every teacher of physical education in giving guidance to secondary school pupils is the constant, persistent problem of having too many boys or girls in one class. How can an administrator expect the teaching and learning process to be carried out at its highest level when there are seventy-five pupils in one class which meets only two times a week? This, indeed, is a fundamental problem with which administrators and physical education teachers have failed to deal adequately.

In the guidance of young pupils, the purpose to provide proper opportunity for abilities to develop rather than to discover what abilities are possessed should mark the policy of the teacher. Long before young children are able to take part in organized games, they play alone or in small groups. At times their play becomes dramatic in character as they assume roles and create situations in which they act according to their imaginations. The teacher's part in this kind of dramatic play is to make sure that the maximum benefit is derived from the facilities provided. The act of guidance and teaching is identical at this time as the teacher gives help to the child in getting a firm grip on climbing apparatus, in learning to take turns, in cooperating with another child for a desired end, and in every possible way helping to make the experience contribute to the development of the whole child.

Moreover, the teacher is faced with the opportunity at all levels to help pupils appraise realistically their abilities. Unwilling to require that pupils be always right, unwilling to condemn failure, unwilling to accept good intentions for good deeds, the wise teacher will make clear, at all times, that no one is always right, that every person makes mistakes, and that the goal of intelligent endeavor is not the avoidance of mistake but rather of its stupid repetition. Growth in responsible personality will occur as failure is regarded as an incident and not as a catastrophe, as purposes lead to action, and as the varying abilities of individuals are accepted by each as starting points for additional effort and continued devotion to growth in excellence.

Physical education should provide meaningful experiences in which the pupil can succeed, not only in the school, but also in the recreational field at home and in the community.

In a small, well-to-do suburban town recently, parents, clergymen, and educators met to discuss the problem of six young boys of the community. The chief of police presented the evidence against the young culprits. On the way home from football practice these boys went by a vacant house. For some reason they decided to enter the house. One thing led to another until they had broken every window in the place; had wantonly broken furniture, glassware, dishes, pictures — everything which was destructible. They admitted to this outrageous vandalism, saying that they did not know what had come over them. The parents of these boys were, of course, scandalized and upset because they thought they had failed somewhere in the raising of the boys. They worked with the police and the clergymen to try to find some solution to the problem. The school officials helped in attempting to assess the failure of the school. The coach was not asked however, to help in this matter. The boys were merely dropped from the team and therefore, were no longer under the influence of the team or this teacher. This sad description of a situation is by no means unduplicated in many other communities in the United States. Just where are the failures of parents, the school and the church? It is unwise to point at any one of these institutions the finger of blame. But it is important to recognize that one element in this kind of behavior is lack of respect for property. In some schools children are allowed to kick basketballs, to mar floor surfaces with street shoes, to throw bats and rackets, and in many ways damage or destroy public property. These behaviors are often thoughtless rather than designed, but guidance of the teacher in discussion of such matters could provide a point of view to which young people do respond. The problem is not one of making regulations or issuing threats but rather one of looking at the facts, of consideration of the values in alternative action, and of recognizing the relation of the individual to other persons and the public in general.

We fall quite short in making a keen impact upon the recreational programs of communities or in the home because of the numerous demands made upon teachers. It is not possible to provide meaningful classroom experiences when a teacher is called upon to take charge of cheer leaders, the graduation ceremonies, dancing in the class plays, assembly programs, concessions at football and basketball games, coaching interscholastic teams, conducting intramural programs and taking charge of the cafeteria at noon. The classroom suffers because it is the easiest one to neglect. Yet, the example of one young teacher might provide incentive to others to take a similar place in their communities. This young man recently went to a small community to teach. He knew no one, but he began by getting acquainted with the local banker, the grocers in the town, the members of the Board of Education and the County Health Commissioner. He made his own personal survey of the recreational facilities available in the community. He took what he found and formulated a tentative plan. He kept this plan to himself for several months until he had established himself in the community. Meanwhile he organized two jaunts on Saturdays, for anyone in the school, to a large city nearby to see a professional football game and to see a major league baseball game. Some of the boys and girls who attended had never been to this large city before. Several parents accompanied the pupils, and they had as much fun as did the young people. Saturday night family recreation was initiated by this enthusiastic teacher. The principal and the superintendent agreed to hold these activities in the school. This is now a regular activity of the community, and it has the support of nearly everyone in town. This teacher is also responsible for the idea which led to the building of a community picnic ground near the river which runs through the hamlet. He had the responsibility for football, basketball and baseball teams as well as the teaching of physical education and hygiene classes. He worked hard and long, but his efforts were rewarded when the people voted him (at the end of his first year of teaching), the most outstanding citizen of the community. Here then, is a man who is interested in providing a fine, wholesome, meaningful classroom atmosphere. He also saw the need for outside of school recreation and did something constructive about it.

Teachers who want to be a part of the community can do so if they but put forth the effort which is necessary.

Physical education should help to develop the pupil through self-discipline, self-direction. It should help to develop attitudes of social responsibility.

Physical education has within its games the potentialities for providing opportunities for the development of self-direction and self-discipline. It is not difficult when one misses a basket, or fumbles the ball to become angry and downhearted. It *is* difficult, however, to learn to control one's actions and emotions in the face of error or defeat. Discipline is a word which is fraught with controversy. Some teachers believe that one can preserve "good discipline" by threatening to send the pupil to the principal's office if he does not behave. Others believe that making the pupil stay after school will have a salutary effect upon his behavior in the classroom. Still others think that discipline imposed by an outside authority can have no permanent effect upon the individual. Self-discipline comes from within, and has no authoritarian origin. It may grow and develop, however, because the pupil is motivated by the desire for approval by an outside force.

Young people need help in developing self-discipline and self-direction. They need to be given occasion to learn by their mistakes without being ridiculed. One is reminded of a physical education class in which the teacher always blew her whistle at the end of the period. At this juncture everyone was to sit on the floor. At another blast from the whistle all of the girls were to remove their tennis shoes. One unenlightened pupil mixed the signals, and removed her shoes before the second whistle blew. Before the eyes of the observers the teacher scolded the youngster, made her put her shoes back on, tie them, then she blew her whistle again, and all shoes were removed.

This incident serves to point out the fact that the teacher had no notion whatsoever of the relative importance of things, and that she understood little of the meaning of the terms self-discipline and self-direction.

To help pupils accept social responsibility is not a very different matter from helping them to develop self-discipline and self-direction. Every pupil needs to have pride in his own ability, in his school, and to know that he has a share in making his school a better one. He needs to see the relationship between his behavior in school and his behavior at home and in his community. Teachers of physical education can certainly help to instill this pride in pupils. Frequently, teachers inadvertently cause pupils to do less than they are really capable of doing. It is just as important to be able to see beyond the superficial actions of boys and girls to what lies dormant within them. One example of this may be found in the story of a boy in a junior high school who had been in Juvenile Detention Home several times for minor offenses. He exhibited antisocial behavior in school, and resisted every attempt to help him. He was defensive, surly, and spent most of his school time in the principal's office. Every teacher in the school but one had given him up and had labeled him as a "no good." The teacher of physical education at this school had noticed at noontime that he sometimes came out on the playground and watched. One day, the teacher asked him to help carry some equipment out to the playground. Gradually, they began to talk and the teacher gained the confidence of the boy. He was given more and more responsibility until eventually he became very interested in sports. He was exceptionally able, and as he gained prowess in sports he also made progress in his studies. He finally became a trustworthy member of the school community. The faith and trust of one teacher, when all the rest had completely repudiated him, in the potential worth of the boy had paid good dividends. Not all such stories have such happy endings, but if more time and understanding were used perhaps much could be done to salvage many youngsters who are so unfortunate as to have no one to whom they can turn for help at home, so have only the school left as a possible source for guidance.

If teachers of physical education concur with the foregoing six principles derived from Strang's statement, then they will be contributing their part to making a better school situation for the pupils under their charge. Guidance *is* the responsibility of all teachers, and it has been shown how physical education teachers can share in this process. [3]

[3] Jerome Weber, "Guidance Opportunities in Physical Education," *The Physical Educator*, May, 1963, p. 81.

RECORD-KEEPING

A very important aspect of guidance is the keeping of accurate records. A guidance expert keeps test results, and anecdotal records of interviews so that he can refer to decisions made, and steps which should be taken to help the student arrive at satisfactory solutions to his problems. Record-keeping is not usually looked upon eagerly by teachers, but they should be aware of the fact that records can be of incalculable aid in discussions concerning specific pupils. Some physical education teachers keep records of class participation, intramural and interscholastic participation. Others keep no records at all. Whatever a teacher decides to do about records, he should be aware of the importance of them in the guidance field.

The guidance of pupils also depends in part upon good working relationships with colleagues. Too often, teachers of physical education regard themselves and their programs as unrelated to the general program of the school. It is unfortunate when activities after school keep the teacher of physical education from faculty meetings, and every effort should be made to arrange for substitutes at this time or a different time for meetings. Faculty meetings may be dull affairs at times, but the usefulness of the teacher of physical education in guidance will be enhanced more by hearing other teachers report the problems of pupils than by an activity period. These meetings can lead to unanimous decisions about the best ways to help individual pupils.

Guidance, then, is not a thing separate from the school program. It is not something which is done *to* pupils, nor is it the province for just a few of the teachers in a school. It is every teacher's task.

QUESTIONS AND PROBLEMS FOR DISCUSSION

1. What is meant by the term "guidance"?
2. What are some of the reasons for guidance?

3. How can a teacher of physical education participate in guidance in a school program?
4. Why is it important for a teacher of physical education to have the guidance point of view?
5. What is a guidance expert?
6. How can a physical education teacher make the best use of a guidance expert?
7. Why is it important for teachers of physical education to attend faculty meetings?
8. What kinds of records do you keep about your pupils?
9. Do you have the qualities which make it possible for you to become a fine influence upon your pupils?
10. What does self-discipline mean to you?
11. In your own behavior in school, do you conduct yourself in a controlled, well-disciplined way?
12. Do you know the difference between a superficial problem of a pupil and one which is deep-seated, needing expert counsel? Illustrate.
13. In your physical education program, do you spend as much time encouraging the "dub" as you do with the highly skilled players? Should you? Why?
14. Do you try to find out as much as possible about a pupil who is having difficulties in adjustment in order to help him? How can this be approached?

REFERENCE READINGS

Arbuckle, Dugald S. *Teacher Counseling*. Cambridge, Mass., Addison-Wesley, 1950.

Bennett, Margaret E. *Guidance in Groups*. New York, McGraw-Hill, 1955.

Burton, William H. *The Guidance of Learning Activities*. New York, Appleton-Century-Crofts, 1944.

Cassidy, Rosalind F. *Counseling in the Physical Education Program*. New York, Appleton-Century-Crofts, 1959.

Davidoff, Eugene, and Noetzel, Elinor. *The Child Guidance Approach to Juvenile Delinquency*. New York, Child Care Publications, 1951.

La Salle, Dorothy. *Guidance of Children Through Physical Education*. New York, Barnes, 1946.

McDaniel, Henry B., and Shaftel, G. A. *Guidance in the Modern School*. New York, Dryden Press, 1956.

Mortensen, Donald G., and Schmuller, Allen M. *Guidance in Today's Schools.* New York, Wiley, 1959.

Symonds, Percival. *The Dynamics of Human Adjustment.* New York, Columbia University, 1946.

Traxler, Arthur E. *Techniques of Guidance.* New York, Harper, 1945.

CHAPTER TWELVE

PRINCIPLES OF ADMINISTRATION

We make a ridiculous fetish of health nowadays. . . . Let us, therefore, give play, recreation, and other popular arts their proper place beside the fine arts, and avoid the common error which degrades play to a medical instrument.

Cabot.

As soon as a conclusion is reached as to the nature of the scene of action, a conclusion is also reached as to what the agent is to do, and this decides in turn what sort of agent he is to be.

Dewey.

Sport, which still keeps the flag of idealism flying, is perhaps the most saving grace in the world at the moment with its spirit of rules kept, and regard for the adversary whether the fight is going for or against; when, if ever, the fair play spirit of sport reigns over international affairs, the cat force which rules there now will slink away and human life emerge for the first time from the jungle.

Galsworthy.

THE SCOPE OF ADMINISTRATION

Administration in physical education deals with three areas: program, facilities, and personnel. These aspects of physical education are interrelated and interdependent. The program on paper depends upon the facilities available and comes alive only when persons are effective agents. The facilities, meager or abundant, are useless until they are employed; and personnel are the ultimate and final answer to both program and facilities.

THE FUNCTION OF ADMINISTRATION

The business of administration is to get things done. It does not exist as an independent specialization concerned with its own purposes and devoted to its own procedures. Its only reason for existence is to make effective the program of the school or institution; in this purpose the administrator attempts to arrange conditions and materials so that teachers can teach better, facilities will be provided and used, and the standards of the program will be realized. The administrator of physical education is usually very close to the program; often he is a teacher in it and hence is likely to be aware of the needs and sensitive to the problems of the department.

The administrator should understand the distinction between policies and procedures. It is sound practice in all organizations for a board or faculty or staff to determine policies and for the administrator to select the procedures through which the policies will become operative. Whether the policies are board, faculty or staff policies depends upon the kinds of problems that these groups select for consideration. Thus, a board would consider financial support, salary schedules, building development, and the general direction of institutional effort; a faculty would be concerned with requirements for promotion, graduation, and degrees, with departmental functions, and disciplinary policies;

and a staff would determine policies relating to course content, methods, and similar operational directions. It is obvious that policies of staff and faculty should be in harmony with board policies.

At faculty and staff levels, the administrator selects the procedures that enable him to execute the policies agreed upon. He is not, however, in his position a policy-making individual.

THE PHILOSOPHY OF THE ADMINISTRATOR

The administrator of any social effort has power. He is the top man. What he proclaims shall be done, if possible. The power he uses is inherent in the position of responsibility he holds rather than in his own person. He may not understand this; he exercises power and often that is enough.

This show of power is not characteristic of all administrators. It is a common observation that the uncertain and fearful person acts with great bravado and excessive confidence. The wiser person, with sincere respect for others, neither needs to exhibit his power nor desires to do so. The psychology of this phenomenon is so well-known that it is often remarked that it is the "little" personality that seeks to impress others with his power. On the other hand, the really superior person will be simple in manner, humble in spirit, and eager to learn the opinions of others.

The philosophy of the administrator is crucial because, while large power resides in the position, the achievement of the department is wholly dependent upon persons. The administrator works not with things but with persons. Human relations is the central fact, at the heart of all he does. Great power is inherent in the position of the administrator, but persons are the human tools with which he must work.

Whenever the king and subject idea dominates the philosophy of the administrator, he issues his orders and announces his decisions with finality. It is unfortunate that some persons of this type hold administrative posts in physical education.

They are the heads of departments who use staff members to promote their own reputation, who change courses and assignments arbitrarily, and who show complete disregard for any judgment not their own. One of the most pernicious examples of this type of philosophy is exemplified by the director of athletics who is concerned with winning athletic contests and is indifferent to educational goals, democratic values, and human relations. Even the athlete is a pawn for his ambition, the department of physical education is a recruiting source for athletes, and even the faculty of the institution is a thorn that too often pricks the bubble of his ambition.

The basis of democratic administration, however, is full opportunity for differing views to be heard. Problems of the department are brought to the staff for consideration. At times, the staff will be unable to agree upon a policy or to approve the proposed solution to a problem. At those times, the administrator must take the responsibility for a decision with the clear understanding that the action is tentative and the matter can be reconsidered at a later time after additional experience. The spirit of democratic administration is the lack of finality about policies where disagreement exists. The minority should understand that its views are respected enough to be heard again. Since the work of the department must go on, the administrator must, at times, reach a decision without the help of majority judgment. This is the test of his philosophy, but here again the democratic attitude would avoid any assumption of superior knowledge and would accept responsibility for action with the statement that the policy will be reviewed later.

ADMINISTRATION OF THE INSTRUCTIONAL CLASS PROGRAM

The extensive program of physical education presents many administrative problems. Some of these are of a general character, such as budget and finance, purchase of supplies and equipment, public relations, annual reports, and similar problems. These are discussed later.

Physical education should provide a basic program of instruction in general physical activities for all pupils.

This principle arises out of the nature of the individual and the needs he has for living successfully in the modern world. These facts have been presented in earlier chapters. It suffices to state here that the program should be instructional in character and general enough to provide experience in a number of activities. A program of basketball, or dance, or gymnastics is too narrow; it fails to offer the range of motor experiences necessary for a person to be physically educated. A comparable failure in the English department would be an offering in Beowulf with complete neglect of Shakespeare, Carlyle, Tennyson, and others.

Physical education should be required of all pupils; exemption from the requirement should be given on evidence that the individual is physically educated.

There is little discussion of the policy of requirement of physical education in public schools; state laws usually determine this. And yet these requirements are often partial and inadequate. James B. Conant, former President of Harvard University, in an address to school administrators said,

> I am also convinced that ideally a period of physical education should be required for all pupils in grades 1 through 12 every day. . . . I have already mentioned my skepticism of grouping and scheduling based on band membership, and I deplore the substitution of band for physical education. [1]

At the college level however, there is, from time to time, objection from the faculty to a requirement. The position is taken that college students should be able to engage in "exercise" at their leisure in relation to their desires. The comment is made that college students are not required to take baths or brush their teeth although both these practices are said to be

[1] "Excerpts from Dr. Conant on Physical Education," *The Physical Educator,* March, 1961, p. 14.

good for them. This sort of analysis of the problem is scarcely worth discussion and yet this kind of comment must be answered by the department.

It is obvious that physical education is *not* carried on for "exercise" purposes, that its hygiene is incidental to the fact that vigorous activity is pursued, and that its program is or should be developmental and educational. Our colleagues should be helped to understand that the department is looking at its students in terms of the interests that can be aroused, the skills that will carry over into wholesome leisure, the development of vital systems, and the standards of sportsmanship that can be accepted by them as worthy.

And yet, at the college level, it is entirely possible that some students can justify their request for exemption on the basis of evidence of being physically educated. What might be the items of that evidence? It should be possible for any department to set up reasonable and functional performance standards in a number of activities that would test the individual in his mastery of the fundamental skills and their modifications. If these technical tests were met, then a written examination could appraise the student's competence with respect to a number of associated learnings. Finally, if all the tests were met, then the final test would be the voluntary participation of the student in some form of physical education in a regular way — very much like the activities engaged in by those who are required to do so. Exemption from the requirement should never mean that the student is to be permitted to spend his time either in the library, at the fraternity house, or loafing around town. On the contrary, like all superior persons, his exemption places great responsibility upon himself; an excellent man, he now becomes obligated by his superior endowment to meet the demands, not of a department, but of an inner awareness of what he is. Surely, physical education and its standards do not end when school and college days are over.

The above discussion is based upon the supposition that the required program is rich with vital and interesting activities, that it is taught by competent teachers, and that it is administered in a wise and understanding way. This, however, is not always the case. In some instances, the desire for voluntary participation is based upon dislike of the program offered, of the teaching staff, or of the administration of the program. Any one of these may be adequate reason for objection to a requirement that is stupid in its content, dull and unprofitable in its methods, and distasteful in its human relations. But the answer to this sort of difficulty is not the elimination of the requirement but a radical improvement in the program.

Physical education should provide a range of electives within the required program.

Many programs of physical education now offer to individuals an opportunity to elect the activities they prefer to follow for a semester. The plans vary greatly. All of them may be conditioned by the facilities available, the number and competence of the staff, and by considerations of fitness to enter the activity chosen. In certain instances a proficiency test is administered as a measure of the individual's ability to exercise a choice. In any form of election, the student should be given guidance in the decision. Pupils already proficient in dance should be encouraged to enter the sports program; those proficient in swimming would gain more from tumbling or dance than from more swimming. The principle behind electives is to give opportunity for interest, but if the interest is narrow and restricted, the value of the choice may be so small that the original concept of interest needs to be enlarged to include expanded interests.

While this hope for expanded interests will be accepted by many, there are, of course, a few persons who will wish to specialize because they have far-reaching ambitions for high achievement in a particular activity. After presentation of the department's view, such specialization may be permitted if the student still desires it.

Physical education should classify pupils to provide for individual needs, to insure fair competition, to improve instruc-

*tion, to care for like interests and abilities, and to secure pro-
gram continuity.*

At one time there was considerable effort to classify pupils
according to standard tests. This procedure has been abandoned
in most places; the variables among a group of individuals make
any single test, or battery of tests even, unworkable.[2] The most
common classification in schools is the grade, and while this is
an easy and convenient procedure, it ignores the principle of
individual differences, tends to put the program into a strait
jacket of uniform performance.

When pupils are classified to provide for individual
needs, some pupils can be assigned to classes of adaptive physical education, others to swimming, and to instruction in those
experiences most needed by them.

Attention to this view enables the administrator to be certain that fair competition obtains; it is always a mistake to match
groups that are markedly unequal in ability.

Classification should take into account the fact that a group
of individuals about equal in ability will make better progress
in learning and will improve the quality of the instruction.

It is always a handicap to try to teach a group with a wide
range of interests and abilities. When the grade plan is followed,
this is likely to be the situation during the years of adolescence; marked differences in the rate of maturation will pose
the most trying problems to a teacher with a group organized
by grade.

And finally, classification should consider elementary and
advanced courses; in some instances intermediate levels are
needed. Swimming classes afford an excellent example of this
fact. Pupils who cannot swim at all belong in the elementary
class, those with skill in one or two strokes are intermediates,
and those with mastery of several strokes are advanced and ready

[2] Elmer A. Gross and Jerome A. Casciani, "The Value of Age, Height,
and Weight as a Classification Device for Secondary School
Students in the Seven AAHPER Youth Fitness Tests," *Research Quarterly*, March, 1962, p. 51.

for life-saving skills. This sort of classification gives continuity to a program.

Laurentine Collins and Rosalind Cassidy report on classification in a statement that is an excellent summary of the above:

> Usually the major criterion for grouping boys and girls in physical education will be their social homogeneity. They want and they should have opportunities to be with and to play with friends, to share with them their satisfaction and joy in the activity. This may mean cutting across grade lines, if necessary, in order to place a child with the group to which he belongs. On the whole, boys and girls tend to be with and to have their closest friends in their own grade so that groups will probably be largely by grades. It is very desirable that flexibility be extended to permit groupings on different bases for different purposes. . . . Wherever possible the physical education teacher will group boys and girls according to their expressed interests and desires.[3]

Physical education should control class size in order to make effective instruction possible.

It is always a mistake to assign several grades to one class in physical education. But this practice is not rare. The following notes reported in a school survey[4] give a picture that is all too common:

> A lesson was observed in which 180 girls were assembled in the gymnasium, like sardines in a box, and, although the instructors made fairly good use of the limited space, the task that confronts them each day is discouraging.
>
> A small gymnasium made out of a classroom gives a space of 61 × 26 feet. In this small room was a class of 83 boys. In another space 81 × 60 feet, the average class would run 190 boys.

In these schools the physical education was largely calisthenics and drill; the limitations of the facilities prevented an

[3] Laurentine Collins and Rosalind Cassidy, *Physical Education in the Secondary School,* New York, Committee on Workshops, Progressive Education Association, 1940, p. 51.
[4] Report of a Survey of the Public Schools of Boston, 1944, p. 764.

educational program, even had there been the desire and ability to conduct one. It is imperative that physical education combat the practice of dumping several classes into a small gymnasium. In many instances, no physical education at all would be better than the distorted and sterile activity that masquerades under that name.

As in other laboratory activities, the size of the class will depend upon the facilities available, the number of instructors, and the kind of activity to be carried on.

Physical education should administer a sound plan of excuses.

There are numerous cases of pupils who should be excused from the requirement in physical education for periods of variable length. In some cases, the excuse should be for the school year; in others for a few days. The basis of excuse should be some health condition that would be impaired by physical activity.

It is not satisfactory, however, for the pupil to bring a note from the parent or family physician with the brief statement: "Please excuse John Doe from physical education." The advice of the family physician is not to be taken lightly at any time, but neither is the obligation of the school for the physical education of all pupils. In such instances, it is necessary to have from the physician more information about John and to give to the physician more information about the program as conducted. This sort of violation of the requirement can be avoided by better guidance of pupils and better public relations. Of course, it should be remembered that the desire of some pupils to be excused from physical education comes from the indescribably dull program that is experienced or the dirty locker rooms and showers that are used. Many children are able to recognize a fraud and to resent an imposition. [5]

Physical education should permit substitution of other school activities that insure an equivalent physical education experience.

[5] E. Nemsen, "Specific Annoyances in Relation to Student Attitude in Physical Education Classes," *Research Quarterly*, October, 1949.

All sorts of requests are made by pupils to substitute one activity for another. These may range from work on the farm to military drill, from playing in the school band to membership in an athletic club. In general, it is unsound practice to permit any outside activity to substitute for physical education in the school. The only school activity that may properly be substituted is membership on a school athletic team. This has disadvantages when the substitution is renewed in succeeding seasons of sport, but in certain cases this may be approved. Approval should rest upon such all round ability and satisfactory behavior that the individual meets the standards of the department for a physically educated person. The Representative Assembly of the American Association of Health, Physical Education, and Recreation in its April 9, 1962, meeting resolved that activities such as marching band, baton twirling, and drill teams should never substitute for a student's physical education period.[6]

Physical education should conform to the policy of the school with respect to the giving of grades for pupil performance.

It is possible to grade pupils in physical education as accurately as in academic subjects. If it is the policy of the school to use grades as a sign of pupil achievement, then grades should be used in physical education. In some schools written reports are used instead of grades to indicate a pupil's progress; such records are feasible in physical education.

As to the dispute in educational circles about the practice of giving grades, the teacher of physical education should have his own opinion and express that view in meetings of the faculty of the school. In this way, one's analysis of the problem can be effective; when the policy is decided, however, it is then the duty of the department to follow the policy of the school.

If grades in physical education are to be given to students, careful plans for doing so should be made, and students should be informed about the conditions. The plans should include some precise objectives such as swimming a certain distance in

[6] *Journal of Health — Physical Education — Recreation,* May-June, 1962, p. 42.

a specific time, or performing a snap-up, or doing a kip on the high horizontal bar. In addition to objective measures, the final grade should include a mark for attitude or effort, and a mark for knowledge of and practice in game rules, hygiene, and sportsmanship. Whatever weight the teacher plans to give to motor performance, to effort and attitude, to knowledge and practice, the students should be informed about that.

Physical education should study the reactions of students to the program.

It is important to know the attitudes that students derive from the experiences they undergo. Are any particular activities distasteful? Are any very satisfying? Several recent studies reveal the attitudes of women in university physical education classes[7] and two studies supply suggested forms for ascertaining student attitudes.[8] Recently the following letter appeared in the column of Abigail Van Buren:

> DEAR ABBY: I am a senior in high school and would like your opinion about a ridiculous rule at our school. All the girls must shower together after each gym class. In order to receive credit, you must call the gym teacher over and show her the SOAP on your body. Now I am going to be 18 soon and I know when I have enough soap on me to be clean. If

[7] Margaret Bell, C. Etta Waters, and Staff, "Attitudes of Women at the University of Michigan toward Physical Education," *Research Quarterly*, December, 1953, p. 379.

Marion R. Broer, Katherine S. Fox, and Eunice Way, "Attitude of University of Washington Women Students toward Physical Education," *Research Quarterly*, December, 1955, p. 379.

[8] Carlos L. Wear, "The Evaluation of Attitude toward Physical Education as an Activity Course," *Research Quarterly*, March, 1951, p. 114.

Eveline E. Kappes, "Inventory to Determine Attitudes of College Women toward Physical Education and Student Services of the Physical Education Department," *Research Quarterly*, December, 1954, p. 429. See also Jack Keogh, "Extreme Attitudes Toward Physical Education," *Research Quarterly*, March, 1963, p. 27, and R. S. Adams, "Two Scales for Measuring Attitudes Toward Physical Education," *Research Quarterly*, March, 1963, p. 91.

you refuse to follow this rule, you get a "D" in gym and an "Unsatisfactory" in work habits. What do you think of this rule?

Abby replied: "I think this 'soap survey' is a dirty trick."

This letter offers a good situation for class discussion. What seems to be the teacher's main objective? What might be more worth while? Will her objective interfere with realization of a better objective?

Physical education should be assigned credits for its courses on the same basis as that which prevails in laboratory courses.

It is a common observation that ruling groups express their rule and position through a formula. Kings relied for years on the formula of Divine Right; in the early days of the United States much was heard in Massachusetts and Virginia of those "fit to rule"; and in this generation the formula of "the indispensable man" appeared. It is the function of such a formula to justify the rule of the group. In education the formula is "scholarship," and regardless of such objectives as health, vocational efficiency, wholesome use of leisure time, and similar outcomes, the tradition of the school aims at a training of the mind and a discipline of the intellect as reflected in scholarship.

There are many valid criticisms of the credit system as a measure of educational achievement, but the fact remains that this is the system in operation, that this is the method by which achievement is noted, and that this is the way in which the worth of a school subject is indicated. The reasons given for discrimination against races, religions, and the feminine sex seldom reflect the true motives behind the action. The plain fact behind the discrimination against physical education is the present inability of the academic mind to appreciate the worth of physical activity in the education of children and youth—play can never be understood from an overstuffed chair.

So discrimination against physical education goes on. The profession has been asking for years that this educational poll tax be removed. It asks for a dignified position for this area, not that its personnel may acquire any particular status but that the programs may be improved, standards established, and results accredited. The whole machinery of educational practice is organized around a system of credits and this organization exerts a tremendous effect upon all that is done in the academic curriculum of the school. Physical education is not so naive as to expect that the granting of credits would automatically and at once transform poor programs into good ones, but it does understand the effect of credit upon standards, teaching methods, and programs.

Whenever the question of credit for physical education is considered by the general educator, he invariably asks shall the credit proposed be in addition to the credits now given to other subjects or shall the present schedule be reduced to include physical education in the present total. There are those who believe that physical education can never be brought into the school in an adequate way without a revolutionary change in the curriculum of the schools. These would be disposed to cut certain other areas sharply, and from some of the experiments in the schools of the armed forces it is apparent that much more time is now allotted to some subjects than is necessary for learning. But it is neither the responsibility nor the function of physical education to curtail or circumscribe other areas; it gives them the respect that it asks from them. Rather it is the simple duty of physical education to declare that credit for its program is essential for the proper development of this vital area of education.

A goal must be possible before there is any point in considering it desirable. Credit for physical education is not possible because it is wanted badly or because it appears to be a pleasant recognition. There is, however, no insurmountable obstruction. The difficulty is the attitude of general education personnel. This attitude can be changed.

Physical education should conduct its programs to prevent avoidable injuries but without eliminating significant activities for children and youth.

"Safety First" is the slogan of a movement of very great importance. Due to the tremendous toll in lives and injuries associated with machines, electricity, and gases of the industrial age, it has been necessary to teach the young the ways of caution with respect to these hazards. Many accidents happen that could have been easily avoided by the exercise of reasonable care.[9] In all activities where risks are run the safety movement has exerted its influence.

In physical education, very few games are really safe. Any child running or jumping may fall and break an arm. It is dangerous to carry the safety idea to extremes. It is necessary for children to run a number of risks because of the advantage gained from such activities; it is not necessary to court some injuries that could be avoided by reasonable care and attention. This is the sensible view of safety: Guard against unnecessary accidents but don't sterilize the program.

Alert teachers of physical education will be aware of what is going on in various parts of the playground or gymnasium. The condition leading to an accident is evident often before it occurs. The alert teacher can see it coming before it happens. Groups of children may be playing too close together, children may be standing too close to the batter — innumerable situations may arise that the alert teacher corrects because the condition may lead to an accident.

Children should be instructed to be attentive and alert to what they are doing and to follow instructions regarding the conduct of their play. Many accidents occur because children do not follow their leader, extend their activities into the play areas of other children, and violate the rules regarding the use of apparatus. These failures of children are to be expected but they are not to be condoned. It is through experience that they learn, but a controlled experience may be as instructive as an uncontrolled one.

Some apparatus is more hazardous than others. Unless the units are especially rich in the experiences they afford, the risks are not worth their use. Swings and teeters are of this type. They

[9] Joseph G. Dzenowagis, "An Accident Reporting System," *Journal of Health — Physical Education — Recreation,* February, 1962, p. 24.

offer little in activity beyond the rhythmical swing of the infant's cradle and they are the source of many accidents. Climbing apparatus offers some risks but these are more than balanced by the activity provided. Damaged equipment should be repaired or not used.

ADMINISTRATION OF THE INTERSCHOLASTIC OR INTERCOLLEGIATE PROGRAM

All forms and all organizations of athletics are aspects of physical education. At times, especially in collegiate institutions but also in high schools, athletics have developed as a separate and special interest with its directors, managers, coaches, trainers, team physicians, budgets, equipment, facilities, and policies. The connection between athletics and education has been lost in a welter of confused values about advertising, alumni support, and similar notions that have no worthy purpose and contribute little, as now conducted, to the education of youth. This development of high-powered athletics is unsound. Its evils are notorious. Efforts to extend the pattern of interschool athletics to the elementary school must be continually opposed. The weight of professional opinion is strongly against such extension.[10] As a problem of physical education and education, college athletics require careful analysis.[11] An analysis of the problem yields seven principles for administration of intermural athletics. They are phrased here in the wording of the original statement.

[10] California State Department of Education, *Compilation of Recommendations and Excerpts on Highly Competitive Athletics for Children of Elementary and Junior High School Age*, Sacramento, 1952.

   Division of Men's Athletics, American Association for Health, Physical Education and Recreation, "A Platform Statement of Athletics in Education," *Journal of Health — Physical Education — Recreation*, September, 1962, p. 24.

[11] Jesse Feiring Williams, "The Crucial Issue in American College Athletics," *Journal of Higher Education*, January, 1949, p. 12.

First, all monies budgeted for the expenses of athletics shall be appropriated from the general funds of the college, and all monies received as income shall pass into the general fund.

Second, all coaches shall be selected and staffed in the faculty in accordance with the standards of excellence that operate in the appointment of other officers of the institution.

Third, all coaches shall be appointed by the trustees and hold their appointment at the pleasure of the trustees.

Fourth, all coaches shall receive salaries that are consonant with the faculty rank held, and shall be appointed for full-time service.

Fifth, since recruiting and proselyting of athletes violate the purpose for which athletics exist in education, the full-time service of coaches will be restricted to teaching and administrative duties.

Sixth, since athletics are accepted activities in the education of college students, all bona fide students shall be eligible to participate, and neither scholarship nor social status shall render a student ineligible.

Seventh, since athletic games are close to the interests of students, there shall be no fee or a nominal fee for their attendance at games, and the general admissions shall be small and not competitive with professional prices.

EXTRAMURAL ATHLETICS FOR GIRLS AND WOMEN

Recently an increasing number of women leaders have advocated interscholastic and intercollegiate athletics for girls and women. Support for their position is probably intensified by the success of women of other nations in the Olympic games and also by the larger participation by women in many aspects of the American culture. Anne Finlayson writes:

> The National Joint Committee on Extramural Sports for College Women has established standards and procedures for the conduct of tournaments for college women, and DGWS [Division for Girls and Women's Sports] has publications spelling out policies and procedures, desirable practices, rules of the games, standards, and officiating techniques for use in com-

petitive activities. Schools and colleges using these recommendations can provide wholesome and beneficial experiences to highly skilled students through interscholastic or intercollegiate competition.[12]

ADMINISTRATION OF THE INTRAMURAL PROGRAM

The forces that control intermural athletics have no power over intramural sport. This program is clearly a part of the whole physical education program. It should not be supposed, however, that the intramural program may not be responsive to some of the distorted notions of the intermural disease. There are problems to be met; certain principles of administration arise out of the attempt to meet them.

Physical education should develop intramural activities as an extension of the instruction program with free opportunity for all regardless of race, religion, fraternity or other relationship.

When young people have learned to play a game, then opportunity should be available for participating in the activity learned. The fun of contesting with one's fellows is not the least of the values that can flow from intramural sports. But the opportunity should be free and any disposition to bring into these social experiences the prejudice of race, religion, or fraternity association should be scotched.

Moreover, the standards of behavior taught in instructional classes should be expected to operate in the contests of intramural games. Large responsibilities should be given to students in coaching, managing, and officiating these affairs but the staff should be close enough in touch with them to prevent undesirable practices developing.

Physical education should offer many activities in its intramural programs.

[12] Anne Finlayson, "Basic Issues," *Journal of Health — Physical Education — Recreation*, May-June, 1962, p. 6. *See also:* Thelma Bishop, "Values in Sports," *Journal of Health — Physical Education — Recreation*, September, 1962, p. 45.

A good intramural program will include more than athletic tournaments. While these may be prominent in the program, other interests and abilities of pupils and students should be explored and served. The following are examples of the kinds of items that belong in an intramural program: dance clubs of various kinds, swimming festivals, leaders' corps, clubs for officials, hiking groups, and camping clubs.

ADMINISTRATION OF ADAPTED PROGRAMS

At one time it was common practice to excuse from physical education any child with a physical disability. Today the best practice consists in trying to provide suitable physical education for every child able to attend school. In the best college departments this is often realized; it is less common in public schools. A statement of the Therapeutic Section of the American Association for Health, Physical Education and Recreation follows:

> The student with a disability faces the dual problem of overcoming a handicap and acquiring an education which will enable him to take his place in society as a respected citizen. Failure to assist a student with his problems may sharply curtail the growth and development process. Offering adapted physical education in the elementary grades, and continuing through the secondary school and college, will assist the individual to improve function and make adequate psychological and social adjustments. It will prevent attitudes of defeat and fears of insecurity. It will be a factor in his attaining maximum growth and development within the limits of his disability. It will help him face the future with confidence.[13]

Physical education should conduct an adapted program to meet individual needs that are indicated by the diagnosis and recommended treatment of a medical examination.

[13] *Platform for Adapted Physical Education in Elementary and Secondary Schools and Colleges,* Therapeutic Section, American Association for Health, Physical Education and Recreation.

The care and treatment of the individual who is in any way limited in activity by defect lie properly in the field of medicine. The department should avoid any attempt to do more than sound medical advice would recommend nor should it ever proceed upon an adapted program without diagnosis of the individual condition and prescription of the activity.

ADMINISTRATION OF COEDUCATIONAL ACTIVITIES

Although it is desirable to separate boys and girls for instructional classes after the fourth grade, it is also desirable to bring them together later for common experiences that they can and should share together. These associations are essentially social rather than physical in their purpose; they aim at appreciation and understanding rather than competitive values. In high schools and colleges coeducational experiences in swimming, tennis, badminton, golf, winter sports, dance and similar ones may help men and women later to play together and contribute richly to married life.

Physical education should offer coeducational activities as early as possible, suitable to the level of development and the nature of the participants.

Boys and girls develop antagonisms early in the elementary school and these tend to persist until after puberty. By this time fundamental attitudes are formed which may remain as prejudices that forever render it impossible for either one to accept as equal and worthy the other. Even in the marriage relation old patterns of behavior continue that are essentially an expression of lack of respect for the personality of the other sex. Every agency of the school that can help to eradicate such absurd notions should be used.

ADMINISTRATION OF FACILITIES

There are many reasons why facilities and equipment present administrative problems. In the first place communities differ in their notions of education and the good life. In these places, there is little appreciation of the need for children to learn skills for their leisure time or to develop interest in the out-of-doors. What people do at any time or place is an expression of the ideas they have. When ideas make a pattern of life with all work and no play, then there will be no playgrounds, no athletic fields, no courts, and no swimming pools.

In spite of a tremendous increase in the use of physical education and a growing understanding of its contribution to the wholesome development of the young, there remain many communities and institutions with the most limited facilities.

One part of the difficulty faced by all institutions is the fact that facilities for physical education are expensive. A plant of gymnasiums, pools, athletic fields, courts, and their associated equipment costs large sums of money. The cost is not excessive in relation to the use, but still an adequate plant is expensive.

When facilities are lacking or meager, as in innumerable public schools, then classes in physical education are held in classrooms, corridors, and basements. Such places limit the program. To perform some stilted exercises in these places and to call it physical education is the type of folly that was accepted some years ago, but that has no defense today. When facilities are lacking, children do not learn the skills and coordinations that are essential for their proper development; moreover, in the pauperized program of the corridor they tend to acquire a dislike for physical education which is quite as serious as their failure to get proper development. Buildings, often regarded as dead and lifeless things, actually do things to persons as well as allow persons to do things in them. A poor artist may eat his crust in the attic, but this experience does not make him a painter. Poor facilities serve no useful purpose and impair achievement.

It follows inevitably that lack of facilities has its effect upon the morale of the staff. Teachers can put up with limitations for a time, but to try to meet the needs of children every day by resort to a substitute that is an obvious fraud leaves the teacher disillusioned; this shows in the teaching and again the children suffer.

Physical education should have indoor and outdoor facilities suitable for the educational purposes of the program.

The elementary school should be planned to meet the needs of the neighborhood for recreation. It should be placed in the center of a school-park area so that the school would have access to the park facilities and the people of the neighborhood could use the school for recreational and adult education purposes.

The size of the plot should be determined in relation to the size of the school. Standards for size are set forth in books on administration;[14] most state departments of education also offer standards.

Unsatisfactory facilities can often be improved by proper surfacing, equipment can be repaired, and much done to modernize showers, dressing rooms, and locker equipment.

Bookwalter has formulated ten principles for use in planning physical education facilities.[15] The following is condensed from his original statement:

1. **Accessibility:** Access to facilities for proper groups should be ready, convenient, and direct.

2. **Beauty:** Facilities should be attractive but not gaudy, and should inspire appreciative treatment.

3. **Departmentalization:** Related activity areas and groups should be in a functionally related unit or department.

4. **Economy:** Cost in time, energy, and money should be held to a minimum compatible with effective instruction, and with maximum wholesome participation.

5. **Expansibility:** Increase in range and amount of activities presented and in provision for participants should be readily and economically possible.

6. **Isolation:** The **elimination** of odors, noises, and

[14] Jesse Feiring Williams, C. L. Brownell, and E. L. Vernier, *The Administration of Health Education and Physical Education,* 5th Edition, Philadelphia, Saunders, 1958, pp. 277-286. Also *A Report of a Survey of Public Education in the State of Washington,* Olympia, 1946.

[15] K. W. Bookwalter, *Planning Health, Physical Education, and Recreation Facilities for Public Schools and Colleges,* American School and University, 18th Annual Edition, 1946, pp. 177-183.

moistures, the **segregation** of activity groups, and the **exclusion** of undesirable persons from all areas concerned should be automatic and effective. Maintenance features of lighting, heating, and ventilation should be on a unit basis.

7. **Safety, Hygiene, and Sanitation:** These items of plant and participants must be duly considered in the provision, arrangement, and maintenance of facilities.

8. **Supervision:** The oversight, control, and management of activities and groups should be facilitated by visibility and accessibility of related areas to the leaders and by the exclusion of undesirable groups. There is legal responsibility for supervision of dangerous areas.

9. **Utility:** The usefulness of a plant requires adaptability to multiple use of areas by activity groups within the limits of safe, pleasant, and effective instruction. Seasonal use of space furthers utility.

10. **Validity:** Facilities must be in accord with curricular needs, scientific facts, and legal requirements.

A recent special report on plans for space for physical activities gives many suggestions for the administrator of physical education.[16]

ADMINISTRATION AND PERSONNEL OF THE STAFF

Physical education as an integral part of the process of education requires a teaching and supervising staff which is familiar with the essential purposes of education, its principles, and acceptable procedures. The activity program of physical education is supplemented by training, advisory and examining functions, so that the staff must be thoroughly informed of and sympathetically inclined toward the whole life of the school. Knowledge of the range and duties of the other teachers in the school is required because of the close correlation of programs and the need for enlisting the cooperation of the

[16] *Journal of Health—Physical Education—Recreation*, April, 1962, p. 33.

other teachers in the special objectives of physical education.

For purposes of education, as well as the purposes of physical education, it is never entirely satisfactory to give the responsible direction of the activity program to one who has only a technical training in physical education. At one time most of the teachers of physical education in the schools were trained in the technique of their profession without that basis of understanding which comes only with a broader and more comprehensive education. The tendency at times to place the direction of the physical education program in the hands of a college athlete or a doctor of medicine — persons who lack both the necessary technical and the general educational training — is a serious mistake.

Physical education should select a staff by using three sources of information: recommendations of others, placement bureaus, and teachers' agencies.

In the case of reliable friends or associates in the field, recommendations are likely to be competent. At times a recommendation may come from one who is trying to unload an undesirable staff member; this sort of experience may be avoided by thorough investigation of the case. It is also to be remembered that a thoroughly competent person may not do well in one institution but may succeed in another. If there is complete frankness in the matter, then one may decide to take the risk of appointing a teacher who has not been a success in the last post.

When there is a friend or colleague in the field in whom there is complete and tested confidence, one can do no better than consider seriously any recommendation that may be made. One earns the privilege of being trusted in such matters by using care and discrimination in the recommendation of persons; of course, there will be some failures, but generally the judgment of a tried and tested source can be accepted.

As a rule placement bureaus are most reliable. They collect pertinent data about the candidate including grades, courses taken in college, past experience, interests and hobbies, anecdotal records from the students' major professors, and other personal items. From the reports on several candidates, a selection of one or more may be made for interview. These bureaus are conducted by teacher training institutions and are as eager to serve the schools as they are to place their graduates. This service is usually of excellent quality. It lacks the intimate and personal knowledge of the student that is possible in the case of a personal recommendation.

Teachers' agencies are business enterprises that conduct a placement service for a fee that is paid by the teacher from his salary after an appointment is secured. These agencies can exist only as they make good recommendations and hence the very nature of the business requires service both to the institution and to the teacher. They are less competent in their recommendations than placement bureaus because they are farther removed from the sources of information about the candidate.

The first steps in the process of selecting a staff member may be taken by correspondence, but before a decision is made a personal interview is regarded by many experienced heads to be essential. Both in correspondence and in the interview it is important not to promise more than the head has authority to deliver. Since appointments are usually made by a board on recommendation of the president, dean, or superintendent, about the most that a head can promise is to recommend the appointment. Failure to observe this procedure may cause great hardship to the candidate and severe embarrassment to the head.

Physical education should consider certain qualifications in selection of members for a staff.

There are seven important items to consider: age, professional preparation, experience, personality, skills, appearance, and personal habits.

For activity posts, youth is desirable but for administrative duties and theory courses maturity is an advantage.

The professional preparation of a candidate ought to bear some relation to the ideas he holds, and the kind and level of his abilities. Degrees from some institutions are more promising than similar ones from others. Whatever the institution, the candidate's preparation should have given some competence in the area he proposes to teach, some understanding of the educative process as a social force in society, and some convictions about the significance of teaching.

All persons begin as novices but for some posts experience is invaluable.

In an assessment of personality, one may appraise the interests, disposition, ideals, manner of speech, and attitude toward the position sought. Personality tests are of little value.

Motor skill above the average is essential; in specialization superior skill is required.

Dress is important, as it reflects taste, notions of cleanliness, and the appreciation of example. Physical education should not be an excuse for wearing sweat shirts at inappropriate times.

Habits are personal and yet teaching may require conformation of habits to the work that is to be done. Those unable to accept compliance with the habits desired are not suitable candidates.

Physical education should exemplify in its professional staff the highest type of ethical behavior.

A Committee on Professional Ethics of the American Association for Health, Physical Education and Recreation has compiled a code of behavior for teachers. Copies of this may be secured by writing to the Association, 1201 Sixteenth Street, N.W., Washington 6, D.C.

The significance of ethical standards is suggested when one attempts to answer questions like the following:

Should one accept from an athletic supply house a gift of golf balls or tennis racket? A federal government official thought it proper for him to accept the gift of a ham but not a house.

Should one use the funds derived from a general tax for the athletic development of a few? A federal government official thought it proper to use federal funds to promote his own position in the government.

Should one give a full and complete accounting of gate

receipts and expenditures under all circumstances? A federal government official thought it proper to conceal the source of funds received and the expenditures made.

Should one recommend a close friend for a position when others, not especially friendly, are far better qualified for the post? A federal government official recommended friends for important positions when others far better qualified were available. What does it mean "to play politics?"

Should one recommend the discharge of a teacher who has held the post for twenty years, the fault being poor teaching? What is the relative importance of the person and the institution? How could the institution and the person both be given some protection?

Physical education should follow policies that promote the development of staff personnel.

The young teacher develops through the process of teaching. Maturation plays a sure part in the process, continued study helps, and experience is a great teacher. The head of the department has nothing to do with maturation, he may stimulate the junior to continue his studies, but his chief role is to provide the opportunity for experience. The regular class assignments of the young teacher soon comprise a routine that after some time will yield little more in the development of the individual. It is the sure responsibility of the head to give additional opportunities as they arise.

The young instructor may gain a reputation for good work through the teaching that he does; but there may be other resources that can be revealed by opportunities to work on committees and to represent the department in speaking engagements. The usual requests that come to the department may be met entirely by the head or he may share some of these with juniors in an effort to give them a chance to grow.

The attitude of the staff head toward all members should be one of unfailing fairness. Playing favorites is destructive of morale, interferes with work, and destroys confidence. The effects are as disastrous upon the favorite as they are upon others of the staff. One who is favored has such an advantage that every effort will be made to retain it, so that the behavior of the favorite is not honest, but always obligated and sycophantic. The other members of the staff show the normal reaction of those whose judgments and acts are not interpreted fairly.

The head will secure loyal cooperation from the staff as he shows an attitude of fairness to all at all times. The individual normally desires to be loyal to the organization to which he belongs, it is as natural as being loyal to one's home town, state, or nation. Disloyalty begins when a feeling comes that some persons have advantages not shared by others. The test is fairness.

Loyalty is also developed by belonging to a good team. If the department is ineffective and floundering in its purposes, morale of the group is likely to be low. Getting things done, winning some approval, and planning with confidence for the future will build loyalty of the staff to the work of the department.

And loyalty is developed by example. If the leadership is loyal to the work of the department, gives himself unstintedly for its purposes, and devotes himself to it rather than to himself, his example is contagious.

Physical education should hold staff meetings of its own in addition to attendance upon faculty meetings.

A staff meeting should be a friendly but formal conference, at which the meeting is called to order and disbands with an official adjournment. The head of department is normally the chairman of the meeting and responsible for the conduct of its affairs. At all times he should preside and get the business of the meeting done. The occasion is not a social affair but a professional meeting to which all members of the staff come; their time should be protected and not wasted in discursive, pointless, or inappropriate discussion. If the meeting is called for an hour but the work is accomplished in twenty minutes, then the meeting should be adjourned; it is not a credit course at which the full period must be used.

The agenda of a meeting comprise those items that are to come up for discussion. The chairman should always have an agenda, and it is desirable for the members to have a sheet with the agenda listed. There should always be opportunity for matters to come up that are not listed in the agenda.

Regular meetings are desirable if there are problems to be discussed. In most staffs there is a series of problems that arise in the course of the year and it is wise to arrange for a free period when regular meetings can be held. But if there is no business to come up, then it is a serious mistake to call a meeting and spend the time wastefully. If the head has no agenda, then there should be no meeting.

Extra meetings may be needed and these should be called as necessary, but careful planning will keep these at a minimum. The inefficient administrator will suddenly have to call a meeting about the catalogue, for example, when proper planning would have disposed of the matter weeks earlier. Such problems arise every year in an institution and it is poor administration not to plan ahead with respect to those matters that must be considered by the staff in regular meetings.

Minutes should be kept at all staff meetings. If there is a secretary in the department this person should be present at all staff meetings and record the decisions reached, committees named, matters to come up later, and other pertinent data. These minutes should be transcribed and filed in a binder for permanent use. If there is no secretary of the department, one member of the staff should be appointed secretary of the staff and perform these duties.

Physical education should administer differences of opinion among staff members in a democratic manner.

It is not reasonable to expect that all members of the staff would agree at all times on all questions. Such unanimity would be as undesirable as it is unlikely. The head of the department should welcome different points of view, expecially when they appear in opposition to his own position. What is wanted in the meeting is a full and honest presentation of the facts regarding any question under discussion. Staff members taking opposing positions on questions should be willing and able to present the facts or logic by which they have arrived at the position taken. These differences then are not personal and will not become so if the head welcomes them, encourages their expression, and avoids directing the debate into the atmosphere of personal differences. Much depends upon how the matter is handled.

Differences of opinion may exist on some matter that does not require immediate action. In such instances it is well to appoint a committee of the staff to continue discussion of the problem for report to the staff at a future time. It is important to form this committee so that those who have differed are on the committee or are effectively represented.

When differences exist on some matter that requires immediate decision so that a policy can be announced or appropriate action taken, then a decision must be made at the meeting. There are two ways to get a decision. One is to take a vote of the group. This is traditionally the democratic way and with a majority indicated, the plan or policy may be adopted in line with the vote taken. If there is an equal division of the staff or nearly equal difference of judgment, then the head might make a statement like the following to the staff: "The staff is divided about equally on this question and a vote does not indicate that one plan is more desirable than the other. But we must announce today what we propose to do about this matter, so I shall take the responsibility of deciding. We will continue our present policy until such time as the matter may come up again for discussion."

This decision of the head may seem to favor one group of the staff, but if fairness rules it will not be so interpreted; on another occasion, his decision might be with a different group. As work with a staff proceeds over the years, most questions will be decided by the group and few occasions will arise when arbitrary action is necessary. This method should be used only when the question requires action.

Physical education personnel should attend faculty meetings.

The faculty of an institution varies in its composition. In some colleges and universities the faculty comprises all those who instruct students; in others it is limited to those who have professorial rank. In public schools the faculty comprises the teaching and administrative personnel.

The staff of an institution may be the same as the faculty, but the word "staff" is used generally to designate the instruction force of a department. The distinction is somewhat arbitrary.

The problems considered at faculty meetings are many and varied. Often they seem to have little to do with the purposes and program of physical education. This impression is mistaken. Everything happening in an institution has some relation to physical education and should be of interest and concern to physical education personnel. If the physical education instructors are members of the faculty, they should always attend. Arrangements should be made to that end. If students are discussed, courses suggested, policies developed, it is important that the knowledge and experience of the physical education group be represented.

After some experience in attending faculty meetings, the staff member may note that some proposals are approved and others rejected even when they appear to have comparable merits. As he watches the actions of his colleagues and considers his own responses, it will become apparent that faculty approval or rejection of a proposal depends quite as much upon their judgment of the sponsor as it does upon the facts of the argument. Even meritorious proposals will be rejected when the faculty feels that the sponsor of the project cannot carry out the plan. Moreover, some proposals about which the faculty can know little, because of the technical character of the request, will be approved; this action reflects the sure confidence of the faculty in the person rather than in the plan.

Physical education personnel should attend professional meetings.

In a survey of policies regarding attendance of teachers at professional meetings the Educational Research Service of NEA reports as follows:

> Most school boards believe that these meetings benefit both the individual who participates and his school district. . . .

Meetings to be attended and staff members who will go are selected in a variety of ways. In some school districts the board of education annually approves a list of meetings to be covered, together with the staff members who will be permitted to attend each event. . . . Sometimes only persons in administrative or supervisory positions may apply for permission to attend at board expense.

The complete report of this survey is available.[17] College and university policies in this matter vary widely. In most institutions selection of staff members to attend professional meetings is made by the head of the department. He may follow a plan of rotation in order to give equal opportunity, or he may ignore the needs and desires of junior members in favor of his own attendance.

GENERAL ADMINISTRATIVE PROBLEMS

There are a number of general administrative problems that need sound policies for their solution. There are principles of administration that can help in the solution of problems that grow out of relations with the military department, health education, the athletic department, and the public. There are also minor administrative matters of reports, budget, and office management for which guides are available.[18]

Physical education should make clear that military training is not an equivalent to a modern program.

A superintendent of schools wrote, in an annual report, the following: "Military drill is an inexpensive and effective form of physical training."

Although this statement was made some years ago, its influence in that school system continued for more than

---

[17] National Education Association, Research Division, and American Association of School Administrators, *Professional Growth Through Attendance at Professional Meetings,* Educational Research Service Circular No. 2, Washington, D.C., 1962 (30 pp., $1).

[18] Jesse Feiring Williams, Clifford L. Brownell, and E. L. Vernier, *op. cit.*

twenty years. In a survey of the school system, the following comment was made upon the superintendent's statement:

> Of course, military drill never is and never has been an effective form of physical education; whether it is inexpensive depends upon what you consider, the budget or boys and girls . . . school officials who are responsible for policy should abandon the unwarranted assumption that military drill is an "effective form of physical training." If military drill is retained in the schools the decision to keep it should rest upon those unique and intrinsic values that may be discovered for it and not upon the mistaken idea that it is a worthy kind of physical education.[19]

In some universities, an effort has been made to enrich the military program by adding sports. This is an unwarranted intrusion into an area of instruction that should be repelled. The only sound principle for physical education to follow in relation to the military is refusal to accept military drill as equivalent to physical education.

And yet physical education and the military organization of school or college must cooperate at many points. Often the gymnasium and playing fields must serve both interests, and locker rooms, showers, and towel service must be shared. Cooperation in these administrative adjustments should be generous and helpful. At the curriculum level, however, compromise is impossible for both parties. The military cannot allow the functional physical education activities to substitute for the technical requirements of military life; and physical education cannot allow the military activities to substitute for the educational requirements of civilian life.

Physical education should cooperate fully with health education but keep clear its own distinctive functions.

Some uninformed persons regard physical education and health education as identical fields. This confusion is due in part to the fact that terminology has been used carelessly and

[19] *Report of a Survey of the Public Schools of Boston, Massachusetts,* 1944, p. 767.

in part to the fact that physical education makes a contribution to the health of the individual.

The cooperative action of physical education toward the purposes of health education is justified as much by its own interest in health objectives as in its desire to assist colleagues.

The relation with the school medical officer is direct and valuable in college programs, but in public schools the department of physical education must operate at times without the advice and counsel that medical competence could give. In such instance, every effort should be made to secure examinations of all pupils engaged in interscholastic sports. There are standards of physical fitness for participation in sports recommended by national committees.[20] In addition, the detailed procedures for the conduct of health services in the schools are discussed at length elsewhere.[21]

In the area of practical hygiene and sanitation, physical education should establish standards that are fully acceptable to the hygienist or sanitarian. The locker and shower rooms should be clean and kept clean by proper care. The lockers must not be used to store dirty and foul-smelling uniforms; the curious superstition that regards dirty uniforms as helpful in athletic performance should be corrected. Jock straps must be clean to prevent fungus disease. Administrative regulations and supervision can control unsanitary practices. Swimming pools must be maintained in sanitary condition. Proper methods of chlorination and filtration of pool water, and regulation for those using the pool are important.[22]

Physical education teachers may conduct classes in health

[20] Report of Committee on Standards of Physical Fitness for Students (Boys) Who Engage in Competitive Athletics, *Journal of School Health,* March, 1943, p. 57. *Ibid.* for Girls, p. 33. Also Charles C. Wilson (Editor), *Health Education,* Joint Committee on Health Problems in Education, 4th Edition, Washington, D.C., National Education Association, 1948, p. 169.

[21] Jesse Feiring Williams, Clifford L. Brownell, and E. L. Vernier, *op cit.,* pp. 100-127.

[22] *Ibid.,* pp. 251-262.

but even when they have no direct responsibility for instruction, they will have numerous opportunities to give health guidance. These should be fulfilled.

Physical education should maintain close relationship with a department of athletics.

In those institutions in which there is a separate department of athletics — a most undesirable form of organization — it is important to maintain close and cooperative relationships. In many instances the two departments use the same facilities and at times members of the two staffs teach in both programs. This situation has some advantages and many disadvantages.

Coaches of athletic teams are usually busy only part or parts of the school year. There are terms when their responsibilities are light and they have much free time. In addition, they are likely to be good teachers of activities and of course they know the field as a rule. For all of these reasons it has been logical to assume that the athletic coaches could and should play some part in the rest of the physical education program. The assumption has not always worked well. Frequently, these men have no interest in other than varsity affairs, often they are careless in meeting assignments, and due to indifference, they sometimes do a poor job of teaching.

The problem arises because the class assignment is regarded as incidental or secondary. If it is made clear, at the time of the appointment, what the full responsibilities are to be, the coach might approach the matter with a different attitude. Moreover, often the teaching assignment is merely a device to pay the coach an additional stipend; in such instances, it is not seriously contemplated that he will make a real contribution to this part of the program.

The matter of extra compensation should be handled fairly and not deceitfully. If the individual, as in high school, is carrying a full teaching schedule of the regular session, it is unfair to ask him to do after-school coaching without additional compensation. On the other hand, if the coaching is a part of the normal schedule that operates in the school, then there should not be extra compensation involved. Such matters can very readily be resolved when there is frankness and fairness.

A study of extra pay for extra duties in high school systems made by the Research Division of the National Education Association for the year 1962-63 reports the average maximum scheduled annual supplements for directing extracurriculum activities, and the relationship of supplements for football to those for other extracurriculum activities. The data are shown in Tables 6 and 7. The full report will be found in the *Research Memo* of March, 1963. It is abstracted in the *NEA Research Bulletin* for May, 1963, on pages 50 and 51.

TABLE 6. AVERAGE MAXIMUM SCHEDULED ANNUAL
SUPPLEMENTS FOR DIRECTING EXTRACURRICULUM
ACTIVITIES, 1962-63

	ENROLLMENT OF SYSTEM		
ACTIVITY	25,000 OR MORE	12,000 – 24,999	6,000 – 11,999
Head coach or only coach			
Football.	$754	$799	$845
Basketball	598	713	718
Baseball	463	450	462
Track*	473	487	468
Cross country	217	266	248
Swimming	336	428	416
Wrestling	387	432	414
Tennis	230	281	271
Golf	210	241	219
Faculty director of			
Instrumental music†	565	445	508
Vocal music	483	348	379
Production of school plays	282	238	254
School newspaper	461	217	282
Yearbook	386	265	323
Debating	278	317	246

* Includes both spring and fall track if shown separately in the schedule.
† In some cases the supplement is for directing the marching band, and the supplement for directing the school orchestra is a lesser amount.

TABLE 7. RELATIONSHIP OF SUPPLEMENTS FOR FOOTBALL
TO THOSE FOR OTHER EXTRACURRICULUM
ACTIVITIES, 1962-63

	ENROLLMENT OF SYSTEM		
ACTIVITY	25,000 OR MORE	12,000 – 24,999	6,000 – 11,999
Head coach or only coach			
Football	100.0	100.0	100.0
Basketball	79.3	89.2	85.0
Baseball	61.4	56.3	54.7
Track	62.7	60.9	55.4
Cross country	28.8	33.3	29.3
Swimming	44.6	53.6	49.2
Wrestling	51.3	54.1	49.0
Tennis	30.5	35.2	32.1
Golf	27.8	30.2	25.9
Faculty director of			
Instrumental music	74.9	55.7	61.3
Vocal music	64.1	43.6	44.9
Production of school plays	37.4	29.8	30.1
School newspaper	61.1	27.2	33.4
Yearbook	51.2	33.2	38.2
Debating	36.9	39.7	29.1

Physical education should develop policies for promoting public relations.

In physical education, it is sufficient to define public relations in terms of sound educational policy. The definition follows: *Public relations comprise those measures by which an educational enterprise maintains an awareness of public opinion on the one hand, and reveals to the public its purposes, plans, and outcomes on the other.*

To secure this reciprocal relation the processes of publicity are extensively used.

The public press is engaged in selling news. What is news? The criteria by which news is judged are freshness, human interest, and conflict of some kind. Since the newspaper is one of the chief means of publicity, it is apparent that "What is news?" determines largely the usefulness of this medium in public relations. The athletic contests of the school are news to the papers, but the daily accomplishments of children in growth, self-control, and functional skills are not news. If a survey is made of the school situation and some unusual features are disclosed, the results might be regarded as news but this would depend upon the information revealed.

Reporters should be received with courtesy, and within the limits of the work that has to be done should be given an opportunity to see classes, visit the pool and gymnasium, and have a chance to talk with teachers. If a dramatic story breaks they will be eager to get the news. In many institutions there are policies regarding the announcements that are to be made to the press, and, if there is an officer responsible for this, then his policies should be followed. If there is no policy in the matter then each individual should use his best judgment in answering questions and giving information. It is almost certain that what seems important to the school will appear in small type and what is minor in significance will be in the headlines. There is no conscious desire on the part of reporters to mislead, but merely that educational institutions and the press operate in two different worlds. If there is a quarrel, the press wants to keep it going as long as possible; the school wishes to settle the point and forget the difficulty. If there is a question of the eligibility of a prominent athlete, the press will run his picture and display the opinions of all sorts of persons on the sporting page; the school desires to forget the heroics, have the student get down to work, and concentrate upon the important things, such as the eligibility of the other athletes.

There are many opportunities to reveal the purposes, plans and outcomes of the department in public addresses before local groups. These openings should be used.

Sometimes topics are assigned but if the assignment is not conditioned by the occasion, then the nature of the address should be determined by the speaker. In preparation of a public address, a topic should be chosen that is of interest to the audience, and developed along simple lines with the presentation of two or three points. As a rule the address should be short rather than long; it is better to stop with the audience feeling that the speaker should go on than to continue against their hope that he will soon quit.

THE ADMINISTRATION OF PHYSICAL EDUCATION, HEALTH EDUCATION, AND RECREATION IN A UNIFIED PROGRAM

Successful adminstration of several areas requires that they possess common elements which can be coordinated. The word coordination suggests a basic interrelationship in the structure or forces to be handled; one does not coordinate the unrelated. Coordination of the similar and related is possible because they have a common bond by which they are united; it is this common bond that renders them suitable for coordinating efforts. An interrelationship between areas implies bonds in two directions at least; it suggests a dynamic situation in which action, reaction, and interaction occur naturally. Interrelatedness makes men into a society but they break up into clans, gangs, tribes, and nations. In the process of coordination we engage in policies and procedures, and we rely upon principles to determine the objectives we have in mind. In well-designed administrative units, the structures or forces with which we deal permit coordination of programs or persons when the interrelationships are real and basic. The close association of physical education, health education, and recreation exists because they have mutually supporting motives, incentives, and interests; the association is not the product of mere chance.

Physical education should manifest a broad view in its relations with health education and recreation.

In thinking about the desirability of any particular type of organization of the forces and structures of a community, we are confronted with the necessity of taking a position from which to examine the matter. There are two possible positions that we can take. Suppose that we take the position that concerns itself chiefly with the separation and development of an area. There is an advantage to the advocate of this position. He is able to circumscribe exactly the limits of his efforts, to concentrate on the job to be done, and to pay little or no attention to other forces and structures that are engaged in a similar process of promoting well-defined areas. We see this policy operative in government, in military services, and especially in higher education. Of course, there is sharp criticism of such a narrow and limited position. To still the criticism that is directed against such narrowly specialized efforts, justification is attempted by reference to the opportunity for, or actual achievement in, cooperation, which usually means getting the other person to do what will help you to promote your own program.

Suppose, on the other hand, that we take a position that is not concerned primarily with the development of an area in any exclusive sense but rather is interested to see that the basically related forces and structures in society are brought into a pattern of organization that allows movement forward on a broad front. Instead of seeing a professional job from the valley, suppose that we mount to some vantage point from which the whole panorama of human effort can be reviewed. Suppose this position reveals to us a number of social institutions with penetrating interrelationships, concerned with mutually related objectives, and moving forward in a coordinated attack upon their common problems.

Physical education should seek the development of health education, recreation, and its own program under the leadership of education.

It is necessary and desirable to organize health education, physical education, and recreation under education, to deal with the programs of these three areas as a single administrative unit, and to utilize the forces and structures of this unified organization, not for the development of separate and special areas, but for the extension and enrichment of education in which the gains may be more marked for the institution called the school than for the institutions called the clinic, the gymnasium, or the playground.

Let us look briefly at this institution of the community, the school. No one is very happy about the state into which this institution has fallen. It has failed to realize its potential usefulness to man because of the small and limited purposes to which it has become devoted. It persists in conducting a program for the average child, who does not exist; it pays its teachers such low salaries that it tends to recruit its personnel from the less able and the timid; and it continues a curriculum that has long ago outlived its usefulness. These are harsh statements to which there are many fine exceptions; and in spite of its faults the school is still the most important agency for the development of democratic institutions. It is responsible for the development of the basic skills in learning, it is a socializing force of tremendous importance, it is the strategic place for development of the physique, health, leisure interests, and happiness of each succeeding generation. The areas of health education, physical education, and recreation should be developed under educational leadership because they have vital and abiding interrelationships, because they belong together in the basic drives, incentives, and motives that move people, and because of what these forces can do for the schools. Improvement of the schools is the first step in the realization of what we want to see accomplished in each of the three areas. Certain it is that we cannot begin to solve the serious problems confronting us in health education until the school acts upon the principle that the whole child *does* go to school, and that therefore diseased tonsils and carious teeth, weak muscles and defective vision, fears and phobias go to school, nor can we solve the problem of leisure time when youth leaves the school without skills and interests in recreational activities. It is imperative that in every community we move forward on a broad front, and stop the senseless practice of developing a special organization every time we are aware of some particular need.

Physical education should recognize that much of its practice will be used in the recreations of people.

Important educational bodies have indicated that recreation is a legitimate function of the schools. The movement for a wider use of the school plant, adult education, functional subject-matter, and leisure-time programs are sure signs of educational thinking in this matter. The peacetime uses of atomic energy will so change the mechanics of living that all persons will have an enormous amount of free time; the use we have made of the forty-hour week is not comforting as we consider working less than ten hours a week.

The American Youth Commission declares, "The schools have a responsibility to equip their pupils for fruitful use of leisure which is equal to their responsibility to equip them for useful work." Precisely! But did anyone suppose that this sort of thing can develop in a substantial way if we pull the program apart and refuse to see the necessity of making the school move along with health education, physical education, and recreation in coordinated and interrelated fashion. The school as an institution devoted to the eradication of illiteracy and nothing more is inconceivable in a time like the present; the school as an institution of the whole community is the path of progress.

With respect to the view that recreation should be developed as a separate area of service in the community, there are several matters to examine. First, there is the matter of piecemeal attack upon the problems of community life; the disadvantage of such an approach will appear from what has already been said. Second, there is the problem of facilities. Every community with a school, and there is none without one the length and breadth of this great land, has a start on a recreation program of some kind. Many schools have gymnasiums, shops, libraries, laboratories, home economics rooms, music rooms, and auditoriums. In a facility survey of 628 districts in New York State there were more than 3000 gymnasiums, 1800 play fields, 700 athletic fields, and many other facilities such as dressing rooms, swimming pools, and rooms for crafts and arts. These facilities are meager in many communities and lacking in some, but where they do exist they represent a substantial means for the development of a recreation program. The problem of duplication at the present state of affairs is not the overproduction of facilities but the inevitable competition for the time in which to use them.

In the third place, the school is the only institution in the community that has the ability and opportunity to develop the skills and interests that are indispensable for a leisure-time recreation program. This matter of play is a very simple thing but the essentials seem to escape some who are interested in promoting recreation. With young children the possession of skill has little relation to the participation in play, but as the years of adolescence burst upon the scene, youth is unwilling to engage in activity in which he is a dub. Young persons do not join glee clubs unless they can sing well enough to enjoy it, and choral societies are composed of those who have some skill in music. It is so in sports and all the other activities that are rich in recreational values and appeal. They belong to those who can do them; they are neglected by those to whom their movements are the alphabet of a foreign language. Much complaint is made of the commercial amusements that adults patronize, but few of the critics appreciate that the choice is often made because the individual is unable to dance, to sing, to play a musical instrument, to carve wood, to paint, or to do any of the activities that are so highly regarded as leisure-time avocations. The adult demand for many of these skills is enormous. The extension division of some of the larger school systems offers instruction in many of these recreation activities and generally are unable to meet the demand. But clearly, the school is the one institution in the community that commands and will command the technical skill and leadership to teach people the skills needed for their leisure-time.

And lastly, the teachers of the school are potentially the core of a recreation staff. Many teachers are unsuited for leadership in recreation; they are too rigid and inflexible, too much concerned with marks and school room discipline. But some of them are able leaders of youth and adults, and, as the program develops under the leadership of education, more of that kind can be added to the staff. Moreover, education has high standards for administrative and teaching personnel, which include training in group leadership, individual guidance, and technical skills in many of the activities that are essential for leisure education and recreation. In many communities now, they are using teachers in the sports and dance programs, in music, crafts, and various programs in the arts.

When we accept the principle of coordination of basically related areas, then we can move forward on a broad front in social progress. And physical education will grow in stature because it has served, in intelligent fashion, many of the urgent needs of mankind.

QUESTIONS AND PROBLEMS FOR DISCUSSION

1. What is the function of administration? How does the philosophy of the administrator affect his work? Discuss the concept that human relations are the core of his problems.
2. What is the basis of democratic administration?
3. Why should there be a basic program of physical education for all pupils?
4. Why should it be required? If it is made elective, upon what basis should this plan operate?
5. Describe the person who is physically educated.
6. Why should there be a range of electives within a required program? Discuss the various aspects of this problem.
7. Why should pupils be classified for physical education? What is the most common classification?
8. How important is class size?
9. Outline an administrative plan for excuses. Upon what principle would you act in giving substitutions?
10. Why should physical education follow the school policy with respect to grades? If you think the policy is mistaken, how can you influence your colleagues?
11. Discuss the administrative problem of giving credit for physical education. Prepare an outline of the argument for credit in a debate on the problem.
12. Discuss the implications of the slogan, "Safety First."
13. Discuss the seven principles proposed for the administration of intermural athletics.
14. Why should intermural activities be regarded as an extension of the instruction program?
15. What are the professional dangers to avoid in the administration of the program of adapted physical education?
16. Discuss coeducational activities from the standpoint of immediate outcomes and remote results.
17. Name and discuss some of the reasons for lack of facilities in physical education.
18. Discuss the facilities for elementary schools with respect to the needs of children.
19. What are the ten principles given by Bookwalter?
20. Describe a situation in which the facilities could be improved and specify what should be done.

21. What sources should be investigated to find a teacher of physical education? What are the limitations of each?
22. Discuss the problem of age in a staff member.
23. What weight would you give to the professional preparation of an applicant for a position in your department?
24. How important is experience in successful teaching?
25. Discuss personality in all its aspects as it affects teaching.
26. How important is skill in the ability of a teacher of physical education?
27. Why should a teacher of physical education look the part he plays?
28. What are professional ethics? Give illustrations of behaviors that conform to ethical conduct.
29. Why should the head of the department promote the development of junior staff members? How can this be done?
30. What distinction do you make between a staff and a faculty? Why should there be staff meetings? Prepare an agenda for a meeting.
31. How should differences in opinion of staff members be handled?
32. Why should physical education personnel attend faculty meetings?
33. Why is military drill not equivalent to physical education as a general principle? Describe a program of physical education to which it might be equivalent.
34. What relationships are important with health education?
35. Why is it important to have good relationships with a separate department of athletics?
36. In what ways can physical education promote good public relations?
37. Give the argument for considering the administration of health education, physical education, and recreation in a unified program.
38. What is your understanding of social progress on a broad front?
39. Why is the school an essential institution of society?

REFERENCE READINGS

American Association for Health, Physical Education and Recreation. *Current Administrative Problems.* Washington, D.C., 1960.

Athletic Institute. *Equipment and Supplies for Athletics, Physical Education and Recreation.* Chicago, 1960.

Athletic Institute. *Planning Facilities for Health Education, Physical Education and Recreation,* Revised Edition. Chicago, 1956.

Bernays, Edward L. *Public Relations.* Norman, University of Oklahoma, 1952.

Bucher, Charles A. *Administration of School Health and Physical Education Programs.* St. Louis, Mosby, 1955.

Cutlip, Scott M. *Effective Public Relations.* Englewood Cliffs, N.J., Prentice-Hall, 1958.

Duncan, Ray O. "The Administrator," *The Physical Educator,* May, 1960, p. 53.

Forsythe, Charles E. *Administration of High School Athletics,* 4th Edition. Englewood Cliffs, N.J., Prentice-Hall, 1962.

Gabrielson, Alexander, and Miles, Caswell M. *Sports and Recreation Facilities for School and Community.* Englewood Cliffs, N.J., Prentice-Hall, 1958.

Havel, Richard C., and Seymour, Emery W. *Administration of Health, Physical Education and Recreation for Schools.* New York, Ronald Press, 1961.

Healey, William A. *The Administration of High School Athletic Events.* Danville, Ill., Interstate Printers and Publishers, 1961.

Holbrook, Leona, and Hess, Lewis. "The Realm of Ethical Conduct," *Journal of Health — Physical Education — Recreation,* February, 1962, p. 75.

Hughes, William L., *et al. Administration of Physical Education,* 2nd Edition. New York, Ronald Press, 1962.

Scott, Harry A., and Westkaemper, Richard B. *From Program to facilities in Physical Education.* New York, Harper, 1958.

Voltmer, Edward F., and Esslinger, Arthur A. *The Organization and Administration of Physical Education,* 3rd Edition. New York, Appleton-Century-Crofts, 1958.

Wiles, Kimball, *et al. Supervision in Physical Education: A Guide to Principles and Practices.* Englewood Cliffs, N.J., Prentice-Hall, 1956.

Williams, Jesse Feiring, Brownell, Clifford L., and Vernier, E. L. *The Administration of Health Education and Physical Education,* 6th Edition. Philadelphia, Saunders, 1964.

Zeigler, Earle F. *Administration of Physical Education and Athletics.* Englewood Cliffs, N.J., Prentice-Hall, 1959.

CHAPTER THIRTEEN

EVALUATION — A PROCESS OF ASSESSING OUTCOMES

Never before have we had to rely so completely on ourselves. No guardian to think for us, no precedent to follow without question, no lawmaker above, only ordinary men set to deal with heart-breaking perplexity. All weakness comes to the surface. We are homeless in a jungle of machines and untamed powers that haunt and lure the imagination. Of course our culture is confused, our thinking spasmodic, and our emotion out of kilter. No mariner ever enters upon a more uncharted sea than does the average human being born in the twentieth century.

Lippmann.

Whatever goods may be in existence — it is out of natural soil that they grow and by a human nature, animal in its basis, that they are apprehended and enjoyed.

Edman.

A CHANGING VIEW

In recent years a new point of view has emerged out of the testing and measuring of children. The goal of exact measurement of all achievement has faded into the background and a saner view of the educational process has taken its place. The earlier purpose emphasized the scientific elements in teaching; the later one would use the scientific techniques now available, indeed would seek for additional ones, but also would wish to consider the art elements in teaching and the human aspects of the problem.

When teaching is regarded as an applied science, like engineering, the elements which characterize the mechanical arts are usually prominent. There are certain justifications for this view, of course. Many processes develop in teaching which are susceptible to orderly arrangement, systematic treatment, and mechanical precision. The use of standard tests for classification and tests to measure achievement has tended to reinforce such practice by the exact record of results. Thus, there may be too great devotion to a measure which is final in form but quite incomplete in nature. This is the weakness of the earlier testing methods. If there is neglect of the personal elements in the situation, there is likely to be manifest a consequent disregard of concomitant learnings. In the face of devoted efforts to secure measurable outcomes, such as speed in running or height in jumping, there is the tendency to neglect the social justifications for running and jumping. The coach, driven by the necessity to win games, has a very exact and practical measure by which he judges the players. The obviousness of the measured outcome often hides the indirect values in a situation. If any particular percentage of games won is essential in having a sport season adjudged successful, then one is faced with the necessity in which statistical averages or percentages may completely obscure standards of educational worth based on ideals. Again, the ease with which measurable outcomes manifest themselves renders more difficult the recognition of the intangibles in the situation.

It is clear that a collection of isolated measurable units do not comprise an education, that many items that should never have been selected for attention in education have been emphasized simply because they could be measured objectively, and more importantly, that the usual measuring devices are entirely inadequate to indicate desirable growth of the individual toward some of the most significant goals. All phases of pupil growth are important, and teachers should wish to know the outcomes in habit formation, the kinds of interests developed, and the changes in attitudes as well as the gains that objective tests reveal.

It is becoming evident that the more comprehensive term is evaluation and that measurement is one phase of this process. An adequate evaluation of the individual's effort or achievement will employ the various objective tests and measures that are so valuable, but it will also collect evidence of subjective character from competent persons. The scientist's criticism of subjective procedure in experimentation is proper, but in the art of teaching the subjective judgment of competent persons may be quite as useful in the development of young people as the objective tests now so widely employed.

Many teachers express judgments about their students on the grading sheets they periodically turn in for the record. Judgments should be based on evidence and not be mere guesses. The nature of the evidence varies. Seeking it, identifying it, helping students to identify it for themselves, insisting that the school administration take it into account — these steps will make physical education more functional in the lives of boys and girls.

THE FUNCTION OF TESTS

The realization of values in teaching which are not subject to exact measurement has led, therefore, to a broader view of the functions of tests. At the beginning of the testing movement, tests were regarded as hurdles to be jumped, barriers to separate those who do from those who do not. A more acceptable practice, now highly approved, uses tests of classification and achievement to place better the individual or group in the educational situation, to arrange better the materials of instruction, and to guide better the individual in relation to his capacities and skills.

This use of tests for increasing individual interest in activities, for development of abilities, and for selection of proper materials of instruction means, of course, not a lesser but a greater emphasis upon scientific method in teaching. We need still to know much more about the achievement levels in motor skills of individuals, what programs will produce not only the most satisfactory growth increments but also the most satisfying individual experiences as well as the most acceptable social outcomes. It may be that the social outcomes lie outside the field of a reasonable testing program today, but if this be true there remains the necessity to use scientific tests and measures for the other purposes.

It may be stated, therefore, that tests are not ends in themselves; they are merely means by which teachers may hope to better the work of teaching boys and girls. The test may be an important measure of achievement but the most important aspect of the question is what happens to the individual after he takes the test.

THE BACKGROUNDS OF THE TESTING MOVEMENT

The use of measures to determine anatomical characteristics is quite old. In its crude form it goes back to early beginnings of civilized life. The effort to secure measures of functional capacities is more modern and corresponds with the relatively recent emphasis upon the dynamic as against the static, or the physiological as against the anatomical.

A rough sort of anthropometry was carried on by certain

Greek sculptors, but Quetelet is generally recognized as the originator not only of the word anthropometry but also of its first techniques. In America, Hitchcock at Amherst, Seaver at Yale, Sargent at Harvard, and Leonard at Oberlin carried on exact anthropometric procedures which accumulated a great deal of data on skeletal and muscular measurements of boys. Dr. Delphine Hanna of Oberlin and other women collected similar anthropometric data on college girls. During this period, the physical education program reflected the influence of this movement. Students were examined and on the basis of bodily measurements were given prescriptions of exercise designed to secure a bilateral symmetry in form and strength. If the left upper arm was not as large as the right, the prescription included exercises to increase the size of the left upper arm. Some look back upon this period as highly scientific and doubtless in its procedures it should be so regarded. The anthropometric period in physical education, however, is a beautiful illustration of the way in which scientific procedures may be so selected and used that other values are ignored by the simple process of focusing attention upon one aspect of the problem. Then the emphasis was upon structure. Today, this emphasis of thirty to forty years ago seems quite faulty, highly undesirable, and of little productive value but this present judgment arises out of a recognition of other elements in the problem of educating boys and girls. Now, the emphasis is upon function.

An illustration with similar lessons may be given from present-day experiences. A director of physical education for men in a state university arranged a plan to measure the student's ability in handball. The corners were marked with circles and scores were given for ability to place the ball within the marked areas. The students were induced to practice these shots with the hope that they would be able to play better handball and with the assumption that they could be scored more exactly. The procedure had two results: first, the student might be able to score high in such tests and still play a poor game of handball, and second, the students began to lose interest in the game. The purpose of the department was to promote activities, and hence the test was abandoned since it interfered with that purpose.

The beginnings of functional tests are found in the measures of strength which fascinated so many of those working in the field of physical education thirty years ago. Sandow as the typical strong man had made strength rather popular and public interest could always be aroused in feats of strength long before such contests colored the early social gatherings of our pioneer ancestors. Sargent and others devised ways for measuring the strength of muscles, but Kellogg's strength test, obtained by a rather complicated machine which measured all muscle masses, marked the decline in this interest as other values were recognized. Again the shift of professional judgment was from the static to the dynamic. Not how strong, but what capacity to use strength seemed now important.

Following the period marked by interest in strength tests, a greater variety of functional tests were proposed. Many were designed to measure cardiac function and others to measure athletic ability. This period extending over the past twenty-five years has been largely without critical standards for determination of validity and reliability of the tests. Thus several tests which were supposed to measure the same thing, for example, circulatory efficiency, failed to correlate at all. Many other tests have been lacking in proper definition and the terminology has been indeed confusing.

THE STATISTICAL AND THE CLINICAL APPROACH

Education has its styles as does medicine, architecture, and clothing. A few years ago it was popular to have a deviated septum, then autointoxication became prominent among the ills of man to be followed by acidosis, and more recently arthritis. Statistics in recent years have dominated education. Many think this to be unwise dominance.

The statistical approach to any problem limits the student

to the services which statistics can contribute. Based on the law of averages, this approach is valuable in science where the factors in a situation occur constantly in the same way under controlled conditions. Thus, standards for the broad jump for 12-year-old boys can be prepared by selecting a group of boys, measuring their ability to broad jump under conditions controlled by the research, and then treating the data statistically.

In the field of health, physical education, and recreation, there are a number of objectives, however, which do not lend themselves to the statistical approach. Health offers a good example of such objectives.

Health is a term representing many functional elements in the individual with various compensations and adjustments which correlate toward a unified condition. Health, therefore, is not a unit quantity or quality and it is, therefore, impossible to establish norms for it using statistical procedures until every element in the total can be measured and the adjustments determined. By statistics it has been impossible to arrive at a measure of "normal health," and hence the more acceptable approach to a problem of this kind is the clinical one.

The clinician views the term **normal** with suspicion and prefers to use the word **negative** to indicate that he finds no evidence of disease or disturbance in a particular function. He knows that individuals vary so much with respect to certain qualities that he is skeptical about terms such as average, typical, or standard. He contends further that variation from a statistical norm or standard may not always constitute abnormality. Thus, he prefers to describe an individual by using adjectives which express the characteristics found in the individual.

The clinical approach is the method of choice of the athletic coach. There are numerous statistical measures of precise athletic skills, such as running, jumping, throwing, kicking, tackling, and catching. Most contests, however, require a blending of these skills with certain qualities such as courage, initiative, drive, emotional stability, and analytical thinking in order to achieve success in a contest. The football coach knows that excellence in one or two skills is not enough to guarantee success in the whole performance.

As progress is made in measuring qualities in the individual in addition to the motor skill he possesses, the statistical approach in sports may be used increasingly. Likewise in the area of health—measurement of ability in adjustment and correlation may be combined with norms for red cell count, hemoglobin index, pulse rate, vision, hearing, and numerous other functional norms now available. At present, however, such synthesis into a health norm is impossible.

With respect to all the procedures that are used in teaching, it is important not to become lost in the techniques, the machinery, and the devices. We are often warned against not seeing the forest because of preoccupation with the trees.

Evaluation must be made in relation to the dominant values of the American way of life. Muscle is not an end in itself. Nor is any skill an end in itself. Rather, it is to be hoped that boys and girls may discover the value of fitness and so make a place for it in their lives. Recreation skills, appreciation of good performance, and ability to play with others find their true place in education as they become part of the habits and denote the preferences of people. Holding such a view, the teacher is not likely to become lost in the mechanics of things.

STANDARDS FOR JUDGING PHYSICAL EDUCATION

A standard and principle have similar qualities. Early attempts of man to establish standards were crude applications of body measures such as the "foot," the "hand"—the breadth of the hand used chiefly in measuring the height of horses—and numerous others. Over the years these empirical measures were *standardized* with respect to exact lengths of certain materials kept under exact conditions in a particular place. In education, standards were often proclaimed and, if they appeared reasonable and people accepted them, they acquired a validity that comes from experience.

More than a quarter of a century ago the author proposed four standards for judging physical education. One never knows how well a proposed standard is accepted until it is submitted to one's peers. It may be called a standard but until there is responsible judgment of its worth, it may remain a mere flag out in front of the parade.

Consequently, soon after their presentation to the profession, ratings were secured from experts to determine the worth or value of the standards for judging physical education practice. On two subsequent occasions, the standards were resubmitted to other panels of experts to compare the later judgments with the early one, and to determine more recent trends.

The ratings accorded these standards by experts in the field range from good through very good to excellent, in which good scores 80, very good 90, and excellent 100. This high approval warrants the reclassification of these standards as principles. The four principles follow:

Physical education should provide physiological results, scientifically determined, indicative of wholesome, functional activity of organic systems, and sufficient for the needs of the growing organism.

Because of the nature of man and his biologic needs we are keenly interested in the organic systems. These systems — particularly the circulatory, respiratory, excretory, and nervous are vitally related to the muscles of locomotion and the fundamental muscles of the trunk, which of course in the flatworm were locomotor mechanism.

This principle is justified, therefore, by this dependency of the vital organs upon the fundamental muscles. This relationship and its significance have been variously appreciated in physical education. While accepting the fact, its interpretation has frequently been confused in the practical working out of methods and procedures. The discussion of breathing exercises in Chapter 6 illustrates the point.

Breathing exercises have been mentioned as an illustration of the need to test our practice by a standard that expresses wholesome functional activity of organic systems in the light of physiological results. Scientific evidence is available for most of the determinations of procedure in this respect. The more deplorable is the position, therefore, of those leaders of physical education in state and city who continue traditional practice when the evidence is available to correct their procedure. It is not a matter at all of recommendations of different systems of gymnastics. There can be no such thing as nationalistic forms of truth. There is truth! Scientifically determined fact! If our traditions, our beloved customs, our cherished beliefs disagree with ascertained truth there is only one defensible position for the rational person.

Unfortunately we do not have all the data that we require to apply this standard everywhere. All the needs of the growing organism are not known. Hetherington has indicated the time requirement in big-muscle activities of children from 1 to 20 years of age. This kind of study needs to be continued and additional data should be collected. Moreover, we need correlated studies on the relation of functional tests of physical vigor with the more static determinations of nutrition and growth. Some work has been done, and other studies are in process of preparation.

Finally, it should be pointed out that any program that fails to provide for physiologic activity of the organic systems sufficient for biologic needs is to be criticized. Experiments with different programs show that one type of program is not so useful for biologic growth and development as another. No matter how desirable the program may be in developing other values, it must never be forgotten that the accomplishment of physiological work is not to be sacrified to other goals, except in unusual emergencies.

Physical education practice should have meaning and significance for the individual and should provide a carry-over interest.

It has been a traditional view that physical education dealt with muscles, bones, and ligaments. Our professional students have generally been more extensively trained in anatomy and kinesiology than in physiology and psychology. We have too frequently dissected the human individual and dealt with him in isolated systems and in separate parts. We have taken a position in our field similar to one sometimes held in general educational theory, namely, that the school trained the mind. It has been declared that physical education trained the body. Such positions cannot be defended. The mass of experimental and clinical evidence accumulating in recent years on this point emphasizes the essential unity of man. Mind and body are one. It is entirely unjustifiable to speak or act with reference to any duality in the education of the human individual.

The practice, therefore, of providing exercises without reference to their meaning to the individual, without recognition of the necessity for an intelligent human being to react toward movements made, is a serious mistake. Thus we shall view with some suspicion the application of terms to exercises if this fundamental view does not prevail. For example, it has been quite popular to classify as "hygienic exercises" certain movements of the trunk that were designed to promote hepatic circulation and intestinal peristalsis. This view is focused on that part of the individual below the diaphragm. Irrespective of the effects of such movements on the abdominal organs, it is a misuse of language and a handicap to correct thinking and planning to call them hygienic unless there are health-producing effects upon the organism as a whole. It is indefensible to speak of hygienic effects upon the circulatory system and neglect the nervous system. If the individual while doing such exercises experiences unwholesome (for our purposes) effects in mind, such as dissatisfaction, depression of spirit, dislike, the very opposites of wholesome neural activity, e.g., joy, happiness, pleasure, then irrespective of salutary hepatic effects, the exercise cannot be called hygienic.

Herbert Spencer knew this truth years ago and expressed it as follows:

> Granting, as we do, that formal exercises are better than noth-
> ing—and granting, further, that they may be used with advan-
> tage as supplementary aids; we yet contend that such formal

exercises can never supply the place of the exercises prompted by nature. For girls as well as boys, the sportive activities to which the instincts impel are essential to bodily welfare. . . . The common assumption that so long as the amount of bodily action is the same, it matters not whether it be pleasurable or otherwise, is a grave mistake.

The importance of recognizing that practice must have meaning and significance is attested to by our leading psychologists. Thus James emphasized the need to insure that every sensory stimulus shall result in a muscular or motor response suited to the emergency, and moreover that the response is not complete until the kinesthetic impulses from the movement return to the brain, informing as it were the antecedent sensory impulses of the completion of the act. The essential unity of mind and body demands that movement be viewed in the light of its meaning and significance to the child. The importance of satisfaction in the learning of movements bears on this point and is stated by Thorndike in the Law of Effect. Nowhere in physical education is there greater need for recognition of the demands of the individual that activities have meaning. It is being recognized in the teaching of school subjects where the psychological has supplanted the logical method in teaching spelling, reading, history, and other subjects. Its application to physical education is an immediate need.

Moreover, if meaning and significance reside in the activity, there will likely be a carry-over interest. The spectacle of men and women who have no love for and no skill in physical activity is made ridiculous by the claims of special exercises made palatable by phonograph attachment. This need for learning activities that will function in the life of the individual is justified in the personal and social necessities of modern life.

Physical education practice should provide opportunity for the individual to satisfy those socially desirable urges and impulses of nature through engagement in motor activities appropriate to age, sex, condition, and stage of development.

The need for development of the neuromuscular mechanisms arises out of the ordinary physical acts of life, the leisure time physical recreation of adults, and the joys and satisfactions that come from physical activities well performed. The ability to pick up objects from the floor, to board a train or street car, to walk, to carry suitcases and parcels, to stand, to run at times, to jump occasionally, and many other related activities depend upon skill, strength, and endurance in neuromuscular groups. For leisure-time enjoyment of physical activity there must be enough skill to rank one above the novice, enough strength and endurance to secure the benefits of moderate participation. Joys and satisfactions of real merit to the individual may ensue from activities well executed. The thrill that comes from a finely conceived and well-executed approach shot, the exhilaration of a dive in good form, the exultation in good woodsmanship, in sound horsemanship, in successfully poling or paddling a canoe through rapids, are types of satisfaction of real worth in the inner life, at least, of the participant. For some persons these values will be nonexistent for the same reason that precludes their enjoyment of a Mays, Mantle, Gibson, Graham, Pace, or Hogan. Those who lack motor skills do not understand what athletes talk about; there is no common ground.

Closely related to this third principle is the necessity for excellence in performance that shall carry the individual above the dub or novice class. Continuance of an activity is related to the skill with which it is carried on. We enjoy doing things we do well. The purpose to teach activities that shall carry on in the life of the person fails unless some proficiency is achieved. Participation depends upon attaining a standard of excellence in performance. No mere perspiration standard will suffice. Exercise alone is not enough.

But neuromuscular development is not an end in itself. It is of value and significance only as it contributes to the life of the person. An omnibus driver would not find it worth while to cultivate a high degree of open-field running. These things can easily be overdone. It is important to determine, so far as possible, how much and what kinds of neuromuscular control shall be taught and acquired.

Obviously the first consideration would be the daily physical activities. Walking, climbing, standing, carrying, and perhaps running represent a minimum list, and enough skill, strength, and endurance so that these activities may go on easily. More definite statements are offered in the chapter on objectives. In addition to these utilitarian controls one should acquire facility with at least two leisure-time physical activities. To be able to hike easily and with satisfaction, to play golf, tennis, handball, to swim, to paddle a canoe or row a boat, to skate, these are some of the many admirable forms that will always appeal. It would seem reasonable to expect that one have skills and strength for unusual occurrences. To come down a rope, to climb a tree, to vault a fence, to jump a brook, to lift a heavy timber—these are items of safety education, in addition to other values.

It is true that one may develop the neuromuscular mechanisms beyond any reasonable use, except for exhibitive, vaudeville performances. Thus, juggling, ballet dancing, advanced heavy apparatus, represent extremes. Marathon racing, cross-channel swimming, long-distance dancing are stunt activities without other than commercial or advertising value. For the average professional, business, or industrial worker, moderate excellence in control of the neuromuscular mechanisms will provide all that is essential.

Physical education practice should offer opportunity to the individual under wise leadership to meet educative situations as one of a social group.

Most of the difficulties which we meet as human individuals are related to persons and not to things. We adjust more readily to environmental changes which are foreign to our nature than we do to personal incompatibilities. Ability to live well as a member of organized society is one of the most valuable qualities. Hence the training in moral and social attitudes is a very important business of the home and school. All the values in civilization are dependent upon the process of nurture by which the original nature of man is modified. Such training, however, must recognize fundamental points of view, and while physical education must concern itself vitally with the problem of character development it cannot proceed successfully without clear recognition of the problem.

It is helpful to remember that the more we work with children, the more we learn that we cannot with absolute assurance teach them anything. The best we can do is to offer a desirable situation and to help them to make a response that will be satisfying or annoying to them in accordance with our plan for the formation of bonds.

Aside from the need for physiological activity for the whole child, for situations which are mentally stimulating and satisfying, for the exercise of socially desirable urges, the individual we are training fails unless he takes his place in the life of the nation as a national asset. Physical education has this responsibility for the quality of our citizenry in precisely the same way that it exists for the school in general, but it has it in greater degree than any other department of the school because of the nature of the activities of the physical education program.

What will wise leadership offer? What are the criteria that will guide that leadership?

To meet educative situations as one of a social group may serve adequately as a principle because it asks us to view our program and practice in the light of social and national needs. It bids us recognize that physical education is worthy precisely to the degree that it helps educate boys and girls to become national assets as citizens of these United States of America. Whatever may be our individual concepts of the elements of good citizenship we will doubtless agree that health, strength, vigor, power are never ends in themselves, but only useful means for the realization of service to the world. The notion that the immediate objectives of physical education are to be judged by their relation to general social ends and needs is not simply *ad hominem,* but the inescapable logic of a human world. This point needs further development.

Suppose that we were to judge physical education by its offering in educative situations and should interpret its practice in the light of character criteria. What would we think of the contribution of physical education to the idea of personal attainment? How much of our physical education is just plain exercise, without spirit, without attitudes which inspire boys and girls to live finely? How often do we see physical education morally fervid enough to portray Hall's views when he said, "Physical education is for the sake of mental and moral culture and not an end in itself. It is to make the intellect, feelings, and will more vigorous, sane, supple, and resourceful," or spiritually minded enough to reflect Plato's words of "Body for the sake of Soul." Are there instances where physical education is developing the "coarse, crude, vulgar, self-seeking individual"? How far is physical education offering an opportunity in the gymnasium and on the athletic field for the development of the best in spirit, in personality, in character? This emphasis upon character qualities should not be interpreted as an advocacy of a pale and pallid type of physical education. Physical education aims to reflect life, the best life, and surely a vigorous life. It favors competition and is interested in personal achievement.

Moreover, shall physical education be concerned with equality of opportunity? What do we think of a few athletes monopolizing the gymnasium or athletic field? What do we think about sharing facilities equally between boys and girls? Equality of opportunity if it means anything at all means that play, games, sports, and athletics shall not be the inheritance of a chosen few.

Shall our physical education be free from class privilege? What do we think of educational policy that hires expert, competent teachers for an athletic few, and limits the instruction of 90 per cent of the school population to a few exercises given by the classroom teacher?

In addition, we ought to be interested to observe to what extent physical education practice offers educative situations which shall stimulate each pupil to achieve and shall give opportunity to share responsibility. The personal qualities valued in human character can only be developed in connection with opportunities offered. Else there is no growth, no accomplishment.

To provide opportunity for wholesome activity of organic systems, to offer a practice full of meaning and significance, to utilize the native urges and impulses in developing neuromuscular skills, to present educative situations for the individual to respond to as one of a social group — these need never mean neglect of health and motor training values so frequently sought. If the supervision is adequate, if the opportunities are hygienic and sufficient, these nearer goals will be won, and if the above or similar standards prevail, in actual programs, physical education will help in developing not only muscles, not only lungs, not only hearts, but in truth, individuals of a free and socially minded nation, ready to serve because of health, strength, and power, willing to serve because of the social consciousness that is theirs.

OTHER PROCEDURES OF EVALUATION

The use of standards that serve as criteria by which activities can be judged is an evaluation procedure. There are numerous others. The following are illustrative: cumulative records, personal check lists, questionnaires, inventories, ratings, anecdotal records, and similar subjective data. All of these, like tests and scales, must be carefully selected and properly administered; otherwise, they may be quite meaningless.

Since the clarification and acceptance of goals, knowledge of progress, and use of the proper method are essential to learning at any age, it is very important that techniques be improved, and even new ones devised by means of which goals can be defined, progress indicated, and proper method revealed. In these directions, the techniques of evaluation are most useful in clarifying goals, achievement tests will show progress, and the practical outcomes and realization of objectives will endorse method.

The achievement of administrator's goals are seldom measured, although the techniques of school surveys do indicate how far they have been realized. Both administrators and teachers may find it helpful to conduct continuous surveys of their programs, and the use of techniques now available can greatly increase the effectiveness of physical education.[1]

Physical education should use cumulative records in evaluating pupil achievement.

It has long been recognized as valuable to record the individual's academic achievement. His physical education experience is equally important to record, so that from his entrance into school until his graduation therefrom, a cumulative record of physical education will present an over-all view of the individual in one important aspect of his education. The record should include pertinent data on health, participation in physical education activities and his achievement in them. It will show achievement test and fitness test scores as well as teachers' judgments of progress made in realization of goals in attitudes, interests, and understanding. His participation in extracurricular activities associated with physical education, his membership on teams, and his level of skill attained should appear on the record.

It is important to record the interests that have arisen in connection with the program; does he engage in skiing, sailing, equitation, camping, hunting, or other similar activities? Most schools do not have facilities for instruction in such activities, but alert and resourceful teachers find ways to stimulate interest in them, to help young people organize their own groups for such participations, and even to take part themselves. What

[1] The following reports may be helpful:
Educational Survey Commission and Survey Staff, *Report to the Legislature*, State of Florida, 1929.
Report of the Survey of the Schools of Chicago, Illinois, New York, Teachers College, Columbia University, 1932.
A Report of a Survey of the Public Schools of St. Louis, Missouri, New York, Teachers College, Columbia University, 1939.
The Report of a Survey of the Public Schools of Pittsburgh, Pennsylvania, New York, Teachers College, Columbia University, 1940.
A Report of a Survey of Public Education in the State of Washington, Olympia, 1946.
The Report of a Survey of the Public Schools of the District of Columbia, Washington, Government Printing Office, 1949.

young people do in their free time is a vital educational record; to ignore how leisure is used may well give the impression of indifference, when actually the understanding and responsible teacher cares and cares greatly about the leisure-time recreations of the pupils in his classes.

It is obvious that such cumulative records serve many purposes, and give vital information regarding individual differences. To keep the records requires time and this expenditure of energy is only justified by the contribution of the records to better understanding of individual boys and girls.

Physical education should use check lists.

There is a proverbial saying, "You can lead a horse to water but you can't make him drink." Much that teachers would wish to do for pupils must await their decision to move in the direction that teachers would have them go. It has long been recognized in education that little is learned until the individual sets a goal for himself. The personal check list is devised to stimulate the student to take an active part in planning his own practice, in recognizing his success or failure in achieving definite results, in accepting goals that are desirable to attain, and in making plans for his own long range recreational use of leisure.

The Kozman and Cassidy *Handbook of Physical Education for Girls* gives excellent treatment of the personal check list. It includes a brief statement of various values and provides an attractive and interesting series of outlines in which the girl may indicate her present standing, her aspiration, and her achievement from time to time.

Much simpler check lists may be used with considerable success, if they are well planned. Student participation in their planning may assure greater interest in the project. The check list may take the form of squad cards in which each member of the squad checks certain items which reveal achievement. The items left unchecked are a record of need for more intensive effort and practice. Such check lists help the instructor to individualize instruction more efficiently; they may be used to include the specific objectives of the course. The way in which achievement is recorded depends upon the nature of the item; it may be shown as a score, as a pass-fail, or as a brief descriptive statement showing further needs. Of course, it has no place for giving an excuse for failure.

Physical education should use the questionnaire and inventory.

These two techniques have possibilities when properly used. As means of discovering the interests of individuals they may be quite helpful, but to regard an expression of interest as identical with practice they may be misleading. Recent studies have shown that it is better to discover how individuals actually spend their time than to ask what their interests are, if a record of status is desired. The statement that one is interested in playing baseball, handball, and tennis is very misleading if the individual fails to engage in these activities when opportunity offers. The pragmatic test is practice, against which desire and interest must always be compared.

Physical education should employ ratings and anecdotal records.

These techniques are subjective, but the subjective judgment of competent and fair persons, based on the evidence at hand, is extremely valuable. Such judgments may excel, in usefulness, objective measures which concern themselves with the superficial items of motor experience. In such areas as personality development, social adjustment, and expression of attitudes and interests, they are indispensable.

Skill in writing brief anecdotal reports and good judgment in rating individuals may be developed through training and experience. When the rater or recorder cannot recognize and take into account his own biases, the techniques are useless. Both these techniques have been satisfactorily used by many teachers, guidance and personnel workers, and group work leaders. They offer very fruitful means of evaluating many of the intangibles of physical education.

In writing anecdotal records it is important to state what occurs and not give an interpretation of what occurs.

Physical education should use various measures of skill.

The most satisfying measure of skill is success in the activity. Holding one's own in team games in relation to opponents of known ability, improving one's score as in golf, archery, or bowling, standing on one's head without falling over, skiing on a given slope without a spill—almost all motor activities give objective evidence of success or failure, and of improvement.

Throughout the learning period, however, programs must be organized for results, and some of these can be determined by the use of standardized achievement tests. Moreover, such tests stimulate the learner to practice the parts needed to perfect the whole, and encourage him through knowledge of his performance in relation to that of others of the same age and classification. The teacher should study achievement tests with great care before selecting any for class use, as they vary greatly in validity, reliability, objectivity, and ease of administration.

Physical education should employ measures of fitness.

During or following wars there is inevitably an interest in fitness. The neglect of measures for developing and maintaining fitness results in unfitness for war and this revelation is always disturbing enough to focus attention on the problem. Invariably the term physical fitness is used. This seems to imply the fitness which can be achieved through exercise, although in reality fitness is total. Indeed mental and emotional factors are important in fitness.

Moreover, fitness is specific. Fitness for football and fitness for ping-pong are not the same thing either in kind or degree. Fitness for clerking and fitness for heavy manual labor are not identical. Obviously there is a favorable condition of the individual under which he performs his work—whatever it is —in the most efficient way without undue fatigue and with the least expenditure of energy. Such favorable condition varies for all individuals and in all cases there are several factors, physical, mental and emotional. It is everywhere apparent that there is no physical fitness apart from mental and emotional fitness. Coaches frequently experience the difficult problem of conditioning men in whom there is a disturbed emotional state or non-acceptance of the self-discipline necessary in training.

William H. Solley raises some pertinent questions about physical fitness. His article deserves careful reading.[2]

Tests of fitness fall into two groups: (1) cardiovascular tests, and (2) performance tests. With respect to cardiovascular tests, Metheny recommends that physical education teachers not employ them, believing that they are too dangerous for the ordinary teacher to use. If the physiological demands of a test are great enough to differentiate among individuals, they are too strenuous for persons with weak hearts; if they are too mild for such differentiation, they are useless.

Tests of performance, such as sit-up, push-up, chinning, and Burpee's test, designed to measure the strength of muscle groups or general endurance for exercise have received a good deal of attention in physical education research.[3] The *Research Quarterly* reports many research projects in performance. The U.S. Office of Education has sponsored studies along these lines, the California Pentathlon is this type of test, and the National

[2] William H. Solley, "Critical Questions About Physical Fitness," *The Physical Educator*, March, 1961, p 8

[3] The following works discuss such tests:

Crampton, C. W. "Blood Ptosis." *New York Medical Journal*, November 8, 1903.

Foster, W. L. "Tests of Physical Efficiency." *American Physical Education Review*, November, 1914, p. 632.

Barringer, T. B. "Circulatory Reaction to Graduated Work as a Test of the Heart's Functional Capacity." *Archives Internal Medicine*, March, 1916, p. 365.

Schneider, E. C. "A Cardiovascular Rating." *Journal American Medical Association*, May 20, 1920, p. 1507.

Rogers, F. R. *Physical Capacity Tests*. New York, Barnes, 1931.

Larson, L. A. "A Factor Analysis of Motor Ability Variables and Tests, with Tests for College Men." *Research Quarterly*, October, 1941.

Burpee, R. H. *Seven Quickly Administered Tests of Physical Capacity*. New York, Teachers College, Columbia University, 1940.

Rifenberick, R. H. "A Comparison of Physical Fitness Ratings as Determined by the Pulse-Ration Test and Rogers' Tests of Physical Fitness." *Research Quarterly*, March, 1942, p 95

Section of Women's Athletics (AAHPER) is making a study of high school girls with tests of this character. Tests of this kind should be used with discrimination. During World War II, the armed services devised many performance tests for use with their selected groups. Some teachers have seized upon these tests, with their norms, as authoritative for general use with an unselected population of younger pupils. It should be obvious that tests designed for the highly selected Naval Aviation units, for example, could be dangerous when used in testing less able groups.

It should never be forgotten that one important purpose of performance tests is to arouse in the individual a desire to improve himself. Self-improvement is the ultimate goal in all teaching; while the motive that arouses the individual to take charge of his life may be some kind of test, it is only a means and never an end. What makes a youth train, condition himself, and follow a regimen of personal hygiene? It is the team to which he belongs — an athletic team, a school group, a family, an **idea**. The first approach in developing fitness is therefore mental and emotional and this is followed by or accompanied with the physical. Until this is understood with all its implications for educational practice and governmental policy, fitness will remain a myth which only the naive will clamorously pursue.

It is apparent then that efforts to measure fitness confront the same difficulties faced in measuring health and athletic ability.

Physical education should use measures of function.

The measurement of any function is a more simple matter. If care is taken not to claim too much, one can readily determine how the individual responds to exercise, what improvement he shows, how far to carry the process, and similar exact determinations of functional activity. Thus, anthropometric data will reveal the effects of any program upon skeletal and muscular changes if other elements are controlled, measurement of respiration and circulation will reveal how exercise affects these, and athletic performance tests will show the progressive change in status in simple patterns such as running and jumping.

THE HEALTH EXAMINATION

The term "physical examination" is used to denote the examination of the physical aspects of a person; it does not include the tests or evaluations of the emotional and social aspects of the individual. It came into use when there was little appreciation of the need for a complete appraisal of the whole person and persists, as is the nature of such things, long after the need for a more comprehensive term is understood. To avoid the limitations of the term "physical," it is customary to use the term, "health examination" with its broader implications, although not all health examinations are complete.

In the examination of an individual it is obvious that the body should be stripped during part of the examination. Several examiners may participate in the examination since special techniques are called for, and in some organizational plans, the examiners are arranged in stations through which the individual passes.

A complete examination of the individual will record information from seven areas of inquiry. These areas will yield data that may be recorded in the following categories:

1. Data from the environmental record
2. Data from the disease record
3. Data from the scholastic record
4. Data from the adjustment record
5. Data from the social-intergroup relationship record
6. Data from the health practices record
7. Data from the examination

Physical education should examine data from the environmental record.

These data should give a picture of the individual in relation to his pertinent past and his present environment. Family histories sometimes carefully record the positions of the child in the offspring series, or the fact of onliness if it exists. It is impossible to predict the personality traits of a first born, last born or only child. Onliness is, however, a potential problem. The occupation of the parents with whatever appropriate suggestion that fact may give of socio-economic status is a desirable item, and the marital status of parents may also be illuminating.

Physical education should examine data from the disease record.

These data give some information regarding the experience of the individual with communicable disease, likely immunities, susceptibilities, vaccinations, and inoculations. The record should also include information regarding operations, broken bones, and accidents.

Physical education should examine the data of the scholastic record.

The achievement of the individual in studies is an important datum for the teacher of physical education to know. The scholastic record may be suffering because of too much attention to athletics and this sort of information should be used to secure a better distribution of the pupil's time.

Physical education should study the data from the adjustment record.

The adjustment of the individual to his world may change from time to time. In many children it is made easily and without difficulty, in others there are signs of strain and stress in the organism. These signs may be abnormal bodily movements such as biting the nails, grimacing, stuttering or stammering, twitching facial muscles (tics) and more general nervous movements of the head, arms, and legs. They may appear as abnormal responses to reasonable tasks and take the form of sullenness, tenseness, talking back, or crying. In the effort to relieve emotional conflicts or tensions the individual may show a bullying attitude toward others, a tendency toward pushing and tripping of playmates, and a general disposition to "take it out" on others. In some persons the maladjustment takes the form of wishful thinking, playing the martyr, ready use of the alibi, and similar escapist and defense reactions.

Physical education should study the social-intergroup relationship record.

In the mental and emotional development of the individual, he comes into contact constantly with others who have urges and desires that conflict with his own inner drives. What he can do and is permitted to do depends upon a congeries of forces that he does not recognize and never understands. He strives to find some way out of the difficulties that beset him, and this may take the form of bragging about his great achievements when in fact he can recount nothing of any particular merit. It may take the form of bullying younger children over whom he now becomes superior. He may become most unreliable and be noted chiefly for lying, cheating, stealing, or truancy when these have their rewards in the social setting in which he finds himself. His abnormality may express itself in lack of personal cleanliness, disorderliness in school, disregard for property, disrespect for the opposite sex, and complete failure in sportsmanship.

Any considerable degree of evidence of the above changes may indicate marked maladjustment; in these disturbances there may be mild forms, of course.

Physical education should examine the health practices record.

The way an individual lives determines in part the kind of health he has, and therefore his habits of sleep, eating, exercise, elimination, correction of remediable defects are important.

Physical education should consider the data from the health examination.

The nature of the examination varies with age and sex after maturity; the hazards of the older adult are not those of the young child. For the young person, the important items are: vision, hearing, nasal passages, teeth, tonsils, adenoids, glands, skin, lungs, heart, blood vessels, abdomen, bones, muscles, postures, feet, spine, puberty, height, weight, nutrition, and nervous system.

THE HAZARD OF EVALUATION

From the preceding discussion it should be apparent that fitness—even "physical fitness"—cannot be assessed by one test. It has been suggested that at least nine items should be employed in an appraisal of fitness:[4]

1. Test of medical or health fitness
2. Test of motor intelligence
3. Test of cardiovascular fitness
4. Test of motor fitness
5. Test of skills fitness
6. Test of knowledge about physical education
7. Test of attitudes
8. Test of character or ethical behavior
9. Test of social adjustment and emotional patterns

After all the tests have been made and all the data evaluated, what should be the attitude of the teacher? One can be sure that no measure of the human individual is infallible and that, at best, judgment from all the data should be tentative. The able teacher will use all the techniques available to help in an appraisal of the student but the wise teacher will know that there are in every person capacities that are not revealed, abilities that have not been measured, and resources as yet untouched. If the procedures of evaluation can be used to disclose these capacities, free these abilities, and arouse these resources the goal of all good teaching is being realized.

RESEARCH IN PHYSICAL EDUCATION

Research provides some, and uses many of the tools of evaluation; it assists in the determination of principles, and is a sure source of insight and understanding. Research in physical education properly concerns itself with studies of man's nature, the forces of the environment, and man's reactions to and interactions with the forces that play upon him.

Research in physical education has increased greatly since the formation of the Research Council of the AAHPER. This organization has a tremendous responsibility because the mem-

[4] John F. Bovard, F. W. Cozens, and E. Patricia Hagman, *Tests and Measurements in Physical Education*, 3rd ed., Philadelphia, Saunders, 1949, p. 170.

bers of the Association are likely to look upon its reports as reliable and therefore to accept its pronouncements. In this way the program of physical education may be shaped by the work of the Research Council. A current example is the effort of the Council to develop the "National Youth Fitness Test." Concerning this work Weiss writes, "Through the cooperative work of this group AAHPER has taken a giant step forward in developing national standards for physical education."[5] The fact is, of course, that the National Youth Fitness Test is not a "standard for physical education" at all but only a test of how well boys and girls in grades 5 through 12 performed certain exercises which the Council *said* were "tests of fitness."

Physical education should conduct research in the nature of man.

Past investigations of man's nature have been concerned largely with his mental and emotional make-up. Whenever his motor skills have been studied, only small, easily isolated, muscles have been employed. But the opportunities in this phase of research are enormous if the worker is prepared to pursue the quest. One of the earliest efforts to discover the facts regarding motor ability that might be comparable to the I.Q. in the mental field was made by Brace, whose work gave great stimulus to research in this area.[6] While Brace has never claimed for his test the functional utility that tests of intelligence enjoy, nevertheless his pioneer efforts in this direction are appreciated by all who know the field.

Research in the medical sciences often approaches the human problem through the medium of animal experimentation. Practically all of the modern achievements in nutrition rest upon the work performed in animal laboratories. Similar conditions exist in biology, chemistry, bacteriology, physiology, and pathology. Some work has been done by Steinhaus in animal experimentation projected upon man. Perhaps most is to be gained by actual study of man's learn-

[5] R. A. Weiss, "AAHPER's Scientists—The Research Council," Report of the International Conference of WCOTP, Washington, D.C., 1960, p. 45.

[6] David K. Brace, *Measuring Motor Ability*, New York, Barnes, 1927.

ing of movements, what happens when he runs fast, and similar functional states. Josephine L. Rathbone's work affords an example of how study of individuals may yield significant data regarding the nature of man;[7] Oberteuffer pioneered in the field of hygiene with his study of interests;[8] and Jones in his analysis of learning helped to define a belief that some teachers of physical education have held for a long time.[9]

It is obvious, however, to even the tyro in this field that the surface has scarcely been scratched in the studies that have been made. There are still to be investigated primary studies in balance; the relation of the eye to movement; the nature of rhythm; relation of blood chemistry to strength, endurance, skill, and alertness as well as to fatigue; growth in relation to exercise; accelerations in growth and maturation; and others.

Physical education should conduct research in the discoverable effects of the environment upon man.

The variables are so many and so difficult to control that research in this area has been avoided by most workers. If we were to deal with disease and death, two definite entities, or even with chronological age, sex, redheads, or siblings the pattern would be simplified but even in such a final and complete state as death, nothing more can be recorded than the mortality rate with respect to occupation, social and economic status, urban or rural environment. Researchers are unable to speak precisely about the virulence or strength of the cause or, on the other hand, the resistance of the individual.

When the student speculates about the meaning of the forces, why they act as they do, and what patterns he can see,

[7] Josephine L. Rathbone, *Residual Neuromuscular Hypertension: Implications for Education*, published privately, 1936.

[8] Delbert Oberteuffer, *Personal Hygiene for College Students; A Study of the Curiosities, Interests, and Felt Needs of College Students in the Subject Matter of Personal Hygiene*, New York, Teachers College, Columbia University, 1930 (Contribution to Education, No. 407).

[9] Lloyd M. Jones, *A Factorial Analysis of Ability in Fundamental Motor Skills*, New York, Teachers College, Columbia University, 1935 (Contribution to Education, No. 665).

then such thinking is philosophical research. He does nothing more than to ask questions and to propose answers. The significance of the questions and the cogency of the answers constitute the contribution. The study by Louise S. Cobb is illustrative of this type of investigation.[10]

Physical education should conduct research in the reactions of man to his physical environment and his interactions with his social environment.

The reactions and interactions of man constitute his life. In many respects they are the most interesting thing about him. The worker may study man's reactions and interactions in the past. These will be historical studies. What has been done is not history; it is the recovery and reconstruction of events in a narrative form that constitute historical research. Ethel J. Dorgan's life of Luther Halsey Gulick is historical research because it portrays how Gulick reacted to the forces that played upon him.[11] History depends upon time, and it is the time element that renders Dorothy S. Ainsworth's study significant for women in physical education.[12] Perhaps as good an illustration of historical research is the outstanding work of Elizabeth C. Rearick, who assayed to study the folk dances of the Hungarians.[13] Here was a phase of culture to be discovered, reconstructed, and narrated for Americans. But first the Magyar language had to be learned; then the student had to live in Hungary, and record not only the dances but also the music,

[10] Louise S. Cobb, *A Study of the Functions of Physical Education in Higher Education*, New York, Teachers College, Columbia University, 1943 (Contribution to Education, No. 876).
[11] Ethel J. Dorgan, *Luther Halsey Gulick, 1865-1919*, New York, Teachers College, Columbia University, 1934 (Contribution to Education, No. 635).
[12] Dorothy S. Ainsworth, *The History of Physical Education in Colleges for Women, as Illustrated by Barnard, Bryn Mawr, Elimira, Goucher, Mills, Mount Holyoke, Radcliffe, Rockford, Smith, Vassar, Wellesley, and Wells*, New York, Barnes, 1930.
[13] Elizabeth C. Rearick, *Dances of the Hungarians*, New York, Teachers College, Columbia University, 1939 (Contribution to Education, No. 770).

photograph and paint the costumes, and interpret the findings in the stream of Magyar history.

The reactions and interactions of man may be revealed in the efforts he makes to organize for certain ends. What organizations does he set up? How are they composed? How do they work? Studies in organization may include types like those of Elliott,[14] Jones,[15] Schott,[16] Sharman,[17] and Abernathy[18] in which the research is largely analysis of many complex factors that constitute the problem. Other studies in organization may consider the standards that evolve out of the continual conflict of theory and practice, as shown by the outstanding contributions of Hughes[19] and Luehring.[20] This sort of investigation may be so well done that for a generation there will be none to attempt new statements of standards for athletics or standards for swimming pools.

The reactions and interactions of man may reflect what physical education attempts in the training of teachers. This may include such excellent analysis and invention as that

[14] Ruth Elliott, *The Organization of Professional Training in Physical Education in State Universities*, New York, Teachers College, Columbia University, 1927 (Contribution to Education, No. 268).

[15] Hiram A. Jones, *The Administration of Health and Physical Education in New York State*, New York, Teachers College, Columbia University, 1934 (Contribution to Education, No. 622).

[16] Carl P. Schott, *Physical Education in the Colleges of the United Lutheran Church in America*, New York, Teachers College, Columbia University, 1929 (Contribution to Education, No. 379).

[17] Jackson R. Sharman, *Physical Education Facilities for the Public Accredited High Schools of Alabama*, New York, Teachers College, Columbia University, 1930 (Contribution to Education, No. 408).

[18] Ruth Abernathy, *A Study of Expenditures and Service in Physical Education*, New York, Teachers College, Columbia University, 1944 (Contribution to Education, No. 904).

[19] William L. Hughes, *The Administration of Health and Physical Education for Men in Colleges and Universities*, New York, Teachers College, Columbia University, 1932 (Contribution to Education, No. 541).

[20] Frederick W. Luehring, *Swimming Pool Standards*, New York, Barnes, 1939.

shown in the studies of Duggan[21] and Haggerty[22] or the primary investigation by Scott[23] of professional personnel.

And finally, man's reactions and interactions may present problems in measurement. How fast does he run? How strong are his muscles? How does he learn? These and similar questions invoke the worker's inventiveness. He relies heavily upon accomplishment in other areas but because of the unique character of the materials with which he works, he must frequently adapt the techniques that others bring to him. An excellent illustration of adaptation is Rodgers' fine investigation of method.[24] Beall's study shows the relation between anthropometric data and success in activities.[25] In a few instances the investigator may be such an expert in statistical technique that his research rests largely upon the skill with which he manipulates his data and shows the relationship between them. Illustrative of this is McCloy's study of achievement standards.[26]

Other types of measurement depend upon the unique

[21] Anne S. Duggan, *A Comparative Study of Undergraduate Women Majors and Non-Majors with Respect to Certain Physical Traits*, New York, Teachers College, Columbia University, 1936 (Contribution to Education, No. 682).

[22] Helen R. Haggerty, *Certain Factors in the Professional Education of Women Teachers of Physical Education*, New York, Teachers College, Columbia University (Contribution to Education, No. 741).

[23] Harry A. Scott, *Personnel Study of Directors of Physical Education for Men in Colleges and Universities*, New York, Teachers College, Columbia University, 1929 (Contribution to Education, No. 339).

[24] Elizabeth G. Rodgers, *The Teaching of Team Games; A Study Applied to the Elementary School Level, of Three Methods of Teaching*, New York, Teachers College, Columbia University, 1936 (Contribution to Education, No. 680).

[25] Elizabeth Beall, *The Relation of Various Anthropometric Measurements of Selected College Women to Success in Certain Physical Activities*, New York, Teachers College, Columbia University, 1939 (Contribution to Education, No. 774).

[26] Charles H. McCloy, *Some Achievement Standards in Track and Field Athletic Events for Boys from Ten to Twenty Years of Age*, New York, Barnes, 1932.

procedure devised for securing the data desired. Considerable work has been done to measure skill in sports, but practically all such studies have assumed that aspects of the sport would portray the whole. But experience shows that one may be able to score high in the tennis serve but in a game make many double faults, shoot baskets with precision on all occasions except in a game, throw a baseball with high accuracy at a target but walk the batsman at the plate, and similarly in all sports. Howard devised a procedure for scoring the effectiveness of play in a real basketball game; this constituted a new approach to the problem.[27]

Research in physical education has only begun. The problems that confront human society, concerning which physical education has something to say, are indeed challenging. Now as never before we are confronted with the problems of leisure, health, crime, and community living. How shall we promote leisure interests and skills? How shall the schools serve as real community centers? How shall music and drama, sports and dance, homemaking and the care of children be developed? For ages the only power at man's disposal was fetish. Occult forces moved man and developed tribes and clans. That is past now. Fetish will no longer suffice. Man is still moved but increasingly by truth. We set out to help in the building of fine lives but by preferred choices based on truth. These realities are the concern of all education; they are to be uncovered by research.

QUESTIONS AND PROBLEMS FOR DISCUSSION

1. Discuss fully the change in viewpoint that has come in the field of measurement. How can a measured outcome hide the indirect values of an activity?
2. What are the functions of tests in modern teaching?

[27] Glenn W. Howard, *A Measurement of the Achievement in Motor Skills of College Men in the Game Situation of Basketball*, New York, Teachers College, Columbia University, 1937 (Contribution to Education, No. 733).

3. What were the old purposes of anthropometry? Have you ever had an anthropometric examination? Is there a justifiable use for this kind of measure today?
4. What are the limitations of strength tests? If two individuals show the same total strength, what does that indicate in functional performance of the two, for example in wrestling, golf, or swimming?
5. What are statistical and clinical approaches to a problem? Illustrate.
6. What standard did Hitler proclaim for racial acceptance in Germany? What standard of school attendance is supported by law?
7. What are the four principles for judging a physical education lesson, or program? Discuss the first one.
8. What is the significance of an activity when it appears to the participant to be a dull and uninteresting experience?
9. What was Herbert Spencer's view of activity? Give illustrations of the principle of meaning and significance from the field of dance, swimming, golf, and gardening.
10. What evidence can you give that the individual is impelled by nature to engage in movement?
11. In what fields were Sisler, Chase, Pavlova, Curtis, Mathias, and DiMaggio great performers?
12. What would you consider reasonable performance levels in ten physical education activities?
13. Give an explanation of the statement that most of our problems are with people rather than things. What suggestion has this for teaching social values and human relationships?
14. Discuss Plato's idea: "Body for the sake of Soul." Read Browning's poem "Andrea del Sarto," and give its implications for physical education.
15. What is the deeper meaning of the statement that equality is always won, never inherited?
16. What are the various procedures of evaluation that may be used?
17. What is a cumulative record? What data does it include?
18. How may a check list be used to improve practice?
19. What are some of the limitations of the questionnaire? What is the weakness of a subjective method? Has it any value?
20. What is the value of skill tests?
21. What is fitness? How should it be assessed?
22. What are some of the motives that may urge a youth to engage in a plan of improving his fitness?

23. What is the desirable scope of the health examination?
24. Discuss the importance of data from the environmental record, the disease record, and the scholastic record.
25. Explain how data from the adjustment record might influence a teacher's decision about a pupil's program in physical education.
26. What are some of the aspects of truancy that might be of great interest to a teacher of physical education?
27. Why are health practices of pupils important to a teacher of physical education?
28. What are the usual items in a good health examination?
29. What three areas should be investigated by research in physical education?
30. What contribution has Brace made in research?
31. What is historical research? Give examples.

REFERENCE READINGS

American Association for Health, Physical Education and Recreation. *Evaluation Standards and Guide in Health Education, Physical Education and Recreation Education.* Washington, D.C., 1959.

Bovard, J. F., Cozens, F. W., and Hagman, E. F. *Tests and Measurements in Physical Education.* Philadelphia, Saunders, 1949.

Clarke, H. H. *Application of Measurement to Health and Physical Education.* Englewood Cliffs, N.J., Prentice-Hall, 1959.

Larson, Leonard A., and Yocom, Rachel D. *Measurement and Evaluation in Physical, Health, and Recreation Education.* St. Louis, Mosby, 1951.

Latchaw, Marjorie, and Brown, Camille. *The Evaluation Process in Health Education, Physical Education and Recreation.* Englewood Cliffs, N.J., Prentice-Hall, 1962.

Mathews, Donald K. *Measurement in Physical Education.* Philadelphia, Saunders, 1958.

Meyers, Carlton R., and Blesh, T. Erwin. *Measurement in Physical Education.* New York, Ronald Press, 1962.

Smithells, Philip, and Cameron, Peter E. *Principles of Evaluation in Physical Education.* New York, Harper and Row, 1962.

Spilker, Otto H. *Elementary School Health and Physical Education Standards and Related Variables Compared with Pupil Achievement on Five Items of the AAHPER Youth Fitness Test.* Bloomington, School of Health, Physical Education, and Recreation, Indiana University, 1960.

Van Dalen, D. B. "The Function of Hypotheses in Research." *The Physical Educator,* March, 1957, p. 21.

Van Dalen, D. B. "The Role of Fact and Theory in Research." *The Physical Educator,* October, 1958, p. 105.

Willgoose, Carl E. *Evaluation of Health Education and Physical Education.* New York, McGraw-Hill, 1961.

INDEX

505